SAGAS, SCHOLARS, & SEARCHERS

— OR —

WHY THE BIBLE IS THE ATHEIST'S BEST FRIEND

Published by:

 Clear Faith Publishing LLC
22 Lafayette Rd
Princeton, NJ 08540

ISBN 978-1-940414-11-9

Printed in the United States of America

First Printing July, 2015
Cover and Interior Design by Doug Cordes
Scala, Sagas, & Searchers is typeset in Jupiter Pro and Mercury

SAGAS, SCHOLARS, & SEARCHERS

— OR —

WHY THE BIBLE IS THE ATHEIST'S BEST FRIEND

— IN MEMORIAM —

Jerry Trageser *and* Pat Connor, S.V.D.

WILLIAM J. BAUSCH

Clear Faith Publishing LLC · Princeton, New Jersey

All Scripture is inspired by God. (2 Timothy 3:16)

- St. Paul, 1st century New Testament writer

Whatever you read in the Old Testament, even though it actually happened, you must interpret spiritually and glean from the truth of history the sense of spiritual understanding.

- St. Leander, 6th century Catholic bishop of Seville

All the senses of Holy Scripture are built on the literal sense alone and not from allegorical passages can argument be drawn. The spiritual senses bring nothing needful to faith which is not elsewhere clearly conveyed by the literal sense.

- Thomas Aquinas, 13th century theologian

Doubt is not a pleasant condition but certainty is absurd.

- Voltaire, 18th century enlightenment scholar

The Bible is true. It's not entirely factual, but it's true. That's hard for a lot of people to understand. Fact and truth are not the same... Some of the Bible is history and some is story and we don't always know which is which.

- Madeleine L'Engle, 20th century prize winning author

If only it were true that Jesus was born in Bethlehem,
  in a manger
And that three kings came from afar, from very far,
Bringing gifts of gold, frankincense and myrrh.

If only it were true what they wrote, Luke and Mark and the
  two others:
The miracle of the wedding at Cana and the miracle of Lazarus.

If only it were true what parents tell their children in the
evening before they go to bed,
When they say "Our Father, Our Mother."

If only it were true I would say yes, surely I would say yes
Because it is all so beautiful when one believes....
    that it is true.

- Jacques Brel, 1960's beat poet

"Just because scripture and tradition say something is wrong doesn't necessarily mean it's wrong."

- Gene Robinson, 21st century, twice married, twice divorced
(first a wife, second a husband) gay Episcopal bishop

We have constructed an environment in which we live in a uniform, univocal secular time, which we try to measure and control in order to get thing done. This "time frame" deserves, perhaps more than any other facet of modernity, Weber's famous description of a "stahlares Gehause" (iron cage).

-Charles Taylor, A Secular Age

CONTENTS

Foreword

It should be noted that difficulties with the Bible often start with the clergy. The more they study as seminarians, the more they learn as ordained clergy, the more they discover that scriptural criticism involves deconstructing the Bible's sacred texts, the more the doubts creep in. More than one clergyperson is harboring doubts even as they preach "the word of God". Noteworthy is a *Religion News Service* article (2010) that cites a study in the journal, *Evolutionary Psychology*, concerning the loss of faith among Protestant clergy, even though, understandably, many remain closet unbelievers because they need the job. What is significant is that the report shows that a common denominator among pastors who claim to have lost their faith is exposure to the study of the Bible using what is called the historical-critical method (the method used by the experts in this book.) It's a method currently criticized but still held by many, including the Catholic Church. Still, if the ministers are losing faith in the Bible, how about the average person?

He does not seem to be far behind. A 2010 survey on religious knowledge by the Pew Forum on Religion and Public Life found that the average Catholic polled answered less than half the religious questions on a 12-question battery on the Bible and Christianity correctly – outperformed by atheists, agnostics, Jews and Mormons. What is apropos to our discussion are the remarks of Dave Silverman, president of American Atheists: "I have heard many times that atheists know more about religion than religious people. Atheism is an effect of that knowledge. I gave a Bible to my daughter. That's how you make atheists." [1]

These atheists are growing and get full support from the culture. For some three or more decades now the public is used to the major weekly magazines like *Newsweek, TIME, US News & World Report* and the monthlies like *The Atlantic Monthly* and *Harpers*, etc. and the TV documentaries *especially* around holiday times – routinely display on their covers the latest lead story of a new artifact found, a manuscript discovered, a novel theory proposed that shows or "proves" something in the Bible is faked, forged or fabricated. Sprinkled over all, like confectioners' sugar, are thin suggestions of duplicity and deceit, cunning and conspiracy. We have come to expect several slick pages of text and artwork undermining the traditional interpretation of the Bible. They always ending with a few paragraphs indicating that, yes, other reputable scholars disagree.

Although there has been some shameless jockeying for ratings and profit – one thinks of *National Geographic* showcasing the discredited Gospel of Judas – or the controversy over a fragment concerning "Jesus' wife" (currently also discredited), the fact is that scholars have found an incredible amount of new materials that have shed light on the Bible. Ever since the cracking of the Near Eastern languages in the late 1800s, the startling discoveries of Gnostic writings at Nag Hammadi in Egypt in 1945 and the unearthing of the Dead Sea Scrolls in the '40s and '50s along with discoveries of other new manuscripts (some still awaiting translation) and artifacts, the Bible will never be the same. The stunning advance of technology has helped scholars to more accurately assess all these things and to construct a whole new approach to the Bible. The old linear pattern, the idealized straight line from Abraham to Jesus, has apparently been broken. The Bible, it appears, is a much more convoluted, complicated and circuitous than anyone ever thought. It appears to be much more the product of a social evolution from the common stories of other ancient Near

Eastern peoples with whom it shares so much (even its gods) than a singular revelation from on high. The Bible in reality is an unfinished mosaic of ceaseless interpretations right up to the present day.

This book, written by a non-scholar, has a modest agenda: to show what is "out there" in current biblical discovery and commentary. What are the scholars saying? How compatible or non-compatible is what they tell us with traditional understandings? How do liberals and conservatives react? Why are people confused? Why do some sincere people find a literal reading of the Bible indigestible, yet a metaphorical reading unanchored? How do we read the Bible in a modern age? Above all, in these days of dwindling religious affiliation (at least in the western world), what is the Bible's authority? Keeping up with the Bible is an ongoing and ever shifting enterprise. This book is a frozen snapshot in that flow to give the reader a chance to catch up.

The book is divided into four parts. Parts I and II are titled "The Hebrew Sagas" and "The Christian Sagas" respectively. The choice of the term "saga" is deliberate. The word implies, not a frozen text, but an ongoing storyline over the ages with developments in terms of plot, understanding and characters –and interpretation – with a thread that unites it all: in this case, faith in YHWH, the Hebrew God. The dynamic inherent in such sagas has caused many, even some Evangelicals, to abandon a static literalist reading and accept a metaphorical one. Not all are happy with that.[2] Part III is entitled "Tensions" because it takes on – sometimes arrogantly – the average person's (my alter ago) common sense questions necessarily raised by the first two parts especially in such hot button areas as abortion, anti-Semitism and gay marriage.

The brief fourth and final section, "The Searchers", reflects uneasily on the issues of how we attempt to make sense of the tensions today within our modern scientific context, how we struggle to find some middle ground, why partisans preface the word Bible with "holy" and put the word for their God in the upper case and others' gods in the lower case while modern nonpartisans, dogmatically tolerant of diversity, relativism and individualism and intolerant of certainty, authority and community, do the opposite. The biblical study world is a challenging one.

Three notes: First, as for the subtitle, "Why the Bible is the Atheist's Best Friend", while it is germane, it is frankly there for PR purposes. Second, although this is not a scholarly book – I don't have the credentials – I have adopted the scholars' standard use of YHWH, LORD, Ba'al and Qur'an just to jolt the reader out of overfamiliarity. Third, by design there is a fourth "S" omitted in the main title, that "S" standing for "Saints" as in *Sagas, Scholars, Searchers & Saints*. The Saints (as St. Paul uses the word) are the believers for whom the Bible, for all of its problems, is the Word of God. They live by it and have a weighty tradition on their side. Their point of view – mythos instead of logos as we'll see in chapter 26 – is a worthy antidote to the neutral and sometimes skeptical view of the scholars and searchers represented in this book. Hopefully, then, this book with its short-comings and limitations will provoke the Saints to come up with, not simple condemnation but better answers, and answers no longer couched in the traditional churchy language of an Aristotelian un-derstanding of nature and a Judeo-Christian faith that no longer shapes our culture. They must not critique or condemn using words that have lost their setting in life as it is lived today. A new language, a new apologetic, is needed. If that happens, then this book will have fulfilled its purpose.

I wish to thank the following who have encouraged the writing if not necessarily what was written: Ed Ciuba, Tom Ivory, Pat Connor, Joe Farrell and Jim Knipper, the last also generously seeing this book to print.

PART I

THE HEBREW SAGAS

Chapter 1.

THE HEBREW GENESIS

About two centuries ago the traditional foundation on which the Bible stood began to crumble. In the 19th century a brilliant and brave young British officer, Henry Rawlinson, perilously scaled a formidable cliff at Behistun in Iran to painstakingly make copies of the long three-language inscriptions in cuneiform that ultimately revealed the deeds and accomplishments of King Darius of Persia. The copies, now manageable, allowed scholars to unlock the languages of Old Persian, Elamite and Akkadian. This remarkable feat in turn eventually opened the doors to old exotic Near East languages heretofore unknown and untranslatable. It was a breakthrough. The discipline of deciphering was born. The literary Near East was at last an open book.

One of the translated works turned out to be the famous Gilgamesh epic. It was written some 2500 years before the Bible, and it was fascinating, not only because it told the story of man's perennial fear of death and search for immortality, but also because the epic itself clearly had a history of development. That is to say, the Babylonian text went through a long, long editorial process centuries ago before anything like a standard final copy emerged. It was apparent that over time different folks and civilizations had their hands on it. Incidents were highlighted, plots were elaborated, the narrative expanded and other traditions and interpretations were added. It also became clear to scholars that even if there were actual historical characters like Gilgamesh behind all the literary styles, they got co-opted into largely inventive fictional stories. In short, the Gilgamesh epic, as we know it today, is the product of a long literary process, the result of many anonymous authors, redactors and editors, each reflecting the interests, biases and background of the era they were writing in. There were other texts around that gave us some semblance of genuine history of course, but even here that history, it was soon discovered, was decidedly slanted and scholars had to be careful to separate possible fact from political fancy.

It soon became startlingly apparent that the Bible went through the same process. It didn't drop down from heaven intact. It, too, developed, as we have seen, over a very long period of time and, like the Gilgamesh epic, reflects additions, corrections and revisions from a vast number of eras, places and perspectives, a process guaranteed to offer varied and contradictory voices without any attempt to reconcile them.

What most intrigued the scholars was that among Gilgamesh's several literary accounts were creation and flood stories very similar to those found in the Bible. That's why the poem *Enuma Elish* is sometimes called "The Babylonian Genesis." This discovery in 1872 by George Smith, a former bank note engraver turned Assyriologist, caused a sensation and upset those who thought that the Bible was the only divinely revealed source of these events. Then for a long time afterward most scholars thought that the Hebrew Genesis simply borrowed from this Babylonian poem and many still do today. But more recently some scholars, admitting parallels, see the Hebrew effort, not as a borrowed tale but as a rewritten one. There are indeed similarities, but the differences are greater. In any case, both the Babylonian and Hebrew accounts have so many parallels with all the other Near East myths (Mesopotamian, Egyptian and even Greek) that it seems evident that even if they didn't directly influence one another they were part of a general pool of similar stories. If there's any similarity, and there is, it's a similarity of common sources.

Another text intrigued. It is called the Uruk Prophecy, a work that gives a series of prophecies for the Mesopotamian city of Uruk concerning a series of eleven kings, the last one of whom would rule the world. The interest of these "prophecies" is that they turn out to be what is called pseudo prophecies or *ex eventu* prophecies or, simply, "after the fact" prophecies. That is to say, the so-called prophecies were written *after* they occurred, the authors pretending to commit to writing a prophecy predating the book. I mention this here because, as we shall see, we have the same situation of after-the-fact prophecies in some of the biblical books, most clearly in the Book of Daniel. Initially, the Uruk Prophecy was thought to be historical but it turned out to be historical fiction also. So too with several other ancient works such as the Neo-Assyrian "The Sin of Sargon" and the Sumerian and Lagash King Lists. These King Lists recorded the names of kings accompanied by how long they lived, with some actual historical kings engaging in legendary stories like King Etana who was "a shepherd, the one who ascended to heaven" (If that sounds familiar, think of Elijah and Jesus).

The point of mentioning these ancient texts that predate or are con-temporary with the Bible is that many of them have the appearance of history but turn out to be fictional stories involving at best a few historical people. Each has gone through centuries of development in the hands of many authors and even where they might be accu-rate, they are shaped by the background, agendas and biases of the authors; and, since many works were palace sponsored, they are often bent to propagandistic royal needs. In a word, the Bible, as biblical scholars emphasize, is like an archaeological site with strata of additions and revisions accumulated over time. It belongs to the Near East literary complex of such collections.

So to the Bible we now turn fully realizing now that, in order for its contents to make sense, contemporaries were already familiar with ancient concepts of deities, of divinely created order and is-sues like good and evil, authority, justice, mercy and other themes common to the Near East but we are not and we will have trouble deciphering its meaning.

THE HEBREW EPIC

The Pentateuch, the first five books of the Bible, were once thought to be a complete, unified work of one author, Moses. Today we generally consider the Pentateuch, like the Gilgamesh epic, to be the product of multiple authors over many centuries. It is skillfully pieced together by editors around the 7th, 8th and 9th centuries B.C.E. and was not organized in the order of its composition. For example, the second chapter of Genesis was written long before the first. Moses was hardly its sole author as once thought (a position that is still held by some conservative Evangelicals). The book speaks of his death for one thing (how could Moses write that?), and, for another, everything is written in the third person: Moses said this or that rather than "I" said this or that – a rather strange way of writing if Moses were the author.

There are also anachronistic passages that clearly come from a time later than Moses, events he could not have known about. Such as mention of the Philistines and the Arameans who came at least a century after Moses' time would be an example. There are references to the kings who reigned in the land of Edom "before any king reigned over the Israelites" (Gen. 36:31). The Israelite kings were to come several centuries after Moses, so how could he reference that? Clearly someone from the time of the monarchy or later wrote those words. They would make no sense to contemporaries of Moses. There are chronology problems, too. In the Hagar-Ishmael story, for example, (Gen 16:16; 17:1) we are told that Hagar carried her infant son into the wilderness, but according to the chronology of the story itself, he turns out to be sixteen years old! Quite an armful. More than twenty times domesticated camels are mentioned in the patriarchal sagas (for example in Genesis 24 Abraham's servant goes via camel to seek a wife for his son Isaac), but historically they did not make their appearance until centuries after the patriarchs lived.

Then there are too many contradictions, too many points of view at variance with each other, too many opposing agendas, too many distinct voices, vocabulary, styles and "personalities" of YHWH to defend a single author. In Exodus 2:2-3, for example, God said to Moses that he appeared to Abraham, Isaac and Jacob as El Shaddai and did not reveal his name of YHWH to them. But Genesis 4:26 quite clearly states that people began to call God YHWH in the time of Adam's grandson! There are two accounts of creation, two versions of the flood story, two accounts of Abraham's dealings with Hagar, two accounts of the naming of Beersheba, differing accounts of the crossing of the Red Sea and different accounts of the revelation of the Ten Commandments on two different mountains (Sinai or Horeb, a word which simply means wilderness). And there are more examples. These duplications obviously come from different sources and different time periods.

SOURCES

Since there are so many styles of writing and vocabulary and so many anachronisms in the Pentateuch, scholars set out to discover the different sources and, for each contributor, determine where they came from, when they wrote, and what agenda they followed. Soon they developed profiles of each source author (who could be a single person, or a committee, or several redactors over the ages.) Theories were not long in coming. Some held that the Pentateuch was composed of fragments, big chunks of traditions that somebody cobbled together. Others held that the Pentateuch simply grew by additions over the ages expanding like all good stories do. The most popular hypothesis is the "Documentary Hypothesis" which identifies four separate authors called J for his use of YHWH for the name of God (J being from the German word, Jehovah), E for using Elohim for God's name, D for the Deuteronomist, and P for the Priestly author whose interest was the priestly class. Their documents were eventually merged with one another to create the Pentateuch. Each source has its specific agenda and, because each has its own politically sensitive and sacrosanct traditions (some originated in

Israel in the north, some in Judea in the south), the biblical editors, ever in awe of ancient traditions, let them stand side by side as is. This tolerance accounts for the, repetitions, duplications and contradictions in the various accounts.

The Documentary Hypothesis is still the most popular explanation for the Pentateuch's kaleidoscopic text. The hypothesis has been challenged, changed and refined over the years but no matter what its status, one truth holds firm: Moses did not write the Pentateuch. Others clearly did and they have left us a rich tapestry of views, theological perspectives, and agendas. The Documentary Hypothesis may have some holes in it, but today no one denies that the biblical texts are composites that incorporate many different layers from different eras and no one denies the heavy cultural absorptions and borrowings from its neighbors, so heavy that it's hard to tell them apart sometimes.

In the Beginning

Genesis is a collection of etiology stories, that is, stories that provide explanations of why things are the way they are. How did creation happen? Let me tell you about YHWH. What is the origin of evil? Let me tell you about the snake in the garden. Why do we suffer? Let me tell you about the fall. Where do the different languages come from? Let me tell you about the tower of Babel. A salt pillar, if you squint your eyes, looking like a person? Let me tell you about Lot's wife. A flood? Let me tell you about Noah. And so it goes. Since scholars revealed Genesis' scientific improbabilities of the stories, they are more likely today to identify this book as "creation poems" or myths, in the sense of creative stories that serve up truth too vast and complex to put into prose. In other words when the Hebrews or any of the ancients came up with their myths they had no intention of seeking or giving a literal explanation for natural phenomena. Their myths were simply poetic attempts to express wonder and to link such wonder to their own lives. Their myths, steeped in the conviction of the presence of unseen forces, were metaphorical attempts to describe a reality that was in fact indescribable. These mythologies were kept alive not only by repeating and embellishing the stories orally or literarily, but especially by liturgy – reenactment in song, poetry, dance, and ritual that made the event alive and present again.

With this in mind, concerning the Hebrews' "creation poems", there are two things to note. First, there were obviously no eyewitnesses to the birth of the universe which came into existence some 13.7 billion years ago. Second, the biblical account of its creation is an adoption and adaptation of old legends and myths common to the Near East reshaping them here and there to fit its particular theology, that theology being that the writers did not really know how the world was created but only that their God, YHWH, they insisted, was responsible. Thus Genesis begins: "In the beginning God created." This is the traditional translation we have from the Greek Septuagint. However, this time-honored phrase, while defensible, is a suspect translation, out of sync with the myths it copied, and one influenced by John's opening Gospel line. "In the beginning was the Word." The more acceptable translation of Genesis' opening line among scholars is:

"When God began to create, the heavens and the earth (or, more literally, "In the beginning of God's creating"), the earth was a formless void and darkness was on the face of the Deep and a wind from God was swooping over the face of the water, then God said..."

In other words, the meaning is, "When God began to straighten out the cosmic mess that was around, God said..." In the more accurate translation, there is preexisting (but chaotic) matter that God shapes into some kind of order. (Where that preexisting matter — Big Bang stuff — came from is the ancient and modern cosmological conundrum.) In short, like many other ancients, the Israelites assumed that the raw, undefined material was there from all eternity, and God gave it shape and meaning. I mention this because it flies in the face of what we have been taught, namely, that God created *ex nihilo*, out of nothing, a position still taught by the Catechism of the

Catholic Church: "We believe that God needs no pre-existing thing or any help in order to create, nor is creation any sort of necessary emanation from the Divine substance. God creates freely 'out of nothing' (no. 296)."

And the Catechism goes on to quote the Church Father, Theophilus of Antioch, who asks, "If God had drawn the world from pre-existent matter, what would be so extraordinary about that?" The Catechism further quotes (no. 297) the late book, Second Maccabees (7:22-23, 28) a canonical book for Catholics but considered apocryphal for Jews and Protestants, which says, "Look at the heaven and the earth and see everything that is in them and recognize that God did not make them out of things that existed."

Yet, modern scholarship differs. The translations, "In the beginning of God's creation" or, as the New Revised Standard Version expresses it, "In the beginning when God created the heavens and the earth, the earth was a formless void and darkness covered the face of the Deep..." are all saying that God imposed order on preexisting chaos, not that God started from scratch (*ex nihilo*) and that the poet had it right after all:

> When Love Divine, with brooding wings unfurl'd,
> Call'd from the rude abyss the living World
> 'Let there be Light!,' proclaimed the Almighty Lord,
> Astonish'd Chaos heard the potent word;
> Through all his realms the kindling ether runs
> And the mass starts into a million Suns.[1]

TWO ACCOUNTS

In the biblical version of the creation stories, God appears quite sovereign and remote in chapter 1, and even has a different name than he does in chapter 2. (That was the first clue that there are two sources here.) Here, God simply speaks from on high and, so powerful is God's word that things happen. In chapter 2, however, God is more "human." God's like a craftsman walking about in the garden talking to human beings and even making leather clothes for Adam and Eve. The first account has no Garden of Eden, no tree of life, no disobedience or divine punishment, and the second account has no seven days and no divine rest. Sometimes the accounts contradict each other. For example, one account says that man was created "before any wild plant was on the earth," but the other account says plainly that plant life was created on the third day long before any creation of man on the sixth day.

The other author seemingly represents a transition point of view. That is, people were getting settled and were moving away from being on-the-move hunters to the beginning of agriculture and settled villages. People had to work, plant crops, eat, wear clothes and live in groups or families. The serpent story serves as the explanation of this transition from hunter to farmer, from the forest to the stubborn fields. Both versions are laced with common Middle Eastern folklore, for example, talking snakes and trees with special power. I might add that, in an all-too-clever insight, the ancient interpreters of this story deduced that God spoke Hebrew. After all, at the beginning God said in Hebrew, "Let there be light," "let there be man," etc. and since neither the Hebrews, nor anyone else were around at that primeval time, God couldn't have been speaking to anybody. He just spoke and out came Hebrew, his native language! "Obviously" all other languages are corruptions of Hebrew.

COMPARISONS

The older Mesopotamian creation myths are uncommonly close to Genesis, especially, as we mentioned, the one called *Enuma Elish*. According to this account, the Babylonian god Marduk created the world by overcoming the primeval sea monster called Tiamat and cleaving her body into two parts, thus separating the heavens from earth thereby making space for creatures. The god Ea designed human beings and the design was carried out by Marduk, who formed them from the blood of a defeated demon. Note the comparisons. Marduk defeated the waters. YHWH hovered over the waters. Creation came about by splitting the waters. God separated the waters from the "firmament." In *Emman Elish,* the creation of heaven and earth was followed by the creation of the heavenly bodies and humanity and God does the same. The biblical account also has a tree of life reflecting the Mesopotamian life giving plant that was stolen by the serpent. Eden's paradise reflects the paradise of Sumerian literature. The result is that "the recycling of Near Eastern myths and motifs by the biblical authors raises serious questions about the traditional view that the Pentateuch provides a perfect historical portrait of human origins and early human history."[2]

That's an understatement. The biblical account of creation has to give way to a radically different interpretation if it is to be credible. That, as we shall see, is precisely what will happen.

The Higgs Boson theory notwithstanding, as noted in the Bible God is presented as creating all things by the power of his spoken word, "Let there be light. " But scholars point out that this kind of creative process was common lore where creation-by-verbal-command plays a basic role. Nanna the Mesopotamian moon god, has his creative word praised and in the Babylonian *Enuma Elish* Marduk's words can create and destroy. Many Egyptian texts speak of creation beginning with a verbal command and, moreover, that creation also begins with the creation of light. It's the same sequence as the Bible. The Egyptian god Ptah spoke things into existence. The forbidden fruit motif comes from a Sumerian myth and, as far as the serpent in the Garden goes, we find Egyptian pictures of a cat with a stick bruising the head of a serpent that dwells in a Persian tree. The cat is Re, the sun god, and the serpent is Apep, the enemy of Re who tries to swallow the sun at the end of each day. The bruising of the serpent's head, by the way, is precisely what God directed Adam to do to the serpent and its progeny after the expulsion from Eden. (This is not to mention that the serpent as spoiler is also found in the Epic of Gilamesh!)

The firmament arising out of the waters (Gen. 1:6-7) is a copy of the primeval mountain arising out of chaos in Egyptian myth. The Sabbath rest appears to come from a later time (and inserted as the "third commandment") since there is no record of Israel observing it prior to the Exodus. And, moreover, the reasons given for the Sabbath differ. The Exodus version says the Sabbath must be observed because God Himself rested on the seventh day of creation. This copies the Babylonian myth where, after Marduk created humanity, the gods were free to rest. The Deuteronomy version says that the Sabbath must be observed because it's a reminder to Israel that God liberated the Hebrews from servitude in Egypt, not because God rested on the Sabbath. There are, in short, some close contact points between the Babylonian and biblical accounts.

The two trees in the Garden of Eden reflect Egyptian deities and the forbidden fruit motif comes from Sumerian mythology. The expulsion of Adam and Eve from the garden and resulting punishment reflect the common Mesopotamian myth of Adapa, fragments of which have been found in a 14th century B.C.E. library (i.e. pre- Exodus) and a 7th century B. C.E. library in Assyria attesting to its antiquity. The Cain and Abel story has roots in Egyptian and Sumerian myths and people spoke different languages long before the tower of Babel incident. As a matter of fact, the Tower of Babel narrative, sandwiched as it is between two lengthy genealogies, is considered a folktale. It opens with the words that the "whole earth had one language and the same words" (Genesis 11:1), a statement completely contradicting what has just been reported more than once in the preceding genealogy which specifies, "...in their lands with their own language, by their own families." (This is the kind of thing that provoked the Documentary Hypothesis.)

So it is agreed: the biblical creation story has parallels with other Near Eastern literature – and, when you come right down to it, the Bible's version, like all the others, is all about one-upmanship. This quote sums it up:

"The ancient Near East was full of conflicting claims to supremacy of this or that god or city over all others. The Bible is part of this polemic. The biblical authors borrowed from foreign creation stories in order to make the best case possible for YHWH, God of Israel. They were participating in a contemporary international debate on the basis of data considered basic and agreed upon by all."[3]

This is true enough and the biblical authors, children of their time, rightly made use of communal myths and storytelling to make their points about their God, the beginning of the world and their own origins. For them, it was history in the broadest sense of narrative beginnings and bonding with their God. Genesis is obviously not historical in our sense. It is the product of religious imagination and fundamentally, the Hebrews' appropriation of the popular Babylonian myth of creation. It is an account of origins guided and brought about by the national god of Israel in contrast to the god of the Babylonians. Genesis, in other words, along with the Exodus and the Covenant, is a foundational myth – and, we should remember that it is the *Hebrew* foundational myth, one bequeathed to Christianity. Others do not share it. And even within Judaism and Christianity, it is (still) much debated what this myth means and how it holds up under scrutiny.

MODERN VOICES

That scrutiny means that, in our day, there are those who loudly dismiss the Genesis myth entirely. Physicists like Stephen Hawking, Lawrence Krauss, and others argue that modern cosmology's quantum mechanics show how our universe and everything in it could have spontaneously emerged out of nothing. The universe, they say, is self-originating and self-sustaining. Hence, there is no need for God. All of which may be an overstating act of scientific faith since w really do not understand anything about the moment of the Big Bang that appears to be a unique since event that voided all of nature's laws - not to mention the obvious that we do not have any data prior to or at the instant of the Big Bang.

Others remind us that up until fairly recently, people held that the world was some 6,000 years old. (Some fundamentalists still hold this.) The 6,000 figure comes from the calculations made in 1650 by Archbishop Ussher of England, who arrived at it by counting up the lifespans of everyone descended from Adam and Eve. He went further and gave us the precise date of creation: October 23, 4004 B.C.E.. Science, with its vast array of ancient fossils and rocks, disputes this.

Some aver that the Genesis story is dismissive and irrelevant because it is too self-centered, too constricted. The world it portrays is too insignificant for this world of ours, and turns out to be a very, very minor speck in the incomprehensible vastness not only of the universe but of the universes. In 1996 and again in 2004, astronomers pointed the Hubble telescope at two "dark" spots in the universe, spots the size of a grain of sand held at a distance, spots where there was a dark "nothing." They did this for ten days in 1996 and 11 days in 2004. They ultimately recorded their findings in 3-D. What they found were galaxies some 13 billion light years away containing over a hundred billion galaxies with hundreds of billions of stars. These numbers are almost meaningless because they are so mind-blowing. We have no frame of reference for such numbers, no way to hold them in our heads. We simply can't grasp the age or the vastness of the universe, the literally countless galaxies, stars, and planets that exist including those that might support life. Then there are the convictions of some cosmologists about the existence of other universes and parallel worlds different from our own. Whatever the case, the planet Earth, where human life began in Africa some paltry 200,000 years ago, started migrating out of Africa around 70,000 and began to exhibit modern traits around 50,000, occupies a very, very, very tiny place in the heavens. This leads some modern scientists, for unsupported reasons, to bend their scientific writings into atheistic manifestos that undermine the poetry of Genesis.

THE FIRST FAMILY

Adam is formed from the dust or clay of the ground – or, as some scholars prefer, "dirt clod" — and God's breath. Eve is formed from Adam's "rib", a word that is an ambiguous guess of an odd word in Hebrew. Their tale is identical to the Mesopotamian and Babylonian accounts in which humanity is also made from clay mixed with the flesh and blood of a slain god or pinched off a goddess (so they too have something of "the image and likeness" of a god within them). One version of the Adam and Eve creation story (the Priestly account) simply has God create humankind: "male and female he created them" as if God created a pair. In another strand (the J account), God seems to go through a kind of trial and error scenario as he parades all the animals before Adam. None seem to Adam's liking until at last he finds a partner from the woman taken from his rib.

Adam and Eve being formed from soil, as noted, is a common motif in the ancient Near East (Egyptian, Babylonian), and the trees of life and knowledge of good and evil are common Near Eastern themes. So are the questions Genesis wrestles with – creation, the origins of evil, and so on. They are not unique, but rather are common human issues pondered elsewhere, perhaps no more so than in the famous *Epic of Gilgamesh* which finds resonant motifs, not only in the Bible but in Homer, as well. Michael D. Coogan notes the similarities:

> "This summary of the epic of *Gilgamesh* has highlighted a number of plot elements in Genesis 2-3. These include the presence of a snake, its association with a plant that gives a kind of immortality, and a preoccupation with the inevitable fact of death. Perhaps most significant are the parallels between the account of the seduction of the man and the woman in the garden. Like Enkidu, at first the man and the woman are in harmony with nature. Enkidu loses his own closeness to nature through intercourse with the prostitute, but in doing so he also becomes humanized – wise, like a god – and thereafter is no longer naked but clothed. Similarly, after having eaten

the fruit of the tree of knowledge of good and evil, the man and the woman realize they are naked, cover themselves up with fig leaves and are eventually clothed by the Lord God. At the same time, however, they have become like God (see Gen, 3, 22), and among their punishments is that the soil from which they were formed becomes resistant to their efforts."[4] This quotation, as much as anything, gives us a flavor of the commonality of the Near Eastern myths with the Bible and how the biblical writers retold them to fit their theology. Anyway, the scenario is familiar: Adam and Eve are placed in the Garden of Eden, given freedom to do what they wish except eat of the apple. The serpent tempts Eve. She tempts Adam. They eat, are expelled from paradise, he to sweat it out teasing a living from unforgiving soil and she to bear the pains of childbearing. It's a story to explain why we have a congenital talent for messing things up.

That's it, and that's all. Really. The biblical interpretation of the Adam and Eve story dates back only to the Hellenistic era (323 B.C.E. to 100 B.C.E.). It's a story that we moderns very much identify with, but in reality it has nothing of the weight that Christians attribute to it. The Adam and Eve saga is not a central story. It's comparatively late written in the 9th century B.C.E. in contrast to the first creation account written three centuries earlier. It is hardly ever referred to elsewhere in the Bible. It has no bearing whatever on the major themes of the Old Testament biblical writers. The only other reference to Adam in the Old Testament is at the beginning of the Book of Chronicles, where he is named as the first human being, and you have to wait all the way to the 2nd century B.C.E. Book of Sirach to find an allusion to both Adam and Eve. That's a big hiatus. As for Eve, she get also gets very little mention. She is named only one more time in Genesis when she bears Cain. She is additionally named once in the Book of Tobias (not in the Protestant Bible), where she is identified as Adam's partner, and only twice in the New Testament where Paul blames her for Adam's sin. The author of 1 Timothy says outright that Adam was formed first and that it was the woman who was deceived and sinned, and so Eve has ever since been remembered as secondary, the guilty party and temptress. The bottom line is that the Adam and Eve story never gets into creeds or prayers. It never serves as an interpretative tool for other biblical passages. It never bequeaths to Judaism a pessimistic view of humanity (Christians would adopt that). And that news brings us to the enigma of original sin.

ORIGINAL SIN

We start off by pointing out that Judaism, which gave us this story and contemplated it for three-thousand years, has no concept of any original sin. Catholic scholar Bruce Vawter affirms this by noting that the traditional doctrine of original sin is not to be found in Genesis and another scholar (Peter C. Bouteneff) says that neither in Paul nor in the rest of the Bible is there a doctrine of original sin, wherein all are proleptically guilty in Adam. Genesis, in fact, really has nothing to say about the origin of evil. It gives no explanation for it (Brueggemann). We should add that the ancient and venerable Orthodox Christianity also has no doctrine of original sin and it is likely the Jew, Jesus, did not believe in it.

And yet, for Western Christians, as far and Adam and Eve go, they are necessary for the whole Christian theology of salvation History, the Fall, Original Sin, and the need of a Redeemer. For such Christians, the whole scene in Genesis 3 became a kind of future Gospel, whereby there was a fall that demanded a redeemer who will "crush the head of Satan." But this theme did not exist in pre-Christian times. These theological themes emerged much later and influential theologians like St. Augustine made original sin a standard Christian concept. In trying to give a Christian explanation for evil he found "proof" for an "original sin" in Psalm 51 ("indeed I was born guilty"), and Ephesians 2:3 ("we were by nature children of the wrath, like everyone else"), and in Romans 5:12 (noted below), and in the general wretchedness of the human race full of evil inclinations, especially renegade sexual desire. Indeed original sin was passed on though intercourse. We're all involved in Adam's sin. We're all an innately corrupt human race stemming from our first parents.

We should not fail to note how radical this concept is. While all previous centuries and cultures considered sin as a wrongdoing that somehow violated relations with the divine, here for the first time we have a shift from the belief that sin is something one does to something that one is born into. (As a related sidebar, we note that St. Augustine proposed the teaching that the only legitimate sexual act was one that was explicitly linked to procreation, this despite the fact that there is no theological basis for this statement. But his teaching stuck with the Catholic Church, which has taught that there is something "intrinsically" evil about deliberately infertile sex, a stand that has embroiled the Church in the current contraception controversy.)

Augustine's pessimism prevailed (for example, over the optimism of Pelagius), and so whatever the story may have meant originally, the Adam and Eve story has been interpreted as the story of the Fall by our original parents, and became a sacrosanct foundational Christian doctrine. St. Paul innovatively sums it up, "Therefore, just as sin came into the world through one man and death came through sin, and so sin and death spread to all because all have sinned...."Therefore just as one man's sin led to a condemnation of all, so one man's act of righteousness leads to a justification and life for all." (Romans 5:18) And "As all die in Adam so all will be made to live in Christ" (1 Cor 15:18 & 21). Again, the "fall," the temptation by Satan, the guilt of Eve, a passed-on "original sin" are not explicitly stated in the biblical text, and the second creation story makes no mention of Satan (It was late Jewish Apocrypha that identified the serpent with Satan, an interpretation wholly accepted by the Christians) or the forbidden fruit or sin. All that is interpretation read into the text and only by Western Christianity, not by the rest of the world.

But there's a more basic question here, Adam and Eve themselves. Are they a pair after all and the first pair at that? Adam, in modern terms, is not necessarily a single human being. True, there was his clan: Eve, and two sons, Cain and Abel but there is no Mrs. Cain or Mrs. Abel. There had to be some others to preclude incest. What if Adam were not unique? What if there were several first parents? (Their children would provide Cain and Abel with wives.) What if there were pre-Adamite folks who roamed the world? There has been a recent discovery of a tiny being on an Indonesian island thought to be about fifteen thousand years old. Suppose he turns out to be a genuine branch of the hominid line though different from us? How does he/she fit into the story of Adam and Eve, the Fall, and the atonement?

EVOLUTION AND ORIGINAL SIN

One and a half centuries ago, Charles Darwin gave a very rational explanation of the origins of the universe that contradicted the Genesis account of individual creation. His theory was, in the words of Pope John Paul II, "more than hypothetical." Since Darwin's time, we have learned that modern humans evolved to our present state about 195,000 years ago from our earliest primate ancestors of 55 million years ago (long before the Genesis time frame) — maybe the successful outcome of many experiments for all we know — and we, *homo sapiens*, given a million or so years, arrived. Such a speculation that we evolved from predecessor species over tens of millions of years – and the human genome sequencing has verified that – obviously poses a real problem for the Adam and Eve story and the doctrine of original sin as an event of a singular, one-time, moment in actual history, a moment that necessitated an atonement, namely, the death of Jesus, to reverse the Fall and take away the sting of death provoked by our first parents. Yet, if death were a result of the Fall, the theory of evolution tells a contradictory story by demonstrating that death was around a long, long time before Adam and Eve.

Yes, death is a natural part of all living things, a part of the evolutionary process of the survival of the fittest, part of "natural selection." It's not a penalty for disobedience in spite of the famous passage in Romans 5:12, where St. Paul states that "sin came into the world through one man, and death came through sin, and so death spread to all because all have sinned." The point is that while in the pre-evolutionary mindset, human death was divine punishment for sin. Modern evolutionary theory presents a viable alternative for the death of all living things and, to that extent, dismantles the whole theological foundation of the Fall, sin, Redemption, blood atonement and the narrow necessity of being "baptized into the death of Jesus." We should not be totally surprised at such speculations. After all, note the subtle changes in Catholic thought about limbo. Once a part of the old equation, it has now quietly disappeared from the official Catechism of the Catholic Church.

Then there's the sacrament of Baptism with its traditional emphasis on its absolutely urgent role in washing away original sin, lest one be barred from heaven for eternity. Mark's Jesus says quite plainly, "The one who believes and is baptized will be saved; but the one who does not believe will be condemned" (16:16). John's Jesus is no less emphatic, "Truly I tell you, no one can enter the Kingdom of God without being born of water and Spirit" (3:5). Over the centuries, this urgency has led Catholic students to learn how to baptize in case of an emergency (water must flow, no sprinkling; melted snow will do), devout nurses to clandestinely baptize endangered babies of any tradition and countless depressed mothers whose infants had died before Baptism. In 2007 the Vatican softened all this based on "the strong grounds for hope that God will save infants when we have not been able to do for them what we would have wished to do, namely, to baptize them into the faith and life of the Church." Baptism today has given way to the Rite of Initiation emphasizing entrance into a community fellowship of believers and downplaying original sin. We can note the latter's new lower-case status when a popular Franciscan preacher and author, Richard Rohr, writes that we grow spiritually more by fumbling than by getting it right all the time noting, "I actually think it is the only workable meaning of any *remaining notion* of 'original sin.'"[5]

But let's return to that Pauline phrase cited above, "because all have sinned." It means literally "as a result of which." But in one of those world-changing moments (we'll see other examples in the case of Mary's virginity and Assumption) there was a mistranslation from the Greek into the Latin where the phrase "as a result of which all have sinned" got transformed to "*in whom*" all have sinned giving way to St. Augustine's understanding that everyone, in solidarity with Adam, has sinned. We are consequently all born in original sin which would require a "new Adam" to atone for it. "As one renowned patristic scholar J.N.D. Kelly noted, the Old Latin version of the New Testament gave an exegesis of Romans 5:12 which, though mistaken and based on a false reading, was to become the pivot of the doctrine of Original Sin."[6]

THE HUMAN BURDEN

Once more, the whole issue at hand is basically the ancient Hebrews' attempt to come to terms with what everyone else struggled with: how to explain death. The Bible's answer was that it came through human beings' own fault not God's. After all, God had warned Adam and Eve that if they ate of the fruit of the tree of the knowledge of good and evil "you shall die." Adam and Eve brought death upon themselves. Death is the penalty for human failure, not God's doing.

With all these tensions in play, some scholars today ask if a literal transmitted original sin from a single pair can be squared with evolution. The eminent scientist (and director of the National Institute of Health), famed atheist-turned-Christian, Francis S. Collins, along with Karl W. Giberson, wrote a book called *The Language of Science and Faith* in which they announce that the concepts of Adam and Eve as the literal first couple and the ancestors of all humans, simply "do not fit the evidence." The magazine *Christianity Today*[7] had for its cover story, "The Search for the Historical Adam". The article reports that the claims of recent genetic research indicating that the human race did not emerge from pre-human animals as a single pair, as an "Adam and Eve," because the complexity of the human genome requires an original population of around 10,000. A Catholic priest, John Mahoney, SJ, started out his book by noting that Pope John Paul II had asked scholars to begin reviewing Christian doctrine in the light of evolutionary theory, has also written a cautious book entitled *Christianity in Evolution: An Exploration*, saying that if evolution is true then original sin cannot be.

A lot is at stake with some defenders of the Christian faith suggesting that maybe Adam and Eve were the leaders of that original population of 10,000 or that the physical form of human beings did evolve, and when two of them reached a certain optimum stage God infused a human soul into them and they became the first humans, Adam and Eve. In other words, whatever the evolutionary process and however long it took, God was presiding over it, infusing it. Evolution, then, far from upending God, gloriously reflects God's creative power and dynamic incarnate presence. In other words, God creates through evolution. As cosmologist Brian Swimme wrote, "The earth was once molten rock – and now sings operas." All of creation, therefore, participates in the dynamism of divine being, and this concept may be a more fruitful approach to the question of our first parents and original sin. And as for the historically obvious disruption in human goodness, many theologians today would adopt the notion of the Greek Fathers that eschews physical transmission or genetic predisposition to sin in favor of humankind's cumulative sinful choices carried forward by each generation creating a culture, a society, in which sin abounds.

SIBLINGS

Let's move on to the siblings. The Cain and Abel story seems straightforward enough although we are never told why YHWH preferred Abel's offering to Cain's. Naturally, interpreters filled in the blanks, but the text itself remains silent. The theme of rival brothers is an old one. It runs all through ancient and modern lore and is a staple of folktale, from Kings Richard and John in "The Adventures of Robin Hood" to the "Corsican Brothers" to John Steinbeck's *East of Eden*. The Bible itself has lots of examples, from Noah's sons and Jacob and Esau to King David's sons. In our story here, one brother is jealous of the other and kills him. Period. That's pretty unsettling and the rabbis could never tolerate this, although the theological conclusion eventually drawn was that the fratricide was the horrendous consequences of sin. Still, they could never have a son of Adam turning out to be a murderer, so they provided and ingenious interpretation. They seized on the phrase "Adam knew his wife, Eve" but they did not read it in the usual sense that of that word, that he had sex and a child was conceived. No Adam did not know his wife, but rather he knew *that*. He knew *that* she had conceived and, obviously, it was by someone else, not him. And who else could be that someone be but the devil himself? No wonder devilish Cain killed Abel! This Jewish interpretation caught hold and was passed down to the Christian Jews. Read, for example, 1 John 3:10-12 in the New Testament: "[These are] children of the devil, whoever does not do right is not of God, nor he who does not love his brother.... we should love one another and not be like Cain who was of the evil one."

The story also functioned as an etiological tale (we'll see this shortly) by explaining why, in the Genesis writer's time, those neighboring Kenites were so fierce. How could they not be? They were descended from bad seed, that bad seed being Cain. This kind of putdown, as we shall see, is common in the Bible. The Hebrew authors, rather nastily, made sure we knew that Ammon and Moab are the descendants of an incestuous union between Lot and his daughters, the Edomnites who were descendants of the nerd Esau, the Ishmaelites descendants of Hagar's son, Ishmael who, it is hinted, engaged in homosexual activities.

We note that Cain does not seem to be punished for his deed. There is no account of his death, a fact that suggests a long life, the usual sign of divine blessing. In fact YHWH warns that anyone who kills Cain will suffer seven vengeances (4:15). Some ancient interpreters were unhappy that Cain got away with it so they had him die in Noah's flood. In later Christian apologetics, however, Cain became a symbol of the Jews while Abel, the good shepherd who dies at the hand of the evil Jews, represented Christ. There is no end of inventive expansion once an interpretation takes hold leaving the literal text, which harbors no such thoughts, to languish.

THE STORY OF NOAH AND HIS BLESSING

The flood and ark story is found all over the Near East literature. It exists in many versions, the oldest being from around 1900-1600 B.C.E. A recently (2009) deciphered cuneiform tablet of the flood and the ark dates to around 1750 B.C.E and envisions a circular ark.[8] They're all produced around a thousand years prior to the biblical account. Especially noteworthy, as we mentioned, is the Bible's association with the Babylonian *Gilgamesh* myth. Both stories, of course, fall into the category of myth since no geological evidence exists of a world-wide flood such as those described in these works, although obviously there is some memory of a giant flood of some sort. They are simply a part of the cosmological myths of all the ancient peoples. The Noah story obviously combines two sources into one. We immediately note in the Noah account the influence of the source called P, or the Priestly writer. He likes to divide things into neat epochs and is concerned about liturgy. This means that when he writes of the flood episode he cannot have Noah take seven pairs of animals into the Ark. Why? Because in his scheme of things dietary laws and rituals do not come into effect until after the Sinai covenant. So he allows only two animals each for the simple reason that the rest are not needed for sacrifice that, to him, is, at this point, anachronistic. The Yahwist author's version is not interested in such time frames and has a different agenda. He has Noah take on seven pairs so that he can have some left over for sacrifice, which indeed Noah offers as one of his first acts of arriving on dry land. One source has Noah enter the ark seven days after the flood starts; another has him enter the same day it starts.

When Noah had landed, he planted a vineyard and eventually made wine. He drank too much and passed out, and lay there in his tent naked (Gen. 9:20-28). His son, Ham, saw him and did nothing. His other two sons, not looking, walked in backwards and covered him up. As a result, Noah blessed his two sons, but cursed his son Ham and *his* son, Canaan: "Cursed be Canaan, lowest of slaves shall he be to his brothers." He also said, "Blessed by the Lord my God be Shem; and let Canaan be his slave. May God make space for Japheth and let him lie in the tents of Shem' and let Canaan be his slave." Here we have the initial biblical justification for slavery. This account provided favorite texts for Jews, Muslims, and Christians, especially for the slave trade to the New World. The Muslims listed the black races among Ham's descendants in spite of the Bible's clear curse on Ham's son, not Ham himself. It was the Portuguese Jewish philosopher, Isaac ben Abravanel, who suggested that Canaan's descendants were black while those of his uncles were white. Christian slave owners were happy to accept this. In the original context, however, all this was another projected putdown. It was politically convenient, to say the least, for the author writing in the 8th century B.C.E. to have his nation's current nemesis, the Canaanites, cursed at the dawn of Israel's history and declared destined to be slaves to the Israelites. They may share the same DNA, but right now they are enemies and that status is projected back into the Noah story.

Intertwined with the biblical flood story are other mythologies such as the "giants" or "sons of God" having sex with humans (Gen. 6:1-4) and the genealogies with their fantastic life spans: Lamech lived 777 years, Noah 950 years and the all-time biblical champion, Methuselah 969 years. Included among these is the fabled Enoch who lived 365 years, one year for each day of the year. We're told that Enoch "walked with God" apparently meaning that he did not die but, like the prophet Elijah, ascended into heaven. In later Jewish lore Enoch returns to give details about the end of time. Actually, these fabulous life spans are small potatoes compared to other Near Eastern sources where kings live nearly a quarter of a million years! What is significant is that in the Bible each succeeding generation lives shorter and shorter as human depravity grows longer and longer. The story of the tower of Babel is mixed in here as well, an etiological story to explain the multiplicity of languages, a punishment from YHWH, according to this story, because humans were always trying to violate the boundaries between themselves and God, trying to take over, as it were, his prerogatives, for example, building a tower to get closer to heaven.

Chapter 2.

THE SAGAS OF THE PATRIARCHS

The Bible places the Patriarchs around 1800 B.C.E. Their stories give the impression of being recorded near that time. Both assumptions are wrong. According to archaeology, what the writers of the patriarchal sagas do reflect fits much better into the time slot of around 1200 B.C.E. Moreover, their narratives were written very late. One reason is that, significantly, there is very little reference to them in the later 8th and 7th centuries B.C.E. prophets like Isaiah, Hosea, or Jeremiah. That's a huge omission. What this says is that these basic, foundational stories are missing all that time, but then they pop up in writings that come from the 6th century or later. This can only mean that the stories of the Patriarchs, as we now have them in the Bible, come *after* rather than *before* the first great Hebrew prophets of the 8th and 7th centuries — which, in turn, validates this truth: the Bible, as we have it, was rewritten in the time of the late monarchy and exile and its foundational stories, totally steeped in these later writers' theology and political agendas, are projected to the past. Indeed mainstream biblical scholarship holds that the Deuteronomistic history (Joshua, Judges, Samuel and Kings) was composed in Jerusalem in the 7th to early 6th century B.C.E.

The stories we find in the Pentateuch center around two themes: family histories and rivalries, and exile and return. All the patriarchs, from the beginning, are always leaving and returning somewhere forming a kind of hopeful pattern for those in the 6th century Exile, when most of these books were written. There are some very old oral traditions here signaled by the many repetitions: three times a patriarch in a foreign land passes off his wife as his sister, twice Jacob puts one over on Esau and twice Hagar is forced to leave Abraham's household. It is also obvious that some of this ancient material is sometimes misunderstood and sometimes wrenched from its original purposes and reworked into other contexts. Evidence of folktales abound in these patriarchal accounts and many of their plots have parallels in other ancient literature: going to other lands, childless ancestors, divinely promised offspring, journeying to seek a wife, the visiting of shrines, and so on. It would seem that the Bible's authors and the Canaanite authors used common motifs and plots. Why not? As we shall see, they are the same people writing in two dialects. Ultimately the separate folk tales about Abraham, Isaac and Jacob coalesced and were woven into a single related family of father, son and grandson. In short, they are inventions at worst or reconstituted traditions at best.

Because Israel's ancestors were a minor migrant shepherd people always on the fringe of the great empires, there is no mention of any of the people in Genesis — and that includes the names of kings from Abimelech to Melchizedek — outside the Bible, no extra-biblical source. In turn Genesis itself does not mention any historical figures from outside its self-enclosed biblical accounts.

Michael D. Coogan sums it up:

> "With regard to Abraham and Sarah, Isaac and Rebekah and Jacob and his family, we are for the most part in the realm of legend, and it is extremely difficult to determine if any of the traditions concerning them in Genesis 12-15 have a historical basis. An analogy from British history is King Arthur, who may have been an actual person, but the repeatedly retold legends about him are our only sources, making historical judgment difficult.

"The quest for historicity is complicated by several factors. First, biblical chronology itself is essentially unreliable, given the ages attributed to the ancestors, and has its own internal inconsistencies. Second, because so many stages of composition and editing have shaped the narratives, they are often anachronistic, since each generation of storytellers, writers and editors added elements from their own times. Third, because of the use of different sources in the final form of the narrative, many inconsistencies are found."[1]

ABRAHAM

Abraham, the hero of three great religions, is a shadowy figure and a controversial one. He first appears as a stable figure out of nowhere in chapter 12 of Genesis after eleven chapters of total chaos, evil and corruption: Adam and Eve disobey God, prefer the snake and are tossed out of Eden. Cain murders his brother. Noah gets drunk. Ham violates a taboo. Arrogant people build towers to heaven. The wickedness goes on and on. No wonder that by chapter 11 YHWH deeply regrets that he started the whole human enterprise.

Then comes Abraham. According to the Bible, for reasons not given, he was called by God. Since there was no reason given for the choice interpreters supplied one. They concluded that Abraham was called because he did not worship other gods and this had antagonized his neighbors who threatened his life. So he had to flee. As the first monotheist, his famed journey was symbolic in that he was leaving the old way of thinking. But it's not that simple. Text-wise, there is no hint whatsoever that Abraham lived differently from his contemporaries. There is not a word in the Book of Genesis that actually says Abraham or his descendants believed in one God only. Rather, the text makes it quite clear that, on the contrary, Abraham's God was one among many. At no point in Genesis does Abraham claim an exclusive God. In fact not only Abraham but Isaac and Jacob all worshipped El, the Canaanite deity.

Yes, Abraham may have worshipped YHWH but likely as one god among others, not as the sole God. Abraham was technically a mono-latrist (there are other gods, but mine is chief of them all or more powerful than all others) not a monotheist (there are not other gods whatsoever.) Abraham doesn't deserve the title of first. The title "The First Monotheist" – that's what Freud called him — may actually belong to Pharaoh Akhenaten (Amenophis IV, 1353-1337 B.C.E.). In his lifetime he was known as the "Heretic Pharaoh" precisely because he recognized only one deity, the Egyptian sun god, Aten. That's why he moved his capital from Thebes to a new site called Akhetaten. (Fifteen years later his successor, Tutankhamun, reversed him and reintroduced the old gods and moved the capital back to Thebes.) The truth is that Abraham's reputation as a monotheist comes from lore found centuries later in old Jewish apocryphal books from both before the Common Era and from the rabbinic period at the beginning of the Common Era, where Abraham is depicted as de-stroying his father's household idols. Ironically, the only place where Abraham appears as an unapologetic monotheist is in the Qur'an.

THE PROMISE

> "Go from your country and your kindred and your father's house to the land that I will show you. I will make of you a great nation, and I will bless you, and make your name great, so that you will be a blessing. I will bless those who bless you, and the one who curses you, I will curse; and by you all the families of the earth will bless themselves". (Gen. 12:1-3)

It is with Abraham that the theme of promise emerged, a theme that would be a major unifying cry among the Jews to this day (especially in the endless Middle Eastern wars). The promise of the land was made unconditionally in one biblical tradition (Gen. 13:15; 17-18), and conditionally in another biblical tradition (Ex. 20:12; Deut. 5:16). The promise is often said to be unilateral but it was hardly so. Abraham, after all, was required to leave his home in order to receive it, and circumcision was a condition for its fulfillment. Circumcision, by the way, is a borrowed practice. It was in existence in the Near East long before the rise of the Israelites. It was far from exclusive to them and only became their special sign at the time of the Babylonian Exile. (Later on, Muslims would adopt it.)

As an aside, one can't help but speculate that if God wanted to give Canaan to Abraham, why wait for 75 years to order him to do so, and at the precise time Canaan was experiencing a famine so that, as soon as Abraham got there, he had to leave? Anyway, Abraham obeyed and started out to traveling to the Promised Land of Canaan. He appears to have gone the wrong way by moving in a southward direction towards Egypt (Canaan is westward). He came across his nephew, Lot. Lot had gone to the infamous Sodom and Gomorrah, mythical cities that never existed, and are variously described in the Bible as being located in a well-watered fertile plain in one place and as "full of slime pits" in another (Gen. 14:10). (The Sodom and Gomorrah story reappears in another form in Judges 19-21).

There is no question that the promise of land formed, and still forms, a fundamental conviction of the Jews (and Christian Zionists). It was a land with a long history of prior settlers – all those Hittites, Perizzites, Amorites, Canaanites, etc. — that make up the usual litany of Israel's enemies. The land ran from Dan in the north to Beersheba in the south and crosswise from the Mediterranean Sea to the Jordan River, a mass about the size of Vermont. It had coastal plains and hill country and mountain ridges, a river, a valley, the Dead Sea and semi-arid land. The boundaries varied in different books of the Bible, its most idealized version being from "the wilderness of Lebanon and from the river, the river Euphrates, to the Western Sea." (Deut 11:24). This over-generous description reflects the time of the monarchy and its control over a rather large area. During the Persian period, however, the land included only a tiny part of the region around Jerusalem (Neh 11:25-35). In reality, the boundaries variously ex-panded and contracted to reflect the political situation at different periods of history. That's why, for example, YHWH delineates the boarders of the land with great precision for Moses when the people are camped at those borders (Numbers 34:1-15), but modifies them considerably at the beginning of the Book of Joshua (Joshua 13:4).

Meanwhile, there is a related convoluted subplot going on that will have far-reaching effects. Sarah is sterile so she gives her slave, Hagar, to Abraham to bear his child as his concubine. Later, Sarah herself becomes (miraculously) pregnant and bears Isaac. So, according to one scenario, to neutralize the competition, she drives Hagar and her son, Ishmael into the desert. An angel prophesies the child's fate: "He will be a wild ass of a man, his fist against all and everyone's fist against him." (Gen.16:12). Ishmael becomes the classic outcast ("Call me Ishmael" is the famous opening line of Melville's *Moby Dick*). The point is that the Israelites would descend from Isaac and the Arabs from Ishmael. In due time, the prophet Mohammad was not thrilled at this interpretation and so he tapped into another part of the confusing Hebrew biblical tradition. In the same account in the Bible, the pro-Persian Priestly editor had inserted another interpretation. This storyline raises Hagar from a mere concubine to an equal "wife," and in this account this polygamous marriage has Sarah's blessing and also suggests that, far from giving birth alone in the desert, Abraham is present and he himself named the baby. If in one place Ishmael is "a wild ass of a man" in another YHWH says of him, "I will bless him and make him fruitful and exceedingly numerous; he shall be the father of twelve princes, and I will make him a great nation" (Genesis 17:20). Ishmael doesn't get the covenant promise but he's close, so close that, in Mohammed's version, Abraham and Ishmael wind up in Mecca of all places where they build the Ka'ba, the most sacred shrine for Arab polytheists and the goal of the world's largest pilgrimage, thus enabling Mohammed to tap into two traditions from which to build his empire.

THE PROMISE REVISITED

Let's revisit that promise. "Go from your country and your kindred and your father's house to the land that I will show you...by you all the families of the earth will bless themselves." Or, as the standard Jewish translation renders it, "And all the families of the earth/ Shall bless themselves by you." (Gen 12:1-2) And with these words a new start after the chaos of the first eleven chapters is offered. The sagas of Abraham, Isaac, Jacob, Moses, and the kings begin: in short, the story of Israel. Not to mention that eventually half of the world's population would trace its spiritual lineage to Abraham.

One would think that such a common ancestor would be the great unifier among the three Abrahamic religions but in fact, as Jon D. Levenson argues[2] the opposite has happened. It all hinges on those words of promise and how one interprets them. If the Jewish translation says, "All the families of the earth shall bless themselves by you," the King James Bible translation is, "And in thee shall all the families of the earth be blessed." And therein lies the controversy. For the Jews, the words simply mean that Abraham is a token byword, an iconic comparison, like: "May you be as good a dancer as Fred Astaire!" or "May you be as rich as Donald Trump!" So Abraham's blessing is basically a byword for good luck and favor. That's all that "all the families of the earth shall bless themselves by you" means.

But Christians, namely St. Paul in Galatians, put their own unique interpretations on these words. They render the meaning as saying that God's blessing goes not just to believing Jews but through them to all who believe. The Abrahamic blessing, premised on faith, is a conduit to believing Gentiles. More than that. Since the Jews fell into unbelief, the promise got transferred totally to the Gentiles. Indeed, in them and through them (the Jews) "shall all the families of the earth be blessed." Thus St. Paul: "And the scripture, foreseeing that God would justify the Gentiles by faith, declared the Gospel beforehand to Abraham saying, 'All the Gentiles shall be blessed in you.'" (Gal. 3:8) Yes, in this interpretation, Abraham is that first believer, the one according to Paul, justified by faith alone (not works; indeed, the Mosaic code with all of its 613 laws was in the distant future), who set the stage for all believers, namely the Gentiles, not just his physical descendants. The blessing of Abraham the believer passed to the Church, the home of the new believers, especially since the Jews apostatized. Obviously, the Jews don't see it that way.

Thus began the origins of the split between Jews and Christians and eventually Islam and Abraham, claimed by all three faiths, has divided rather than united them. We see here also what we shall come across time and time again: the Bible is a collection of ongoing interpretations, some quite creative, some bearing little relationship to the original passages they're interpreting, most reflecting the agendas of the interpreters.

TEST TIME

Abraham is put to a lot of tests: leaving his native land, losing his wife, and, of course, the great one: sacrificing his only son, Isaac. This incident is known in rabbinic texts as the Aqedah, or the binding of Isaac. (Jewish lore says the Aqedah became the site of the Jewish Temple.) This story has intrigued scholars forever, for it leaves much more unsaid than said. For one thing, asking Abraham to sacrifice his son was not an unusual request; offering one's firstborn son was common among the ancient peoples, where people believed that the first born was the offspring of a god and human, and so the first child was being returned to his divine parent. This belief was part of the common culture that included the Hebrews. For example, early on there are the commands in the Book of Exodus (22: 28-29) where YHWH ordered, "The firstborn of your sons you shall give to me...the same with your oxen and sheep." That "giving to me" phrase means "sacrifice to me." This command was later modified by allowing the son to be bought back or redeemed. Then there were kings, like Ahaz (2 Chronicles 28:3) and Manasseh, who offered their sons as burnt sacrifices (the expression was they made them "pass through fire").

There was even a place outside Jerusalem where children were burned as victims, although nothing has been found in Jerusalem's Hinnom Valley to suggest child sacrifice. In Ezekiel 20: 25-26, God chillingly says, "Moreover I gave them statues that were not good and ordinances by which they could not live. I defiled them through their very gifts, *in their offering up all their firstborn*, in order that I might horrify them, so that they might know that I am the LORD." The fulminations against the practice from prophets like Jeremiah testify to its existence (32:35).

Although it was a later Hellenistic insertion added to the Deuteronomistic story, who can forget the chilling story of Jephthah (Judges 11), who sacrificed his daughter because he had made a promise to sacrifice the first one to come out to meet him and here his daughter walks through the door? So YHWH's asking Abraham to sacrifice Isaac was not unusual. What is interesting is that, unlike Deuteronomy which condemns child sacrifice, Leviticus forbade it (18:21), Genesis is altogether silent. Strangely, Abraham, who would later persistently and passionately bargain with YHWH to spare the people of Sodom, says nothing about sparing his son, especially within the dramatic subtext that if Isaac dies, so does the Promise. Some Jews take this incident as an occasion to judge God's moral character. How could he allow this? They conclude that YHWH is not morally perfect – he's still insecure and imperfect — and has yet to grow into the job. Christians, raised in the Greek notion of the perfection and unchangeableness of God, find this shocking.

Still others point out Abraham's incredible faith because in sacrificing his only son, as we just mentioned, he is sacrificing his promised future of an heir and a nation. Yet he was willing to do this, and so, in the long run, proved himself worthy of the promise. The writer of the New Testament Book of Hebrews (11) took it this way, seeing the incident as an instance of Abraham's trust and faith. But others were not so sure and tried hard to finesse the story. Later Jewish works such as the 2nd century *Book of Biblical Antiquities*, for example, has the adult Isaac tell his father that he had been born to be offered as a sacrifice. That was his destiny. The 5th century *Genesis Rabbah* portrays the event as a dispute between Isaac and Ishmael about whose devotion to God was greater. Some Islamic renditions suggest that it was Ishmael rather than Isaac who was to be sacrificed. In any case, the story is troubling in some respects. For one thing, as we noted, Abraham shows not one wit of inner anxiety or sorrow at having to dispatch his son. He just goes along coolly, calmly. For another, Isaac is a lad who clearly was old enough to ask questions and carry a load of wood. Therefore, when he got the drift of things, he could have easily fought off his aged (over 100, according to the Bible) father when he tried to tie him up or could have easily outrun the old man. Since he did none of these things there evolved the interpretation (it's not in the text) that obviously Isaac must have been a willing victim –and from this it was an attractively easy jump for Christians one day, ever alert to such motifs, to identify Isaac with Jesus, to make Isaac a foreshadowing of Jesus' Crucifixion – with, of course, the usual anti-Semitic commentary. Thus the 2nd century church father Melito of Sadis wrote, "But Christ suffered. Isaac did not suffer, for he was a type of the Passion of Christ which was to come." Basically, what he is saying is that the Aqedah episode is diminished by its real fulfillment in Christ in the same way as Judaism is rendered null by Christianity.

Finally, a modern note: commentators of today's intricacies of modern Israeli politics still engage in the endless heated debates of the practical ethics of the story. In blind obedience must Abraham ignore the profound violation of ethics in the killing of his son and obey God? Does God's command override the command of the ethical? For some, the answer to both questions is yes. Among them are some modern Zionist Jews who identify their cause with God's will. This belief is reflected in the State of Israel, which does not have and never will have a written constitution because its authority would conflict with God's. This is also why every new soldier in Israel receives a copy of the Bible along with his first gun. In short, the Jewish State *is* "God's will" and obedience to the state's decrees is absolute, no matter how immoral or unethical its orders. The Abraham-Isaac story confirms this. Naturally, others dissent and cite the interference of YHWH's angel and say that this shows that one must disobey the state's unethical commands. Some point out that the army manual "black flags" immoral actions (like killing innocent civilians), and others simply dismiss the story as irrelevant mythology. Clearly, no matter what one's take on it, the Aqedah still has resonance.

ABRAHAM AS PARADIGM

Finally, ancient interpreters find in Abraham's life a foreshadowing of the Exodus event from Egypt (Genesis 12), a prefiguring of the Passover meal (Genesis 18 and 19), and a precursor to the paschal ransoming of the first-born son (Genesis 22). It's easy to see why they would see the Exodus event prefigured in Israel's founding father. After all, knowing that Abraham, the founder of the nation, went through his own Exodus gave the people a connection not only with the past but also a connection to the future. YHWH promised Abraham that, although his offspring will be strangers in a foreign land and be enslaved, they would be delivered (Genesis 15: 13-14), and that storyline was good enough to motivate future generations, languishing in exile, to hang in there.

Bottom line: Abraham comes to be known as a man of faith par excellence. "Abram believed in the Lord, and he credited to human righteousness" (Genesis 15:6). St. Paul with his peculiar theology made much of this and over the centuries Abraham has transmuted into the paragon of ready belief (that is, trust in its original meaning.) But, according to the biblical story, he was anything but that. When God promises him (Genesis 12) great rewards such as the status as the father of a great nation Abraham balks complaining that he can't even start a family much less a nation. He doesn't have a son, only a distant cousin far away. He only believes when he gets a cosmic display by YHWH and the promise of a son. When God insisted that his wife would bear a son, we all remember how post-menopausal Sarah laughed at this possibility, but completely forget that Abraham fell on his face and also laughed at the thought of his ninety-year-old wife conceiving (Gen.17:17). He even winds up hedging God's word by impregnating his slave girl. Just in case. This is man of fragile faith, hardly great faith. At least, it didn't come easy for him. Then, too, he was not above deceit. Recall his travels in foreign lands several times passing off Sarah as his sister so as protect himself from the hostility of the local rulers, but when the rulers who take Sarah discover who she really is, they send her back to Abraham along with tons of gifts. Abraham becomes a very wealthy man.

When all is said and done we are still rather ignorant of Abraham. It is odd, as we said, that that none of the 7th and 8th century prophets ever refer to him. Not a word. They do talk about everything else in Israel's history – Sodom and Gomorrah, Jacob and Esau, the Exodus, etc. but leave Abraham out. Strange. Did he exist? As we mentioned at the beginning of this chapter, many scholars think that Abraham, like all the patriarchs, is a legend, a figure who evolved over the centuries as layers of interpretations and storytelling piled up. As they put it, the epigraphic and archaeological evidence are non-existent. The long oral tradition is another thing. Still, as we shall see in chapter 25, for some, it doesn't matter if Abraham existed or not. It's the thought that counts, the myth he embodies.

THE EARLY PRIESTHOOD

Patriarchal accounts had God follow the people wherever they went as befits a nomadic people. That's why, wherever they went, the patriarchs built altars to God, often under the name of El, a common designation of God among all peoples and the specific name of the god of the Canaanites. The patriarchal habit of building altars here and there, by the way, made it tougher later on for the Deuteronomist author to insist, as he never tired of doing (unsuccessfully), that the Temple of Jerusalem was the sole and only legitimate place to worship YHWH and all other altars or shrines must be destroyed. It was a tough sell because the patriarchs had legitimized the other places.

Speaking of altars, interestingly, there is no mention of priesthood in all of Genesis, in spite of its very elaborate and specific later institution. There are lots of altars built, but there's little sense of sacrifice. Oddly, the one and only mention of priesthood is the incident (Genesis 14) where Abraham gives a tithe to the pagan priest of El Elyom, who blessed him. This priest also happens to be the king of Salem or Jerusalem (at that time an old Canaanite city) and called "king of righteousness." The Canaanite priest-king's name is Melchizedek. He, the priest of another god, blesses Abraham (showing Melchizedek is superior) and they share bread and wine. Some Christian commentators tried to make a Eucharistic connection here, but the writers of the Christian scripture don't pick up on it and it likely had no such association. On the other hand, in a very creative piece of writing, his superiority over Abraham would be used in the Christian Epistle to the Hebrews to show that, *therefore*, Melchizedek is also superior to Abraham's descendant, Levi; that is, the Levitical priesthood. This was scoring a theological point because the writer of Hebrews was claiming Jesus as a priest, but clearly, since Jesus was not from the tribe of Levi (according to the order of Levi), the claim had to be moved to higher ground; rather, he is "a priest forever according to the order of Melchizedek." (Heb. 7:17) Christian theology has picked up this phrase as a bit of typology and made it part of the liturgical ordination of the Catholic priest, but it remains an interpretative stretch.

THE COVENANT

God makes a covenant with Abraham. The Covenant is a cornerstone of Jewish faith and is the foundation of their claim to the Promised Land. "On that day the LORD made a Covenant with Abraham saying, 'To your descendants I give this land" (Genesis 15:18). Then follows an elaborate ritual of cutting up animals – a three-year-old heifer, a three-year-old female goat, a three year old ram, a turtledove and a young pigeon – and burning them to seal the Covenant. As James

Kugel points out, discoveries of ancient covenant practices show that what was really happening in this story was that Abraham wanted, so to speak, the Covenant in writing. In other words, the Covenant's animal sacrifice ritual, according to standard Near Eastern custom, was a legal political act, binding God to a legal agreement. It is saying that the Hebrews have a right to the land and, moreover, they had a "document" to prove it. It all sounds too convenient and contrived and some scholars hold that the claim via the legal fiction of the ritual "document" validating the claim to the land is a self-justifying invention, much the same way the that popes of the middle ages laid claim to Rome and the western part of the Roman Empire on the basis of the "Donation of Constantine," a decree purportedly given by the Emperor Constantine I, but later proven to be a forgery.

As part of this Covenant, as we saw in Genesis 12, God famously makes the gift of land to Abraham, a promise repeated many times subsequently. It must be remembered, however, that these words were written in the time of the monarchy precisely when, at last, Israel was a small but unimportant kingdom, yet a kingdom nevertheless, and so in effect the authors are telling the people, "We've arrived! We're the fulfilled promises! Look around you!" In short, these words aren't so much telling the future as affirming the Israelites' present status. And they can thank YHWH for that. It was all "foretold." They were the Chosen People:

> Praise the LORD for the LORD is good.
> Sing a psalm to his name for he is loving.
> For the LORD has chosen Jacob for himself
> and Israel for his own possession.

(Psalm 135)

THE CHOSEN ONES

Being chosen by the deity over others (especially one's enemies) is a great boon. It validates every political move. And Israel's chosenness was uncompromisingly linked to the land, a link that ultimately provided for the foundation of Zionism though its roots were thoroughly secular. The Messianic impulse of Judaism is found here also. We see this today with fundamentalist Christians who vehemently protest the erection of statehood for Palestine as a violation of the promise made to God's Chosen People that they would possess the land forever (Genesis 13:15). We likewise see this today in some young radical Muslims who also have a deep sense of being chosen by Allah to wreak destruction on Israel and the West and are deeply desirous to be martyrs. History is full of people who claimed they and their people were chosen by their gods.

The emperor Theoderic held that the Roman Empire was part of the divine plan, chosen by the gods to bring humankind to its full potential. When the many gods gave way to a singular Christian God, the mission was recalibrated to spreading the Christian Gospel. The Aztec god Huitzilopochtli chose his people and led them out of the wilderness.[3] In ancient China, the people during the Zhou dynasty (c. 1050-1221 B.C.E.) had a deep sense that they were a chosen people. Then there were Genghis Kahn, Attila the Hun, Mohammed, and so on, all claiming to have been chosen by God. Our own U. S. history is full of the concept of evangelical chosenness linked to the land. One thinks of Thomas Jefferson, Andrew Jackson, James Polk, Theodore Roosevelt, the whole Manifest Destiny theme, and also today's ideas of "American Exceptionalism."[4] And if God chose one people (because he loves them, he says in Deut. 7:7-8) he excluded others:

> " I have loved you, says the LORD But you say, "How have you loved us?" Is not Esau Jacob's brother? says the LORD. Yet I have loved Jacob but I have hated Esau."
>
> (Malachi 1:2-3)

Of course these words were written at a time when the Jews were angry at the Edomites (Esau's descendants) who snatched some of their territory when they were at a low point.

Recall that others, in an effort to mitigate the darker side of election, point to the saying that "all the families of the earth" will be blessed through Abraham and, therefore, Israel's election eventually means universal election. How this would happen is not disclosed. Later prophets like Isaiah seem to extend YHWH's invitation to other nations (19:19-25) if they accept the offer of salvation. Isaiah's initial expansion, however, contracted severely when, after the exile under Nehemiah, the need for identity shoved the Jews into a sharp separatism, including the draconian decree to dismiss their foreign wives. Gradually, the universal scope of YHWH's election of the nation of Israel gave way to individual election. This notion is quite prominent in the Dead Sea Scrolls, a notion that Paul seems to follow in his epistles and which the early Christians took up. The Pauline thought was that not all Jews were chosen to believe in Jesus, only "the elect" were, along with "elected" gentiles. The early Christians expanded the notion of election (for some like Augustine, it was a matter of predestination), and today's candidates for the RCIA are called "the Elect of God" and they must sign "the Book of the Elect." In the Mass Catholics still pray that they may be counted "among those you have chosen," and the words of consecration, "This is my blood shed for many" (not for "all" as it was for centuries) make us wonder who is left out. Being chosen is constitutive of any religion, or else it wouldn't be different from the others. The whole notion of biblical election, like so many biblical notions, has obviously been reinterpreted.

When all is said and done, the concept of divine election remains, again like so much in the Bible, intriguing. God actually does show favoritism to one group over another. He does choose some to come to faith in Jesus, but he does not choose all (Romans 9:16). The rabbis and the early Christians wrestled with it. It was a source of major controversy during the Reformation time, when people were deeply concerned about who is chosen, who is saved, and Paul's epistle to the Romans became a hot place to search for answers. "How do I know I am chosen, predestined?" was an especially burning question for Protestants. The best some could do was to suggest that being wealthy was one sign of God's favor, and today's flourishing Gospel of Prosperity churches have enough biblical quotes and stories to justify them.

For moderns, indoctrinated with political correctness, the issue is moot. Rabbi Michael Kogan spins it: "I believe God chose the Jewish people. But who said God can make only one choice?" He goes on to remark that the Jewish people are *a* chosen people, not *the* Chosen People.[5] Other modern Jews, haunted by the Holocaust, are conflicted. Being chosen has nearly led to their extinction, and so they want no part of it. If being identifiable as elected Jews leads to persecution and death, then better to assimilate. Secularized Jews have chosen to be unchosen as evidenced by their extremely low birth rate, their high intermarriage rate, and their likelihood of being converted to other religions. The fictional rabbi, Shamon Haretz, in the movie "Defiance" is presiding over a grave, and he prays this prayer:

> "Merciful God, we commit our friends to you. We have no more prayers, no more tears; we have run out of blood. Choose another people. We have paid for each of our commandments; we have covered every stone and field with ashes. Sanctify another land. Choose another people. Teach them the deeds and the prophecies. Grant us but one more gift: take away our holiness. Amen."

An honest prayer that provokes the ultimate question: Why should being chosen be so arbitrary? No one knew the answer beyond that that's the way life is. Mother loved me more than you. Live with it.

Chapter 3.

THE SÀGAS OF THE GRANDSONS

Abraham's reputed grandsons, Jacob and Esau, from the beginning, from the womb, never got along. There's a reason for this. Although not in the text, interpreters found it necessary to make ancestor Jacob the hero and Esau the villain. Why? Because Esau's descendants, the Edomites, were, at the time of the composition of this story, mortal enemies of the Israelites, and so the interpreters had to demonize them by making their founding father an uncouth scoundrel from day one. (We just saw the same etiological device in the Noah saga. Noah's daughters had sex with drunken Noah, and produced Moab. The hated Moabites were also bitter enemies but, after all, says the foundational story, what can you expect from a bunch of bastards?) Need I add that powerfully determining in all of this is the arch theme of election?

Of course, Jacob himself, as a liar (he lied to his father, "I am Esau, your firstborn") and cheat, and manipulator of his starving brother, was far from admirable, but interpreters would play that down and see nobler and deeper meanings in his deceits. Anyway, in keeping with the way stories grow, Esau's wicked reputation expanded in succeeding centuries and new charges were added in later biblical pages that never appear in Genesis. No matter, the equation stood: from the beginning we (Jacob/Israelites) are good, and they (Esau/the Edomites) are bad. Again, this dichotomy stems from the current fact that at the time of the writing of Genesis the Israelites were disunited and militarily inferior while, the Edominites were strong, powerful, and superior. But, do not despair: the weaker, younger brother will prevail, as indeed he did for a brief period under King David who conquered Edom. That's when the biblical writer put into Rebekah's (their mother's) mouth one of those pseudo-prophecies (ones pretending to be written before the event but actually written after it) that "the older will wind up serving the younger."

Finally, to mix it up some more, some have noted that the Jacob and Esau saga corresponds to the Egyptian gods, Horus and Set, who also struggled in the womb and fought over who would lead the nation. A clue to this connection is found in the fact that the Egyptian god, Set, Horus' rival, was covered with a lot of red hair just like Esau (or, more to the point, vice versa). Jacob's deceit in getting the birthright also reflects an Egyptian story and his renaming as Israel finds two conflicting accounts in Genesis that reflect political rivalries. One naming is at the wrestling incident at Penuel and the other is a Beth-El, two power centers trying to claim a foundational hero and political legitimacy. That brief wrestling incident, of course, has been fodder for all kinds of literary imaginings and "Jacob's Ladder" has lent itself to many exotic interpretations and questions. (Scholars think that the word ladder really means "mound" and, therefore, a more accurate rendering would be "staircase," reflecting the image of a Mesopotamian ziggurat). Is there hope for release from this "valley of tears?" Is it better to move on than to stay like Jacob? Who is Jacob's opponent? YHWH? His alter ego?

JACOB'S BLESSING

One day, Jacob becomes old and is ready to die. Before he does he gives his prophetic blessings to his sons:

> "Reuben, you are my firstborn...Unstable as water you shall no
> longer excel because you went into your father's bed...Simeon

and Levi are brothers; weapons of violence are their swords...
Cursed be their anger...I will divide them in Jacob, and scatter
them in Israel. Judah, your brothers shall praise you; your
hand shall be on the neck of your enemies; your father's sons
shall bow down before you. Judah is a lion's whelp... The
scepter shall not depart from Judah, nor the rulers' staff from
between his feet. His eyes are darker than wine, and his teeth
whiter than milk." (49:3-12)

And so it goes. In contrast to his older brothers, Judah is praised
and, although fourth down the line, he will rule over his brothers.
(The election theme again.) Reuben is disqualified because of his
illicit sexual activity with Jacob's concubine (a political act signaling
that he was taking over. Absalom, David's son, would make the same
gesture when he revolted against his father.) The actuality is that,
by the time of this composition centuries later, the tribe of Reuben
had all but disappeared and was in no position to warrant an eternal
blessing back then. Next, Levi and Simeon are disqualified because
they are people of violence (although there is no indication of such
conduct prior to Jacob's words, so later scribes inserted the terrible
story of Dinah to provide such an episode of violence to discredit
them). That effectively removes the first three contenders for leadership and leaves Judah, who just happens to be the ancestor of the
current writers' reigning king, King David. This is another instance
of the present being justified by a contrived past. Once again we are
reminded that, although the stories of the Patriarchs take place in
the 11th or 12th centuries B.C.E., they were in fact written hundreds
of years later; although there is some very ancient material here and
there, their stories were heavily edited to conform to current religious
and political situations. On the whole matter of Jacob's blessing, this
comment in the *New Interpreters' Study Bible* is apropos:

> "Jacob's final words to his sons are from an archaic poetic
> composition inserted into the narratives of Jacob's last in-
> structions and blessings. Much of the Hebrew text is dif-
> ficult, and many of the images are obscure; but some of the

later realities of the Israelite tribes and of their relationship with one another are reflected in these brief statements about Jacob's sons. Here, as elsewhere in Genesis, Jacob's sons represent the *later Israelite tribes* that bear their names. *Thus the fortune of the sons described here are in fact the fortunes of their tribal descendants.* Since Judah is given the preeminent role among his brothers (v.8), *this composition reflects the period of the monarchy*, when the family of David, from the tribe of Judah, established dynastic rule over Israel in Jerusalem."[1] (My emphasis).

So, once more, the average person may be scandalized to learn that a political agenda is at work. That, in order to validate the status quo, current political realities are creatively read back into the nation's beginnings. This is an instance (one of many) of nationalistic propaganda that we didn't realize was an intimate part of the Holy Bible.

One can sense another pseudo prophecy put into the mouth of Jacob. He says to Judah, "Your hands [will be] on your enemies neck and even your brothers bow before you. Judah is like a lion's club...like the king of beasts, none dare challenge." Indeed, at the time of this editing, David had subdued the other tribes and his enemies, and so Jacob was "predicting" what had already taken place. In short, the blessings of Jacob, as old as the core event is, go back to the time of David and Solomon. But there was a problem about that promise made to Judah. The promise was that Judah's kings should rule *forever* ("the scepter shall not depart from Judah"), but in fact it did depart. The Davidic dynasty died out in the 6th century B.C.E. under the Babylonians. Faced with this prophetic dissonance later interpreters had to come up with an answer and the answer they proposed was that Jacob's blessing really meant was that the scepter would not *depart* forever. Temporarily, perhaps, but not forever. So that meant that at some point in the future it would return. As a neat recovery this interpretation was to fuel the hopes of the Jews in exile or under occupation. Thus was born the notion of a future Davidic king, God's anointed, the Messiah. Yes, Jacob was actually predicting a future Messianic king who would bring back the glory days of

David. (This was a critical point for the evangelists so they strongly underscored the point that Jesus was from the tribe of David and, in fact, was born in David's town even though, as we shall see, most mainline scholars hold that Jesus was actually born in Nazareth.)

As a sidebar, we're not through with Jacob (nor politics), because the Bible goes on to say that his wife, Rachel, was buried "on the way to Ephrath, which is Bethlehem" (Gen. 35:19), but in 1 Samuel, 10:2, the Bible says that Rachel was buried in the territory of Benjamin. She couldn't be buried in both places, of course, but the contradictory claims represent a feud between Israel and Judah. Claiming such a matriarch would go a long way in determining who would rule over whom. (Something like having Jesus born at the southern royal-line David's Bethlehem instead of where he really may have been born, northern Nazareth, out of which "nothing good could come".) It is easy to detect rivalries and politics and partisanship in the authors' hindsight accounts.

THE TRIBES OF ISRAEL

According to the biblical account, Jacob, tricked by a very sleazy father-in-law named Laban, winds up marrying two of Laban's daughters and two of his female servants. From this foursome come the twelve tribes of Israel (although the tribes from the wives would, of course, always outrank the tribes of the concubines). Thus was born the nation of Israel. But the scholars are skeptical that an entire nation was descended from one ancestor. Certainly, all we know about the twelve tribes – and it was apparently a fluid number – indicates that they were scattered all over the place, seldom had unity with one another and often fought one another. They really appear to be separate and unrelated, and their numbers and names vary in the Bible. The tribe of Simon is missing, for example, when Moses blesses the tribes. The listing differs from that given in the Book of Judges where four tribes are omitted. When Deborah sang her song to rally the tribes of Israel, the tribal names are different from Jacob's. The four tribes of Reuben, Gad, Levi, and Issachar are absent. The tribes, such as they were, were notoriously at odds with one another. They came together (briefly) to fight a common enemy, and eventually this (temporary) unity was validated by the myth of a common ancestor, a common artifice in many ancient societies. Mostly they were associated with parcels of land assigned in the time of Joshua. By and by, they dissolved into the protection of the centralized monarchy.

The whole Abraham-Isaac-Jacob saga has been fascinating, but it turns out not to be as simple and direct as once thought. That old linear paradigm of the promises made to Abraham and renewed and passed on in an unbroken line to Isaac and Jacob and through the prophets to David culminating in the Messiah, Jesus, doesn't hold up, especially, in spite of Christian apologists, where there are (as we shall see) no clear cut prophecies of the Messiah. In fact, as we noted, scholars hold that Abraham, Isaac and Jacob never existed much less were related. They are fictional characters not attested to outside the Bible. Some scholars concede that there may have been some figures in the past, some local heroes, as attested to by oral tradition, who correspond to this trio, but they are lost in folklore. So, concerning the Patriarchs, this last word is in order: "The Bible biographies are not magnificent portrayals painted by artists onto canvas but the work of a mosaic-maker who selected, fashioned, and arranged colorful stones until a well-planned and deliberate work emerged."[2] These words, of course, refer also to the entire Bible.

THE JOSEPH NOVELLA

The story of Joseph, one of Israel's heroes, is a beloved one, even though he started out as an arrogant prig and caused some raised eyebrows among later Jewish commentators by his marriage to a foreigner, the daughter of an idol's minister no less. (Their solution? Joseph converted her!) Anyway, this story of Joseph of the multicolored (actually, "long-sleeved") coat has all the earmarks of a folktale and, indeed, there is a similar story found among the Egyptians and other biblical fictional stories where Jewish heroes survive in exile in a foreign court (Daniel, Esther, Tobit). It's an engaging story with puzzling geography, so much so that scholars sense it's not only a work of fiction – Joseph is not mentioned in Egyptian annals as we would expect of Egypt's most important official next to the Pharaoh himself – but one strongly affiliated with and adapted from Near Eastern literature, especially Egyptian and Canaanite lore. This biblical version supplies the bridge to the next story by explaining how the Hebrews wound up in Egypt.

Genesis has been quite a trip. Once more, what we have to keep on remembering, is that book was written hundreds and hundreds of years after the purported events it describes. Like most biblical books, it represents hindsight writing. That means, being written by scribes during the exile, the time of their captivity by the Babylonians, Genesis is basically an attempt by the Hebrews to define themselves as above and separate from their captors – their religion, their gods, their values. That is why Genesis is written theologically (not scientifically) the way it is. To add to its mystification, from the beginning it has become continuously overlaid with more theological interpretations to the point that the average person – and a good many scholars – cannot read the text without reflectively reading someone's interpretation of it, an interpretation that, more often as not, has nothing to do with the literal text. As John Collins remarks of Genesis, "More than most stories, these chapters of Genesis have been overlaid with theological interpretations that have little basis in the Hebrew text." [3] So when Jews or Christians read the Genesis story – and, indeed, the entire Bible – they are reading it filtered through centuries of interpretations rendered by the Rabbis and Church Fathers, interpretations that often have solidified into orthodoxy and Church doctrine, even though the literal text does not always support either.

Chapter 4.

THE EXODUS SAGA

Moses becomes the hero of the next books in the Bible, following the Joseph story. (We have no idea how long the Hebrews really were in Egypt.) As a result of his parents sidestepping orders to kill all Hebrew newborns, Moses is saved from the Nile by Pharaoh's daughter, raised in the Egyptian court, and called by God at the burning bush to lead a huge throng of enslaved people to freedom after ten spectacular plagues devastated the Egyptians. (Later on, evangelist Matthew, in his effort to make Jesus "another Moses" will give us his version by having another Pharaoh-like king, Herod, decree the killing of newborn babies.)

From the beginning, scholars have doubted this story. For one thing, the story of Moses' rescue from the Nile is clearly and verifiably an old folktale. It reflects many similar contemporary stories from around the world, such as that told of King Sargon I, king of Akkad, who conquered Babylon around 2300 B.C.E. Legend says his mother, a priestess, left him on the bank of the Euphrates in a basket made from rushes and tar. The river took him down the canal, where a gardener called Akki, the "drawer of water," rescued him and reared him as his own, and he became a powerful leader. All this is a reminder that all the ancients were storytelling peoples and so events automatically became stories, with all of their impulses of color, exaggeration and comparisons. Perhaps, then, the inclusion of a revised Akkadian story is simply meant to say, storytelling-wise, that Moses, like Sargon, would grow up to be a great leader.

The Moses account, then, is clearly not historical. In fact, if read literally it has some glaring storyline gaps, such as: if the order was to kill all the Hebrew males, how did Moses' brother Aaron and other males of Moses' generation escape? More than that: if Pharaoh was so concerned about Hebrew overpopulation why didn't he logically order the death of the Hebrew *females*? Then there's the name "Moses." It is an Egyptian name, and it is very likely that Moses was an Egyptian. Since that embarrassing fact about his name is true, the Hebrew writers had to work around it. So they wrote that the name Moses means, "drawn out of the waters," an inaccurate explanation. Moses' name is a very common Egyptian name and it means, "to be born," and many Egyptians carry the names as a suffix, as in "Thutmoses."

Moses, like Abraham, is not exactly a sterling character. He kills an Egyptian, hides the body, and flees to escape persecution. In his new country, he has a mythic dialogue with YHWH at the famous burning bush scene. Moses' call and his protestation in this encounter are part of the stereotypical storyline of all such calls that elicit the "I am not worthy" response. We see this with Jeremiah, Isaiah, Gideon, Oliver Twist, and Harry Potter. One of Moses' excuses is that he's not a good speaker, but his brother is. This dialogue is basically a veiled political boost by the Priestly editor, who had a vested self-interest in heightening Aaron's status. Notice that YHWH *also* spoke directly to Aaron (Numbers 18:1. 8. 20), just as he did to Moses. Aaron also winds up in the Priestly rendition as the one who tells Pharaoh, "Let my people go," and it is his staff that turns into a snake, not Moses' (Ex. 7:2 and 9:9-10). Recall, too, that when YHWH ordered a staff from each tribe to be placed overnight in his tent to determine which one should have the priestly leadership (the one that blossomed would be his choice), Aaron, being of the tribe of Levi, didn't possess a staff, so Moses gave one to him alone. In the morning Aaron's staff not only blossomed, but sprouted almonds, as well! What this tells us is that there was constant jockeying all throughout the Bible as to who would claim the powerful priestly role, and the propaganda here is quite apparent.

Whatever the literary maneuverings, Moses still comes off as the flawless hero of liberation, the reputed author of the Pentateuch and undisputed leader of the people. Well, not entirely flawless, because his marriage to a foreign Midianite woman proved to be an embarrassment when, later on, such foreign marriages were forbidden. His own brother and sister, Aaron and Miriam, confronted him on this issue (Numbers 12). Others also contested his leadership, and one of Levi's descendants named Korah, supported by some others, wound up being swallowed up by the earth (Numbers 16) for challenging Moses. YHWH and his chosen leaders are not to be trifled with.

Doubts

Scholars who question or reject the story of Moses and the Exodus usually divide into four camps: (1) it didn't happen because of the lack of corroborating archaeological evidence in Egypt and Sinai; (2) the whole story reeks of myth, legend and folklore; (3) the narratives were written so many centuries after the purported events, and therefore they are theologically and ideologically shaped to the point where you can't detect any real history anymore; and (4), while the story is quite fictitious, there is, in the words of Israel Finkelstein, a "germ" of reality to it (a stubborn oral tradition?). Like so many other books, the books that tell the story of the Exodus are the composite products of many hands over many years.

Indeed, the scholars are on to something. Those who insist on the literal history genre, rather than the story one are faced with the facts: there are no Egyptian records of such a mass movement as the Exodus depicts. Some counter by saying that Egypt could hardly be expected to advertise such an embarrassment but, in fact, all peoples, including Israel, *did* in some way advertise their embarrassing losses. They simply put them under the category of judgment from their gods. For example, Egypt makes mention of its defeats by the Hyksos and the Sea Peoples, and Israel vividly recalls its near-annihilation by Sennacherib (2 Kings) and both freely interpreted them as a punishing act by their gods for their infidelity. And, then too, for Egypt not to mention, even in a veiled way, the death of a whole generation is hard to imagine. Moreover, other peoples of Mesopotamia have no record of the march of such an incredibly vast number of people, with the biblical Book of Numbers giving a population of over 600,000 and Exodus 12:37 offering a figure of "about six hundred thousand men on foot, besides children. A mixed crowd also went with them, and livestock in great numbers." If you add one wife (some had more) plus two children (some had more) for each man that adds up to over some two million people! That is larger than the population of all of Egypt at the time. The land simply couldn't support that many people. How did so many people manage to survive in the desert and, most of all, why is there no archaeological evidence of that many people in the desert? Certainly some two million people could not have entered Canaan without notice or archaeological trace. As a report in the *New York Times* puts it: "Archaeologists who have worked here [North Sinai, Egypt] have never turned up evidence to support the account [of the Exodus] in the Bible. And there is only one archaeological find that even suggests the Jews were ever in Egypt."[1]

That report reflects the situation in modern Israel after the Six Day War in 1967 which opened up historical and archaeological sites formerly occupied by Jordan, Syria and Egypt. These sites included Jericho, the Golan Heights, Banias, the site of Caesarea Philippi and Sinai. It was hoped that the archaeologists could now find the Exodus route. But during the thirteen years (1967-1980) that the state of Israel occupied the Sinai Peninsula and Israeli archaeologists combed the Sinai for evidence of the Israelites' 40-year sojourn, the bottom line is that there was simply no evidence of any large-scale migration. The Exodus, on the scale and the manner the Bible describes, simply did not happen. So, what is going on here? The answer is storytelling, as described by Franciscan scripture scholar Leslie J. Hoppe:

> "The story of the Exodus as found in the Bible is the product of the Persian Period (sixth century B.C.E.), about six hundred

years after the events described. The geographical details of that story reflect sixth-century B.C.E. knowledge of the Sinai. The narrator was heir to the tradition that the Hebrew slaves made their way from Egypt to Canaan, across the Sinai Peninsula. The contribution of the narrator was to provide a more detailed geographical setting for the story of how God guided the Israelite tribes through the desert.

"The theological value of the Exodus story is its portrayal of the God of Israel as one who takes the side of slaves over their oppressive masters, thus turning the social order on its head...The descendants of the Hebrew slaves – those who first heard or read this story in the Persian Period – found it to be a source of hope and consolation. It is an affirmation that God's love for Israel is not undermined, even by Israel's lack of faith and commitment.

"The 'good news' is something the Jews of the Persian Period needed to hear...What God did once, for the generation of the Exodus they hoped God would do again in their own day..."²

BITS OF HISTORY

So the Exodus – an event that happened in 1200 B.C.E., according to most scholars – is also a late propaganda piece elaborated from old traditions. For all the obvious monarchic constructions in the story of the Exodus, some maintain that there are pieces of reality that constitute the outline of the myth. There are indications of foreign Semitic herd peoples (pastoralists) present in Egypt during the times of the Exodus. There were POW's, the fruit of various military exploits, present in Egypt. There were famines that drove others there. So there may be something valid in the memory of what may have been originally a real but minor event of a handful of people escaping into the desert. After all, the idea of liberation from oppression is an old one. It has roots in other Near Eastern cultures; for example, the worker-gods rebel against the oppressive rule of the high god Enlil in the Babylonian *Atrahasis Epic*. As for Israel, modern scholars now speak of Exoduses in the plural – that is, Exodus 1, Exodus 2, Exodus 3, and so on – to underscore their belief that there were several minor escapes or departures that were literarily coalesced into one major celebrated event. There may be something here, for it seems unlikely that someone would concoct a foundational tradition that presents its ancestors as slaves.

A bit of historic irony: the Exodus saga has become the iconic motif of liberation inspiring the cries for the rights of ordinary people. In reality, that liberation was far from a democratic victory as we moderns understand it. It was a distinctly patriarchal concept of "freedom," for the enslaved Hebrews, once free, drove the Canaanites from their land, owned slaves when they got there, and oppressed women. The patriarchal pattern that the Bible left us later became the basis of the divine right of kings. Any opposition to the king was an opposition to God. Authority definitely flowed from the top down, as it did in the Bible. With its interpretation of Matthew 16, the Catholic Church fully adopted this model. That authority would flow from the bottom up, from the people, was a radical concept derived from the pagan Greeks, not from the believing Jews, who firmly upheld a top-down authority. Likewise, the principles of freedom and tolerance, in almost total opposition to the Bible, were gifts from the secular Enlightenment of the 18th century of our era, not from the Christians. In brief, nowhere in the Bible, outside of a few thin references (Paul's "there is neither male or female," etc. or the "good" Samaritan) is there any scripture promoting equality, tolerance, or freedom the way we understand them. The Exodus as liberation for all is more PR than truth, more motto than reality. On the contrary, it was YHWH/-monotheism or death, Jesus is Lord or the Inquisition. It was only by *undermining* the teaching of the Bible, and the practices of Jews and Christians derived from it that we get modern tolerance:

> "...Freedom from authoritative rulers had to wait until the Bible's own authority was worn down by the radical questions of the freethinkers of the Enlightenment, including several of

our founding fathers. The Bible had to yield its own political authority in order to prepare the path for freedom."[3]

MOUNT SINAI?

Standing like the mountain it is, Mount Sinai (sometimes called Mount Horeb) also figuratively stands as the epicenter of all these divine-human encounters. It is commonly thought to be a high mountain, and is pictured as so in popular lore and movies. But in fact, nowhere in the Bible does it say it is high, and indeed some traditions hold that it was low, to reflect its humility. Whatever it is, scholars, especially the archaeologists, are not sure the present site identified as Mt. Sinai is the real one. Nor is anyone sure why this mountain was chosen for the encounter between YHWH and Moses. There's no historical reason for it. The origin of its choice seems to come very late. It comes from the mid-3rd century Christian monks who settled there and who began the tradition. By the 4th century the peak called Jebel Musa was the best contender. When the Emperor Justinian replaced a church with a monastery in the 6th century, the identification of the Mountain of God with Sinai finally became fixed in Christian belief.

But modern archaeologists balk. That's because, scour as they might, they can find no evidence of a large group of people who might have settled there. How can some two to three million people leave no trace? Even if the number were more modest, say several hundreds, how could they survive in uninhabited Sinai (barring the miraculous manna and quail)? More pointedly, if Mt. Sinai were the actual site, how come it never became a place of Israelite pilgrimage – unlike, say, Shiloh, where the Tabernacle was placed in the time of the Judges? So, although there are a number of theories for Mt. Sinai's location, the fact is none of the candidates are supported by archaeological evidence. Maybe, some think, Mt. Sinai isn't even in the Sinai Peninsula but elsewhere, leading some archaeologists to speculate that a more likely site is the comparatively lower and flatter Midian area. It has a lot going for it. Recall it is the place where Moses fled after killing the Egyptian taskmaster and which became the home of Moses' wife and father in law, Jethro, who also guided Moses in his escape from Egypt, and where his son was born. In short, there's a very rich connection between Moses and Midian. In addition, the Bible speaks of earthquakes, shattering wind, and fire emitting from Sinai's peak. It is a veritable volcanic mountain, but in the Sinai Peninsula there is no evidence of any volcanic activity – but there is in Midian. The holy site is up for grabs.[4]

OTHER PUZZLES

The seemingly miraculous event of crossing the Red Sea (three versions are given, and they are incompatible with one another) and the ten plagues do provoke skepticism. Questions arise over one account that says that God had Moses use his staff to part the waters (Exodus 14:15), but then a few verses later, another account says the strong east wind did the job (Exodus 14:21-22). Like Ba'al, the storm god, YHWH is also depicted as a storm god who uses the wind through his nostrils to cause the sea to roil. Which was it, God or nature? Later biblical books – Psalm 77, Isaiah, Nehemiah, and Wisdom (which don't always agree) – opted for the miraculous and the whole event, like any good story, eventually blossomed over the centuries with cinematic details. Further, as Joseph F. Kelly points out, can you see Pharaoh, savvy monarch and strategist, ruler of much of the Near East, coming upon those huge walls of water and actually being foolish enough to think that Moses would actually keep the water walls intact while he crossed? He couldn't be that incompetent. Anyway, most scholars believe that the crossing was not at the Red Sea, an awkward detour, but rather at a watery reed marsh which would allow for people on foot to cross but mire heavy chariot wheels. Besides, the crossing of a river and its wondrous drying out is an old device in ancient hero stories. You have the account of the

Assyrian ruler Ashurbanipal crossing the Ulai River, Kroisos' crossing the Halys River in Herodotus' *Histories* and Xerxes' crossing of the Hellespont. For the Israelite authors who wrote the story, it was, as it must be, a victory for YHWH, the great warrior God, the One who would not only conquer Israel's enemies but show his mighty power over the waters, a theme reflecting an old Near Eastern belief that the waters were the homes of Sea Monsters (Rahab and the Leviathan in the Bible) who were defeated by YHWH (or Ba'al in the Canaanite version). The point always remains that YHWH is the chief actor, and in every ongoing contest between the gods, YHWH will always be victor. His promises will be kept.

THE PLAGUES AND THE DESERT EXPERIENCES

As for the ten plagues, it is interesting that later biblical books not only omit certain plagues but also mix up the order given in Exodus. Besides, there seems to be eight, three or five of them, not ten, depending on the source (J, P, or E). There's an old papyrus, called the Ipuwer Papyrus, that contains ancient material that describes, during a time of upheaval, almost the same happenings as the plagues. Certainly that last ferocious biblical plague, the death of the firstborns in all of Egypt, would hardly have gone unrecorded or unnoticed, yet outside of the Bible, there is no mention of it anywhere.

In the desert the Hebrews were attacked by the Amalekites under King Amalek (There are no extra-biblical references to them.) In the emergency Moses went up on a hillside and there, whenever he held up his hands, the Hebrews won. However, when he got tired and lowered them, the Amalekites won. This folkloric incident made the biblical interpreters nervous. It comes off too much as a bit of magic. They quickly explained it away by saying things like that Moses' upraised hands inspired the soldiers to think of YHWH and that gave them an extra emotional push or that his hands were held up as a sign he was praying to YHWH. When he lowered his hands, the prayer stopped and victory stopped. The point was being made that YHWH, not Moses was the agent of victory. No magic here. The Christians, when they had their turn, saw something else. They saw in Moses' outstretched hands a sign of the cross. Amalek was, in their eyes, just as clearly the devil and the whole incident was a kind of coming attractions of how Christ's cross would defeat him. To them, as always, the Old Testament was a prototype of the New.

Also in the desert, as we know, the complaining Hebrews ran short of food and water. Water came from the rock and manna from heaven supplied the lack. Modern scholars pause to observe that the manna story is a bit of an embellishment. The fact is that manna need not drop from heaven for it is a quite natural food from earth, a sweet substance excreted by insects that the Bedouin use to this day. It is also written that YHWH went before them guiding them as a pillar of fire by night and a cloud by day (Exodus 13: 21) but an Egyptian carving shows that when the Egyptians went into the desert to do battle, they carried two very high stanchions in front of the troops, that is, very long poles with a platforms on top of them. One platform held a container for fire and the other a container for fire with a lid that dampened the fire and made smoke. The fire platform at the front of the column leading the Egyptian soldiers was to guide them at night. The smoke platform was for guiding them by day. Moses, who, after all, reputedly lived in Egypt for decades and knew Egyptian ways and was in fact a superior military leader, used the same stanchion method of leading the Israelites in the desert. This was YHWH's "presence" in the fire and cloud.[5]

In the desert, a Covenant was forged creating a bond between YHWH and the Hebrews, whom he chose above all other peoples. It strictly followed the usual structures and basic treaty patterns of Israel's neighbors, especially the Hittites and the Assyrians. In fact, the Hebrew Covenant follows the Hittite version so closely that it has caused some scholars to wonder why God had to use someone else's format on this auspicious occasion instead of something more uniquely creative. Even the injunction, "You shall have no other gods before me" has a direct comparison to the injunctions that the Hittite and Assyrian rulers laid on their subjects.

The book of laws

The infallible sign that this Covenant was intact and working was the keeping of the laws. From this point on laws – all 613 of them – move front and center. To observe them was to court YHWH's favor; to break them was to run the risk of severe punishment, usually in the form of oppression and conquest by surrounding kingdoms. More than that, breaking them offended God, wounded a sacred relationship, and became, not just a transgression, but a sin. The laws both the written and in time the Oral Torah, were never really about hygiene but about identity, about separating the observant and nonobservant Jew, between Israel and the unclean gentiles.

The laws were comprehensive and minute and not always clear as to their reasons. As expected, scholars say that Moses could not possibly have written all those laws. For one thing, there are several collections scattered here and there: we call them the Priestly Code, the Holiness Code, The Deuteronomic Code, the Covenant Code, etc. They often repeat the very same materials. Why would they do that if they came from the hand of one author? The laws sometimes contradict one another; for example, the burnt offering altar in one place must be made of earth and in another place of wood overlaid with gold. The rule in one place is to boil the Passover meat, and in another it must be not be boiled but roasted; "do not boil it" (Ex 12:8-9). Nor do they always make sense. Why, for example, may the Israelites eat sheep but not pigs? The purity laws seem more to do with taboos than with common sense. And they were often harsh: rebellious sons must be stoned by the community (Deut 21: 18-21, Exodus 21:17, Leviticus 20:9), a young woman who loses her virginity before marriage must be stoned (Deut 22:13-20), illicit sexual relations bring stoning (Lev 21:10, adulterous couples are to be stoned

(Deut 22:22, Lev 20:10), and a father has absolute authority over his children and can even sell them as slaves (Exodus 21:7-11). Whether these penalties were actually applied, or served as mere scare tactics to protect what was basically commercial marriage alliances, nevertheless they are presented as direct divine commands.

Further evidence that the Mosaic laws were neither unique, nor from Moses' hand, came at the beginning of the 20th century when archaeologists found other older and similar collections, for example, the codes of Lipit-Ishtar, the Hittites and especially the Babylonian law code of Hammurabi dated centuries before the Exodus collection. We should note that, as in the Bible, the Mesopotamian gods had similarly authorized Hammurabi to make those laws. These laws had striking similarities to the Exodus list to the point that some laws and their wording were identical. As in the case of finding other similar versions of the flood, so, once more, the Bible was found to be no different from its surrounding cultures and it is obvious to scholars that, for example, the collection of cases found in Exodus, chapters 21 and 22 are derived from already existing Canaanite laws. Once more, it became quite clear that another hand had appropriated and inserted all those laws, that chapters 21, 22 and 23 are in fact much later additions. The idea of all these later additions was, of course, to imprint the aura and authority of Moses on them, much like later anonymous Christian writers would write epistles and attribute them to St. Paul. All of this obviously hands the notion of Mosaic authorship a setback. In any case, the God who gave these laws is highly reminiscent of the God of Genesis in his compulsive demand for order. Just as YHWH brought order out of chaos in creation so, with exact blueprints, he brings order to the sacred space of worship in the desert.

THE TEN COMMANDMENTS

The desert was also the place of the Decalogue, the Ten Commandments. Moses traveled up the mountain to get them. (The fact that he travels up and down the mountain so frequently in this chapter of the Bible is evidence of its highly composite character.) The Commandments were inscribed on two stone tablets which Moses carried down the mountain, although it has been noted, that they could have fitted on one tablet. Naturally, having two tablets provoked all kinds of interpretative speculations. It should also be noted in passing that, not only are the Commandments written in the second person masculine – which means they are addressed to males only, thus reflecting the values of a patriarchal society where animals, wives, children and slaves are described as property – but they are also particular to their time and place.

The Ten Commandments, in imitation of the contracts of other ancient peoples, are a form of contract between YHWH the over-lord and his subjects. In the Bible there are three versions of them. They are found in Exodus 20, Deuteronomy 5, and Exodus 34. Two are close but not identical and one is very different. Lacking any background reference to the monarchy, especially King David, all three versions likely came from the time when Israel was a loose confederation of the twelve tribes, and so that makes them very old.

At times, God is the giver, at other times Moses is the transmitter. Jews and most Christians follow the Deuteronomy versions. Catholics and Lutherans follow the Exodus version, which is why they have different numberings. The Exodus version alludes to the account of creation in six days, with God resting on the seventh and so people should, in imitation of God, also rest. In the Deuteronomy version there must be rest but from a different motivation: in order to give the slaves time off. All this reflects two different sources and, as we noted before, it was all right to include them because the understanding was that it is better to preserve the traditions than to reconcile them. Still it is noteworthy that, while the origins of the Sabbath are unknown, Israel seems to be the only group in ancient society that set aside one day a week for rest.

Many of the commandments are likely Canaanite in origin and were early on absorbed by the Israelites. For example there exists an epic poem written in Ugarit from around 1400 B.C.E. that antecedes the "honor thy father and mother" commandment by describing a son's duties towards an aging parent.

What intrigues us is that the Commandments, in practice, seem to be loosely observed. In the Book of Numbers, for example, Moses, in spite of the prohibition against graven images, commands a bronze serpent to be made, and all those who looked upon it were freed of the serpent's venom. (21:9) Later, King Hezekiah, in a vendetta against idols, would ground Moses' serpent to dust. (Kings 18:4) The throne of YHWH was adorned with cherubim that YHWH himself had ordered and designed. Solomon had oxen and lions adorning his temple. Jews and Christians continued to disregard the prohibitions of graven images. Even in biblical times, the threat of transgenerational punishment was rejected by Ezekiel and, later, Jesus. (John 9:1-3) Christians freely changed the day of rest to Sunday. It seems that everyone felt free to reformulate, interpret, ignore or reject one or another of the 10 Commandments.

Perhaps the best summary is this:

> "Although the biblical writers did cloak the three Decalogues with the myth of divine authorship, as is the case for the rest of the Bible, we can scarcely credit the deity with such inconsistency and repetition. Instead of an allegedly divinely revealed set of universal moral codes, we have variants of historically conditioned texts, none of which in their present form go back directly to Moses, let alone to God. If there was a proto-Decalogue, as it were, it is no longer recoverable. Nor did this seem to matter to the biblical writers, for whom the actual words of the Decalogue were not as important as its underlying principles: love of God and love of neighbor." [6]

THE PASSOVER REINVENTED

According to the Bible, it is at the time of the preparation for the great escape from Egypt that the Passover was born. Eat a lamb, do not break its bones, and sprinkle some of its blood on your doorposts so the killing angel can "pass over" your house to strike the houses of the Egyptians. Modern scholars see it differently. The Passover, they say, is a combination of two old, separate festivals, the Feast of the Unleavened Bread and Passover. The Feast of the Unleavened Bread is one of the three pilgrimage feasts of Israel, and is reflective of a settled agricultural community. This celebration was intended to bring a good harvest. The other, the Passover Feast, borrowed (as so many other of Israel's rituals) from their neighbors, involved slaughtering an animal. An animal, bones intact, was sacrificed to ensure a good flock and ward off evil as the people began their migration to another feeding plain. They also used unleavened bread and bitter herbs from the desert plants to season their food.

These feasts were totally separate, so much so that even passages in Exodus (23:14-17 and 34:18-23) talk about the Unleavened Bread, yet make no mention whatever of Passover. These two feasts, both spring activities, merged when these festivals moved out of the homes and into the various temples. At one point in history they were definitively joined together, picked up and inserted into the Exodus story although here and there, the biblical books inadvertently speak of the Feast of the Passover and the Feast of the Unleavened Bread as two separate feasts (Leviticus 23:5-8, Numbers 28:16-25 and Exodus 12:1-20), and there are other discrepancies in the directions for preparation. The New Testament reflects this dual origin because there the Feast of the Passover gets two names: the Feast of Passover and the Feast of the Unleavened Bread, testifying that the two had merged into one and were by this time synonymous. In the Gospel of John, the Passover figures as a central theme. The other three evangelists have Jesus dying on the day *after* Passover, while John, who has his own mystical agenda, has Jesus dying on the day *before* Passover, the Day of Preparation on which the lambs were slaughtered thus identifying Jesus as the Paschal Lamb as Paul did earlier in 1 Corinthians 5:7.

The Passover, as we understand it today, clearly did not originate with Moses. Interestingly, while we're at it, we might mention that a critically important feast, the Day of Atonement, is never mentioned in the Book of Exodus. According to the scholars, it started out as a ceremony for the priestly purification of the Temple sanctuary after it had been defiled. Very similar purification procedures were found elsewhere in the Near East, especially in Babylonian lore. Thus, the procedure originally had nothing to do with God forgiving people their sins once a year. It started out as just a sanctuary cleansing ceremony.[7]

FAMOUS LAST WORDS

The forty years wandering in the desert are coming to a close, and Moses, not allowed to enter the Promised Land, gives his long valedictory. Among his words is the famous "Shema," with its commands that "you shall love the Lord your God with your whole heart, soul and might.... Teach my words to your children.... Attach them to your hand, before your forehead, and on your doorposts and gates." Often the latter words were taken literally and gave rise to leather cases housing scriptural words adorning the headbands, shawls and doors. In addition, Moses attached multiple dire warnings and really terrible curses to the violation of any of the commands and laws he had left, forty-four long verses worth of threats! What catches the scholar's eye is how many of the curses' wordings match those of other nations whose members might violate *their* Covenantal agreements.

In all of this, we cannot but notice the one recurring motif: YHWH's relationship with the human race. Genesis is replete with the human race's unstoppable sinfulness and at YHWH's despair at ever correcting it. The inclination to disobedience is almost genetic (Genesis 1-11). Adam and Eve, Cain and Abel, humans and angels mating, drunken Noah, a dissimulating Abraham and Isaac, a deceitful Jacob, an arrogant Joseph, jealous brothers. No wonder that YHWH, by the end of Genesis, has given up on the human race. The characters in the Book of Exodus fare no better with their backsliding, murmuring and idolatries. They marry foreign women and sacrifice to Ba'al (Numbers 25). Yet, although YHWH is quite murderous in his response, he doesn't give up on his people as he did in Genesis. He seems to have learned his lesson and, except for one instance when he was tempted to throw in the towel, come to terms with his people's innate weaknesses. He allows his relationship with them to continue and maybe that's the meaning of the story.

CONCLUSION

The biblical stories are based on oral traditions and that is their fundamental problem: there are few or no parallel sources to test the accuracy of the stories. The questions always are: How much truth was retained in the transmissions, and how much inflation and distortion? Moses and his story is an example. He is a complex character whose existence and achievements are found nowhere outside the Bible, and his story and his attributed books (the Pentateuch), as we have seen, are rife with material from later authors. That's why some consider him (like the patriarchs) a fictional character. Most disagree. Acknowledging the fact that he and the Exodus experience are so normative, so ingrained, so central to all biblical traditions that most scholars feel there is probably an historical individual behind the inflation of propaganda. Underlying the traditions and interpretations, they feel there was some kind of Moses person who, more than anyone else, founded the religion of Israel. In any case, the Exodus story itself, true or not, would fall into the world's vocabulary as paradigm of the rallying cry to move from oppression to freedom. Pentateuch texts would transcend ancient contexts to motivate present day realities that pitted the power of God against the power of men. All kinds of people would be dubbed "another Moses" from Martin Luther King Jr. to the Underground Railroad heroine, Harriet Tubman, the "Moses of Maryland".

I cannot end this chapter without referring to the intriguing incident found in Deuteronomy 18:1-5. YHWH announces to the people that someday he will raise up a mediating prophet like Moses. Yet about a dozen or more verses later we read, "Never since has there arisen a prophet in Israel like Moses" (34:10). Since that seems to clearly exclude all the prophets who followed Moses, then who is this foretold prophet? This obviously undermines what was said in 18:1-5. So, again, where, who, is this prophet? The answer eventually took the form for both Judaism and Christianity that the not-yet, post-Moses, prophet was someone forever expected. Indeed, he became the forerunner of the Messiah. We see this understanding, for example, in the Gospel in John 1:21, when the priests and Levites ask John the Baptist if he is "the prophet." In the same Gospel, the people mistake Jesus for "*the* prophet" more than once as, for example, when he performed the miracle of loaves and fishes and they commented, "This indeed is the prophet who is to come into the world." If so, that meant the Messiah could not be far behind.

Chapter 5.

THE SAGAS OF JOSHUA AND THE JUDGES

The Book of Joshua was supposedly written by Joshua himself or by the prophet Samuel or the priest Eleazar – John Calvin's guesses (none of them is likely). The book presents the happy ideal of a harmonious Israel, whose twelve tribes were loyally united in the worship of YHWH alone, gloriously triumphant under the divinely appointed successor of Moses, Joshua. Nothing could be further from the literal truth.

Let's start with Joshua's makeover. Right away, we see the Deuteronomistic creative agenda at work (once again, the people who long after the event, wrote the book) because Joshua, a quite minor figure in the Pentateuch, gets elevated to the status of another Moses. Why? Because, literarily, he *is* another Moses (as Moses is another Abraham and Matthew in his Gospel would make Jesus another Moses). He is transformed into a loyal follower and noble figure because everything Moses did, he does. "As the LORD had commanded his servant Moses, so Moses commanded Joshua, and so Joshua did" (Josh 11:15). Thus: Moses sent out spies, so did Joshua. Moses led the Israelites out of the wilderness through the piled-up waters of the Red Sea, so did Joshua lead the people through the waters of the Jordan, whose "waters stood still..." After the crossing of the water, Moses celebrated the Passover and so did Joshua. Moses interceded with YHWH when he was angry with the people, and so did Joshua. Moses held up his hands and the Israelites defeated the Amalekites. Joshua held up his sword and his followers defeated the people of Ai. Moses mediated the Covenant at Sinai, Joshua at Shechem. Moses delivered a farewell address, and so did Joshua. With all this Mosaic overlay, it becomes hard to detect the real historical Joshua who in actuality was likely a minor local hero, if he existed at all.

THE "CONQUEST"

The beginning book, the Book of Joshua is a pure, non-stop victory account. The book follows the normal pattern of contemporary conquest accounts common to the Near East nations, especially those of Assyria. Like those accounts, it plays a role in court ideology and the legitimization of the occupation of another's territory. They are hardly real descriptions, and are full of stereotypes in the give and take of psychological warfare. The storyline is that the Israelites enter Canaan under YHWH's genocidal orders to slay a population that seems to have done no wrong except be in the land that YHWH wants to give to his Chosen People, but a promise is a promise: "From the wilderness and the Lebanon as far as the great river, the river Euphrates, all the land of the Hittites, to the Great Sea in the west shall be your territory" (Josh. 2-5) The Book of Joshua indicates a clean sweep, a dazzling movement of stunning campaigns that swiftly bring about a complete takeover of Canaan. It's a total success. The Promised Land was theirs. The Canaanites were annihilated. For a long time, this version was accepted as accurate and historical, but as expected, modern scholars have shown that that's not quite the way it was and the Book of Joshua is more propaganda than reality, more fiction than fact.

For example, archaeology clearly demonstrates that one of those campaigns, the trumpet-blasting takeover of Jericho, couldn't possibly have taken place. Joshua could not have leveled the city. The reason is that the records show that it had been destroyed centuries before Joshua and didn't get resettled until about six centuries after him. It simply did not exist when the book said it did. (As an aside, it strains credulity that Joshua had his soldiers circumcised before the attack on Jericho. An army of sore soldiers is no way to begin a military campaign!) There's more. Other listed "conquered" Canaanite cities show no signs of conquest at all at this period. Still other Canaanite cities, some quite important, appear totally untouched. Furthermore, there is no sign anywhere of more than two million Israelites (the Exodus estimate) coming in and displacing the native population of Canaan. There is certainly no extermination of the Canaanites. On the contrary – in the Book of Judges itself, which follows the Book of Joshua, the "annihilated" Canaanites turn up all over the place, and Judges blithely speaks of the Israelites as "living in the midst of the Canaanites" (Judges 1:27-35; 3:5-6). Even in the book itself, YHWH informs Joshua that "very much of the land still remains to be possessed" (13:1). If there were any kind of so-called conquest, it obviously covered only a small portion of the country. It seems that some later writer took a few victories and expanded them to include the entire nation. No, the Canaanites remained and the Israelites remained – or they never left since they likely were Canaanites – to develop tribally and culturally as a separate people. Some scholars even say that "Canaanites" is just a pejorative term for the ruling elite whoever they were (like we would call some CEOs "barbarians"), and what you have here is basically a peasants' uprising perhaps led by Joshua.

In any case, what seems more likely was that the takeover of Canaan – if you can call it that – was a long gradual process of assimilation. That's why some scholars hold that the real origin of the Hebrews is not from Abraham, Isaac and Jacob – (all fictional etiological figures) – but rather from a blend of these semi-nomadic grazers who mixed in with the native peoples. It would appear, therefore, that the Israelite tribes were formed, for the most part, from the people who lived in Canaan and who had also fled to the safety of this lightly populated area to escape the inter-Canaanite wars. Then, as Leslie Hoppe speculates:

"Religious undergirding for this withdrawal from the obligations to the oppressive Canaanite regimes was provided by
the ideology of a small group of Hebrew slaves who escaped
from Egypt. These escaped slaves spoke of a God who took
the side of the poor and oppressed against their overlords.
The peasants of the Canaanite hill country, scattered in small
villages on the hilltops, made the ideology of the Hebrews
their own. The Canaanite villagers identified with the escaped
slaves and, in time, adopted their story of the Exodus and
Sinai as their own."[1]

THE CONQUEST REVISITED

A comment like this is why, according to the explanation of modern
scholars, the Book of Joshua is pure propaganda. No wonder modern
scholars give it a familiar spin. This careful summary from Richard
Nelson is a good example:

"Joshua is a typical product of Israel's scribal tradition of re-
using the literary legacy of previous generations to meet the
needs of new audiences. The individual stories in Joshua
began as oral folktales about local victories tied to local
places such as city ruins or commemorative markers. Later
these tales were written down and gathered into a connected
narrative as the triumphs of a unified Israel... Joshua is describing an idealistic and theoretical picture of Israel's origins
in Canaan, not factual history..."

Nelson goes on to speculate on the real propaganda purpose of the
Book of Joshua. He writes:

"In fact, the book of Joshua actually appeared as a way of
dealing with Israel's persistently weak and vulnerable
position, not as a celebration of its imperialistic triumph and
dominance. The communities who wrote and read Joshua
were constantly threatened by the loss of their land or

dispossessed exiles hoping for its return. Attack from outside and foreign oppression repeatedly endangered Israel's possession of the land..."

"In other words, it was usually Israel who played the role of an indigenous people menaced by politically and technically superior foes. It was Israel whose culture and religion were endangered by hostile outsiders and the alien groups with whom Israel shared the land. The book of Joshua was part of Israel's reaction to the danger posed by its enemies. Joshua evokes this continuing threat by describing enemy kings with iron chariots and cites with impregnable walls. Retelling stories of past heroes was one way of conceptualizing and strengthening Israel's title to its homeland. In this way, Joshua served generation after generation of readers as a claim on the endangered land that they believed God had promised them."[2]

USE AND MISUSE

Indeed, the first eleven chapters of Joshua are in fact a prime example of the ancient Near East literary genre in which such themes of the occupation of a nation and the linking of the group to one man (Joshua) are literary devices to stress the successful control of events, usually by a great king. Still, one wonders and grieves why all these long centuries we did not understand this literary quality. One cannot help but think how often the Book of Joshua has been used to justify invasion and genocide. One thinks, for example, of our own country, when the English settlers, fleeing European suppression, arrived here in this land that they felt God had given them. They were here to found a "New Jerusalem" in this new "Promised Land" and, of course, like Joshua, their treatment and near-extermination of Native Americans were biblically justified to achieve these goals. The truth is, the Book of Joshua appears to be one more extended etiological story explaining how Israel got control of the Promised Land. There are a lot of such etiological stories in Joshua mostly old legends that purport to explain the terrain (the existence of old ruins and odd landscape formations) and, in the fascinating story of Rahab the prostitute, how a Canaanite group became a part of Israel in spite of the divine order to kill all Canaanites and never intermarry with them.

I can't resist a gossipy footnote on Rahab. She was supposedly a prostitute, the movie kind with a golden heart, compassionate as well as deceitful and shrewd. She, a native of Jericho, shelters Joshua's spies and helps them escape in return for protection for herself and her family. She converts and becomes an Israelite, and from then on her rehabilitation shoots off in many directions and she becomes pretty much whatever you want her to be. In the New Testament, in his creative genealogy, Matthew makes her an ancestress of Jesus! Later, the author of Hebrews uses her as a sterling example of justification by faith while the author of James uses her as an example of justification by works.

THE BOOK OF JUDGES

The Book of Joshua has two or possibly three conclusions that somewhat clumsily attempt to make that book a transition to the Book of Judges, which itself has two introductions. The Book of Judges is a reality check to the Book of Joshua. It presents a period of incessant anarchy, civil war, and chaos among the tribes. To expand on what we wrote in chapter 4, the so-called twelve tribes were in no way related, in spite of the biblical fiction of making them twelve brothers and half-brothers from the common patriarch, Jacob, and the weaving of a prehistory of Jacob, Isaac and Abraham as relatives. As we indicated before, the most likely thesis about the beginnings of Israel is that a small group of slaves, of whatever nationality, escaped from Egypt. They attributed their deliverance to their god, YHWH, a local god they adopted from other tribes and settled in Canaan. There they eventually converted some of the Canaanite groups to adopt their god and eventually, through intermingling and intermarriage, these Canaanites emerged as conjoined groups centered around the symbol of the Ark of the Covenant, and then a confederation of tribes named "Israel". This Confederation obviously was a military as well a political and economic, benefit. Israel's use of Canaanite words, names for God, attributes of God, rituals, shrines, festivals, laws, children's names, Temple design, and so on betray Canaanite beginnings. Israel, in a word, is a late composite, not the product of an ancient linear descent from the prehistory of Abraham, Isaac, and Jacob to the recorded history of David and his dynasty.

The Israelite Confederation would seldom really unite. They tended to go their own way and would religiously revert all too often to the old worship of Ba'al, and that failure forms the theme of the Book of Judges that laments: "Then the Israelites did what was evil in the eyes of the LORD and worshipped the Ba'als" (2:11). Then would begin the rhythmic pattern of apostasy, oppression, cries to the Lord, repentance, another local hero to deliver them, a time of fidelity and peace, and then the cycle would begin over again. This repetitive cycle reflected the unfailing Deuteronomist theme of YHWH's disappointment with Israel's performance and his determination to use the people of the land to plague them. Militarily, the Israelites were not successful, because their confederation proved to be too decentralized, too sporadic, uniting only in time of need. Ironically, the only time the confederation really did unite was to gang up and punish one of their own, the tribe of Benjamin! They lacked continuity and stable leadership. Certainly they were no match for the disciplined standing army of the new threat on the block, the Philistines.

It is interesting that all through Judges you catch the refrain of a later editor (who was at the time living under an established kingship) lamenting that all this chaos was happening because "there was no king in Israel." Their disunity would benefit them for a while, but in time, in the face of sophisticated and united enemies, disunity became a luxury they could not afford and someday, under a ruthless leader like David, they would unite.

THE JUDGES THEMSELVES

The Book of Judges, replete with the usual legends, folktales, and etiological stories, is basically a chronicle of local heroes or local chieftain leaders. It's the stuff that belongs to folklore, and not much can be verified by sources outside the Bible. The plot, as we mentioned, is always the same. The people sin, God sends punishment by granting victory to their enemies, the people repent, a local hero arises who throws off the enemy. There are, significantly, twelve of these judges, whose stories are presented back to back. (The number twelve is given to reinforce the Deuteronomist's view that not just some tribes were guilty for the tragedy of the Exile, as some held, but all of Israel.) Were this true – the stories being consecutive – it would all add up to some four centuries, not the actual two centuries between the Exodus and the monarchy. The Book of Judges also contains passages of dubious moral value. There is Gilead, who takes the Canaanite name of Jerubbaal and who makes an idol from the gifts the grateful people have given him. There is Jael, a Canaanite woman who hospitably invites the Canaanite general Sisera into her tent and then proceeds to kill him by pounding a peg through his head while he is sleeping. Jael is not an Israelite, an enemy, and she grossly violates one of the Near East's most defining rules of hospitality by killing and shaming her guest. Yet she gets a thumbs up from the biblical author and is even called, in "The Song of Deborah," "most blessed of woman" (5:24). It depends whose ox (or general) is gored.

The sad story of Jephthat (10:6-12:7), as we recall, is about his vow. He swore, under the spirit of the LORD it is specifically noted, to sacrifice the first one to come out and meet him if YHWH would let him win the battle. Well, that person turns out to be his only daughter, but he has to follow through and so he sacrifices her. Sure enough, he wins the battle. There is no judgment whatever in the story that Jephthat did any wrong. On the contrary, not only did he make the spirit-inspired vow, but YHWH apparently accepted the sacrifice of his daughter because he granted him victory. Then there is the grisly Sodom-like story of the Levite who takes his runaway concubine to the city of Gibeah in the territory of Benjamin. There the inhabitants want homosexual sex with the Levite, but the man who has taken him in offers instead his own virgin daughter, and the Levite offers his concubine as replacements. The concubine is thus handed over, gang raped all night long, and found dead in the morning. So the Levite hacks her into pieces and sends a piece to each of the tribes, who take up arms of revenge against the city of Gibeah. They eventually slaughter all but 600 of the Benjaminites, and since the other tribes will not give their daughters to them to help revive their numbers, they are allowed to kidnap and assault other women at Shiloh. We observe that in this whole sordid story there is never any thought of the women, who in every instance are repeatedly treated as throw away objects.

Probably, thanks to the movies, most people remember Samson, who, it turns out, rather resembles the Greek heroes of the Aegean peoples he was battling, the Philistines, and indeed some scholars think he is a borrowed figure. His birth to a sterile mother is quite reminiscent of the birth of Samuel, John the Baptist, and Jesus. He, a veritable Heracles, does all kinds of heroic deeds. He's an amoral brute of a fellow with a taste for Philistine women, Delilah to be specific. That's why it's hard to swallow the author's description that Samson was endowed "with the spirit of the LORD" (13:25) and to fathom what was in the mind of the Christian author of the Book of Hebrews (11) who praised Samson as one "who through faith conquered kingdoms." And it's probably no surprise, given, as we have seen, the Christian habit of seeing everything through Christological eyes, that some even considered Samson a type of Christ. After all, look how he suffered and notice how he died with his arms outstretched. Just like Jesus.

A note: in the Christian canon, the Book of Ruth follows Judges. It really doesn't belong here. It doesn't have the tone or the theology of the Deuteronomistic historians. For example, Ruth was a Moabite, one who could have no place in Israel's history. Why it found its way to its place after the Book of Judges comes solely from its opening line, which the people who put the Bible together took literally: "In the days when the Judges ruled." In the Hebrew canon, Ruth is placed among the Writings.

Chapter 6.

THE SÀGA OF YHWH

This is a bit challenging but it is time to interrupt our survey to take a look at the chief character in the biblical saga, YHWH, the common god that the tribes adopted, the one whom the Deuteronomistic historians would identify as the God who led Israel out of Egypt. But, as we should expect by now, it's not that simple. YHWH, it turns out, seems more of a gradual evolution of society rather than a singular original revelation to a particular people. Reading the Bible even casually, one can see how the character of YHWH evolves quite radically in the course of its pages. YHWH appears to be in the trajectory of the Egyptian god Aten, or the Mesopotamian god Marduk (the god of the city of Babylon), both of whom gradually moved towards being a universal god by replacing the other gods or making the other gods their subordinates or eventually mere aspects of themselves. As some scholars speculate, this process seems to be a result of changing times. As technology advanced and as nations became more and more aware of other people, it became politically, militarily and economically wise to get along by recognizing other gods (as Israel did), and eventually to move towards the concept of a universal god as a platform for common ground. These Egyptian and Babylonian experiments didn't last, but the trends of assimilation and extension had been started, and they paved the way for the day when YHWH would gradually replace (or, more properly, absorb) the Canaanite god El.

YHWH, at the beginning, was hardly the transcendent deity we have come to acknowledge today. At the beginning when we first meet him in the Bible, he was not yet the sole omniscient God of the universe because, for the most part, the biblical writers portrayed YHWH as mostly concerned with Israel as with no other people. Only peripherally does he figure in the destinies of the other nations, and even then only in relationship to Israel. He was, at first, far from transcendent but quite earthy. He was decidedly hands-on, the craftsman planting the Garden of Eden, tailoring clothes for Adam and Eve, and strolling in the garden and not quite as omniscient back then, since he had to ask Adam and Eve where they were hiding. As Israel coalesced into a tribe or nation, he gradually moved to the role of powerful warrior, destroyer and punisher. At the same time, YHWH was also but one of many of Israel's domestic gods, part of Israel's pantheon. Notice the biblical record: *"Let us* make man in our image, after our likeness," or, after the sin, "Behold, the man has become like one of *us...*" and at the tower of Babel building, "Come, *let us go down*, and there confuse their language." Later, Psalm 82 would declare, "God has taken his place in the divine council; in the midst of the gods he holds judgment." Interpretations making these "gods" angels or part of God's army don't hold up. These gods were precisely that.

So the Bible, abundantly fortified by archaeology, shows that initially the Israelites were polytheists and remained so for most of their history. YHWH was but one God among other gods only, as their patron, more powerful to them. Moses himself, for example, says, "Who is like you among the gods?" (Exodus 15:11) and later his father-in-law exclaims, "Now I know that the LORD is greater than all the gods." (Exodus 18:11) and various psalms extol YHWH as "greater indeed than all the gods" or ask, "who among [the other] heavenly beings is like the LORD?". So YHWH was one among many, although supreme.

GODS, INC.

All this reinforces the fact that, way back then, Abraham, Isaac and Moses himself were indeed monolatrists, not monotheists. That is to say, they recognized the primacy of their God while freely admitting the existence of other gods. Even the first commandment's "you shall have no other gods besides me" does not refer to monotheism, but to monolatry: "There are other gods, but I am uniquely yours and you shall not hanker after the others". Moreover this God, given the current needs of the oppressed tribes, had to be a warrior God, "YHWH Sabaot," the "Lord of Hosts" or the "Lord of Armies" and the early biblical literature and the Psalms are replete with that image. It's used some 250 times in the Bible. Interestingly, to the chagrin of the pacifists, if they knew about it, we still use the military phrase, "Lord of Armies" or "Lord of Hosts" in our liturgy: "Holy, holy, holy, Lord God of Hosts." God is consistently depicted as a warrior whose right hand shatters the enemy, who marches in the fields, drives his horses and chariots to victory, leads at the head of his army (cf. Psalm 68) and so on. It is even this God who determines the moment of attack in Judges and passes on orders like a general.

In this regard YHWH was basically not much different from other gods. The Philistines had Dagon, the Babylonians Marduk, and the Moabites Chemosh. Concerning the latter, chapter 3 of 2 Kings depicts a battle between King Mesha of Moab and an Israel-Judah coalition. When the military leader Mesha was losing the battle, he took his first born and offered him as a burnt offering to his god. It worked. Chemosh accepted the offering and the tide turned. Israel was routed. Recall YHWH did the same thing when Jesophat sacrificed his daughter and, as a result, YHWH also granted victory. In the 19th century archaeologists found what is called The Mesha Stone which gives Moab's version of the battle. In it we find these words: "Omni was the king of Israel and he oppressed Moab for many days, *for Chemosh was angry with his land.* And his son succeeded him and he said, 'I too shall oppress Moab.... but I got to see his downfall and that of his house, and Israel was lost forever.'" The point is that just like YHWH, Chemosh becomes angry with his people and so he too hands them over to his enemies. Just like YHWH in Joshua and Judges and elsewhere, Chemosh signals his people the moment of attack. YHWH was Israel's Chemosh.

SYNCRETISM

There were in Israel's life, as we indicated, lesser domestic gods in evidence but later writers would circumvent this embarrassing reality by transferring the domestic gods to foreign ones, and so blaming Israel for worshipping foreign gods or imitating the idolatry of their neighbors. In short, the early Hebrews *were* polytheistic and had a wide variety of home-grown lesser divinities. That's why we should note that the great, frequently quoted, passage from Deuteronomy, "Hear O Israel, the LORD is our God, the Lord alone," did *not* originally mean that YHWH was the only god in the same sense that it would come to mean later on. For many centuries it was taken for granted among the Israelites that they would have other (lesser) gods and that the other nations would also have their gods. To interject Bruce Feiler, author of popular books on the Bible:

> "Even the *shema*, the holiest words in Judaism and what one commentator calls 'the great text of monotheism', *seems to imply that other gods exist.* The traditional translation is 'Hear, O Israel! The LORD is our God. The LORD is One.' But the words, which come from Deuteronomy 6, are considered vague by Bible scholars and are often translated today as, 'Hear, O Israel! The LORD is our God, the LORD alone.' God, the words suggest, should stand apart and above other gods, meaning that he is the superior god but not the only god."[1]

We should note here, also, that the *shema* itself is not unique in its command of love:

> "Hear, Israel: YHWH is our God, YHWH is One. You shall love YHWH your God with all your heart, with all your life and with all your might... Keep these words that I am commanding you today on your heart and teach them to your sons."
>
> (Deut. 6: 4-7)

This is basically no different from the Neo-Assyrian command:

> "You shall love Assurbanipal...King of Assyria, your lord, as yourself... you shall not seek any other king or other lord against him...this treaty ...you shall speak to your sons..."

The authors of the Pentateuch, as we have mentioned before, apparently copied the Neo-Assyrian theology and its various treaties and transferred them to YHWH. There was probably a subversive point to be made. By transferring covenants and treaties from the Neo-Assyrian culture to theirs, the authors of the Deuteronomistic history were subtlety saying that Judah's master is not the Assyrian king but YHWH. We will find this transfer later in the New Testament where heavenly signs and the high sounding titles of Caesar Augustus are applied to Jesus. Moreover, in the injunction, "You shall love the LORD your God with all your heart, and with all your soul and with all your might", the word "love" does not mean affection or feeling. Despite many a pious commentary, it simply is a synonym for total loyalty, a command to total allegiance, the same as it is in other ancient Near East covenants as we see from the vassal's promise, "the King of Assyria, our Lord, we will love."

THE WAY IT WAS

Conversely, other nations did not deny the reality of YHWH as the Jews' national god. When Sennacherib threatens Hezekiah, he claims that the LORD, as Israel's national god, cannot defend Judah against him any better than the national gods of other now defeated nations have managed to do. In fact, Sennacherib claims, the LORD has said to him: "Go up against that land and destroy it" (2 Kings 18:25; Isa. 36: 10). For ancient Israel the issue was competition between the different deities at their various shrines.

Prior to the 8th century, YHWH was, as it were, the "divine patriarch", the head of a family of Israel's deities. By the time we hit

Isaiah, however, he is so no longer, and the choice becomes, worship me or worship nothing. Until that time, we repeat, monotheism, in the way we know it had not reached that point of understanding and, all along, as the records show, whatever loyalty there in fact was to YHWH, it did not prevent belief in and worship of other gods simultaneously, especially Ba'al. Popular piety, particularly among the subsistence farmers (they were taking no chances), continued to venerate the gods of the fields and fertility. Female figurines and open-air shrines are often found at Israelite archaeological sites. There have even been discovered two inscriptions from the divided monarchy period that clearly show that some Israelites venerated the goddess Asherah (whom we have seen before) as YHWH's consort. She was a goddess familiar to the people around Israel, and is even reflected in some parts of the Bible.

SIMILARITIES

The fact is that, until Moses' time, God was "El Shaddai or other "El" combinations, "El" being the name of the Canaanite god and to whom YHWH bears a striking resemblance. This god was seen as a bull (a raging warrior), yet he was also called "El, the Compassionate" just like YHWH who is pictured as a fierce warrior giving no quarter, but who shows compassion to his people. Both spoke through prophets, both are paternal creator gods, and, often, the Hebrew word El appears in the Bible as the word for God. This is not to say necessarily that YHWH started life as El, but to suggest there is a close link. "I am YHWH. I appeared to Abraham, to Isaac, and to Jacob as El Shaddai ..."
Even YHWH says he started out with the name of El although this does not have to refer to the Canaanite god. Maybe the words suggest a theological merger.

The discovery of the Ugarit texts going back to the time before Moses, clearly shows the Canaanites using El as the supreme deity (for example, Psalm 82:6), and that the Hebrew God had exactly the same characteristics as the El and the Ba'al of the Canaanites. Scholars couldn't help but notice, for example, that the Hebrew Psalm 29 is so similar to an Ugaritic paean to Ba'al that they have suggested that the Hebrews simply deleted the name Ba'al and substituted YHWH in its place. Genesis gives us the El referred to above, and El seems to be Israel's original deity, not YHWH. Why else would we have the word "Isra-el" and not, as might be expected, Isra-yahu? (It seems ironic that the State of Israel is named after a non-Hebrew Canaanite deity.) Was YHWH at one time a secondary god who wound up displacing El? Sometimes El and YHWH are identified with one another, sometimes not, but finally they blended: "I am YHWH. I appeared to Abraham, to Isaac, and to Jacob as El Shaddai, but my name is YHWH I did not make known to them." (Exodus 6:3)

BA'AL

Adding to the influence of El, scholars also see a bit of the Canaanite god Ba'al (who replaced El) in YHWH. Ba'al was a storm god. In time, YHWH picked up some of his characteristics as evidenced in Psalm 29 where it is stated that, like Baal, the Israelite God of glory "thunders" and the voice of YHWH "flashes forth flames of fire". Even the famous crossing of the Red Sea reflects Ba'al's dominance over the waters. The storm god Ba'al is also depicted as the god who is the "rider upon the clouds" and so, in time, YHWH is described as the God "who rides upon the clouds". The point being that anything Baal could do, YHWH could do better. Yet, as much as YHWH absorbed his rivals' attributes, slowly he drops them; for, as time goes by, he doesn't need the pyrotechnical displays any longer. He moves to a more gentle and transcendent mode. He's no longer in the fire, storm and wind, but in a gentle breeze. The hands-on God who walks around the garden begins, so to speak, to shed his flesh. The one who builds, plants, sews and smells begins to disappear, becomes more abstract. He is on the way to transcendence.

The 8th B.C.E. century B.C.E. prophet Hosea advances the movement. He, fiercely hostile to foreign nations in a time when international trade was expanding, breaks ground by moving closer to monolatry and sets up the path to monotheism. YHWH, he insists, is *not* just another god among many. He is better than all the rest of those foreigners we're dealing with now. The prophet, Zaphaniah, joins in the chorus. So there's a movement here from polytheism where one god is as good as another, to my god is better than the rest (monolatry), even though their adherents are free to worship them. In time the trajectory will lead to monotheism.

ORIGINS

As far as YHWH's particular origins go, one theory holds that the biblical texts indicate that the origin of Israel's God goes back not to Palestine or Canaan but to various sites to the southeast of Israel, the land once inhabited by the Kenites and Edomnites. YHWH is not native to Israel. In Deut. 35:2, for example, it says, "The LORD came from Sinai and dawned from Seir [the mountain of Edom]" or in Judges 5:4-5: "LORD when you went out from Seir...the mountains quaked for fear of the Lord, the One from Sinai..." So, it is held, YHWH originally came from places located far from Israel and was, over time, imported to Canaan where the Hebrews settled and mingled. Some scholars speculate that it all goes back to Moses' father-in-law, Jethro. In the Bible he is called a priest of Midian, a place near those southern regions. He must have introduced his God, a Midianite deity named YHWH, to Moses, who in turn brought this deity to the Israelites claiming that this was the God of their ancestors.

This Midianite Theory is discredited today but still the question arises, why didn't the biblical writers clean up the biblical text? That is to say that, since the biblical writers so freely invented or rewrote stories to suit their agendas, why didn't they just omit the YHWH of the mountain from foreign Sinai and say YHWH came from the mountain of Zion right smack in their own country? Yet consistently YHWH's first appearance is always outside his homeland and no pre-Moses text ever mentions the name of YHWH. Then too, one must ask, why should the Israelites copy others' concept of God as a suzerainlike figure, a conqueror from elsewhere? Why not pattern him after their own native king? The answer seems to be that, as far as Israel knew, YHWH really *did* come from elsewhere. YHWH is originally an imported deity not a home-grown one.

Other scholars have suggested that a group of wandering Kenite no-mads entered Canaan, bringing with them the worship of YHWH who eventually became the deity of most of Canaan, including the assimilating Hebrews. Obviously it took a while to catch on for the fact is that, as far as into the time of David, the biblical record shows that people were naming their children after El or Ba'al not YHWH. This may only prove that change comes slowly and the Israelites would take a long time to break with the polytheism of the times. The path to true monotheism was a long one, not a singular epiphany. Monotheism did not emerge in one dramatic moment at Mt. Sinai when God spoke to Moses. As far as Israel's deity goes, there was, as we said, no revolution. There was evolution as the Israelites partook of the larger ancient Near Eastern cultural matrix. This is shown by the stunning new access to the Canaanites' Ugaritic liter-ature demonstrating how much the Bible is reflective of that culture and giving strength to the claim that the Israelites were originally Canaanites.[2]

Further indication that this is so is that scholarship has also shown that the Hebrew language is written in the Canaanite alphabet and was until the Babylonian captivity. The discovery in 1928 of the city Ugarit in Syria (located in the northern part of the Mediterranean) unearthed the dominance of a northern Canaanite dialect and provided the suggestion for understanding Hebrew as a southern dialect of the same Canaanite language. That's why Isaiah could ex-claim, "On that day... the land of Judah will become a terror to the Egyptians...On that day there will be five cities in the land of Egypt that speak the language of Canaan and swear allegiance to the LORD of hosts." (19:17, 18). As one scholar puts it, "As with language and the alphabet, so with culture generally: Ancient Israelite culture was in many respects a subset of Canaanite culture."[3] In fact, it is obvious to scholars that the biblical writers in their allusions and references fully assume that their audiences are quite familiar with Canaanite Ugaritic literature and, often, the scholars use the Ugaritic texts to understand passages in the Bible. In short, there is an unmistakable connection between Ugaritic literature and the Hebrew Bible.

The Canaanites had gods such as El, Asherath, Ba'al, and the lesser Resheph and Deber (reduced to the lower case of "pestilence" and "plague" in the Hebrew Bible to clear the field for YHWH cf. Hab. 3:5). They had angels and rituals, poetic styles, literary traditions and the same constellation of names and titles as Israel. The worship of El, for example, appears in Numbers 23-24 and in Genesis 49. First Samuel, as we indicated before, contains El names. In terms of such literary features as parallelism, word pairs and religious motifs, Israel copies Canaan. It seems, then, that the Israelites evolved from a loose coalition of Canaanites and other tribes who slowly defined themselves by way of ritual (circumcision), covenant, and a special deity. As someone has put it, the Ugaritic texts and other ancient histories form "the Old Testament of the Old Testament" in much the same way that the Old Testament became a backdrop for the New Testament.

The bottom line seems to be that the Israelites were not an independent tribe to whom YHWH uniquely revealed himself in the desert, taking this raw, pristine people and instantly consolidating them into the Chosen Race by way of divinely given rituals and laws. Rather they were, it seems, evolved Canaanites and who knows what else, who over time assumed the identity of a people set apart with their own rituals and, ultimately created their own mythology.

It is apparent that it was a long process of incorporating other deities' characteristics into "YHWH." Concerning the (composite) nature of YHWH John Miles offers this litany:

"The God whom ancient Israel worshipped arose as the fusion
of a number of gods whom a nomadic nation had met in its
wanderings... Here the sky blue of El, there the earth tones
of 'the god of your father', over there the blood red of Ba'al
or Timiat or the evergreen memory of Asherah.... Historians
have generally recognized the powerful originality of Israel's
religious synthesis even when they did not also believe on
religious grounds that this originality was revelation from
God himself. (pp. 20, 21)....The most coherent way to imagine
the Lord God of Israel is as the inclusion of the content of
several ancient divine personalities in a single character."
(p. 72) ... Moreover, this Lord God of Israel was not the sole
deity and this God was quite tolerant of other gods at the time
of Adam, Noah, Abraham, Jacob, and Joseph. Suddenly, with
Moses and Joshua he becomes 'jealous' and even though,
once you have the book of Deuteronomy with its prohibitions
of further fusions of various gods into Yahweh, the syncre-
tism continues."[4]

It seems that the undeveloped YHWH cult evolved from interaction
with the local cults. We can readily deduce this from Joshua's speech
at Schechem when he commands the people "to put away the gods
that your ancestors served beyond the River and in Egypt and serve
the LORD" (Josh. 24:12). It is interesting that he makes this speech
at Schechem where Jacob had built an altar to honor "El, the God
of Israel" (Gen, 33: 18-20). Schechem was also the site of the temple
of "El-berith" or God of the Covenant and of "Ba'al-berith", Ba'al
of the Covenant. So obviously the God of Israel was not the first to
dwell there and it's no stretch to see that he may have derived his
concept of a covenant from the site's older residents. In Judges, we
note that Gideon was called Jerubbaal and Gideon repeatedly had
to be reminded to trust in the LORD of Israel, and that he winds up
worshipping an ephod. Jephthah engages in human sacrifice, as was
practiced in most Near Eastern religions, including that of Israel
(Genesis 22, 2Kings 16:3; 17-17; 21:6. 23:10). Micah worships an idol.
In short, as indicated above in Jack Miles' quote, the other religions
and gods all contributed to the composite identity of Israel's God.

Who they were is no mystery. Judges 10:6 conveniently tells us: "the Ba'als and the Astartes, the gods of Aram the gods of Sidon, the gods of Moab, the gods of the Ammonites and the gods of the Philistines." To these we could also add Ashera, Hadad and the Philistine storm god, Dagon.

TRIUMPH

Finally we must ask, why did YHWH ultimately (roughly during the monarchy) prevail over the others? The most likely answer is because of the influence of the kings. Israel's kings had a special affinity for YHWH. As part of the Israelite pantheon he, was not only the national God but he was the one who gave legitimacy to the king. YHWH, therefore, was the court favorite and those in the know named their sons after him. Accordingly, it was only YHWH's prophets who were welcomed at the court. The king could not tolerate other prophets running around prophesying in the name of Israel's other domestic gods. That would be the enemy of consolidation and centralization and that seems to be the motivation. The king had to control access to the divine will. It was only a matter of time, therefore, that a special bond was forged between YHWH and the king with YHWH even calling him "son"(See Psalm 2). The seeds, as we shall see, of the royal ideology leading to the concept of a Messiah were being planted.

This strong privileged position naturally tended to submerge Israel's other gods. The court needed to stay on point, and this political necessity went a long way towards hastening the leap from polytheism to monolatry and then, in due time, to monotheism. It was above all King Josiah who officially put the final nail in the coffin of polytheism with his thoroughgoing (failed) reform designed to bring about absolute centralization. Any worship of other gods must be stopped and any worshipper of these gods must be killed even if it's a member of one's own family (Deut. 13: 6-9; 13:15; 18:19-20). All allegiances of Israel to other gods were transferred to YHWH and items used in the worship of the other deities, domestic or foreign, were burned. That was the ideal. That other domestic gods were still on the scene is bolstered by the fact that such items were found in the Jerusalem Temple itself. The priests obviously considered these gods as a part of the YHWH pantheon (2 Kings, 23:4).

A BOOST FROM THE EXILE

If we remember that the Deuteronomistic history was written before and during the Exile, we can see why that tragedy also pushed along the cause of monotheism. The big question then (as it would be after the modern Holocaust) was why did the destruction by the Babylonians of their beloved Jerusalem and the Exile happen? Or, in their terms, how could Marduk defeat YHWH? As expected, answers differed. Jeremiah for once hit a familiar theme by saying that the tragedy was due to Israel's infidelity to YHWH. Devotees of other gods countered saying that it was the other way around. The Exile was punishment from the Queen of Heaven (a popular domestic goddess) for abandoning her in favor of YHWH. The latter had a point for under her rule things were great but the moment Josiah started pushing "YHWH alone," things went downhill. (Jeremiah 44:17-18). Jeremiah and a cadre of other prophets held fast, however, and said that although Josiah did proscribe other gods, nevertheless, as we saw, some of the folks at home secretly kept some of the household gods and that's the reason for the disaster. And, as a backup, they tossed in the fact that some of Josiah's successors were not as faithful as Josiah himself and that added to the anger of YHWH. Nor, said these prophets, revving up the argument, should people forget the terrible infidelities of Josiah's predecessor, the wicked (in the historians' eyes) polytheistic Manasseh whose legacy still lingered to poison the atmosphere. So cumulatively YHWH had a lot to be angry about. But angry or glad, the concept of YHWH as more than a local deity and the only deity had been put forth. In time monotheism would become the norm but as always, minor gods would not go away. They simply morphed into the patron saints of fertility, house sales and lost objects.

SUMMARY

YHWH, an import (from the south?) became the subsidiary, tribal god of the Hebrews. He went national, so to speak, during the monarchy after the division of the kingdom into northern and southern entities. He emerges as a counterpoint to and in competition with Ba'al with whom he shares many traits (rider of the clouds, dwells on the mountain, giver of rain and fertility, etc.). That competition probably started with the northern kingdom's King Ahab who adopted his wife Jezebel's Phoenician god, Melqart. This provoked the Elijah-Ahab conflict and the promotion of the rival god, YHWH, as evoked by the prophet Hosea. The YHWH alone campaign got a boost when northern Israel fell to the Assyrians in 722, indicating that the god there was inadequate and the true YHWH was with the southern kingdom.

When the Babylonians superseded the Assyrians the monarchy was dethroned. The Temple was destroyed. The land was occupied. External identity-belonging marks were erased. Other ways had to be found for Jews to express themselves. For one thing, the Jews had to rescue YHWH from the status of a local tribal god. As long as he was confined to that it logically meant that he had just been defeated by Babylon's local tribal god, Marduk. YHWH had to become more universal than that. The writer called Deutro Isaiah begins the process. YHWH is the only God, he proclaims. Others are false or imaginary "I am the first and the last; besides me there is no god" (44:6). From the exile forward the faith is officially monotheistic. This is a radical departure from the polytheistic past and in practice not followed everywhere. A Jewish colony in the south of Egypt (Elephantine), for example, still worshipped YHWH as one of a triad of deities in the 5th century B.C.E.

Another makeover demanded that the old prophetic books had to be reworked and whole new books had to be created. The Deuteronomists with their "fidelity to YWHH equals victory and prosperity and infidelity equals punishment and conquest" took over. Drawing on some ancient traditions they created from whole cloth the story of Moses down to the destruction of the kingdom of Judah. The constant theme was that disaster was never far off when the people and the kings were not willing to worship YHWH, who is always powerful. Downfall follows the infidelity of the people. These books were basically propaganda works with the hidden theme that, yes, things are bad – we've lost our land, Temple, monarchy and priesthood – but look what mighty deliverance YHWH brought to our ancestors in the stories we give you in the Pentateuch. Take heart. He will rescue us again.

In time, the triumph of universal monotheism would turn out to have unintended consequences in two serious ways that are with us today: first, projecting tolerance, peace and good will to all nations coming together under one universal (Israelite) Father monotheism inevitably developed a heavy intolerance and severe punishment for those who refused to accept a jealous God. In other words, horrific intolerance often became the flip side of monotheism. Second, in contrast, the monotheistic god of Judaism, Christianity and Islam is a solitary male. He is alone and cannot engage with other gods, cannot be a part of a sexual relationship that defines the totality of human beings and so embrace all aspects of life. In contrast the Hindu god Shiva needs his consort Parvati. Karen Armstrong explains the problem:

> "In the monotheisms, particularly in Christianity we've found questions of sex and gender difficult. Some of the faiths that start out with a positive view of women, like Christianity, and also Islam, get hijacked a few generations after the foundation and dragged back to the old patriarchy. I think there's a big difference, however, in the way people view sexuality. When you see sexuality as a divine attribute, as a way in which one can apprehend the divine, that must have an effect

– you see it in the Hindu marriage service, where this is a divine act. Questions of gender and sexuality have always been the Achilles heel of Christianity, and that shows that there's a sort of failure of integration here, a failure to integrate a basic fact of life."[5]

The fact is, though God is genderless and some biblical passages imagine God as female, for example, "the God who gave us birth;" there is no doubt that the biblical God is overwhelmingly male. The prophets speak of YHWH as the husband of Israel, the Psalms praise him as king and father. Jesus directs us to pray "Our Father". The Church's universal creed proclaims forthrightly, "I believe in God, the Father Almighty". The doctrine of the Trinity gives us Father, Son, and Holy Spirit and, with delicious irony, while *The Catechism of the Catholic Church* proclaims that "God's parental tenderness can also be expressed by the image of motherhood ...[and] God transcends the human distinction between the sexes", it continues with, *"he* is neither man nor woman: *he* is God. *He* also transcends human fatherhood and motherhood" [239, 252, 255]. Even subconsciously we can't get around God's maleness.

Finally, notwithstanding the fact that it is almost impossible to find "a single monotheistic statement in the whole of the Pentateuch" (Armstrong's phrase), the trend to monotheism had been started. Its thrust was not only the result of the trauma of the Exile, but also simply from a rise in human consciousness (a notion we will explore later.) Each era would subsequently create a god that reflected it values. In the last hundred years of our own times God has moved from the stern, all seeing, all watching, fire and brimstone deity so dear to the 19th century circuit riders to a gentle, loving Father who, like Sergeant Schultz of TV's "Hogan's Heroes," sees nothing and forgives all. In some circles God today is not even a solitary he, but a solitary she. Rabbi Margaret Moers Wenig, a lesbian with two grown daughters from a previous marriage and now partnered with another lesbian rabbi, and who teaches at a seminary of the Jewish Reform movement, published a famous sermon called "God is a

Woman and She is Growing Older" portraying God as a loving if long-suffering mother.[6]

Still, for all that we have written, as we close this chapter, we must recall the Bible's legacy of a unique relationship between YHWH and his people and how YHWH, unlike other deities, was so desperately concerned about the Israelites' response to him, how "imperfect" he was compared to the changeless and impervious gods of the Greeks, how, like lovers, they fought and made up. There was never a God like that.

Chapter 7.

YHWH IN A BAD MOOD

There's an old Bob Newhart routine where Bob plays the scientist Wernher von Braun, the father of rocket science, and at an interview one of the reporters asks him, "Doctor von Braun, is it true that at one time you worked for the Nazis?" Von Braun, via Newhart, exhales, "That one again!" And that's the way it is with the perennial question of YHWH and his propensity to violence. That issue again: the Israelite God, YHWH, who at times is hard to tell from the bloody Canaanite god, Ba'al. Which is to say, he is frighteningly revengeful and violent. He swings from compassion to revenge and, in this respect, the Bible is like the Qur'an: both contain passages of tolerance and passages of genocidal annihilation, and both religions still work hard trying to reconcile the two.

Let's begin with YHWH at the beginning. For one thing, he destroys the world he created with a massive flood. Then there is that enigmatic episode which no one can satisfactorily explain and still perplexes commentators, namely, that YHWH sought to kill Moses:

> "At a night encampment on the way, the LORD encountered him [Moses] *and sought to kill him.* So Zipporah took a flint and cut off her son's foreskin, and touched his [Moses'] legs [genitals] with it saying, 'You are truly a bridegroom of blood to me!' And when He let him alone, she added, 'A bridegroom of blood because of the circumcision'" (Exodus 4:21-26).

WHAT KIND OF GOD IS THIS WITH MURDER ON HIS MIND?

Then it is recorded: "The LORD tossed the Egyptians into the sea" (Genesis 14:17), and "Thus says the LORD the God of Israel, 'Put your sword on your side, each of you! Go back and forth from gate to gate throughout the camp and each of you kill your brother, your friend and your neighbor.'" (Exodus 32:27). YHWH goes on to grandly announce his proclamation of genocide as he reveals his plans for the "ethnic cleansing" of Canaan. YHWH in no way appears to be angry at the Canaanites. It's just that they're in the way. Their only offense, it seems, is that they worship their own gods and live on land for which the LORD has other plans. No matter. They are doomed. They will not be offered the option of conversion nor given the offer of coexisting with Israel and maintaining their own ways. It's YHWH's unilateral decision to exterminate them.

In Moses' speech to the Israelites about to invade Canaan he tells them to enslave the people if they surrender and kill all the males if they don't, take the women as booty and "do not let a soul remain alive" (Numbers 20:10-18). Again, unlike the Egyptians, the Canaanites are never presented as guilty of anything or of any offense against Israel. They are just in the way of its expansion and they may pose a threat to Israel's religion. They, the inhabitants of some thirty-one cities, are merely the unlucky victims of genocidal slaughter.

MORE ATROCITIES

YHWH thunders from Sinai, revs up the loss of life in Egypt, imposes a virtual reign of terror on his own people, slays all the scouts but two when they bring back news from Canaan (Numbers 11) and disallows Moses to enter Canaan. When a fresh rebellion breaks out against Moses and Aaron the LORD punishes the rebels by having the earth swallow them alive. (Numbers 16:30). The next day the LORD slays

14,700 of them. He visits the iniquity of parent upon children and children's children to the third and fourth generation and grim is Israel's fate if they do not observe God's law (cf. Numbers 28:47-57 for ghastly details.)

The Book of Judges is, as we saw, a collection of stories of guerilla bands. In chapter 19, as we have mentioned before, it even pits the Israelites against one another over the horrible gang rape of a concubine to whom her owner shows no pity (19:25-28). At one time, the great future king, David, was actually a leader of the opposition, a group of bandits who fought against YHWH since David was in the employ of the Philistines who were fighting against Israel. The Philistines themselves marveled at the savagery of David's raids against his own people.

Then there's the story of Phinehas in Numbers 27. The Israelites have sex with the foreign Moabite women. When Phinehas spots an Israelite taking a Midianite woman into his tent for sex, he follows them in and runs them through their bellies with his spear. Why did he do this? Because he was on fire for the LORD and his statutes. "He was zealous for the Lord," reports the text. His action made atonement for this sin and stopped the YHWH-sent plague (which killed 24,000 people). And, the Bible says, YHWH rewarded Phinehas praising him:

> "Phinehas...has turned back my wrath by manifesting such zeal among them on my behalf...I hereby grant him my covenant for peace. It shall be for him and his descendants after him a covenant of perpetual priesthood, because he was zealous for his God, and made atonement for the Israelites". (10-13).

Phinehas, obviously a hardliner as we would call him, came to be in too many instances the ideal disciple of the LORD who wielded the sword on his behalf. Much later the second century Maccabees would invoke Phinehas as their model of resistance to the Syrians, and the 1st century Zealots, who assassinated people in their fight against Rome, would take their name from Phinehas' "zeal" for the LORD. Phinehas was only one of the first with spear in hand to show an attitude of intolerance in the name of religion. And YHWH rewarded him.

Then there are Samuel's words to King Saul:

> "I am the one that the LORD sent to make you king over His people Israel. Heed therefore what the LORD has said to me, Thus says the LORD of Hosts, 'Now I will punish the Amalekites for what they did in opposing the Israelites when they came up out of Egypt. Go attack Amalek and utterly destroy everything that they have; do not spare them, but kill both men and women, children and little babies, oxen, sheep, camels and donkeys.'"
>
> (1 Samuel 15:1-3)

How about Elijah's confrontation with the prophets of Ba'al (1 Kings 18)? Having proved that his YHWH was more powerful than their Ba'al, he has them all slaughtered and for his zealous deed – slaughtering his opponents in the name of YHWH — he, too, in later tradition is likened to Phinehas. Even Elijah's protégé, Elisha, is the source of Jehu's slaughter when he kills King Ahab's descendants and all those associated with him and every worshipper of Ba'al in Samaria (2 Kings 9), justifying it all by appealing "to the word of the LORD that he spoke to Elijah." The Book of Maccabees approves the killing of unfaithful Jews. Even women take up the sword: Deborah pushes Barak to war, and Judith kills an enemy general with her own hand. Jeremiah's God is a fearsome creature. He scapegoats women as a way of speaking of sin (2:1, 3:25). He is an angry, unforgiving punisher of the people. He is unspeakably cruel and abusive (6:8). Jeremiah's book is full of what we might call war poems where a devouring army acts on YHWH's orders as "LORD of Hosts". YHWH is a Commander-in-Chief, who issues rallying orders against the Israelites who have brought destruction on themselves for they are "skilled in doing evil, but do not know how to do good" (4:22): "Cut down her trees; cast up a siege ramp against Jerusalem. This is the city that must be punished. There is nothing but oppression within her" (6:6). The Psalms have their share of prayers beseeching divine violence such as Psalm 58 which asks God to "break the teeth in their mouths" and good folks will rejoice.

In the New Testament Jesus makes a whip and drives out the Temple merchants. He tells a parable in which God will take revenge on wicked tenants and trade violence for violence (Matt. 21:12-17); and there is no missing the implied violence in Matthew 25:41: "Then he will say to those at this left hand, 'You that are accursed, depart from me into the eternal fire prepared for the devil and his angels.'" In the Book of Revelation there will be the casting into the "lake of fire" those not found in the book of life. In the Acts of the Apostles, God kills the husband and wife team of Ananias and Sapphira, two members of the Church, because they cheated in a real estate transaction (Acts 5: 5-11). Christianity's history, as has been often acknowledged, is a particularly violent one, one often inspired by verses in the Bible.

A PROBLEM

The Bible is a bloody anthology in many ways. It raises, in every age, the question of God's cruelty and injustice and no one seems to have a satisfactory answer. Like the acceptance of slavery, God's punishment for infidelity is replete throughout the Bible. It is a constant Deuteronomistic theme. Many have tried to work around the dilemma of a biblically revengeful God. Here are some responses. The 2nd century Gnostic teacher, Marcion, just eliminated the problem by tossing out the whole Old Testament as presenting a monstrous Old Testament God incompatible with the loving God of the New Testament. Some Church Fathers — Origen for instance – made the whole issue an allegorical one and so bleached out the question. For some, YHWH had a tutorial agenda: he allowed mass slaughter to show that lingering torture and humiliation were wrong. By acting as Commander in Chief, YHWH took war out of human hands. By forbidding booty, YHWH was saying you couldn't go to war for gain. By exterminating the Canaanites, the Israelites would not be deterred from seeking their destiny. In short, YHWH tolerated a lot of cruelty in the interests of shaping a people as his own. These are creative responses that do not satisfy everybody. Let us see other theories.

JOSHUA REVISITED

To begin with, a revisit of the Book of Joshua is in order. Joshua's conquest of Jericho (fictitious as we saw) begins as he instructs his soldiers that "the city and all that is in it shall be devoted to the LORD for destruction' (6:17). This is called *herem*, a religious act, and was practiced by other nations. The troubling thing with Israel is that *herem* is presented as a religious ideal and you have all kinds of sacred language tied in with the savagery. And it's all justified by divine command, something to glory in and write songs about.

It is generally believed that the Book of Joshua was written at the time of dwindling Assyrian rule and under King Josiah's reign. It was written to provide legitimization of Josiah's expansion policies under an Assyrian warlike YHWH. These biblical books of divinely mandated warfare and massacre of whole peoples are written in the context of Israel's need for ethnic and religious identity which, in the context of the Babylonian captivity and exile, required the absolute centrality of YHWH and the denigration of all other gods who fought for their people. It's a defensive posture presented in arrogant, aggressive language. Foreigners who are chipping away at that identity must be annihilated. Scribes writing in the reactionary times of Ezra and Nehemiah felt the need to revise the old documents of Israel's history to justify exclusion and that's what they did for the Book of Joshua.

Powerful Assyria was, as in so many ways, the standard paradigm of acting (recall the Covenant treaty as a takeoff on Assyrian treaties). Therefore, YHWH is portrayed as Israel's military general in the spirit of King Assurbanipal and Assyria's terrible warrior god, Sargon. In other words, since the warrior god was a feature of the dominant Assyrian period YHWH was presented as such, thereby upending the Assyrians with a more powerful version. Furthermore, like Assyria's god, Sargon, YHWH too miraculously intervenes to grant his people victory. In short, the Book of Joshua, with all of its divinely mandated horrors and extermination of a native people, is a knock off of Assyrian propaganda and, therefore, is not to be taken literally. Its aim is anti-Assyrian. It is meant to show that YHWH is stronger than the gods of Assyria. This explanation seems the most satisfactory though, in hindsight, it turned out to be a dangerous device because subsequent ages, armed with such literal sacred texts, legitimized warfare and atrocities. The three Abrahamic religions, Judaism, Christianity and Islam, are full of both. Yes, other images of a benign and gracious God are present in both Testaments—images much in vogue today – but historically, in the name of God, other days of the unbearable suffering of wars, genocides and enslavements cannot be washed away.

Barbara Orn sums it up:

> "This is clearly rhetorical language and has its own internal logic. The history was written when worship of Yahweh-alone was beginning to emerge among the Israelites. The language of war is strong, excessive to the modern ear, but underlines the importance of exclusive worship of Israel's God. It also belongs in a culture that understood war and conquest and the custom of kings to impose their own gods on conquered groups. The main difference between the Deuteronomistic idea of conquest and that of surrounding nations is the emphasis on exclusivity and intolerance for other gods."

> "Thus the historian imbued with the theology of Deuteronomy sees Israel as a conquering force which will wipe out any vestige of alien worship, leaving the field clear. Logically, if God gave the land to Israel the other nations must have been

dispossessed and this must have been accomplished by war (how else?); therefore the acquisition of the land must have been by military conquest. Conquest must have been swift and comprehensive since this was Yahweh's war after all. If other gods belong to other nations those nations must have been destroyed so that Israel could start with a clean slate. Thus Deuteronomy's admonition and the Book of Joshua's reconstruction of what must have happened, based on this theological understanding."[1]

MORE THEORIES

Some evangelical theologians appeal to God's sovereignty. After all, God is the author of life. Since he created it, he logically has every right to take it away. That's surely God's prerogative. So theologically there's really no problem with YHWH's orders to slay and destroy men, women, and children. St. Paul, for one, certainly goes along with this:

> "Is there injustice on God's part? By no means! For he says to Moses, 'I will have mercy on whom I have mercy, and I will have compassion on whom I have compassion.' So it depends not on man's will or exertion, but upon God's mercy. For the Scripture says to Pharaoh, 'I have raised you up for the very purpose of showing my power in you, so that my name may be proclaimed in all the earth'. So then he has mercy upon whomever he wills, and he hardens the hearts of whomever he wills".
>
> (Rom 9:14-18)

There's a logic here that escapes us moderns but one that works quite well for the ancients. That is to say, the biblical writers so embraced the fundamental conviction that God indeed was intractably sovereign and omnipotent over the entire world that they were quite able to see him as the author of good and evil. "I make weal and create woe"

Isaiah has him saying (45:7). That's why they can blithely write that he hardened Pharaoh's heart, "incited" David to take a census and then punished him for taking it (although the author of Chronicles cleans it up and says that Satan incited the taking of the census) and caused the prophets to speak lies to lure a king to his death (1 Kings 22). That's why, since Israel's enemies, the Amalekites, were bent on destroying Israel, YHWH had every right, in view of the necessity for Israel's survival, to annihilate them. He is LORD of all. And this makes sense once you see their terrible logic.

The late Catholic scripture scholar, Father Lawrence Boadt, weighs in by reminding us that the Bible is not an ideal picture of a saintly community and, with its mixture of traditional stories, laws, poetry and other types of literature that record experiences with God in the past and express issues and practical problems for the present and future, we should expect it to be somewhat inconsistent, messy and often dealing with uncomfortable subjects. Besides, since the Bible is propaganda, we should expect some exaggerated, highly persuasive, passionate and extreme language that voices fear, sorrow, rage, and the desire for vindication.

"Israel, used battle language to emphasize God as the one who brings down the violent and exalts the humble and lowly. Violent pictures are used as rhetorical emphasis to teach that God upholds the right at any cost and that salvation involves turning to God in trust. And don't forget the majority of passages about the forgiving and merciful God…"

DOUBTS REMAIN

Did our forebears understand it this way? How many, officially and unofficially, took such words literally and acted on them? History gives ample testimony to church and state's literal embracing of such words. And, as far as those passages showing warrior YHWH's forgiveness and mercy, in this he is not far from the Canaanites gods. There has been found a Babylonian prayer to Marduk who is addressed as "warrior Marduk, whose anger is the deluge, whose relenting is that of a merciful father." (Abba is not new with Jesus). The Canaanite head god "El" (later replaced by Ba'al) is called in the Ugaritic literature "the kind and compassionate," a phrase taken over by the biblical writers. So the stereotype of a unique YHWH as a merciful, tender, forbearing father who is a contrast to all those other "pagan" gods depicted as monstrous, vicious horrors who torture children is more from the movies than from history.

Noted Catholic Scripture scholar Richard Clifford offers his solution.[2] He reminds us that evil in the Old Testament is imagined concretely, that is to say it is embodied in a particular people, in this case, Israel's enemies, though we may ask, why were they Israel's enemies? Because they were fighting over the same territory? But in that case, from the Canaanite point of view, Israel was the enemy. After all, the Canaanites were there first and they were protecting their land. Or was it because the Canaanites worshipped false gods? But, again from their point it view, it was the Israelites who were worshipping a false god. The Canaanite "scripture" would no doubt have a different take on the whole situation. Since we're reading one nation's partisan account, it's no surprise that they would demonize their enemies, those people of the "Evil Empire." Evil must be eradicated and that's what the Joshua story is all about. The Israelites really didn't exterminate the Canaanites. The account is really an allegory saying that God hates evil and leads the charge against it and that makes the story a theological statement, not an historical one. The story really portrays the LORD as a righteous fierce warrior who roots out evil by commanding his Israelite armies to destroy, root and branch, a particular people, the personification of evil. War and extermination are but devices to portray a just God's judging or ruling justly. Likewise praying fervently that the LORD take vengeance is really a way of placing all wrongs in God's hands.

A LITERARY CONSTRUCT

Clifford seems to be telling us that the biblical revenge stories are, thus, a literary construct about justice. All the warring and genocide, etc are but literary devices to establish this notion. The accounts and orders from the deity are not to be taken literally. Remember, the LORD is also revealed as merciful and forgiving (that is to be taken literally). Holy Wars really did not take place, but their execution was portrayed as a dramatic fictitious instance of the singular LORD's singular justice. After all, the sacred writers identified YHWH as the author of good things, so why not credit him with saving things? Why not credit him as the LORD who drove out Israel's enemies, their patron deity who fought for them as they readily understood that Chemosh, for example, fought for the Canaanites? Their God is YHWH Sabaoth who protects and cherishes them and he simply had to be invoked as their champion and so those terrible deeds he commanded and those armies he led and those genocidal orders he gave are all an ancient people's expressive way to speak of his proprietorship.

So what all these "solutions" are saying so far is that it's all basically allegory and metaphor. It's a familiar, across-the-board, reaction. Note, for example, that long ago the Hindus removed barbaric passages from the opening scene of the *Bhagavas Gita* where the god Krishna, like his biblical counterpart, encouraged believers to slaughter an enemy even their own kin. Gandhi, the non-violent Hindu, was quick to also pronounce those passages as metaphor, explaining that they mean that we should strike at our darker side. Moderate Islamic scholars benignly reinterpret the awful "sword" passages of the Qu'ran. It seems that every tradition, religious and non-religious, parses away contemporary embarrassments but none of it lessens the body count.

OTHER VIEWS

Others suggest that all this Divine Warrior or Lord of Hosts (Armies) scenario is but a literary variation for God as Creator General; that is, God creates by winning the battle over military chaos just as he waged "holy war" over the primal elements. YHWH is a restorer of order. Triumph over enemies is but a literary code for triumph over the waters of chaos and its nasty sea monsters. This sounds pretty thin. As does the suggestion of others who say that the order of *herem*, killing everybody down to the last infant, is a variation of the notion of sacrifice due to the deity in a sacrifice culture. As we saw, human sacrifice was indeed carried out in Israel and its neighbors, else why have mention of it and why the restrictions against it? All those victims are offerings to God.

Some, like Walter Brueggemann, note that Israel was hemmed in on all sides and had an almost unbroken history of subjugation. Many times it was nearly extinct. Therefore, its aspirations and dreams for a happy future would naturally mean the removal of its persistent enemies. They constantly dream, as they must, of freedom at last and for them, who can bring that about but YHWH? Since YHWH is master, is strong, has authority, why should he not use his attributes against Israel's enemies? An oppressive system calls for oppressive measures and so the slaughter – or at least wishful projections — is justified. Others have pointed out that it was a customary Near Eastern practice to obliterate one's defeated enemies. Such obliteration was a religious act, a way of dedicating by sacrifice of all life to the Lord of the winners.

For some, concerning God-led violence, there is the dialectic or "trajectory" response. Some opted for the "trajectory" thesis (which we'll see later), whereby revelation was progressive and God simply accommodated himself to the stage and mentality of the Hebrews where they were at that stage of moral consciousness. He would bring them along some day and, when they were ready, reveal that all that violence was wrong. Scholars thus point out the opposing biblical views of war and genocide. The Israelites were a diverse people and diverse voices are heard in their writings. One voice extols conquest and slaughter. Another voice preaches compassion. Multiple voices on many issues surface in the sacred text and they were allowed to have their say. Those voices promoting violence and those uneasy about it are present. The idea is that the reader is to enter into this dialectic conversation, to reflect and come to terms with the issues of war and violence. In other words the mixed voices are there to invite us to conversation about these issues and ask hard questions.[3]

Philip Jenkins has an interesting take on this view. He says that the very fact that such violent texts in the Bible are considered something we have to cope with itself proves their success. That is, the very fact that the violent excerpts of the Bible cause us to shudder today proves, in the final run, the nonviolent aspects of the Abrahamic faith else why would we be so bent on explaining them away?[4] The message of the Bible works! We refuse to accept violent passages at face value. There is something in the biblical religion, after all, that makes us critique them and not extol them. Or, we might add, was religion just catching up with the Enlightenment's programs of the abolition of slavery, freedom of conscience and religious tolerance?

Still, once more, there is no denying that Christians have done their share of extolling. They have taken the violent words of the Bible literally. They have embraced them and have argued not only that God permits war but, in some cases, demands it. Wars became crusades on behalf of God. Again, the pages of two thousand years of Christian history are stained with biblically approved blood shedding, for example:

> "Verden is a small north German town near the confluence of the Weser and Aller rivers nineteen miles (30 kilometers) south of Bremen. On a spring day in 782, it became the scene of a horrible massacre during which more than 4,500 Saxon warriors were beheaded between dawn and dusk. The perpetrator of this barbarism was Charlemagne. He waited until the Saxons surrendered their arms and then slaughtered

them... [According to the *Royal Frankish Annals*] he was determined 'to persist in this war until they [the Saxons] were either defeated and forced to accept the Christian religion or be entirely exterminated.'"

"This was just the worst of a number of outrages committed by both sides in a thirty-two-year long war as the Franks tried to subdue Saxony. While for us this was cold-blooded murder, the emperor saw himself acting like a biblical king on behalf of God. He was much influenced by King David, who after the defeat of the Moabites killed two out of every three men he captured, or like Saul, who defeated the Amalekites and killed 'man and woman, child and infant, ox and sheep, camel and donkey' (1 Samuel 15:3). Charlemagne felt he had biblical precedents."[5]

Or, take some five hundred years later (1202-1204) when during the Fourth Crusade Catholic Crusaders ravaged the Catholic city of Zara (Croatia), then besieged and sacked the Orthodox center of Constantinople. Or some 250 years after that the 16th century Spaniards forced young Native Americans to work in the silver mines of Potosi (Peru) in the freezing high altitudes of the mountains where they contracted pneumonia and mercury poisoning, or around 1600 when "the death rate soared among the local Indian communities, tens of thousands of Africa slaves were brought to Potosi to replace them.... they too, died in large numbers."[6] In Mexico, with the help of those subject peoples the Aztecs had conquered, the Spaniards destroyed the Aztec civilization. Warfare plus devastating European diseases killed about 90 percent of the population. In modern times professed religious leaders like Joseph Kony and his religiously named "Lord's Resistance army" slaughtered many in Uganda. The long biblical legacy of divinely sanctioned warfare, understood or misunderstood, has remained intact.

I repeat at this juncture that the best thing is to keep remembering that these biblical "horror" stories are not factual. They are all fiction to begin with. All are made up propaganda revisions inserted into a former narrative to score points against the gods of the Assyrians and

Babylonians, namely, our God can outperform, outdo anything your gods can do. The stories, in other words, are drawn from the ancient Near East matrix of actions, symbols, metaphors and storytelling that say, tit for tat, wonder for wonder, battle for battle, miracle for miracle, power-play for power-play, cruelty for cruelty, YHWH can match and exceed the deities of Assyria and Babylon.

BIBLICAL POLITICS

Without cynicism, it is to be noted that the ire of YHWH fluctuates in the Bible as Allah's ire does in the Qur'an. That is to say that, when Israel feels disadvantaged, it becomes quite tolerant of its oppressors when suing for peace. Thus to the Ammonites: "Should you not possess what your god Chemosh gives you to possess? And should we not be the ones to possess everything that our god YHWH has conquered for our benefit?" (Joshua 11:24). Here the Israelites are the soul of tolerance. On the other hand, when they feel advantaged and expansionist, the Israelites are told by God to "annihilate" its enemies "so that they may not teach you to do all the abhorrent things that they do for their gods..." (Deut. 20:16-18). When they needed allies or were in a position to profit from live-and-let-live situation, both the Hebrews and the Muslims could turn quite ecumenical; when they didn't need them quite genocidal. In other words, in the question of violence and genocide, the choice between accommodation and annihilation had as much to do with politics and economics as with theology and that accounts for the various conflicting strands in the biblical books.

A JEWISH VIEW

Let's turn to Robert M. Seltzer, professor of Jewish history at Hunter College. In talking about the bloodletting in the Book of Numbers, especially Numbers 31 and its story of the slaughter of the Midianites, he wonders how God could have ordered such a massacre. One rabbinical opinion, he says, is that maybe the story is not accurate for it seems implausible that an army of 12,000 Israelites could slay every male in an army with five kings without losing a single soldier themselves. Then, too, he says the account doesn't dwell on or depict bloody details but the Bible surely does elsewhere. Check, for example, the truly awful descriptive warnings of Moses against unfaithful Israelites in Numbers 28. Seltzer simply adds:

> "The late Orthodox commentator Joseph Hertz, the chief rabbi of the United Kingdom was reduced to saying, 'We are no longer acquainted with the circumstances that justified the ruthlessness with which it was waged, and therefore we cannot satisfactorily meet the various objections that have been raised in that connection.'"

> "How can we attribute to God an order to 'set mercy altogether aside'? ... Confronting this tale links us obscurely to the very beginnings of Jewish heritage, when it had to confront a inhospitable and threatening world, but physical and religious survival require of us much more discriminating means of self-defense that are respectful of the essential humanity of the foe. The lesson is that we read this story in order to remember to forget it."[7]

And maybe that's the best we can do. You can sense that everyone is trying to come up with something and no one is totally succeeding. The Rabbi is right: forget it and be content with noting in passing what John Miles says: the divine bloodthirstiness is but a stage in the development of YHWH's character. He'll get better as time goes by. Still, meanwhile, we can't shake the issue because it surfaces in our times with some radical Islamists' application of Shariah law. As an example, radical Islamists in Mali (a country in northern Africa) amputated the hands and feet of four young men accused of robbery. Interesting, because the explanation of one of the perpetrators is so biblical sounding: "We cut their right hand and their left foot. We cut all that today. It is not us who ordered this. It is God."[8] Joshua could have said that—and did. And that's the problem.

Chapter 8.

THE SAGAS OF THE PROPHETS

Christians believe that the Bible is the Word of God, just as Muslims and Mormons respectively believe that the Qur'an and Book of Mormon are. There are about four hundred references to that phrase, "word of God," in the Old Testament. God speaks and communicates a great deal. How this communication happens is not entirely understood. There is, for example, ample evidence of divination (the use of omens), even though it was officially forbidden as a means of divine contact. In practice the prohibition never stuck. Divination was simply too popular among the common people, a holdover no doubt from its thousand-year use in Mesopotamia. It even snuck into official use when the priest juggled the *urim* and *thumimim* (Exodus 28:30) to discover answers in time of crisis and was used to determine if God was unhappy with Saul. Nor should we forget that in the New Testament the casting of lots determined who would fill Judas' place. We should also observe that, like the Delphic Oracles in Greece, the interpretations were often ambiguous, guaranteeing a win-win situation.

Prophets were an institution everywhere in the Mideast, including among the Canaanites, and prophecy is well attested to in Mesopotamia, Phoenicia and other places. These foreign prophets are recorded as also receiving messages in a dream or at their temples like Samuel did. They all seem to use the same devices as Israel. They were closely connected to the kings, used divination including consulting the dead (remember Saul calling up Samuel?), checking out the liver, shaking arrows, casting lots, using sacred objects such as the *urim* and *thummim* (parts of the vestment of the priests), music, ecstasy, and so on. Cities were arising five thousand years ago and social stratification and inequalities were rising. Egyptian sages developed a concern for justice, and the kings of Mesopotamia proclaimed the establishment of "righteousness" or "justice:" or "equality." In Persia, the prophet Zarathusta (or Zoroaster) taught that the one supreme God, Ahura Mazda, had created all good things and wanted people to practice truth and kindness. Some scholars think he lived around the time of the Hebrew prophets and may have influenced them (this is debated), but there are, in any case similarities with them. On the other hand, the other nations seem to have nothing as well-drawn as the Israelite prophets who advised and reproached kings alternately – prophets and kings were the yin and yang of the monarchy; one did not exist without the other – and who penned those powerful and colorful words we associate with their books (although, as we shall see, whether the books we have reflect their actual words is problematic.). No other nation has such a great collection of prophetic writings and such strikingly poetic cries for justice as the Israelites.

Still, all was not smooth on the prophetic front. Perhaps John Collins gives us the best summary about the state of the prophets and prophecy:

> "It is of the essence of prophecy that the prophets addressed specific situations in highly concrete terms. Nonetheless, like many of the Assyrian prophecies, the biblical oracles come to us embedded in collections that were made for later generations. Moreover, the biblical prophetic books are often edited with later situations in mind. There is inevitably tension between the words of the prophets in their original context and the 'canonical shape' given to their oracles by later editors....

> "The historical prophets whose oracles are preserved in these books were often highly critical of the political and religious

establishments of their day. The scribes who edited their books were part of the establishment of later generations."[1]

In other words, as so often happens, we have a conflict of interest. The prophetic books, like all the other books in the Bible, are hindsight productions. This means that they are heavily edited, reworked, and readjusted books made to conform to current ideology and to support current propaganda needs. Those doing the editing and adjusting often had very different attitudes and agendas from the prophets themselves, so we're not sure whose words we have – the prophets' or the partisan editors'. Certainly we know that the editors of Jeremiah, for example, did not share his hostility to the institutions of his day. We note also that his book is a composite one. Further, it has come down to us in two texts, the Hebrew and Greek. The trouble is that there is a substantial difference between the two, so we really don't know which one is authentic. Scholars used to think that the Greek text, being far shorter than the Hebrew, was an abridgment but the Dead Sea Scrolls reveal that the Greek version either preserved an older text or that the Hebrew text is an expanded version of the Greek. Maybe both existed together. Most notably, there is some conflict between the oracles of Jeremiah and his prose sermons. They give off two different messages. All this is symptomatic of the book's very complicated history, a book that doesn't always speak with one voice – and symptomatic of how fragile it is to speak of the Bible as "the Word of God" when we can't figure out what that word is.

It seems that what the prophets meant in their oral original tradition, and later in their early written tradition and as we have them now in their final scribal incarnations may be two different things. Our general caution is that quoting any portion of our current Bible as the Word of God is a highly circumscribed and chancy thing, for who knows what the original words were? For some this doesn't matter. It's the final edition, the final product, that matters, the Bible we have today. For others, the composite revisions reflecting shifting and often conflicting agendas and the inscrutable and contradictory perspectives of the Bible with human fingerprints all over it make it suspect as the Word of God, and how misguided it is to claim that it is so.

THE PROPHETS, TRUE AND FALSE

Be that as it may, let us turn to the Hebrew prophets. What about them? Again, they are a part of a long tradition of prophets current all throughout the Middle East: the ancient archives of Mesopotamia, Assyria, for example, show that they had an abundance of male and female prophets. So the Hebrew prophets are counterparts to the shamans of other civilizations before and after them, that is, people who have a special gift, or claim to have a special gift, to be in contact with the numinous. As such they were sought after by paupers (is this a good time to plant?) and princes (is this a good time to go to war?). They spoke to kings and the people and, we should remember, they always spoke from and to a particular historical context, for example, the monarchy or the Exile. They, therefore, exercised considerable power – as long as their batting averages held up. The prophets of Israel who wielded great influence were not immune to the law of averages, and after the Exile they declined and fell into disrepute. Maybe one reason for this disdain is the fact that, after the Exile, the words of the great prophets of old had become canonized scripture, and latter day prophets began to quote *them*, for God's word was increasingly considered as written for all time and here to be interpreted throughout the ages.

Besides that there were no more kings around that prophets could be the conscience of, there may be another, more basic reason the prophets went out of style: credibility. What they foretold, what they prophesied, simply didn't come true. They kept on saying, "Thus says the LORD," and whether those words were actually and truly the actual communications of the LORD himself or simply their own words wrapped in the authority of LORD, they failed to pass the acid test: they were wrong. One thinks, for example, of Amos who predicted that King Jeroboam would die by the sword (7:11). Never happened. Or the prophet Huldah who predicted that King Josiah would die in peace (2 Kings 2:20). She was wrong. Josiah did not die from old age or "in peace," but was violently killed by the Egyptian pharaoh Neco in the battle at Megiddo. Or how about Ezekiel? In 26:7-21 he predicted as a word from the LORD that Nebuchadrezzar of Babylon would destroy the city of Tyre so thoroughly that it would never be rebuilt. It never happened. Ezekiel appears to have realized his gaffe so he makes a second prediction saying that since Nebuchadrezzar did not seize and conquer Tyre, YHWH would give him Egypt as a consolation prize (29:18-20). This didn't come true either and, even though some three hundred years later Tyre was conquered by Alexander, the city of Tyre was, contrary to YHWH and his prophet, rebuilt and to this day is thriving as Lebanon's fourth largest city. Then there is YHWH's promise via the prophet Hosea, "I will not again destroy Ephraim; for I am God and no mortal, the Holy One in your midst and I will not come in wrath.'" (11:9). But Ephraim was destroyed again and two chapters later, we get an outright contradiction of the previous promise: "I will destroy you, O Israel; who can help you?" (13:9). Assyria conquered the northern kingdom of Israel in 722 B.C.E. and in turn was defeated in 612 B.C.E. by a coalition of Medes and Babylonians. The prophet Nahum exalted in Assyria's comeuppance and after saying "so there, take that!" to defeated Assyria prophesied of Israel, "Nevermore shall you be invaded." (1:15). Fifteen years later it was by the Babylonians.

Here are some apropos comments from Jack Miles:

> "True, most of the marvels that Isaiah and the other prophets predicted for an Israel returned from exile never came to pass. The failure of prophecy, a fact of massive importance in the history of Israelite and then of Jewish religion, is a personal failure in the life of God. .... The promises God made through Isaiah and the earlier prophets have clearly not been kept. The reason why prophecy is passed over in silence (in the Psalms) is almost surely also the reason why it died out

and why the prophet Zechariah himself looked forward to its dying out – namely, that what the prophets prophesied had, in very large measure, not come true."[2]

No wonder commentators resort to allegory when they attempt to explain to us the words of the prophets or (as we shall see) the rest of the Bible, for that matter. Still, lest I seem to misrepresent them, the prophets' main role was decidedly not to predict the future. Their main role, as noted above, was to be the conscience of the people, to bring them back to basic principles, to YHWH. They were there to make the people and the people's leaders realize that their current actions had future implications. In every sense of the word they were the community's reformers.

THE GREAT PROPHETS

We can jump ahead chronologically in our commentary and consider the Major Prophets such as Isaiah. Penning the Book of Isaiah are at least two major authors (maybe even three although that opinion is becoming less common). This is to say, scholars have detected several hands spanning the centuries in the composition of this very long book. (Its length assured that it would be one of the most frequently quoted books in the New Testament and among the Essenes, both of whom saw themselves as the communities who fulfilled Isaiah's end time visions.) You have, for example, the so called 8th century Isaiah talking about things that take place two centuries later, namely the fall of Jerusalem to the Babylonians and the rise of the Persian king Cyrus (chapters 40-50) who would conquer Babylon. How could Isaiah's name appear not at all in those chapters 40-55 while it is quite frequent in chapters 1-39? How could an 8th century author write of a 6th century reality: "Leave Babylon, flee from the Babylonians! Announce this with shouts of joy and proclaim it." (48:20). Even if fundamentalists insist that, after all, Isaiah was a prophet and saw into the future, it's still hard to think of what his 8th century contemporaries would make of a reference to a country that didn't exist and they never heard of (Persia) and why weak Babylon was such a threat. And who was Cyrus? It's an obvious after the event prophecy, and was written by the anonymous Second Isaiah after the exile – or at least it was perhaps a real prophecy but one directed to current exiles.

Isaiah rather exuberantly calls Cyrus, who allowed the return to Judea, God's Messiah, the one who "shall build my city and set my exiles free" (45:1-13). Isaiah's pronouncement is made some 150 years before it happened. As we said, none of this would make any sense in the 8th century and so it was clearly made in the 6th century to the Jews in exile. If such a prediction were made in the 8th century then why didn't Jeremiah, who was always looking for ammunition for his side, reference it? If Isaiah's prediction had been around for a hundred and fifty years that would surely be a potent citation in favor of Jeremiah's case. As a big-city prophet living in Jerusalem, the capital of scribal activity, he could not fail to know about Isaiah. He had to have known about First Isaiah, but obviously not about Second Isaiah, and this supporting citation. Again, the case is clear: large portions of Isaiah were not written by him and did not exist in the time of Jeremiah.

We might add that all this praise of a "Messianic" Cyrus leaves the impression of the magnanimity of the man. It may be deserved. On a clay cylinder, Cyrus (or his scribe) wrote what has come to be called the "first declaration of human rights." It announced his renunciation of terror, his efforts at peace, his release of slaves and the right of people to worship as they pleased. A replica of this cylinder rests in the United Nations. Cyrus was also a practical conqueror, allowing all exiles, not just the Jews, to return to their homelands. In the case of Palestine, it had been severely ravaged, and that meant that little or no taxes would be collected there. So Cyrus sent the exiles back in the hope they would restore and refresh the land, and so restore some measure of prosperity and, therefore, of revenue. As for Second Isaiah and the exile, he was not much concerned about its theology or cause. He knew restoration was coming just as he knew that life for many Jews had become sweet and profitable in Babylon and few would want to return to a devastated land. So he set about to reveal why God decided to bring the exile to an end and restore the people to the land.

Isaiah is also the one who gave us a dazzling view of heaven as a vast sanctuary above the clouds where YHWH, surrounded by his council (of lesser gods?), was served by a myriad of angels and elders and the message-bearing Seraphim who cried out ceaselessly, "Holy, holy, holy!" (That council, by the way, reflects an enduring concept among all the ancients of the chief god surrounded by lesser ones who carry out his bidding. Notice that at the end of Isaiah's vision God pointedly says, "Who will go for us?" This kind of slipped in from force of habit.) One day this triple refrain would be picked up in the Christian Book of Revelation, and later, when the doctrine was formulated in the 4th century, interpreted to refer to the Trinity. As St. Jerome put it, "For whatever we may read in the Old Testament we will find as well in the Gospel...the Trinity is announced in both Testaments." That bit of Christian chauvinism would surprise the ancient Hebrews (and later Muslims). We might also notice that, contrary to a strong tradition (Exodus 33:20) that no one can see YHWH and live, Isaiah survives.

As we have noted previously it is in the Book of Isaiah that, for the first time, we really get unambiguous monotheism. Until that time, as we have seen, monolatry was the practice: one main god with others allowed. Monotheism was not fully spelled out until the time of the monarchy when it was projected into the Sinai scenario. Anyway, along comes Isaiah, and not the 8th century one at that, but the second author, likely a 6th century anonymous writer, who presents monotheism unequivocally. The motivation was that the Judeans, living for nearly two generations in Babylon, had fallen in love with their captors. Babylon, after all, was a much nicer place than Palestine, certainly more cultured and it seems that the Babylonian god, Marduk, was doing a good job. The Jews prospered there and the prophets had a hard time convincing them to return to the home-land. Kugler and Hartin describe the problem nicely:

"After two generations most Judeans in Babylon had happily accommodated to their context. They had settled comfortably in the rich and fertile land of Babylon and had even prospered there. It seems certain they had even begun to make a certain peace with the main god of Babylon, Marduk, who, after all was worshipped through a single New Year festival and in response provided enormously fertile crops. By contrast their God required constant faithfulness and had responded to their infidelity with exile from their homeland. They also no doubt saw the clear advantages of the rich farmland of Babylon over the difficult land of Judah, and the city of Babylon over the ruins of Jerusalem...."

"These were the challenges faced by the author of Second Isaiah. As for the idea that Marduk was preferable to the God of Israel, Second Isaiah announced for the first time in Israelite history that there was, in fact, but one God alone. Until this time the biblical authors...understood their God to be one divinity among many worthy of worship. Second Isaiah overturned that notion, denying the existence of other gods altogether (41:21-29; 46:1-13)."[3]

ISAIAH AND THE NEW TESTAMENT

Because Isaiah with its 66 chapters is such a long book and is full of lush and powerful poetry it became a favorite of Jews and Christians. Christians mined it for Messianic motifs. They could point out how Isaiah, in his prophecy to Ahaz, "foretold" Jesus as the Messiah. Later when that Messiah was put to death on a Roman cross, these same Christians were able to cite Isaiah's Suffering Servant as an answer to that embarrassment. Christians have often referred to Isaiah as "the Fifth Gospel" because they perceive in his writings almost a perfect description of Jesus – or was it the case, as some scholars think, that Jesus' Passion was made to fit Isaiah? In this regard, let us take a look at the famous Isaiah 14:10- 16 passage:

"Again the Lord spoke to Ahaz saying, 'Ask a sign of the Lord your God; let it be deep as Sheol or high as heaven.' But Ahaz said, 'I will not ask, and I will not put the LORD to the test.' Then Isaiah said, 'Hear, then, O house of David! Is it too little for you to weary mortals, that you weary my God also? Therefore the LORD himself will give you a sign. Look, the young woman is with child and shall bear a son and shall name him Immanuel. He shall eat curds and honey by the time he knows how to refuse the evil and choose the good. For before the child knows how to refuse the evil and choose the good the land before whose two kings you are in dread will be deserted.'"

The background is this: King Ahaz, threatened on either side by Damascus and Assyria, is inclined to enter into an alliance with Assyria as his only chance of survival. Isaiah is against this and tells Ahaz not to fear. It's all bluff. So he says, in effect – to translate the above quote – take a young mother. Her baby, like all babies, puts everything in its mouth, but, says Isaiah, by the time it takes this child to grow up and learn the difference between oatmeal and sawdust, ("by the time he knows how to refuse the evil and choose the good"), the political threat will be gone. So don't worry and don't enter into any alliance with Assyria. Trust in YHWH. That's all the passage says and means to say. There is not a hint of a future Messiah in this passage. The child to be born (Hezekiah) is no more than a successor to King Ahaz or was Isaiah's own son.

Eventually this passage was made to say more due to a single word in the passage, the Hebrew word for young woman. In the Hebrew passage, the "young woman" ('almah) is either the prophet's wife (cf. 8:3) or Ahaz's wife, an assumption based on a word from a Canaanite parallel. However, in the 3rd century B.C.E. Greek translation of the Hebrew Bible (the Septuagint), the scholars translated the word 'almah in this passage by the word "Parthenos," a word meaning "virgin." This word simply meant an unmarried woman who would get married and have children the normal way. Matthew, in his Gospel, following the Greek translation, chose the word virgin:

"Look, a virgin shall conceive and bear a son and they shall name him Immanuel" (1:18:25). This was an acceptable translation and the Vulgate Bible of St. Jerome in the 5th century followed suit ("Behold the virgin shall conceive and bear a son.") and, as the standard Bible for Christians for centuries, laid the foundation for the doctrine of Mary's perpetual virginity and the medieval veneration of Mary, with Isaiah held up as the great prophet of the Virgin Birth. (Here we may note that the United States Bishops, aware of this history, in their recent revision of the New American Bible, have replaced virgin with "young women.")

That birth elicited, two chapters later, this familiar paean:

> For a child has been born to us,
> a son given to us;
> authority rests upon his shoulders
> and he is named
> Wonderful Counselor, Mighty God
> Everlasting Father, Prince of Peace

Once more these verses either celebrate the coronation of a king, probably Hezekiah, or the birth of Isaiah's son, nothing more, nothing less. The descriptions (Wonderful Counselor, etc) are symbolic throne names. It reflects Isaiah's strong pro-monarchy stance. Christians seized on this verse, not legitimately as a literary analogy, but as an actual prophecy of the Messianic king to come, namely, Jesus.

And how about:

> A shoot shall come from the stump of Jesse
> And a branch shall grow out of his roots.
> The Spirit of the Lord shall rest upon him,
> The Spirit of wisdom and understanding,

> The Spirit of counsel and might...
> The wolf shall live with the lamb

> The leopard shall lie down with the kid
> The calf and the lion and the fatling together
> And a little child shall lead them (11:1-9)

This is an oracle of the ideal kingship, the "peaceable kingdom," the golden age brought about by a new ruler. Yes, little lamb Judah, harassed by the wolves and leopards of more powerful neighbors, under the right ideal leader, one day will live without fear among them. That's all it says. It's all about Israel's vision of a restored, purified kingdom. The point is, all these passages were talking about the prophet's own era – after all, if Isaiah's signs to Ahaz were to be intelligible and meaningful, they had to be fulfilled in his own time, not some seven hundred years later – and when things didn't turn out this way, it's easy to see how they could be used to look to the future, to a Messianic age, as a prediction of a Messiah, an Anointed King, who would succeed in making all things new again.

THE PASSION ACCORDING TO ISAIAH

For Christians, the most evocative words in Isaiah are those associated with Jesus' Passion: the Suffering Servant motif (chapters 42 -53).

> He will not cry out or lift up his voice,
> or make it heard in the street.

And again:

> I gave my back to those who struck me,
> and my cheeks to those who pulled out the beard
> I did not hide my face from insult and spitting.

> And, all this on behalf of other people:
> He was despised and rejected by others;
> A man of suffering and acquainted with infirmity

and as one from whom others hide their faces;
he was despised and we held him of no account

Surely he has borne our infirmities
and carried our diseases...
He was wounded for our transgressions,
crushed for our iniquities
Upon him was the punishment that made us whole,
and by his bruises we are healed (53:3-6)

Not even in Judaism were these words ever meant as a Messianic prophecy until after Christianity. The Suffering Servant is simply collective Israel and many passages state this. Later, as these things evolve, one of the late 1st century B.C.E. Jewish apocalyptic books does have a Messiah that dies but, before the Christian era, mainline Judaism had no notion of Isaiah's Servant as referring to any kind of Messiah. For Christians it was a different matter. They quickly seized upon these passages to interpret Jesus' shameful death, not as a failed Messiah, but as a suffering one, one "explicitly" foretold in Isaiah. Modern scholars dismiss this and hold to the original text and Jewish understanding. The Servant is not Jesus foretold, nor Jesus the suffering Messiah. Indeed, as Joseph Fitzmyer, S.J. writes, "The idea of a suffering Messiah... is found nowhere in the Old Testament or in any Jewish literature prior to or contemporaneous with the New Testament. It is a Christian conception that goes beyond the Jewish Messianic tradition." This does mischief to all those gorgeous Advent readings, but it's accurate.

HOPES

What is clear is that the Book of Isaiah reveals a prophet living in the days of the Babylonian rise to power who predicted Israel's impending doom and coming exile and yet, at the same time, the restoration of Israel's fortunes, meaning a restored priesthood and a restored Davidic dynasty. An unnamed king would care for his people just like David. These were failed prophecies. Israel was hardly "restored to its fortunes." It never regained its independence and languished as a minor province in the Persian Empire and later the Roman Empire. Of course, true to form, when the State of Israel was formed in 1948, those committed to the assumption that the Bible cannot err said, see, the prophet was right. It took a while, but he "clearly" predicted the restoration of Israel.

SECOND THOUGHTS

The conquest, the destruction of the Temple and Jerusalem, the exile of the elite to Babylon – all this trauma forced the people to rethink the Covenant. Some Chosen People! How could all this happen? The people turned to the Deuteronomistic view that when they're good, God will bless them and when they're bad he will punish them. So they figured they must have sinned just like Israel to the north obviously did causing them to be swallowed up by Assyria a hundred and fifty years earlier. Yes, it was their sins that brought the Exile about. God had abandoned his Covenant with them. The prophet Jeremiah, however, comes along and reminds them that God had *not* broken his word. Rather, God would renew the Covenant, a New Covenant, but this time one on the inside, in the heart, (31:31-34) where the Torah (not the temple) must be cherished and scrupulously lived. This was a turning point. From this time on in their history, the proper interpretation of and fidelity to Torah became Israel's religious mainstay. Through utter fidelity to the Torah, they would be truly a new covenanted people.

It wasn't long before different groups all claimed that their interpretation of the Torah made them the authentic heirs to the true new Covenant. Communities like those at the Dead Sea would claim that they alone possessed the new Covenant. Christians would come along and, vis-à-vis the Sadducees and the Pharisees and the Essenses, make the same claim. *They* would be the New Testament, the new

Covenant people. The writer to the Hebrews would claim that God "has made the first one [Covenant] obsolete. And what is obsolete is growing old and will soon disappear" (Hebrews 8:7-13). Jesus at the Last Supper would proclaim, "This cup that is poured out for you is the new covenant in my blood" (Luke 22:20). Eventually this whole notion of the Covenant being taken away from Israel and given to Christians became the foundation of "superinsessionism," the notion that Israel was replaced by Christianity. The seeds of Christian anti-Semitism were accidentally planted.

SHORT TAKES

Ezekiel was a member of a priestly family preaching in Babylon (unlike Isaiah and Jeremiah, who preached in Judea). He employs bizarre visions and weird symbolic actions, to the extent that some have suggested that he was unbalanced. His elaborate language and visions laid the groundwork for the world of apocalypticism. Archaeologists have unearthed Syrian hybrid figures of human bodies with the heads of eagles, lions, etc., the very same identical figures found in Ezekiel's famous vision of the four creatures. Ezekiel needed no special vision to come up with these icons. They were around the corner, so to speak, again pointing up how much of the Bible simply reflects its surroundings, how much the Hebrews have borrowed and how much the biblical writers, like their contemporaries, saw everything through theological eyes, although there is a natural explanation at hand. Germane to this observation is Ezekiel's prophecy in 12:1-12 where it speaks of Zedekiah who will be taken into exile. He sneaks out of the city, but was captured by the Babylonians before he could make good his escape. What catches our eye here are the words of a Catholic commentator who writes concerning this passage, "Because many of the details are supported by historical record, some scholars think that this prophecy was written after the fact." That the commentator would offer this opinion rather than assume true literal prophecy is surely a support to all we have been saying.

Ezekiel is also the one who gives us the famous "Valley of the Bones" drama (37:1-14) where the bones take on flesh and skin to form a mighty throng, in reality, as YHWH tells Ezekiel, renewed exiles back in the homeland. This raising of the bodies is not an actual Resurrection but a symbolic one. This did not prevent later Judaism and early Christianity to press it into proof for a bodily Resurrection.

Ezekiel's original writings, like all the other prophetic writings, were later rewritten and expanded and it is clear to scholars that the text has suffered in the transmission to the extent that its interpretation is frequently uncertain. As scholar Eugene Maly notes, "Ezekiel is probably the most difficult of all the prophets to understand."[4]

We can't leave Ezekiel without briefly mentioning Gog and Megog only because of the fundamentalists' end-timers fascination with them. For them, Gog is Russia which poses a danger and will band together with Israel's neighbors (Iran, Pakistan, etc.) to battle Israel but, take heart, Israel will triumph just like the Bible predicted it will. As far as history goes, there never was a Gog or a kingdom of Gog. He seems more to be a stereotypical prototype of a tyrant, but in the Bible he does comes from way up north of Israel, and what could that northern place be but Russia? The fact is, in Ezekiel's time, no "Gog" appeared, no defeated mighty foe unless it was Babylon. This empire was eventually defeated, not by God's power, but because the Persian Empire was stronger. Yes, Israel did return home, but not as victors but rather as a poor subject people once more.

We need only mention in passing here some pertinent aspects of two Minor Prophets. Amos, for example, the 8th century prophet from the northern kingdom whose book, as usual, contains material by later editors, is famous for his oracles against the nations and for being the first to use the phrase, "the day of the LORD." He meant it as a kind of military motif indicating that the warrior, YHWH, will fight against Israel's enemies and "the day of the Lord" will be a victory day. The phrase, as often happens, took on a different meaning in later Jewish and Christian apocalyptic literature, morphing into the day of judgment at the end of the world. Amos, along with Isaiah,

Jeremiah, Hosea and Micah spoke harsh words against ritual and sacrifice giving strong indications that there were no ritualistic sacrifices following the Exodus period – a perplexing claim. They all railed against social injustice and corruption with Amos leaving us the famous, "Let justice roll down like water and righteousness like an ever-flowing stream" (5:24). Hosea, the antimonarchist, is known not only for his marriage metaphors and his picturing God as a parent and Israel as his child but for his seeming awareness, in the 8th century during which he was active, of old Israelite traditions concerning, for example, Jacob, Moses, the covenant and the desert wanderings. This suggests that not only were these traditions very ancient but also that the Deuteronomistic writers who were active centuries after Hosea were influenced by him in the way they depicted the relationship between YHWH and his people.

For all of the threats against Israel and its corrupt priesthood (for example, Micah 4 and Malachi 2), the prophets generally foresaw the restoration of Israel. It is Malachi who predicts a forerunner to announce the day of the LORD, the day of judgment, the restoration of Israel. This forerunner was eventually identified as Elijah who, according to tradition, did not die. In turn Elijah, in the New Testament, would be identified with John the Baptist (John 1: 19-23).

In summary, the prophetic writings have been so consistently and severely edited, added to, reworked and redacted throughout the centuries that it is difficult to claim that some of the prophets ever existed or, for those who did exist, that we have their actual words. As we have them today some of their writings are frequently notoriously difficult to interpret and understand which would seem to undermine any notion, not to mention the purpose, of divine revelation.

Chapter 9.

THE SAGAS OF THE MONARCHY AND THE MESSIAH

L et us return to our proper chronology as we come to the monarchy. Unlike previous periods, there is a relatively abundant store of historical and archaeological material for the age of the monarchy, not so much for the monarchy itself, which lasted only some seventy-five years, but a great deal more for the divided kingdom. (In fact, some 50 people mentioned in the Bible have been confirmed archaeologically.) We start at the less documented beginning with the books of Samuel and Kings (formerly one book), that had access to court records. People, places, names are often authentic. We might interject here the usual instruction that not only are 1 and 2 Samuel, like all the other books of the Bible, composite works but the sources for the books are quite mixed and ambiguous. There are Masoretic and Septuagint versions of 1 and 2 Samuel, and the problem is that they differ in many places and frequently offer different stories of the same event. We have in effect, two witnesses to the books of Samuel. Which one is right? Some scholars used to prefer the Septuagint as the more authentic and held that it deserved priority. Others insisted on the Masoretic version as primary. Then the discovery of the Dead Sea Scrolls in our time produced a very early *Hebrew* manuscript that favors the Septuagint version. All of this proves once again that there existed alternate editions of these books, and others as well. All of which also displays, once again, the illogic of a literal, each-word-inerrant reading of the Bible, because we really don't know for sure if this is the original word. Even for those who read the Bible metaphorically there is no certainty what the original metaphor was and this, as we shall see, severely challenges the authenticity and authority of the Bible.

We must also remember that historical people and places are always pressed into the service of the historical biases of the Deuteronomistic historians (covenant fidelity leads to covenant blessing, but covenant infidelity leads to covenant curse/punishment). Scenes and dialogue are staged to score ideological points. Further, so sacred were old traditions that conflicting and independent ones, some of which outright contradict or duplicate each other, are allowed to stand as they are. Yet, they too, are shaped and edited to serve the Deuteronomistic perspective, even when it's a conflicted one and the authors are highly ambivalent about the material. Examples of this ambivalence would include the establishment of the monarchy (lots of arguments pro and con), the construction of the Temple (YHWH does not want a Temple yet, in the next breath, David's successor will build it); David as hero and rogue; YHWH's Covenant with David as unconditional (contradicting Psalm 132 which likely goes back to the time of David himself, where it is conditional: "*If* your sons keep my Covenant.... their sons also, forevermore, shall sit on your throne.") The writers obviously kept these conflicting traditions because they were genuine and too well known, too venerated, to skip over. (This doesn't mean they were factual, just that they were preserved.)

THE TIME WAS RIPE

Once the Israelites got into Canaan and after the period of the local charismatic Judges, Saul is made Israel's first king. The timing was right. The superpowers were either in decline or busy regrouping at home or fighting enemies elsewhere. The resulting political vacuum allowed the smaller groups in comparatively tiny areas to unite under a king. Israel was no exception. The Philistines were a continuing threat, and the disunity and rivalry of the tribes were dangerous handicaps. Israel needed a united front under a uniting king to face the enemy. Not all were happy about this flirtation. After all, YHWH was the Warrior God, King. He would deliver them as he delivered their ancestors from Egypt. It was a slap in the divine face to have another king besides YHWH. Nevertheless, the time was ripe for Israel's first king. Saul was chosen precisely because he was a mighty and effective warrior. The prophet Samuel, a highly idealized figure – seer, judge, priest, military leader (and crank) – is the king-maker.

Samuel is a strange figure and one wonders why the two books were named after him since he figures so little in them. Concerning his beginnings we are told that he is the answer to his mother Hannah's prayer. She, like her biblical predecessors – Sarah, Rebekah, Rachel, Samson's mother — is sterile (an old storytelling device to show the power of YHWH). Her prayer is answered indicating an unusual child, the future prophet, Samuel. Hannah sings a song of joy. (In another age, her song will be lifted by the evangelist Luke and put into the mouth of another childless woman, Mary of Nazareth.) The only thing is that scholars have noticed that, linguistically, the Hannah-Samuel saga gives every indication of really belonging to Saul's beginning, and that most likely the story was transferred to Samuel both because of his central role in the establishment of the monarchy and because of the Deuteronomistic historians' consistently negative view of Saul. Whatever, Samuel served as a prophet, priest, and judge who was illegally grooming his own low-brow sons to succeed him (judgeship could not be hereditary). He also functions, as we said, as a kingmaker. And to Saul he turns.

SAUL AND TRAGIC NARRATIVE

Saul is a very complex figure. He was an effective military leader approved by YHWH: "the spirit of God came upon Saul" (1 Sam 11:6). He piles up victories. His soldiers loved him. His beginnings vary. One story has Saul, "a handsome young man standing head and shoulders above the others," searching for some lost donkeys, and eventually he enlists the seer Samuel's help in finding them. (Must have been a slow day for Samuel.) Then, Samuel, who had received a prior message from the LORD to do so, anoints a reluctant Saul as king. ("I am only a Benjaminite from the least of the tribes of Israel and my family is the humblest of all the families of the tribe of Benjamin"). In spite of the protest, Samuel proceeds. Note that Saul is the first king of Israel to be so anointed (christened or "Messiah-ed"). In another account, Saul is chosen by lot. Whatever the tradition, Samuel has done his job and retires. But not for long. He reappears later to chastise Saul for violating the etiquette by offering sacrifice himself instead of waiting for the priest, who was tardy. (Yet, other kings offered sacrifice without censure). The consistent Deuteronomist's point comes across in this incident: success comes from obedience and failure from disobedience to YHWH. Ritual comes before strategy and, on top of that, in another swipe at the monarchy, the judgeship of Samuel is the preferred form of leadership, over the kingship of Saul. Later on, as we noted in the previous chapter, Samuel scolds Saul for not following the law of *herem*, killing all his captives. Saul had fallen out of favor.

The Bible gives two versions of his death. One, the official (and suspect) Davidic court version, was that he committed suicide and the other is that Saul, at his own request, was slain by a stranger who then brought Saul's crown and bracelet to David who was at camp and who, after hearing his account, has the stranger slain. Conspiracy theorists consider this question: why did the stranger, an Amelekite soldier, bring the crown and bracelet to *David* and not, logically and fittingly according to protocol, to Saul's son, the heir apparent to the throne? Think about that. Could it be that he was David's hired assassin? Did David, who would not scruple to shamelessly kill Bathsheba's noble and innocent husband to cover up his adultery, have Saul murdered by this hired assassin and then killed him so he couldn't talk? Sounds like a Mafia tale but it wouldn't be too far off – for David, in spite of the "media makeover," was, as Raymond Brown called him, little more than a Mafia chieftain.

DAVID

Saul rides high in the narrative, until David appears on the scene. Then, in the view of the sacred writers, Saul can do nothing well. He's a total failure and God's spirit departs from him. He becomes moody and psychotic and obsessed with David and no longer could contain the Philistines. How much of this is true is hard to say. For example, the text says that Saul "loved David very much and David became his armor-bearer" but, not very long after that statement, Saul is presented as never having met David. One suspects that Saul is the victim of the historians' negative propaganda and obsession with their hero, David. (Note how parts of 1 Samuel refer to Saul as prince and reserve the title of king for David.) Anyway, Saul comes and goes and is succeeded by David, the slayer of Goliath. (Or was he? 2 Samuel 21:19, it says that Elhanam slew Goliath — whose armament, by the way, contains elements from a later era.) After "David" killed Goliath, the text says he brought Goliath's head to Jerusalem during Saul's reign. This can hardly be true. During Saul's reign, Jerusalem belonged to the Jebusites. Jerusalem, according to the Bible itself, did not come into Israelite hands until after David became king. YHWH's choice of David from Judah over Saul from Benjamin is meant to legitimize the Judean dynasty against the Northern monarchy.

It is no surprise to learn that there are three different independent stories on how David rose to the top and was anointed king – obviously, again, three traditions heavily laced with the various authors' agendas. It does seem, though, that David was an opportunist who, according to the Bible was apparently willing to kill his fellow Israelites (1 Sam 25:13, 34) and even fought on the side of the Philistines against his fellow Judeans and their God if it profited him. Sharing his booty with his fellow Judeans, he bought his way to the kingship and took over in a military coup. As for the Bible's account of the northern tribes beseeching David to be king over them because he is their own "bone and flesh", this reeks of invention, because if there was one thing David was not, it was a Northern Israelite. He was from a different tribe in a different region with different interests altogether.

David was king and set up his capital at Hebron. Then he acted. He slaughtered Saul's family. He was exceedingly cruel against the Moabites, killing two thirds of their soldiers. He burned to death the Ammonites in brick kilns, he excluded the blind and the lame from his capital, committed adultery and murdered the husband Uriah by proxy. He couldn't seem to control his sons. He is dethroned by his son Absalom, who killed his half-brother Ammon because he raped his sister. In the end David was like "the Lion in the Winter," an old man, a tragic figure, unable to control anything. Not quite Michelangelo's paradigm statue.

Whatever flaws David has in the Book of Kings, he gets a makeover in another book, the Book of Chronicles, which *The New Jerome Biblical Commentary* (Prentice Hall, 1990) describes "as a proper exegesis of the books of Kings, wherein the author, [likely a Levitical cantor], injects his own personality and convictions chiefly by suppressing or slanting a given narrative." In short, Chronicles airbrushes David (as it does Solomon), and it is interesting to track how this book omits his rise to power, his conflict with Saul, his alliance with the Philistines, his affair with Bathsheba and the disintegration of his family. The reason for this extreme adulation of David was that the author of Chronicles was trying to provide a firm blueprint for life after the Exile. He was interested in centering the recovery squarely on the David-Temple-Levites (hence his strong interest in Levites) centralizing triangle so he concocted his own distorted and sanitized version of what was written in the Deuteronomic histories. In other words, he needed to emphasize the Covenant with David in its role of legitimizing and establishing the Temple and its cult as the cornerstone of a new Judaism. Once more, we are made aware of the propaganda of the scriptures and how carefully we have to read and assess them.

Thus reading between the lines, what seems indisputable is that David was by all accounts an excellent strategist and military leader and, as we said, with the superpowers temporarily distracted, he subjugates his enemies and brilliantly extends his kingdom, though hardly as wide and influential as the text would make it. (Remember that the territory promised to Abraham, not surprisingly, corresponds to the same territory ruled over by the monarchy.) But David's and Solomon's power was felt. This political peak forms the basis of the ideal Davidic kingdom that the Israelites would forever aspire to. The United Monarchy, even though it lasted less than a century, was the quintessential "Golden Age," much the same way Christians, especially Protestant Christians, looked upon the apostolic age as the apex of Christianity, when miracles abounded daily, equality reigned, everyone loved one another and all shared everything in common. (Both myths would eventually not stand the examination of history.) It was also at this time that the Deuteronimistic historians elaborated the major theme of the everlasting dynasty of the House of David. YHWH would unconditionally guarantee it. David was indeed a giant – or became one – and the most important biblical figure next to Moses. Having morphed from a local petty Semite chieftain to Michelangelo's universal Apollo-like god, he has been innocently placed in the pantheon of the "Great Men of History."

Many archaeologists and biblical scholars, however, believe that David was not the mighty potentate of biblical lore whose power was felt from the Nile to the Euphrates, but rather he was a mercenary who carved out what was at most a small duchy in the southern highlands around Jerusalem and Hebron. His capital city of Jerusalem (which replaced Hebron) was not an oriental Disney Magic Kingdom, but likely a rather small village covering some 15 acres with a population of perhaps a few thousand. The real bottom line in all of this is that there is no way of knowing whether the David of the Bible and the actual David match. It's hard to separate the facts from the myth, the metaphor from the prose. He's certainly a legend celebrated in story and art. Still, the sheer variety of traditions about David give firm evidence of his standing in the memory of Israel. So it seems that, at this stage, the consensus is that David did exist as an historical figure but that the biblical accounts, as usual, must be taken with a large grain of ideological salt.

The Messiah

With David and his interpreters was born what is called the Royal Ideology, or the David-Zionist theology. It deals with the concept of a coming Messianic figure. That ideology was a quite common one, shared with the rest of the contemporary Near Eastern nations. Scholars speculate that the Israelites got it from the Phoenicians, whose terminology and temple plans (recall that Hiram, the Jerusalem Temple contractor, was king of the Phoenicians) Solomon mimicked. You catch the inadvertent connection in Psalm 48 that describes Jerusalem thusly:

> His holy mountain, beautiful in elevation,
> is the joy of all the earth,
> Mount Zion, the heights of Zaphon.
> is the city of the great king. (vv. 1-2)

Zaphon, it should be noted, is the home of the Canaanite storm god, Ba'al.

The Royal Ideology was pretty much a copy of common Mideast ideology where the king was held to be a manifestation of the gods (for example, in Egypt). It was natural, then, that when Israel opted for a king he too would also have to be a "manifestation of the gods" or, within the monotheism of Israel's theology, God-related in a very special and close way. This relationship blossomed into a Father-Son paradigm and eventually became concretely embodied in the dynastic promise that assured forever YHWH's blessing on David and his descendants. (2 Samuel 7). Recall the Father-Son paradigm in Psalm 2.

> YHWH said to me.
> You are my son
> Today I have begotten you.

Some scholars contend that this kind of father-son talk, found in the Hebrew writings like Psalm 110, are the origins of the trajectory of imputing divinity to the title "son of God," and eventually putting Son in the upper case and, further down the biblical road, eventually ascribing this elevated title to Jesus. This frequent "upgrading" process is deeply embedded in Jewish thought.[1]

That is to say that the Royal Ideology conveys the notion that the king becomes a kind of adopted son of God. That relationship in Covenant terms soon became unconditional. The Davidic dynasty would never end. God had chosen the dynasty and its capital and its Temple and they would endure. That was the meat of the new Royal Ideology: the king was now the basic mediator between God and the people (not Moses). He stood in special relationship to YHWH, and he had a special mission. David and his descendants were to represent the rule of God in the world. The Davidic kings were YHWH's representatives who should "judge the poor with justice, and decide aright for the land's afflicted" (Isaiah 11:1-9) and "He shall...govern wisely, he shall do what is just and right. (Jeremiah 23:5-6) These qualities would mark the ideal Davidic king and, as we shall note shortly, the early Christians, were quick to apply them to Jesus.

In the way of the ancients but puzzling to us moderns, Luke, in the speech he puts into Paul's mouth in Acts 13:30-33 (very much like the speech Luke puts into Peter's mouth in Acts 2:14-36), has Paul say, "We announce to you the good news that what God promised our fathers, he had fulfilled for us their children in raising up Jesus, according to what is written in the second psalm, 'You are my son; this day I have begotten you.'"

Paul turns the standard ancient formula of adoption, whereby in this royal coronation psalm the king became God's son (see above), to a prophecy of the Resurrection of Jesus. As we shall note subsequently, it's a form of exegesis that, though foreign and puzzling to the modern mind, was apparently accepted by Paul's peers. Psalm 2's application to the king's coronation and Paul's application to Jesus' Resurrection remains for us problematic. The fact is that, to this day, that Pauline passage is used in our liturgy during Easter time with its full force of a Resurrection prophecy "according to what is written in the second Psalm".

THE CITY ON THE HILL

To return to an aspect of the Royal Ideology, we must appreciate an interesting side effect, namely the linkage between YHWH and the king and his capital city. It was a singular novelty. You can see this in the growing pumped up references to Jerusalem: "From Zion shall go forth instruction/And the word of the LORD from Jerusalem," wrote Isaiah (2:3). For ancient Israel and later Christians, Jerusalem became the center of the world, the navel of the universe, specifically the temple atop Mount Zion. Jerusalem quickly evolved into the great mythological city, the all-embracing symbol of divine presence, hope and restoration. That's why, many centuries later, the Christian Book of Revelation speaks of a "New Jerusalem" coming down from heaven. It's the old Davidic Ideology fulfilled. Jerusalem's Mt. Zion replaces the desert's Mt. Sinai as the place of official revelation. (Ironically, Jerusalem was probably named after Shalem, an ancient god). Not surprisingly, references to Sinai (or Horeb) and the Ark of the Covenant – the two touchstones of the old Mosaic tradition – quickly peter out in the monarchy accounts and the books that follow. Not everyone was happy with this replacement, and some prophets, like 8th century Amos and 7th century Jeremiah, minced no words over their disapproval. All this transformation, of course, had as its aim political and religious centralization in contrast to the free floating confederation of the previous times. Mythical Jerusalem joined Cuzco, Peru, Mecca, Saudi Arabia, Pacanda, Mexico, the Sierra Nevada de Santa Marta, Columbia, the Fame Islands, Greenland and Baboquivari Peak in Arizona as contenders for the navel of the world — not to mention Brooklyn, New York.

> The Lord is great and worthy to be praised
> in the city of our God.
> His holy mountain rises in beauty,
> the joy of all the earth.

> Mount Zion, true pole of the earth,
> The Great King's City! (Psalm 48)

THE ROYAL IDEOLOGY REBORN

This Royal Ideology hung on even after the fall of the Davidic dynasty in 586 B.C.E., and became fodder for the concept of a Messiah, an Anointed One, a Son of God. This Messiah was to come from David's royal line and restore the kingdom. There was hope when the Persians allowed the Jews to return to Judea and rebuild their temple and David's descendant, Zerubbabel, was placed in charge. But, as we shall see again, he passed silently from the scene and so did the Messianic hopes for several centuries. Eventually, every time something was said about a past or present anointed king, the reference got transposed to the future. The term Anointed One or Messiah was reinterpreted as the promise of a future leader sent by God to restore the Davidic kingdom in unending peace and prosperity. The term was not read as a current statement but as prophecy, and those prophecies "clearly" foretold the coming of this Messiah.

By the time of Jesus the notion had become complicated, with some expecting a Davidic political Messiah and others a heavenly figure who would usher in God's Kingdom (Daniel 7) and still other several end-time figures. One thing was clear. The early followers of Jesus saw him as the fulfillment of God's promise to David. He was their Messiah (the Christ), a word that occurs over 350 times in the New Testament in reference to Jesus. Mark's Gospel put it most bluntly. He has Andrew say, "We have found the Messiah". Peter makes his confession at Phillipi: "You are the Messiah." (Mark 8:29; Luke 9:20; Matt. 16:16.) To this day we use the Messiah or the Anointed One as Jesus' last name (*Christos* in Greek), Jesus, the Messiah.

A SECOND LOOK

A couple of scholars clarify the trajectory and raise interesting questions. The Deuteronomic writers, when they came on the scene, were unhappy about all this since, after all, YHWH had made a Covenant with *all* the people, not one individual, and they tried to sabotage the kingship whenever they could (1 Samuel 8; 2 Samuel 11-20), especially after the fall of the kingdom and the Exile. Noting that, these modern scholars make a summary comment on the trajectory:

> " ... The royal ideology did not disappear so easily from the Israelite imagination. Psalm 89 is a powerful testimony to one response to the Exile: it demands that God exercise proper justice and demonstrate his character in relation to other gods by renewing and bringing to fruition his promise to David. And better known is the *transformation of the Davidic promise in the Greco-Roman period into Messianic expectation*, the hope that God would one day raise up a deliverer to lead Israel in victory over her imperial rulers. In time this was adapted in early Christian circles to understand Jesus as a Messiah." [2]

Indeed, Jesus' followers firmly believed that Jesus was the kingly son of David who fulfilled the traditional job description. We see this in Luke's Gospel, where Jesus begins his public ministry commenting on a passage from Isaiah that originally refers to the anointing of the prophet, but which Jesus takes and applies it himself: "He anointed me to bring glad tidings to the poor" (4:18). Thus like a good Davidic king, Jesus would heal the sick, share table fellowship with the marginal and give special care to the oppressed and needy. This Davidic king motif was intentional and consistent. At the end of his life, Jesus was acclaimed king on Palm Sunday (as we would call it), disputed with Pilate over the term, and was Crucified under the sign "King of the Jews."

Moreover, as noted in the last chapter, Jesus becomes the *suffering* Messiah who "died for our sins according to the scriptures." (1 Cor 15:3). Drawing on Isaiah (52:14-53: 12), the passage about the Suffering Servant (which of itself has no Messianic connotations whatsoever, as we also saw in the last chapter), Christians saw a suffering Messiah. Luke, in his Gospel passage of the famous Emmaus walk, has Jesus say, "Was not the Messiah bound to suffer all this before entering his glory?" (24:26). And Peter in Acts (17:3a; 26:23) said that God saved Jesus from the dead, thus bringing to fulfill-ment "what he announced long ago through the prophets that his Messiah would suffer." We repeat: the idea of a suffering Messiah is found nowhere in the Old Testament or in any Jewish literature prior to the New Testament. The great theologian, Yves Congar states firmly that a suffering Messiah is without foundation. It's a Christian concept with no roots in the Old Testament tradition, even though Luke writes about "Moses" and "all the prophets" and "all the scriptures" testifying to it. Nevertheless, although there was nothing in the Old Testament to associate the Messiah with suffering, the early Christians combined the royal figure of the Messiah with the suffering servant of Isaiah and also added that Jesus would come at the end of time, and people have been guessing at a timetable ever since. Consider the Passion narratives, according to Matthew 26:23-24, "He answered and said, 'One who dips the hand with me in the bowl, this one will hand me over. The Son of Man goes as it is written about him.'" Daniel J. Harrington S.J., the great New Testament scholar, comments on this verse:

> "As it is written of him, there is *no specific one reference* to the suffering and death of the Son of Man. The fulfillment is tied to the person of Jesus taken as a whole, not to one title for him. The verse simply expresses the early Christian convic-tion that Jesus' suffering and death took place 'according to the Scriptures.'" [3]

Perhaps the evangelists' words were necessary to counteract the embarrassment of Jesus' criminal death ("Cursed be the one who hangs on a tree") just as they had to counteract the rumor of Jesus' illegitimacy by invoking the Holy Spirit. Anyway, how are we to deal with the constant refrain in the New Testament that Jesus' death was "according to the scriptures," by which the writers meant the Old Testament? How are we to think of the ritualized orthodoxy we call the liturgy when it unfailingly prays on Easter Sunday:

God our Father, creator of all, today is the day of Easter joy.
This is the morning on which the Lord appeared to men
Who had begun to lose hope
And opened their eyes to what the scriptures foretold:
That first he must die, and then he would rise
And ascend to into his Father's glorious presence...

A LATE CONCEPT

It is important to note again that all this talk of an Anointed One or
Messiah in this sense came very late in Israel's history. As J. Becker
says, "There is no evidence for true Messianism until the 2nd century BC."[4] On the contrary, prior to the 2nd century, wherever the
term "Anointed One" or "Messiah" is used of David or any of his descendants, its context is always the current celebration of the king's
ascension to the throne or the everlasting character of the Davidic
throne. In the Old Testament, the overwhelming majority of cases
that speak of an anointed person refer to the king. Nothing more.
Most of the recorded rituals of "Anointed Ones" (Messiahs) usually refer to the reigning king, simply indicating that he has been
designated as an agent of God to guide and lead the people. Any
claim that such references refer to a Messiah as we understand it is
an ideological interpretation. As Joseph Fitzmyer puts it:

> "In the foregoing seventeen Old Testament passages [in the
> books of Samuel] which refer to pre-Exilic times (despite
> an occasional later formulation) the use of 'Anointed One'
> [Hebrew letters] has always been applied to a king reigning
> in the undivided monarchy of Israel. In none of them is the
> religious literal meaning even hinting at a "Messiah" or a
> "Messianic expectation" – despite the way that some of them
> are interpreted at times by commentators."[5]

The point is that in the Old Testament there is never an instance
of anointing any "Messiah" in any narrow sense as an awaited or

future agent of God, and all those citations of a "clearly" foretold Messiah are really late Jewish and early Christian interpretations. As Fitzmyer calls it, any attempt to speak of Isaiah's Messianic prophecies "are still-born." In this he echoes Raymond Brown, who said, "There are no predictions of Jesus, as we know him, anywhere in the Hebrew Scriptures." So, then, if this is so, how does one view all those marvelous Advent antiphons, glorious musical compositions and splendid liturgies when one realizes that they are the products more of innocent piety than of reality, more of interpretation than of text? Yes, that second Advent preface in the Catholic liturgy is off the mark when it states, 'Jesus' future coming was proclaimed by all the prophets." Or, in the revised liturgy, "For all the oracles of the prophets foretold him." That, according to the scholars, is simply not so. Nevertheless, we use such "predictions" heavily in our liturgical books and we justify them as a case of the *sensus plenior*," that is, a fuller sense that even their authors were unaware of when they spoke or wrote them but which we know God intended. The trouble, as always, is one of criteria. The trouble is that anyone can play the "fuller sense" game, as evidenced in the fervid certainties of the end time scenarios of the biblical fundamentalists.

Even regarding the psalms, so often interpreted as prophecies of an end-time Messiah and which gave rise to talk among some Christian commentators about "royal Messianism," Fitzmyer quotes the Jewish scholar Mowinckel: "They [the royal Psalms] are in fact not prophecies but prayers issuing from a real, contemporary situation, that of the poet or the worshipper himself; and they express what he then felt, and thought and said. The fact that the worshipper is in many instances a historical king of Israel does not alter the fundamental fact that the Psalms are not prophecies but prayers with contemporary reference."[6]

Yet the early Christians determinedly found many such references to the Messiah that "clearly" pointed to Jesus (they called him Jesus, the Messiah or Jesus Christ and made sure he was of the house of David). Yet even though there are no passages in the early Bible that can be said to be Messianic in their original meaning, all this changed by the time of the Second Temple period. What happened is a familiar theme – reading into biblical words what one wants to see or building a case on faulty translations (we shall see this again and again, especially in the case of Mary, Jesus' mother). An instance is the Balaam story in Numbers 24:17. Hired to curse Israel by King Balek, Balaam unleashes a blessing:

> I see him, though not now: I behold him though not near.
> A star shall advance from Jacob, and staff shall rise from Israel
> That shall smite the brows of Moab, and the skulls of all the Shuthites...

Note that there is no Messianic vocabulary here, only the prediction of a future blessing through some kind of royal figure. This would not do for the early Christian Fathers, who took this as a precise Messianic prophecy even though this passage is cited nowhere in the New Testament itself which, if so obviously pointing to Jesus, raises the question, why not? For the Fathers, it was a no brainer: the star is Jesus as is the staff. They came to this conclusion by a misreading of scripture. In the Greek Septuagint the Hebrew word "scepter" is translated as "a man" coming forth from Jacob. This, plus a few other word changes, ultimately gave us this: "A ruler shall not depart from Judah...and he is the expectation of nations." In this changed form this is a sure fire reference to a future Messiah but, as scripture scholar and Dominican Stephen Ryan, observes: "We can see from this example that a passage that in its original language and context had little or no explicit Messianic content, through a long process of translation and interpretation came to be seen almost universally, by Jews and Christians, as Messianic."[7]

As we have seen and will see many, many times again, wrongful translations, the frequent misunderstanding or misreading of scripture to support dogma, tends to undermine confidence in the teaching of the churches. It appears that these faulty interpretations have hardened into accepted belief, are used as proof texts, and get gloriously enshrined in our song and prayer. The fact is, we are believing, not so much pristine revelation as an interpretation by persons with vested interests. We call it "tradition." We should also add that, to the degree that such "prophecies" were so "obvious," how shamefully dense must those be who don't see it:

> "While [the Pontifical Biblical Commission's document on Jewish-Christian relations] suggest that messianism was not a central motif in all currents of first-century Judaism, it does not emphasize explicitly enough the significant differences between the Old Testament and early Jewish notion of messianism and the messianism of early Christianity. Early Christian writers *sometimes projected the centrality of the Messianic idea in the New Testament into the theology of the Hebrew Scriptures and early Jewish religious text* imagining that every Jew of the first century was eagerly awaiting the coming of 'the Messiah.' That the vast majority of Jesus' Jewish contemporaries did not accept him as the expected Messiah was *therefore explained as sinful obstinacy* (for example, Acts 7:51). Certainly one of the roots of Christian anti-Semitism was the apologetic problem caused by the Church's confession of Jesus as the fulfillment of Jewish Messianic expectations, while those whose faith was supposedly shaped by those expectations did not make such a confession."[8]

Let us pick up on those words of the scholars: it's "an early Christian conviction that Jesus' suffering and death took place 'according the Scriptures,'" and "Early Christian writers sometimes projected the centrality of the Messianic idea in the New Testament into the theology of the Hebrew Scriptures...." So there is no question that the royal psalms were given allegorical or typological interpretations in later Judaism and early Christianity. The antecedents of Jesus as a suffering Messiah are not to be found in the ancient text. The notion is an interpretative "conviction" and definitely a later development. It's not hard, though, to see how that development happened. The reality was that David's dynasty fell and Jerusalem fell and the people were sent into exile. There, as would be expected, they began to long for "the good old days," and in this longing the hope of the restoration of the Davidic monarchy grew. When the Davidic restoration did not happen, there developed late in Israel's history the expectation of a Messiah in the narrow sense who would restore, if not the political kingdom, a spiritual one, but only after several centuries. So the truth is that, in Israel's life, the notion of a spiritual Messiah was quite limited and, beyond the Qumran community, which talked of two Messiahs, most Jews did not subscribe to it. Still, the Qumran community demonstrates that there existed a variety of Messianic beliefs from the second century on. The topic in some quarters was a hot one, and messianism was "in the air" when Jesus arrived on the scene.

THE ISSUE

I have spent some time on this issue because the evolution of Israel's king as imitative of its neighbors, a kingship that was innately connected to the gods, to a special relationship, to promises of perpetuity, to a promised Messiah, to Jesus as that Messiah, are emblematic of the dynamics of a kind of interpretation that does not always rest easily with the modern mind. The modern mind balks at such heavy projections that appear so freewheeling and partisan. Put simply: seeing a perfectly normal and understandable evolution of the notion and need of a Savior-Messiah rooted in the desires and projections of a perennially oppressed and occupied people, how does one handle the literalism of liturgy, catechism, creed and councils which elevate all this to some kind of a divine plan of "salvation history" and see "manifest" prophecies going back to the time of Abraham, and especially the time of David, that announces and celebrates in clear and certain terms the coming of the Messiah in Jesus? How does one view all those elegant seasonal liturgies when one realizes that they are the products more of innocent piety than of reality, more of interpretation than of text? Of course some hastily affirm that they are only metaphors through which we describe Jesus but the truth is that both officially and unofficially we stopped at the metaphors. We made them proofs, not epiphanies. Still, all this is not to say that Jesus is not the suffering Messiah – not at all – but it is to say that we must be always aware that it is a faith belief that he is, a belief that draws upon interpretations of scripture's metaphorical language, interpretations not everyone will or can subscribe to.

As we end this chapter, it is not amiss here to remind ourselves that the notion of a savior-Messiah is not unique to Israel. Every civilization has memories of a "golden age" and a longing to return to it – a longing, ever delayed, never realized, that ultimately births the creative interpretation of some promised savior who will make it all possible at the end of time. The latest expression of this can be found in the intractable cauldron of Mideast tensions where the *New York Times* reported the return of a certain Moktada al-Sadr, an anti U.S. cleric, to Iraq. Here is part of that report:

> "Mr. Sadr set out from his office in the style of a Baghdad potentate, riding in a convoy of silver BMWs, escorted by sport utility vehicles. A few miles away, at a mosque that is hallowed ground for the movement, his supporters spoke in millennial terms of Mr. Sadr as a savior and a herald of the coming of the Hidden Imam, who will reveal himself at the end of time, bringing order and justice and taking revenge on God's enemies."[9]

That could be straight out of the Bible.

Chapter 10.

THE SAGAS OF SOLOMON AND THE DIVIDED KINGDOM

S olomon becomes king although he is the youngest not the eldest son of David. David is near death and imparts to Solomon his wise counsel on how to be a good and faithful king (1 Kings 2:14). (By now we should be alert to the Deuteronomic editor's theology in this episode: a successful king is one who is wholly faithful to the Mosaic law). Even with the highly selective accounts and mixed reviews of the Deuteronomistic historians prevailing, Solomon comes across as a ruthless conniver (eliminating his brother and his father David's oldest surviving son, Adonijah), a pragmatist, master builder, an insatiable accumulator, and a high roller. We are told that he engaged in international trade, drank out of golden goblets, outfitted his soldiers with golden shields, maintained a fleet of sailing ships to seek out exotic treasures, kept a harem of 1,000 wives and concubines, and spent thirteen years building a palace and a richly decorated Temple to house the Ark of the Covenant. The only trouble is that, to this day, in spite of the blockbuster movie (made and remade) "King Solomon's Mines," not one goblet, not one brick, has ever been found to indicate that such an exotic reign existed. Jerusalem was, in his time still a very tiny place, the habitat of a local chieftain and accounts of his expansive kingdom may well be read back boundaries of the territory promised to Abraham.

Solomon, who ruled roughly from 988 to 928 B.C.E. is nowhere mentioned in any other known sources from ancient times. If he had such an extensive empire, fabulous Arabian Nights wealth, renowned wisdom and ruled for a full 40 years, why is there no mention of him outside the Bible? If he engaged in international trade and imported luxury goods, why are so few of these goods found in his supposed fortresses of Hazor, Gezer, and Megidio? Why are there only meager remains from his supposed capital of Jerusalem? His building expansion centerpiece existed. In 2012, archaeologists in Israel unearthed a trove of artifacts dating back to the monarchy, artifacts that they say closely correspond to the description of Solomon's Temple in the Book of Kings though not necessarily indicative of famed extravagance. The fact is, as we mentioned before, that Jerusalem in the time of Solomon was a small town. Only later did Hezekiah greatly expand it, probably due to the immigration from the northern kingdom after its fall. Do we have here history or legend about him and his house? In 1896, Egyptologists discovered a reference to Israel in an inscription from the reign of Mernepath (1212-1202 B.C.E.) and in 1993-1994 archaeologists excavating at Tell Dan discovered two fragments of an inscription that may refer to the "House of David." We are not to get our hopes up:

> "Yet when all is taken into account, the epigraphical evidence pertaining to ancient Israel is meager and disappointing. After the mention of Israel in Mernepath's inscription – only a passing reference and difficult to interpret – there is silence for the next two-and-a-half centuries. Abraham, Isaac, Jacob, Joseph, Moses, Joshua, Samuel, Saul, David, Solomon —none of these biblical characters turns up in any ancient written sources outside of the Bible. Nor are there any clear references to the Israelite exodus from Egypt, the conquest of Canaan or Solomon's empire. Not until the mid-ninth century BC, the time of Ahab and Jezebel, does reference to Israel turn up again in non-biblical sources. From that point on there are, with one or two notable exceptions, only sporadic references to Israelite and Judean kings, mostly in Assyrian and Babylonian sources, and usually mentioned along with

other petty rulers of the day. In short, were we dependent upon the epigraphical sources alone for information about ancient Israel, we would know little more than that an entity known as Israel existed towards the end of the 13th century BC, and that two minor kingdoms called Israel and Judah, existed alongside each other in the central Palestinian hill country after the mid-ninth century BC. We would know further that Israel was destroyed by the Assyrians toward the end of the eight century BC and that Judah survived longer, but eventually was destroyed by the Babylonians early in the sixth century BC."[1]

Because of assessments like this and the many imitations of the Neo-Assyrian literary traditions, some scholars hold that the "Solomonic empire" is altogether a fiction incorporating realities from the Neo-Assyrian empire and projecting them as a glorious past for Israel. Other scholars say that there was a kingdom, but such a fabled one is more hindsight projection than reality. As Lesile Hoppe puts it:

"The scholarly debate between those who uphold the historical value of biblical narratives and those who do not sometimes becomes heated and personal. There are some scholars who seek a middle ground. While they are willing to characterize the biblical stories as often fictional and sometimes propagandistic, they also believe that the stories do contain actual historical information. Unfortunately, there is no consensus as to how to differentiate the fictional from the historical."[2]

THE TEMPLE SOLOMON BUILT

Continuing in the same vein, the whole building of the Temple – the centerpiece of the Deuteronomistic history — is very much a story of very human partisan agendas. In 2 Samuel 7, God is indifferent to any building. He doesn't want one. Then he changes his mind. Solomon finally builds it with slave labor (1 Kings 9:15) and with the help of King Hiram of Tyre, his builder, to whom he became so indebted that he had to pay off Hiram with land in the northern part of his kingdom. It is not without irony that the Jewish Temple is an exact copy of the pagan temple to Ba'al. In fact, it turns out that the Temple is very much the same as Canaanite temples excavated elsewhere in the Near East. Its very layout, the nature and types of sacrifices, the priestly officials, the rules of purity, the hymns and prayers – all line up pretty much with those of the Canaanite temples. Even the very site of the Jewish Temple, said in the Bible to be a threshing floor (very unlikely), was probably already a sacred area once used by the Jebusites for worshipping their gods. This is not quite the dramatic and cinematic story of the Bible. Once more we are faced the claims of modern scholars with their diggings and comparative religions versus ancient interpreters with their faith assumptions. Whatever the story, the Temple became iconic, the only valid place for the sacrificial worship of YHWH, and as such it was clearly a project designed to support the monarchy. Its eventual destruction changed dramatically the religion of Israel, as it moved from being a people of the stable Temple to a people of the portable Book.

As to the significance of the Temple, we repeat that it soon became, in the theology of the Deuteronomistic historians, *the* one and only place of worship. Such centralization was part of the move towards the concentration of political and religious power in Jerusalem. The Temple, in reality, stood at the end of a long history. At first, the Israelites could worship wherever they chose, even though the ever alert Priestly writer insisted that this was not so, but claimed that there was a portable tabernacle that provided the legitimate place for worship. This tabernacle, along with the Ark of the Covenant, was eventually moved into the Tent of Meeting, which in turn was placed in the center of the camp. The Ark of the Covenant was originally a simple wooden box containing the written covenant. Because YHWH was considered to accompany the Ark it was carried into battle (as other peoples did), the Ark became a powerful icon and in the time of the monarchy, Solomon moved it into the Temple,

YHWH's site of his "glory." During the Exile, it was Ezekiel, ever concerned about ritual purity, who mulled over how God could have permitted the Babylonians to violate the Temple where he dwelt. His solution was to say that YHWH abandoned the Temple before it was desecrated and to make his point Ezekiel combined the images of the Ark, cherubim and throne stool into a movable Ark and said that represented the true presence, the glory, of YHWH. Because it was now a special presence spot, the simple wooden Ark needed to be elaborated with gold plate, two winged cherubim and other accessories.

The Temple naturally brings up the priesthood. The best thing we can say is that its origin is unclear and the Pentateuch reflects this lack of clarity. From what scholars can garner, however, it seems that, before the Exile, any worthwhile man could offer sacrifice from any tribe. (Think of Samuel, David.) Somehow, the priesthood, at least from the 7th century B.C.E., became limited to the tribe of Levi, and then, during the Exile, became even more limited. The problem was, according to Ezekiel at any rate, that most of the Levitical priesthood had defiled itself with idolatry, leaving the field open to only one Levitical family, that of the Zadokites with the other Levites assisting them but not doing the main work. Later on, as we shall see, in the time of the Maccabees, the high priesthood was sold to the highest bidder and removed from the tribe of Levi altogether.

THE KINGDOM DIVIDED

It wasn't long, therefore, before Solomon's (shakily) united kingdom fell apart. It was a matter of time, because Solomon was unfaithful. He began almost immediately to disobey the conditions as set up in Deuteronomy 17:14-20. He conscripts horses for his army, amasses huge wealth, marries foreign wives, tolerates their gods and all the rest. Research, however, shows less theological causes. Although there was some military and commercial expansion, the economy was highly imbalanced, with the wealth going into the hands of the few while the majority of people sank into debt and poverty, all this rendering the Solomonic kingdom weak and quite susceptible to a growing Assyria, which eventually came and gobbled up the northern part of the kingdom.

So Solomon's kingdom split into the northern kingdom of Israel under Jeroboam, and the southern kingdom of Judah under Rehoboam. If we recall that the Deuteronomistic historians were from the southern kingdom of Judah and were writing after the fall of the northern kingdom, we are not surprised that, for them, the northern kingdom fell because of apostasy, and they never tired of preaching this message. Their sermonizing about Israel's apostasy is incessant. Not one of the northern kings is decent or faithful. Look, for example, they say, at Jeroboam, who sinned by making two golden calves and setting up shrines at Dan and Bethel so that his people wouldn't have to traipse to the Temple at Jerusalem and perhaps be won over to the king there. The fact is, there was no single central Temple for the whole country when Jeroboam lived. That came two centuries later, under Josiah. Those golden calves were no more idolatrous than the golden cherubim on either side of the Ark of the Covenant. The one thing we do know about Jeroboam is that he rebelled over Solomon's forced labor program. For his pains, he was persecuted and had to flee to Egypt. In biblical terms, he did his Exodus thing in reverse and fled slavery to go to Egypt, only to return when Solomon died. It is no surprise, given his experience, that Jeroboam made the Exodus myth central to his shrine at Bethel and provided the eventual impetus to connecting it with the YHWH story that became standard biblical lore. Regardless, he fell under the Deuteronimist's condemnation of idolatry.

THE LOST TRIBES

With the fall of the northern kingdom of Israel under the Assyrians and the scattering of its people came the endless speculations, not to mention fascination, about the fate of its ten tribes. Ever since, attempts to trace them have provided enough loony pseudo-histories down through the ages to fill several libraries. Once the Bible was translated into the vernacular after the Reformation, people and nations tended to graft their identities to the biblical tree, or at least use the Bible as the template against which to define themselves and their national policies. Everyone, it seems, by claiming Israelite tribal descent, wanted to write themselves into the biblical story, especially small nations looking for some claim to fame, some "Mayflower" credentials. After all, to trace one's people back to one of the tribes was to claim the blessings YHWH made to those tribes, including being gathered together in God's kingdom at the end of time – not to mention that such "heirs" got to sit on the Twelve Thrones to judge the rest of humanity.

So where did these tribes wind up? According to the never ending legends, literally, all over the place: North Africa, Spain, Central Asia, China, South America, and the Artic. You name it. According to Mormon belief, the American Indians and Pacific Islanders are lineal descendants of the ancient Hebrew Lamanites, although DNA studies decidedly dispute that. Orthodox Jews, armed with their DNA tests, still hope to locate missing tribes in Burma. Even the outrageous Baron Munchausen claimed to have found the lost tribes. Likely, of course, the ten tribes, if they were that, melted into the melting pot of the Near East, including southern Judea and simply disappeared. This is not to say that the romantic search will not go on.[3]

THE FALL OF THE SOUTHERN KINGDOM

By 700 B.C.E. the Assyrians, based in modern day northern Iraq, built an empire that stretched from Iran to Egypt – most of the Middle East – and was the largest empire yet created. Since Assyria had no natural boundaries, they spent huge resources on a large army to police its frontiers. That is why the heavily fortified city of Lachish in Judah, about 25 miles west of Jerusalem and a strategic point on the trade routes, was of interest to them. At one point King Hezekiah of Judah (715 -687) unwisely rebelled against the Assyrians. In 701

B.C.E. the Assyrian King Sennacherib thus seized Lachish, killed its defenders and deported its inhabitants. The Assyrian account of this victory boasts: "Because Hezekiah, King of Judah, would not submit to my yoke, I came up against him and by force of arms and the might of my power, I took 46 of his strong fenced cities... plundered a countless number...carried off 200,156 persons..."

The Bible's account, on the other hand, gives a different whitewashed version. It says that Hezekiah refused to pay tribute. "He rebelled against the King of Assyria and would not serve him." (2 Kings 18:7) Then you have that story of the miraculous slaying of the Assyrian army by an Angel of God (19:35ff) immortalized by Keats. The Bible records two Assyrian campaigns against Jerusalem, but according to the scholars, the whole biblical account is suspect. As they point out, there's a lot of legend interwoven in the account of Sennacherib, including the prophet Isaiah's (unlikely) predictions of his downfall and assassination. The Bible does not mention, for example, that Sennacherib brutally seized the Judean cities until Hezekiah was crushed and paid up. Among the punishments was the deportation of the people to resettle in other parts of the empire, creating the flow of refugees, a phenomenon still with us today in several parts of the world. Hezekiah's son Manasseh succeeded him and became a vassal of Assyria.

It is interesting to note that King Manasseh ruled for nearly fifty-five years (a record for the Davidic dynasty) but, since he was considered an apostate by the Deuteronomistic historians, he rates only a paltry eighteen verses! Here we must interrupt our narrative to point out one of those dissonances common in the Bible. We have two accounts of King Manasseh, one in 2 Kings 21:1-18 and another in 2 Chronicles 33:1-20, and they can't be reconciled. The author of 2 Kings makes Manasseh the Adolph Hitler of his time. He is the arch villain, the most despicable of the Judean kings. He was so evil that he was the cause of YHWH's punishment, namely, the Babylonian Exile and the destruction of the Temple. The author of 2 Chronicles had a problem with this. After all Manasseh *did* rule for 55 years, even longer than David and a long rule, in ancient understanding, is a sign of God's favor. How could God bless such a blatant sinner? So 2 Chronicles has Manasseh movingly repent and so, automatically, he is no longer responsible for the Exile or Temple destruction, and (as a bonus) gets a long life. In one account King Manasseh is so evil he causes major misfortune; in the other account, he is so repentant that he has nothing to do with these misfortunes and is rewarded with a long life. It's impossible to reconcile the persistent evil of one book with pious repentance of another, the cause of the Exile with no cause of the Exile.

Josiah came to the throne and declared independence from a weakened Assyria. Josiah is famous for his religious reform and the "discovery of the book of Deuteronomy." He was killed at Megiddo. Megiddo is dear to the fundamentalist apocalyptic crowd. It's a strategic site defending a major pass. There, long ago, an Egyptian pharaoh had defeated a coalition of Canaanite kings. There, under the Judge Deborah, the Israelites defeated the kings of Canaan. Eventually, because of the number of famous battles fought there, the Book of Revelation elevated Megiddo to a symbol (under the name of Armageddon) of the final battle between good and evil forces (Rev. 16:17-21) and became the leitmotif of pulp fiction and movies.

In due time, the southern kingdom also fell. In 586 B.C.E. Jerusalem was destroyed and the Davidic dynasty ended. A weakening Assyria and Egypt and a rising Babylon were battling it out for supremacy, and the small kingdom of Judah would necessarily be caught in the crossfire. Babylon prevailed, and King Zedekiah being the last king, was blinded and sent to Babylon along with thousands of others. The Exile had begun. As expected, the main view was that the destruction of Jerusalem was divine punishment for Israel's worship of other gods. At least, Jeremiah preached this.

Inevitably, tensions between those who stayed behind and those exiled began. They divided, somewhat petulantly, across status lines, like those who came across to America in the *Mayflower* and those who didn't. The ones who stayed, like Jeremiah, considered themselves loyal to the LORD. They did not abandon the land given to them, and so they validated YHWH's promise of fulfillment. Those who, like Ezekiel, went into exile in Babylon considered themselves the true Israel because, in their eyes, that homeland was now abandoned, empty, and devoid even of YHWH, who went with them into exile as he went with the Israelites into the desert. Jerusalem was no longer the city of God. The truth is that, while much of the population, especially the elite, did go to Babylon, a remnant remained in Judah, and there they eventually left us the Book of Lamentations and maybe the final edition of the Deuteronomistic history. The land was hardly empty.

In time, the Jews in Babylon grew prosperous and wealthy, and Babylon became a flourishing center of Jewish culture and learning. When the time would come to return to Palestine, many of these Jews, much as they grieved for the homeland, preferred to stay put. After all, Babylon was a cultured, elegant city. Who knows what was back home? In this political climate, settled in Babylon, the Israelites clearly had to rethink their understanding of the land and its relation to YHWH. Israel's greatest challenge was now how to identify themselves since the loss of their traditional marks of identity, and how to make any new identity represent Israel's "original" one.

RETURN

After Nebuchadrezzar, the king of Babylon's long reign, he was succeeded by his son and his sons (all assassinated). Down the line, one of them, Balshazzar, was made famous as the king in the apocalyptic Book of Daniel where, by the way, he is erroneously identified as the son of Nebuchadrezzar, a mistake repeated in the Book of Baruch. Eventually, Babylon is conquered by Persia (modern Iran) under King Cyrus, who ushered in the two hundred year "Persian Period," as it is called, until Alexander the Great took over. In 583 B.C.E., King Cyrus, in Israel's version of a New Exodus (Second Isaiah spoke of the return from Babylon as a new Exodus), reversing the pharaoh of

Egypt, allowed the Jews return and rebuilt the Temple. Needless to say the Persian King Cyrus became Israel's hero. We recall Isaiah's exuberant designation of Cyrus "Messiah", the only non-Israelite ever to be called that (Isaiah 45:1). Cyrus, it was claimed, was YHWH's specifically chosen instrument for Israel's return with YHWH declaring, "I have grasped Cyrus' right hand to subdue the nations before him." Yes, it was YHWH who gave Cyrus victory "so that you may know that it is I, the Lord, the God of Israel, who call you by your name" (Jeremiah 10:2). It should come as no surprise that the Persians saw it differently. Recall that on a clay cylinder discovered in 1879, Cyrus says that he had been called to conquer Babylon and the land beyond by the Babylonian god, Marduk, "the great Lord," whom he would now worship faithfully. It all depends on who writes the history books or whose prevail.

The first job was to rebuild a modified Temple to fit current circumstances. All was not well. As in all human endeavors of this kind, jealousies, rivalries and power politics took their toll. The reconstruction of the Temple would take decades, the city of Jerusalem nearly a century. The community was divided over style, leadership and who was in and who was out. The native Samaritans' offer of help was rejected. Nearby neighbors were not happy to see a comeback, much less to observe a rebuilding of the city's fortified walls. Those who never left felt a sense of faithful ownership of the land, while the exiles looked down on them as ones YHWH had obviously abandoned (he took off with the exiles). Even when the Temple's foundation was laid, some old timers wept. It wasn't the same. Some tried to sabotage the rebuilding. Finally, in 515 B.C.E., the Temple was dedicated, and we move into what is called the "Second Temple era," roughly from this time to the fall of Jerusalem under the Romans in the year 70 C.E. All this time, we must remember, we're dealing with a small insignificant little country, a minor blip on the international scene whose population was never more than 10,000 people, the size of a medium American town, and its capital, Jerusalem had about 1000 people. Again we have to resist thinking of Judah and Jerusalem as a grand, exotic country with the size and power of ancient Egypt, Babylon or Persia. It was minor backwater country.

SOUR GRAPES

In general, hopes were dashed for the returnees. Besides internal conflicts, there was an ongoing fight over leadership, with the exiles or those from the Diaspora gaining the upper hand. One of the returnees was, as we mentioned, Zerubbabel, a descendant of David, and so there was an undercurrent buzz that maybe the Davidic dynasty would be restored, but that hope fizzled as Zerubbabel simply disappeared from the scene. Thus, it was only natural that since things clearly were not being returned to their past glory, now maybe it would all come true in the future. More and more, that's where the hope lay: the future. Here, we repeat, especially in the prophetic literature of the time (we've already mentioned Ezekiel) we get the beginnings of apocalyptic literature. We can sense its natural progression from hope for a restored Israel and, when this failed, to the hope of a restored kingdom and, by extension (as dreams evaporated and prophecies failed) to the hope of a restored reign of God once his enemies had been defeated. (Yes, there will be war and a final battle.) Humans had failed. God had to intervene.

In short, there is the march from a specific vindication and restoration of Israel to that remote day of the Lord's universal judgment over the whole world, not just Israel. We get these indications in the 6th century B.C.E. prophet Zachariah with his surreal visions – the trend will be to dip into non-Jewish sources, mostly Persian stories, for metaphors and images – wherein a divine messenger reveals the future. This "divine messenger" figure would turn out to be a stock character in apocalyptic literature, from the Old Testament prophets to the Christian Book of Revelation: Isaiah, Zachariah and others all furthered the genre. They all say the same thing: there is a divine plan, complete with timetable, that will be fulfilled, and you could be privy to this plan if you knew how to unlock the prophets' coded messages. Meanwhile the battle between good and evil continues (there's a pronounced dualism in all apocalyptical literature, right up to the Gnostic writings of Christianity). Eventually, much of this would be fodder for the developing concept of a Messiah who would usher in a new age. To sum it up, apocalyptic literature is basically crisis literature. Hopeless people more readily imagine a future when the tables will be turned.

NEW WINESKINS

At this point, it is time to get more specific and emphatic about what we have mentioned several times before – that is, the role of the Deuteronomistic historians during the Second Temple period. Formerly, as we have seen, the worship of Judah did not differ much from that of the surrounding regions. The official cult was centered in the temple in Jerusalem, where YHWH and other gods were worshipped. Now this monolatry was no longer tolerated. The trauma of the Exile would no longer permit the old ways, the old religion. A radical change was needed; indeed a whole new religion. In the Exilic and Persian period the new religion was created and, to this end, Israel's religious past was radically reinterpreted by the scribes of the Deuteronomistic school. As one scholar notes well:

> "The disaster that had happened was interpreted as punishment for the worship of God/esses other than Yahweh. The Deuteronomisits thus created a (historically quite distorted) picture of the past, in which Israel was constantly at war with the demands of its own religion. This 'intolerant monolatry' was finally transformed into exclusive monotheism that amounted to a thorough break with Israel's own past. The differences are so substantial that the very fundaments of religion had been changed. Israel's relationship with Yahweh was reinterpreted as a covenant modeled on Near Eastern treaties of kings with their vassals; from now on his law (Torah) was the center of Israel's religion. Collective

repentance for past sins was called for so that God would fulfill his promises to the ancestors and turn the fortunes of his people... In the religious world of Deuteronomy, the temple and the cult were subordinated to a written text that demanded constant study and interpretation...The efforts of the scribers (including priestly scribes) led to the gradual emergence of the Hebrew Bible"[4]

Yes, Israel's history was thoroughly reworked from the post-exilic vantage point of the Persian era and projected backward to a thousand years before. This accounts for the historical mistakes and implausibilities we have noted in the various sagas. The whole Exodus-Covenant story, for example, even if culled from some old pieces of tradition, is a bit of creative fiction — "historically quite distorted" – reflecting the axial move from polytheism to monotheism, from permanent cult to portable scripture. Once more, the average person becomes aware of the disjointed, uneven evolution of a book he once thought was a unified, harmonious, seamless unfolding of the story of salvation history.

The bottom line to all of this is that scholars tend to move between the extremes that the Bible has no historical value whatsoever in constructing the history of Israel to admitting that, for all its creative theological and political interpretations, the Bible does contain some kernel of historical truth. This latter view is best summed up by the prominent Israeli archaeologist Amihai Masar of the Hebrew University of Jerusalem:

> "I recognize that the Pentateuch, the collection that the scholars call the 'Deuteronomistic history'... were written and further edited during the Monarchy (eighth-early sixth centuries B.C.E.) and even later during the Babylonian Exile and the Persian period that followed (sixth-fourth centuries B.C.E.). But I also accept the view of many scholars that the late-monarchic authors, and editors used early materials such as Temple and palace libraries and archives, monumental inscriptions perhaps centuries old, oral transmissions

of ancient poetry, folk stories rooted in a remote historical past, and perhaps even some earlier historiographic writings.

> "I also accept the view that though much of the biblical historiographic texts are basically literary works biased by late Judean theology and ideology, they nevertheless contain valuable historical information, which may be assessed on the basis of external written sources and archaeological finds."[5]

So what he is saying is that, yes, there is a gap of several centuries between the time of writing and the events described in the Bible and clearly orally transmitted narratives filled in the gap. The big question is, how credible are these oral narratives? One large problem, we remember, is the lack of parallel sources against which to measure their accuracy. Scholars like Masar would hold that often the details are inaccurate and even anachronistic, but the general political and religious situation, the core event, was accurately remembered.

Chapter 11.

THE EXILIC CHAPTER, THE APOCALYPTIC VERSE

The Babylonians didn't see it coming, but the Persians came along and displaced them. As we saw, the generous victor, Cyrus, with revenue in mind, allowed the Jews to return to Judah to bring the land and prosperity up to snuff so they would have enough money to pay him tribute. Some Jews returned, but many stayed, and we have practically no information of what life was like in the time spent in Babylon, except that, eventually, many Jews accommodated to life there and prospered as they always did in Egypt and in other nations where some kind of middle class existed. For those who did return, the practical questions were, who would be in charge? What would Judaism look like now? The influential "Priestly" author (or authors), whose voice we have acknowledged in Exodus, Leviticus and Numbers, prevailed: order was needed – an orderly society, an orderly practice such as Sabbath observance and, of course, a restored Temple. All this meant the restoration of the power of the Aaronite priesthood. Some Jews were quite glad to accept the priestly oversight across the board, like the prophets Haggai and Zechariah. Some, like Malachi accepted priestly dominance but were concerned about corruption in its ranks. Second Isaiah (55-66), on the other hand, wanted nothing to do with the priestly caste, and saw the day when YHWH would intervene and replace them with honest men.

Another issue that arose was how to deal with what we moderns call diversity. Should Jews convert others or shun them? Ezra and Nehemiah, plus the Book of Proverbs, promoted the isolationist view. Another sensitive issue was, how could the returned Jews hope and pray for the return of a Davidic king without offending their Persian overlords? The Book of Psalms kept this hope alive. It was during these difficult struggles that the Jews were beginning to reinterpret the books that would someday evolve into the Bible.

THE GREEKS

The Persian period lasted from 538 to 333. While there was relatively peaceful coexistence at the beginning, the Persian tax levies on Samaria and Judah had grown increasingly burdensome and oppressive, and so when Alexander the Great swept in and took control of Judah, many were happy to see him come. The Greeks began to homogenize Alexander's vast empire by spreading Greek language and culture. When Alexander died, Judea fell under the wretched rule of the Ptolemaic dynasty, and then under the worse rule of the Seleucid dynasty of Egypt. In all of this, the Jews for the most part were not hostile to Greek influence, despite the danger of assimilation, and benefitted a great deal from it. (One thinks of the Septuagint, the Greek translation of the Bible, and the great Jewish philosopher Philo.) They began to act Greek, as someone put it, without becoming Greek. But there were moments of great tension. Antiochus IV pressed Hellenizing ideals vigorously, to the extent that Judaism was about to lose its identity. Not that many of the upper classes minded – they became enamored with things Greek. The lower classes were more conservative – especially the Hasidim, a group of pious conservative Jews – and resented the erosion of Jewish identity. Tensions were building.

The legitimate high priest's younger brother was as liberal as his brother was conservative. He even changed his name from Jesus to Jason to be more hip, and bribed Antiochus IV to depose his brother and put him in as high priest and head of state. Hellenization now picked up speed under him. The last straw was the building almost next to the Temple of a Greek-style gym where men exercised naked. Such nudity was highly offensive to the pious Jews, but some of the in-crowd often went through a painful and hazardous process to cover up their circumcision. A certain Menelaus bribed Antiochus to depose Jason (notice they both have Greek names) and put him in as high priest. What is notable about this is that for the first time, the high priesthood, which could only be held by one of Aaronic descent, was now given to an outsider (Menelaus was of the tribe of Benjamin). This provoked a scandal among the conservative Jews, a reaction not assuaged by the fact that Menelaus ordered the murder of the original legitimate high priest.

As time went on, Antiochus IV decided to implement Hellenization more deeply, and so he unleashed a program of massacre, pillage and destruction. He ordered the abolition of the Temple cult, and, at the end of 167 B.C.E., built a pagan altar on top of the Jewish altar. (The "abomination of desolation?") This sparked the revolt of the Maccabees in 168 B.C.E. The revolt succeeded. Eventually the Temple was rededicated and a more steady, conservative, Judaism prevailed. But not for long. A new Seleucid leader named Demetrius was bribed by the liberal Jews to dismiss Menelaus, execute him and replace him with one of their own kind. The new leader stupidly executed some 60 Hasidim Jews provoking a reaction by Judas Maccabee who decided to cut free of the Seleucids altogether and seek Rome's help to oust them. Before the Romans could arrive, however, Demetrius defeated Judas Maccabee in a bloody battle. A rival to Demetrius, to curry Jewish support, made Judas' brother, Jonathan Maccabee, the high priest (again, to which he was in no way entitled).

The rest reads like a bad novel. Over the years there was a dreary and repetitive series of struggles among the Seleucids for the throne. The air was filled with shameful intrigues among the Maccabees, who by this time had founded the Hasmonean dynasty. There follows a whole series of assassinations among themselves in the struggle for power.

More invasions, more intrigue, more conspiracy, more murders – brothers killing brothers, a son killing his mother – over the coveted high priest position. Also, over the years, the Hasmonean rule, traveling a long way from its original pious aims, became more despotic (not to mention more Hellenized than the regime it replaced). For example, one of these Maccabee Hasmoneans, Alexander Jannaeus, had 6,000 fellow Jews who threw lemon peels at him slaughtered. Later he had some 800 of his enemies crucified.

Eventually Judea fell to Roman rule and its puppet, Herod, who quickly slaughtered the opposition. Herod had conquered Jerusalem in 37 B.C.E. with the help of Roman legions and set about transforming his capital in specifically Roman style. The Roman architectural techniques incorporated into his grand rebuilding of the Temple won praises from the Jews. Although they hated the Romans, the Jews had ceased feeling threatened by Hellenism for quite a while, and even when Rome destroyed their Temple and would not allow it to be rebuilt, the Jews did not turn against Greek culture. Once more, they comfortably identified with the culture of the oppressor. Herod died in 4 C.E. and was succeeded by his three sons and then by procurators (such as Pilate). Again there were those who collaborated with the Romans and those who resisted. Tensions were always high between the privileged aristocratic members of that society and the common folk. High-strung nationalists were always plotting and there was a rise in fanaticism and Messianic prophets. Corruption and extortion were commonplace.

REVOLT AND REVISIONISM

Finally, it all erupted in the Jewish revolt of 66 C.E. The Romans reacted, and in 70 the Temple was torched and the city burned. Many Jews died. It was a shock every bit as much as the destruction of the Vatican and the slaughter of the pope and cardinals would be for Catholics. There was a second brief uprising in 132-135 C.E., and again the land was devastated by Rome.

This is a sorry thumbnail sketch of a nation's plight, but the fact is that Judea fared no better and no worse than any other tiny country caught in the politics and battles of the superpowers of the day. For our purposes, the difference with the Jews is in their crisis of faith. They were, after all, by their own accounts, a Chosen People. According to ancient lore, faithful YHWH, full of mercy and compassion, had delivered them time and time again, and would do so once more. They had fully embraced the Deuteronomic theology that any misfortune was the result of their infidelity to YHWH. If they repented, surely YHWH would look on them once again kindly, and life would be sweet. The prophets said so, but theory and reality kept colliding, for even when they were good and faithful, they still got plummeted – and so often and so severely and so thoroughly and so consistently! Decade after decade, they had Syrians and Egyptians and Greeks and Romans and other hoards warring on them, conquering them, massacring them. If that were not bad enough, there was the corruption and internecine murders of the Temple priests whose office was sold to the highest bidder. There were the "beautiful people," the aristocrats, who had willingly adopted Hellenistic ways and just as willingly sold off their national souls. There were hotbeds of assassins, the Zealots, who did not flinch at killing their own around every corner. Jewish specific identity as an ethnic group was fast eroding. Times were terrible. What was a faithful Jew to do? More to the point, their patience was wearing thin. Their faith in YHWH and in their special status was evaporating. Where was God who had chosen them?

APOCALYPTIC TIMES

As so often happens, when such dissonance occurs between theory and practice, you do one of three things. You either abandon the theory (one thinks of some modern Jews who left their faith over the Holocaust), dig in deeper, or reinterpret it.[1] Some Jews of the terrible times we're considering concluded that there is not only no

Covenant, there is no God. If there were, how could he have allowed this horror to happen to his Chosen Ones? Others, who wanted to remain faithful to God, sought to reinterpret the biblical experience. Among those who did such a reinterpretation in the era of the Exile and after were the apocalypticists, whose initial writings were in direct response to the dangers of a very seductive Hellenism. Such apocalyptic writings, though hopeful, were basically fundamentalist: let's return to the old traditions that have been despised and forbidden and even criminalized by Antiochus Epiphanes (his self-styled title meaning "the Manifestation of God"; he was soon dubbed by the Jews as Antiochus Epimanes, "the Madman"). There was a culture war going on, one that even affected the Temple priests who "went Greek." Between war, loss of the land, occupation and the seductions of their heritage by Hellenization, these were wicked times. All this would fuel, as we said, the Maccabean revolt and the birth of apocalyptic writing.

Some were becoming hesitant to continue to hold God as the author of such unrelenting evil. I say "continue to hold" because the centrality and sovereignty of God was a given in Hebrew theology. YHWH was the Lord of history. He alone is the source of both good and evil, and often as not, as we have seen, he wreaks evil on his people, including the innocent, for infidelity and tests them in time of fidelity (the Book of Judith). Ironically, monotheism had complicated the problem. As long as there was polytheism, as long as there were many gods, some good and others bad, that handled the problem of good and evil. Now with only one God, the author of all, how do you account for evil? Now there was a single God who claimed,

> I form light and create darkness.
> I make weal and create woe.
> I the LORD do all these things.

(Isaiah 45:7)

And then there is Job: "Should we accept only good from God and not accept evil?" (2:10) and Lamentations, "Is it not from the mouth of the Most High that good and bad come?" (3:38)

But some were chafing under the unfairness. Why should the good suffer along with the bad? In modern terms, why do bad things happen to good people? The apocalyptic writers came up with an answer, a novel theological scenario. It isn't YHWH who sends the enemy to chastise an unfaithful Israel. It's wicked people themselves who do terrible deeds. And one day, goes the new interpretation, God will send another person, a Savior, to defeat such wicked ones and establish on this earth a kingdom of peace for his faithful ones. In time, the generalized "wicked ones" evolved into a specific one: Satan, sometimes known as Asmodeus, Azazel, Mastema or Belial, the Prince of Darkness, and, in the Christian Book of Revelation, as simply the "Devil." We notice the switch when we compare the incident of David taking up a census, a deed that displeases YHWH. In the early version in 2 Samuel (chapter 24) it is YHWH who "incites" David to take a census of the people and then punishes him for doing so. In the later Book of 1 Chronicles, the author, in telling the same story, writes that, "*Satan* stood up against Israel and incited David to count the people of Israel" (21:1). Yes, blame Satan and his minions for the world's evils. The invention of Satan, the fallen angel, according to folklore, helps but does not really solve the problem because Satan is, after all, a created being and could at any time be restrained or destroyed by YHWH.

We take time to note here that Satan goes back to old non-biblical Jewish sources like the Wisdom of Solomon and 2 Enoch, even at times appearing as a snake. Actually, the proper name Satan does not appear in the Old Testament and it's only around Jesus' time that he is so identified. Until then, mostly satan is used in the lower case not as an evil spirit but as a description meaning generally a minor character such as an accuser or adversary, opponent, or some malevolent force. One of the Dead Sea Scrolls (the Psalm Scroll) asks God "let not a satan have power over me, nor an unclean spirit", sounding very much like the phrase in the Our Father. But, as we said, around Jesus' time that changed. Luke's Gospel, for example, (10:18) has Jesus mention upper case Satan as a personal Evil Force and John, in a far-reaching unfortunate phrase, has Jesus say to Jews, who declared that God was their father, "You are from your father the devil and you choose to do your father's desires." (8:39). While the passage does not specifically mention Satan it was assumed that's what he meant and so it was quickly used to justify anti-Semitism. Even earlier, however, in Christianity's oldest book, 1 Thessalonians, Paul says "Satan blocked our way" (2:18), and the Book of Revelation really bequeaths to us the cosmic personal Satan of our tradition.

It was late apocalyptic writings like the books of Daniel and Enoch that suggested that there were evil forces at work in the world, forces that, for God's own reasons, had been given permission to inflict harm on the world. It was becoming clear that victory over such evil forces was not to be had simply by the people repenting. Rather, God himself must intervene to destroy these evil ones and start a new kingdom. It would be an all-out war between good and evil. Borrowing from the dualism in Persian Zoroastrianism (such dualism is found in the Christian corpus in John's Gospel and the books of Jude and Revelation), the new Hebrew apocalypticts saw the world as a conflict between that good and evil, light and dark. The cosmic struggle was played out on earth. On the everyday level, in popular lore, we would all soon learn to absorb the practical dualism of Good vs. incarnate Evil: the Archangel Michael vs. Satan, Holmes vs. Professor Moriarity, Luke Skywalker vs. Darth Vader, 007 vs. Specter, Batman vs. the Joker.

THE APOCALYPTIC ITCH

Although the Book of Daniel was the first (and only) apocalyptic book to get into the Hebrew scripture, and the Christians added to its singularity in the New Testament by including the Book of Revelation, apocalyptic writings are found in Egyptian and Mesopotamian canons. These writings were concerned about what would happen in the general future, while people like the Persians in their Zoroastrian writings were concerned with the end of the world. The Jews, too, were also concerned about the end of the world and what would happen in the immediate days before it wound down and all was over. They would assimilate some of their material from the Persians: end time tribulations, the struggle of God and his Messiah against evil, and so on. But the end time was an especially Hebrew fixation, since most of the ancients viewed history as cyclical and so history would go around and around endlessly.

But the Hebrews had a linear view of history, with YHWH as a God who works through history and reveals himself progressively in it. By necessity, therefore, there would be a beginning, a middle and, someday, an end. So the end of the world was a concern, and the Hebrews, starting around the 2nd century B.C.E., began producing books, like the books of Enoch (which included the Apocalypse of Weeks and the Book of Dreams) and The Book of Watchers. Such apocalyptic books were basically resistance literature composed in response to people like the tyrant Antiochus. The Rabbis, however, distrustful of private prophecies and revelations about the end of the world – especially since rabbinic tradition held that after the Exile there was no more prophecy – firmly disowned all these writings as weird and disorientating and excluded them from the Hebrew Bible. They were the ravings of the fringe groups, such as the separatist community at Qumran. Where it not for discoveries of Qumran at the Dead Sea in the last century, we would never have copies of such apocalyptic writings today. It is in these writings that we get the fullest expression of the novelty of the Messiah, fused with Daniel's "Son of Man" as a heavenly God-sent Savior. (Some apocalyptic writings envision two Messiahs, one from the tribe of Judah and one from the tribe of Levi.)

THE BOOK OF DANIEL SCRATCHES IT

Although, as we just mentioned, there were Jewish apocalyptic books around in the early centuries before Christianity, the Book of Daniel is the only one to get into the Bible and the latest one to do so. The rabbis accepted this book because they really thought that the young prophet from the Babylonian exile, whose name is already mentioned in Ezekiel 14, wrote it. (Christians would do the same: include some weird books like the Book of Jude in their canon because they thought the apostle Jude wrote it). The rabbis didn't know the book was really composed hundreds of years later in the Hellenistic period and completed in the time of the Maccabees around 165 B.C.E. by several anonymous writers. It is a fictional storybook full of standard "court tales." The name itself of the reputed author of the book should have given them a hint. "Daniel" is a stereotypic wise man name. He appears in Ezekiel, as we mentioned above, and also in the Ugarit Epic of Akat, and in similar tales from the East where the Jews were dispersed. The tales themselves and their standard characters – the sea dragon or Leviathan, the Ancient One (a variation of the god El who rides the clouds) and so on – can be found in Greek, as well as Canaanite myths.

Daniel became a pivotal book for both Jews and Christians, the latter even including Daniel among the four major prophets. In reality, it's a mishmash of a book written alternately in Aramaic and Hebrew (only Ezra shares this distinction) with several late additions. It falls generally into two parts. The first deals with court tales about Daniel and his friends – cheerleader fictions urging persecuted readers to hang in there. The second part deals with its famous "predictions" of the four kingdoms that would rise and fall over the centuries until God's final kingdom appears. This is the section so dear to religious fanatics and which to this day nourishes their politically dangerous doomsday fantasies.

The Book of Daniel remains a book of tall tales that defy any foundation in history and perhaps, since it is so out of sync with reality, is meant to be nothing more than a collection of uplifting folktales. For instance, Daniel has King Nebuchadnezzar besieging Jerusalem in 606 B.C.E., but this event wasn't until 598. The book relates that this king was transformed into a beast for seven years. Not really. In one chapter, Daniel presents Belshazzar as the last king of Babylon – he was never king – and identified his successor as king, "Darius the Mede," but there is no such historical person. Think of the four great beasts in chapter 7. They are highly reflective of the old Canaanite myths with its battles between Ba'al and the Sea Monsters. Also appearing in Daniel are two figures, "the Ancient of Days" and another divine figure. They reflect El, a venerable figure with a white beard, and Ba'al, the "rider of the clouds." As to that "Son of Man" (7:13), the best interpretation is that he is Michael the Archangel. Finally it is unlikely that there ever was a Daniel to begin with. In short, there is no history here, just legends. Later additions to this book include the incident of Susanna and the lecherous elders and Bel and the Dragon (named after Dagon, the Philistine god).

What trips it up is that the Book of Daniel claims to have been written by someone named Daniel who lived in the 6th century B.C.E. As such, it uncannily foretold the rise and fall of the four kingdoms of Babylon, Persia, Greece and Rome. It was remarkably accurate and, in simpler days, everyone believed this book to be an example of divinely inspired prophecy. Except for the fact that it turns out that this is another case of predictions after the fact. Since scholars have determined that some anonymous writer in the 2nd century B.C.E. composed this material, it was easy to "predict" the future by reading the history books. What is interesting is that predictions after the 2nd century fall off the cliff. That is to say, the foretold events from that point on were after or contemporary with the anonymous author's time, and he made bad guesses. So, for example, he predicted that God's new kingdom would arrive "a time, times and a half time" after Antiochus came down hard on Jewish practices, but it never arrived. In other words, according to its internal calculations, the Book of Daniel predicted that God's kingdom would arrive during the Greek era, but it never did. The pseudonymous "Daniel" also predicted that the Temple would be re-consecrated some six and a half years after Antiochus violated it, but in fact it took only three years. He predicted that this same Antiochus would be killed in Israel. On the contrary, Antiochus died in Persia. Why people give literal credence to the Book of Daniel is its biggest mystery (except see footnote 1).

OLD SCENARIOS, NEW SOLUTIONS

As we mentioned above, in the terrible conflict between Antiochus and the Jews, the Book of Daniel's message is that the latter are to take heart, for the righteous among them will be lifted up to heaven. So don't fear persecution and death in the fight for right. Forget the simplistic Deuteronomic thesis that the good prosper and the wicked get punished. It obviously doesn't work out that way. No, the good will get their reward and the wicked their comeuppance. O.K., maybe not now, but justice will triumph in an age to come. (Think Jesus' parable of Divis and Lazarus.) Nobody sums up the new solution up better than Kugler and Hardlin:

> "Not everyone responded to the Deuteronomic explanation of the Exile favorably; not everyone was convinced that the Babylonian defeat of Judah was a just punishment for Israel's apostasy. This was surely so in part because not all who had suffered had been unfaithful. Among such devout believers surely the question arose: why should all suffer for the sins of the few? In the exilic work of Ezekiel we have seen a way around that problem in the notion of individual responsibility, but that too struggled to make a full and adequate response to the wider suffering of all Judah, indeed all Israel. In the Persian–era works of Ezra and Nehemiah we saw a response that simply assigned to those who suffered a lower status, an approach that clung fast, against any evidence to the contrary, to the Deuteronomic perspective. In Ecclesiastes from the Ptolemaic period we saw an author who simply saw no way around the problem, who asserted that there was no divine justice and one should not expect any either. So it is hardly

surprising that an author found himself finally compelled in the Seleucid period – in the face of the Antiochene persecution to deal with this challenge in a new way, in the ultimate way Daniel did: God's justice will be proven in a new age to come, when God establishes a time and a place – here on earth – that confirms his justice on all the cosmos and for all time."[2]

So, there you are: a new twist that prevails today. The Book of Daniel, with its message of a delayed reward for the righteous, along with Jesus and Paul (whom we shall note in the next chapter) and the author of the Book of Revelation, has had a profound influence on all of western civilization because of its predictions of the end of the world and a new Golden Age to come. The apocalyptic impulse had been let loose: a looking *beyond* this world for justice in this world. Yes, good rewarded and the evil punished, since it was not obviously happening presently and there were no signs of it happening in the future, were moved to another time beyond time. Yes, someday God would intervene and, furthermore, there were clear signs when that "someday" would be apparent – namely, when things looked so bad, when everything was unmistakably and unbelievably calamitous and clearly falling apart, these were the very signs that God would act, and act soon.

Of course, since every age fulfills that description one time or another and has its prototype horrors beyond all horrors, every age accordingly produces "exact" signs and predictions when Jesus will come again, and that list of such predictions is extraordinarily long, right down to today's Christian Zionists and other fundamentalists who pen best sellers. According to the *Millennial Prophecy Report*, there are some eleven hundred groups in the world today that believe the end is imminent because the world is in such a mess – a sure sign. Newsletters, albums, blogs, books – think of the 1970 best seller, Hal Lindsey's, *The Late Great Plant Earth* (forty years later and nothing he predicted has happened) and Edgar Whisentant's best seller, *88 Reasons Why The Rapture Will be in 1988* (a 1989 edition was published!) – are beyond counting. Magazines like *Midnight*

Call, advertises itself as "America's only international prophecy-orientated publication" and further boasts that since "God's Word explicitly foretells the future" people ought to subscribe and learn what that future is. The editors will reveal it accurately because, after all, their track record is impeccable. They boast, "So how did we know about the fall of Soviet Communism? Because the Bible says, '...all that dwell upon earth shall worship him' (Revelation 13:8). That means a system void of religious freedom had no future, which is why we were able to confidently write that headline." To the editors the logic is unassailable. To everyone else the logic is twisted.

In my lifetime (so far), according to radio preacher Harold Camping, the world was supposed to end on October 21, 2011. With that inevitably failing to materialize, the date was transferred to December 21, 2012. The Y2K and millennium end-of-the world warnings were rampant. The lunar eclipse and its "Blood Moon" in 2014 was clearly the start of something big and billboards by televangelist John Hagee, author of "Four Blood Moons: Something Is About to Change", proclaimed, "The heavens are God's billboard." Doomsday episodes continue to be a staple on television and in the movies. The Mayan-calendar-end-of-the-world crisis was popular, and the election of the new pope in 2013, Pope Francis, was significant because he, according to the prediction made by 12th century St. Malachy, was going to be the last one before the end of the world.

THE NEED

There is something in the human psyche that needs these never-ending predictions. As Diarmaid MacCulloch writes:

> "It is not surprising that so may have sought the Last Days. The writing and telling of history is bedeviled by two human neuroses: Horror at the desperate helplessness and seeming lack of pattern in events, and regret for a lost golden age, a moment of happiness when all was well. Put these together

and you have an urge to create elaborate patterns to make sense of things and to create a situation where the golden age is just around the corner."[3]

It would seem that the appeal of end time predictions is that studying and decoding gives people the illusion of being in control, that having secret knowledge, they can duck the catastrophe. The Book of Daniel, along with the eccentric Christian Book of Revelation (a poorly written, vehemently anti-Roman, feverish work by a second generation Christian Jew, a John of Patmos – not the apostle John – who likely witnessed the horrific destruction of Jerusalem, knew of the devastating eruption of Mt. Vesuvius and felt the long delayed end of the world was near), becomes a blueprint. It provides enough terrifying dreams, exotic figures, special effects and timetables to keep the genre going forever, even though within the Book of Daniel itself, we see backtracking. In one place it's 1,290 days left to the end, in another it's 1,335 days and in another 1,150 days – evidence that as the shorter numbers came and went, new calculations were made. In our time, the phenomenal popularity of the *Left Behind* books and similar publications continue the tradition with about as much factual credibility as Daniel.

In summary: towards the end of the Second Temple period, for many the only hope left was the end of the world, producing an outpouring of eschatological and apocalyptic literature. Attention was diverted from the horrible past to a future time, perhaps not too distant. The consistent theme was that YHWH would send a rescuer, a Messiah, to inaugurate an idyllic new era. The End of Days would be one of terrible warfare, swift punishment for the wicked (the Sons of Darkness), and eventual vindication and salvation for God's faithful ones (the Sons of Light). Such faithful ones who will be saved have been chosen from the beginning. They are the predestined. They are the Elect, a concept easily segued from the traditions of being a Chosen People. In short, during the period of the Second Temple, there was an ever-intensifying interest in eschatological and apocalyptic writings, culminating in full-blown Messianic theories. These books were very much in place when Jesus came, and his interpreters made use of them by having Jesus warn in his "Little Apocalypse":

> "Beware no one leads you astray...you will hear of war and rumors of wars...nation will rise against nation... there will be famines, earthquakes...the love of many will grow cold but the one who endures to the end will be saved. And this good news will be proclaimed throughout the world as a testimony to all the nations; and then the end will come...the sun will be darkened and the moon will not give its light; the stars will fall from heaven...then the sign of the Son of Man will appear in the heavens...keep awake therefore for you do not know on what day the Lord is coming." (Matt. 24)

It is germane here to add that St. Paul was a fervent believer in the end time. In 1 Thessalonians he was full of eager anticipation for what he firmly thought would be the end of the world and the imminent appearance of Jesus, even in his lifetime. It didn't happen. It was the anonymous author of 2 Peter, the last written New Testament writing, embarrassingly faced with what is called "delayed eschatology" – people were getting tired (and skeptical) of awaiting the Second Coming – who backtracked by saying that, after all, God has his own timetable. To God, a thousand years is like a day. What is notable about 2 Peter, however, is that although there were numerous standard descriptions of what those terrible end time days might look like –clouds, trumpet sounds, lightning, blast, earthquake – it alone in Christian canonical writing describes the end as a great conflagration; that is, the world will end by fire. In this the author tapped into an old Persian tradition that found its way into Greek, Roman and Jewish apocalyptic literature.

FINAL WORD

It is easy to sympathize with the psychology of searching for a positive answer when your beliefs consistently don't come true. Either you finally let go of your beliefs in the light of all contrary evidence or you reinterpret them. That's what happened to the Jews. A defunct dynasty got transformed into a mystical dynasty. Justice was transferred to another day. In other words, to the neutral observer, the natural human reaction to the cognitive dissonances of the simplicities of the Deuteronomistic theology – that obedient Israelites garner YHWH's blessing and unfaithful Israelites provoke punishment and exile – was to remove the problem to another time and another space. That was really the only alternative. That is, if they wanted to continue to believe in YHWH. That other time and space was an unspecified moment, heralded by specific cosmic signs, a moment that eventually extended beyond the world to a new and reformed here and now. In other words, YHWH had to triumph and keep his promises – if not, as thought and taught in prophetic books, in the here and now, at least in the there and later. There's a perceptible evolution here in making scripture work even if it takes some creative and corrective interpretation. We still operate on this unconscious understanding: there is so much injustice in this world of ours – this post-Jesus and his kingdom world – that we automatically reference a future world to solve all of life's unfairness (Why did my child die? Why did I lose my job? Why me?). We hope it will all be straightened out there.

One downside of this basically apocalyptic worldview where nothing can be done here and Jesus will have to come and save us is to settle for inaction and just let the wicked world putz along. After all, everything is in God's hands, and the rapture will deal with the wicked and reward the good, why bother to make the world a better place? The upside is that the apocalypse genre should not be entirely dismissed. We live with the fantasy of a normality that is only occasionally interrupted by our daily horrors and social injustices. Apocalyptic writings jolt us out of our delusions and slumber and force us to see the idolatries and injustices that pervade our lives.

Chapter 12.

THE LATE WRITINGS

To give a flavor of what was happening during the Persian Period, roughly from the 6th century B.C.E. to the time the Greeks took over in the 3rd century, we give a passing nod to its considerable gathering of Israel's literary tradition and the considerable amount of updating, revising and editing that occurred. It is during this time, as we noted in the last chapter, that eventually such collecting and editing (and revising) would culminate into the collection we call the Bible. It is also the time of the writing of the loosely called Wisdom books, books that deal with human instruction and insight, morals and manners. I simply highlight points of interest to our concerns.

Wisdom literature, for centuries a common staple in the Near East, found its way into Israel's corpus. Wisdom literature dealt with the everydayness of life. The larger political environment was blithely ignored. Even their own ancient history, the Exodus, Sinai, the Covenant, and so on, was of no interest to the writers of these books. The writings, instead, loved proverbs and poems and collections of them were common. Israel had its books of proverbs and sayings (The Book of Proverbs, The Wisdom of Solomon, The Song of Songs, and Ecclesiastes). Books like that of Proverbs were more like advice from Miss Manners, teaching one how to get along, which fork to use, how not to be a jerk. ("Whoever blesses his neighbor with a loud voice, rising early in the morning, will be counted as cursing", 27:14; that is, wait till the guy has showered and had his coffee before you shout blessings.) Hardly, one would think, the stuff of what would fall under inspired and sacred literature. Women, as usual, get the short stick: they are temptresses. Strange women should be avoided. Marry your own kind. The best kind of woman is the one who serves her husband. It is amusing how often "The Valiant Woman" excerpt is used at the funerals of strong women. Meant to be taken as praise for her leadership and talents, the words, quite to the contrary, praise her precisely for her subservience to her husband and her domestic savvy while her husband sits idly at the gate. The same misapplication befalls the passage from the Book of Ruth, where the well-known phrase, "Wherever you go, I will go" is spoken to the bride or groom, not, as it was originally, to a mother-in-law!

THE PSALMS

In his career, David not only took on the role of priest, led religious rituals, and controlled Israel's priesthood, but he was also a musician so notable that his reputation as a psalmist, author of the 150 Psalms, was launched. That reputation may have arisen from the episode where David is called in to soothe troubled King Saul by strumming his harp. David as harpist may have inspired David as musician; that, in turn, inspired David as the composer of the Psalms. However we know now that he did not write the Psalms or at least most of them. Today, for internal reasons, most scholars have ruled him out as their author. As an example, Psalm 137 speaks those famous words, "By the rivers of Babylon there we sat down and wept as we remembered Zion...there our captors demanded we sing songs [of Zion]... How could we sing a song of the Lord's in a foreign land?" The Psalm is from the Exile, four hundred years after David.

Moreover, like Solomon's Temple, the Psalms turn to be not much different from the contemporary hymns and songs of other nations. The discovery of the pre-Mosaic Canaanite library at Ugarit, it turns out, contains a great deal of material quite consistent with the Psalms. The characteristics describing their gods here are strikingly similar to those describing YHWH. Even that gracious quality of mercy, so extolled as YHWH's special prerogative, turns out to be a standard characteristic of El, the Canaanite god. The very same sacrifices and temples cited in the Psalms can be found in the Ugarit tablets. Even the Canaanite and Hebrew literary styles, their parallelisms, are very close. If one didn't know better, it's sometimes hard to tell the Ugaritic Psalms from the Hebrew Psalms, and some of the later Hebrew Psalms simply borrow whole cloth from the Ugaritic. Indeed, reading the Ugarit text provided corrections for the long held misinterpretations of some words in the Hebrew Psalms. James Kugel in his book, *How to Read the Bible*, gives us an example:

> "Some of the things people have always believed about words in the Bible – including prominently, verses in the Psalms turned out to be wrong. For example, the most common Hebrew word for soul, *nefesh*, means something a little less spiritual elsewhere in the Semitic world: throat or neck... Thus when the psalmist cries out (to quote the old King James translation), 'Save me, O God; for the waters are come into my soul' (Ps 69:2), it turns out what he really meant was: the water is up to my neck!"[1]

The Psalms, as we know them have an interesting history, and are only one collection among several that Israel had. They can be categorized into several genres such as Psalms of thanksgiving or lament, or royal Psalms (the David-Zion theology is particularly well represented in the Psalms). Psalms played a part in Temple worship, but for a long time not exclusively or officially. They were used widely elsewhere before they became canonically associated with the first or second Temples. People began to use them in private settings and, of course, when the Temple was destroyed for the first time and the people sent into exile, the Psalms became the accepted mode of private and communal worship in Babylon; and later, when the Temple was destroyed the second time, the Psalms became synagogue standard fare. So it happened that the Psalms, so intimately connected within the context of the Temple cultic worship, drawing their meaning from it, lost their original home and their meanings along with it, to conform to something new. That is to say, the original meanings of the Psalms transmuted into entirely new meanings not envisioned by their original authors. (Once more, those Psalms that mention the Temple can hardly be David's, since he lived before the Temple was constructed.)

For example, in the all-time favorite, Psalm 23, "The Lord is My Shepherd," which contains the phrase "Surely goodness and mercy shall follow me all the days of my life and I will dwell in the house of the Lord forever," the "house" originally meant the Temple. Now, with no Temple and no Temple context, this line came to be interpreted as referring to life after death: "I will dwell in the house [Temple] of the Lord" that is, in God's abode, heaven, forever." So this Psalm, once referring to the Temple, wrenched out of its original setting, came to be recited at Christian funeral services as a scriptural revelation of life after death. Psalm 23 originally did not mean that. Its phrases "valley of the shadow of death" really means in the original Hebrew," "a very dark valley" and "forever" means simply "for length of days" and "the house of the Lord" in Hebrew always refers to the Temple. In short, what some of the Psalms originally meant and what they came to mean are frequently two different things (thus confirming again and again that the Bible is a collection of interpretations of interpretations).

RESURRECTION?

Kugel points out the same misunderstanding in the prophet Ezekiel. Unlike the Egyptians, the Hebrews had a very foggy notion of what happens after death. People, they surmised, went down to "Sheol," whatever that was. It appears to be shadowy existence where nothing much happened. That's why Psalm 115 reminds us that "The dead do not praise the Lord." Nevertheless, the Hebrews practiced some vague kind of cult for dead people – remember, Saul had Samuel called back from Sheol – and sacrifices to the dead seem to be unofficially practiced. The after death existence was a non-issue. There was no tradition of the Resurrection of the dead in Israel (although the Zoroastrians held this belief). It is interesting, by the way, to learn that the Egyptians, long before the Old Testament, had a much richer and fuller notion of the afterlife than the Hebrews. Their Book of the Dead amply testifies to this. Moreover, they anticipated Christian theology in that for them, there is not only life after death, but there is judgment after death when the human heart is weighed for its good or evil deeds and sentenced accordingly – very much like Matthew 25, where Jesus clearly calls for distributive justice; that is, whether you did the Corporal Works of Mercy or not determines the fate of the kingdom or the fire. (Let his successors argue about grace versus works.) It is interesting to speculate here why, there being such a close parallel between ancient Egypt and the Gospel on the subject of the afterlife, the Old Testament with its distinctly minimalist view of the afterlife is considered inspired, while the much older Egyptian view is not.

It was only much later, in post biblical times, that interest in the afterlife peaked and the Jews began to search the Bible for clues. There were none – except there is that famous passage in Ezekiel about the dry bones, but it was a metaphor about the return of the Northern Kingdom and its eventual reunion with the Southern Kingdom. The Jews in much later times, however, seized on the Ezekiel vision to point to the Resurrection of the dead, and we find such a reference in the non-canonical book of 4 Maccabees, where the mother of the seven sons about to be martyred tells them to remember the words of their father, who spoke of Ezekiel's great question, "Shall these bones live?" Soon Ezekiel's original words about the return of the Northern Kingdom evolved into the biblical "proof" of the Resurrection – another example of how literal texts change their meaning over time and another instance of how we read the Bible not for what it says, but for what it has come to mean via canonized interpretations.

We have the same thing in Hosea (6:2), where the prophet writes:

> Come, let us return to the LORD and he will heal us.
> He has struck down and he will bind us up.

After two days he will revive us; on the third day
He will raise us up and we will live before him.

A typical standard pronouncement of a call to repentance and words of encouragement, this saying was too good to let go by and, again, in post biblical times, the rabbis found hints in it of the Resurrection. The Christians, of course, could not let this slip by either, especially that third day reference. So St. Paul: " For I handed onto you... what I in turn received: that Christ died for our sins in accordance with the scriptures, and that he was buried and that he was raised on the third *day in accordance with the scriptures...* (1 Cor.15: 3-4). (What scriptures?) And Luke has Jesus say, "Thus it is written, that the Messiah is to suffer and to rise from the dead on the third day." (24: 44-46). (We'll come back to that "third day" motif later in our New Testament commentary.) And even though the plural "us" was used – "healing us... binding us up... reviving us ... raising us up" – the Christians simply took the language as meaning the singular "him," saying that they considered those plurals as simply forms of the inflated royal "we," as when Queen Victoria said, "We are not amused." Yet the text really does not talk about an individual. The Hebrew text uses the plural and means the people of Israel who are invited to repentance and its consequent renewal. God will raise them up from their moral sickness. Again, a text is interpreted to mean something different from what is says. Later on, the folkloric story of Jonah was also pressed into prophecy by typologically equating the three days in the fish's belly as the three days of Christ's Crucifixion, descent into hell, and the Resurrection.

It is to be quickly noted that Jesus himself lived in a Psalmatic background. He quotes them – at least according to Luke's revisionist account of Mark – even as he died on the cross. The evangelists put many Psalms on the lips of Jesus, thus causing St. Augustine to comment that Christ indeed stands at the center of the Book of Psalms. Like so many others, Augustine read the Psalms as prophecies about Jesus, even if to modern ears (and modern scholars) the applications sounded forced, as indeed they do in the Gospels themselves. For instance, when Jesus entered Jerusalem to the cries of "Hosanna!", much to the dismay of the chief priests and scribes, (Matt 21:15-16) he countered by quoting Psalm 8:3 as a kind of prophetic fulfillment about himself. "From the mouths of children and of babes you fashioned praise." In short, as one modern commentator says, "The fulfillment of Scripture authenticates the accolades of these children." Anyway, the apostles quoted the Psalms, and singing them was quickly incorporated into the Christian liturgical services, and to this day the clergy and monastic communities recite or sing the entire Psalter.

THE SONG OF SONGS

As we know, wisdom became attached to Solomon's persona. The Book of Ecclesiastes, the Book of Proverbs, and the Song of Songs came to be attributed to him. Scholars are doubtful about that authorship. In Proverbs, for example, there are just too many different dialects seemingly from different eras, and it has a great similarity to the Egyptian text "The Wisdom of Amenemope," not to mention substantial differences in its Hebrew text and Greek translation and their additions. Further, the Book of Ecclesiastes, full of glaring contradictions and about-faces, contains words unmistakably Persian. Its language and style resemble the Mishnah (part of the Talmud), and was more likely written around 300 B.C.E. With its phrases like "vanity of vanities and all is vanity," and other negatives it is an enigmatic book. As for the exotic Song of Songs, it originally had nothing whatever to do with God (other than the Book of Esther, it's the only biblical book that never mentions the name of God) and it is no different from any other love lyrics found in ancient Egypt or the Near East – for example, the 11th century Persian love poem, the *Rubaiyat of Omar Khayyam*. It's simply a part of Near Eastern love poetry and, after some doubt as to whether it belonged, it seems to have slipped into the biblical collection as an allegory of the love between YHWH and his people. The rabbis could not handle the overt sexuality of the piece. In any case, translations of this poem vary, and scholars struggle to interpret the several variations of the Hebrew text in the light of the Septuagint, Vulgate and Aramaic versions. Some of the terms used in this poem are extremely rare and are not found in other Old Testament books. Again, this raises the question of how all this can be the revelation of God when we have an unclear text. In due time the *Song of Songs* was elegantly expanded by Christian writers who ferreted out all kinds of hidden meanings that became part of our tradition. St. Bernard of Clairvaux, for example, turns it into a sensuous valentine between God and man. He's way off base from the original meaning, but it is the meaning we want and the meaning we have adopted and enshrined in our exegesis and our liturgy. It has a life of its own.

Solomon is also reputed to be the author of the Wisdom of Solomon, or just plain Wisdom. Showing its cultural context, it draws heavily on Greek philosophy. It was likely composed in Alexandria in Egypt for the Greek speaking Jews, about a century before Christ. It reflects the Platonic body-spirit dualism, with the body dragging down the soul, and its philosophy was to greatly influence the Church in its first three centuries. The book was meant to encourage Jewish readers, unlike their skeptical Greek neighbors, to see God's stamp on all of creation. The Book of Sirach, much like Proverbs (which it often repeats or modifies), covers the usual practical matters – parents, friendship, children and so on – but is notable for its strident (and misogynistic) reflection of the common Near East attitudes on women. Some samples:

> Any iniquity is small compared to a woman's iniquity (25:19)

> Better is the wickedness of a man than a woman who does good; it is woman who brings shame and disgrace. (42:14)

> I'd rather live with a lion and a dragon than live with an evil woman (25:16)

The birth of a daughter is a loss (22:3)

Then there is this one: From a woman sin had its beginning, and because of her we all die (25:24).

This, of course, refers to Eve, and was written before the Christian era, but Christians picked it up and the sentiment found its way into the epistle to Timothy: "Adam was not deceived, but the woman was deceived and became a transgressor" (1 Tim 2:4), and the whole attitude found its way into dogmatic Christianity for the next two millennia.

REBELLION AND ROMANCES

There were voices, now and then, that challenged the simplistic conventional Deuteronomistic wisdom that held that the obedient will prosper while the wicked will fail. One just had to look around in real life to know that that just wasn't true. The age-old question persists: how can a good and powerful God permit so much evil? Why do the good suffer and the wicked prosper? All ancient Near East literature dealt with the issue. Scholars have found powerful Sumerian, Egyptian, and Babylonian texts that take on the theodicy question. The Book of Job, a bit of folklore frequently edited and revised and probably written in the Persian era, is Israel's contribution. It draws on other cultures, especially works from Mesopotamia. There is, for example, a Sumerian work dating some thousand years before Job called "A Man and His God" that covers the same ground. There are also parallels with several Egyptian texts as well. Wresting with God and the unfairness of life is an old theme.

The Book of Job opens up with Satan – a name whose linguistic roots are "to accuse" and the related "opponent" – appearing in the introduction. He is there as a certified court angel of the Lord, a legitimate member of the heavenly council, where he functions as an edgy troubleshooter, a prosecutor. We see this role, for example, in the Book of

Zachariah where Satan brings a case against the high priest, and in 1 Chronicles where he incites David to conduct a census. He appears similarly here in this Book of Job in his role as advocate testing, in a way both God and Job. It's not hard to see how this "opponent" could come to play the role of a full-fledged opponent to God. As we have already seen, he evolves into the Satan of mythology very late, around the 2nd century B.C.E. appearing (no surprise) in apocalyptic literature under various names. Gradually, Satan becomes the negative counterpart of goodness and light. In short, in a concept borrowed from Persian dualism – a dualism totally alien to Judaism – Satan becomes the dark reflection of the light. He is Prince of Darkness wreaking havoc. There are now two principles of good and evil. We get the first mention of this newly fashioned "devil" in the Wisdom of Solomon, 2:24. From then on, he becomes a conglomerate of all the evil names. So we read in the Christian Book of Revelations, "The great dragon was thrown down, that ancient serpent [resonances of the ancient Sea Monsters in Canaanite lore], who is called the Devil and Satan, the deceiver of the whole world." (12:9) In short, Satan is new on the biblical scene and did not make his debut in Genesis.

A passage from the Book of Job has found its way into the Christian funeral liturgy where are quoted the words:

> But as for me, I know that my Vindicator lives,
> And that he will at last stand forth upon the dust;
> whom I myself shall see:
> My own eyes, not another's, shall behold him,
> and from my flesh I shall see God.

In Hebrew, these verses are extremely difficult to translate, and they do not necessarily refer to a Resurrection of the body, and nowhere else in the Book of Job is this concept expressed. Bodily resurrection does not, in fact, occur until very late in the biblical era. Very near the time of Jesus the Pharisees held it but life after death was not universally held.

PARTING SHOTS

As for that Book of Proverbs again, or as its subtitle puts it, "Sayings of the Wise," a passing remark: the book is, for much of its pages (its "thirty sayings" portion) an out-and-out plagiarism of the Egyptian work, the "Instruction of Amenemope". The author, or one of its editors, simply lifted the Egyptian sayings and transferred them to the Book of Proverbs, much the same way that the authors of the Psalms lifted some Psalms from the Canaanites.

As for Exile literature in general: finding themselves under foreign rule once more, the Jews turned to romance literature; that is, novels with twisty endings, stories of resistance and bravery and exotic predictions of a better future (the realm of apocalyptic writing.) The fictional Book of Jonah gives us a comic plot of a runaway prophet, a large fish and, of all things, an enemy pagan king of Assyria actually listening to the prophet and repenting! The Book of Esther, filled with a few egregious chronological mistakes, and never once mentioning God (an expanded later addition tried to add a religious dimension by adding references to God and prayers), is an exotic tale of a beautiful queen who overcomes a wicked adversary. The Book of Judith, likewise manifesting its share of historical errors, also shows a woman using her feminine charms to lure the enemy into her tent and then beheads him. The Book of Tobit, mimicking the plot of other Near East tales, adds its spin on how to live faithfully in a foreign land. Noticeable here are angels and demons in the cast of characters, reflecting the dualism of the Persians. We have already noted the putative 6th century (actual 2nd century) Book of Daniel. The attractive Book of Ruth, to which we alluded earlier, is set in the time of the Judges (1200-1000 B.C.E.), but its cultural context suggests the Persian period (538-333 B.C.E.). Finally, there is the Book of Lamentations bewailing Israel's sufferings under the heel of the Babylonian exile and the destruction of Jerusalem. What is noteworthy is God's silence. Interpreters come to the rescue by suggesting (1) this shows YHWH is a good listener, (2) he's showing silent awe at the terribleness of it all: it is just too much for words, (3) his silence is a sign that he's not going to rescue Israel anytime soon and Israel will just have to learn to tough it out. In short, Lamentations signals that Israel just needs to get its grief out of its system. It doesn't need answers. This interpretation is one more example of how believers respond to questions unbelievers raise.

Again, this fast-forward glance at these late writings is designed to help us note difficult, opaque texts, constant revisionisms, misunderstood interpretations, assimilated borrowings, and dubious teachings that, along with beautiful poetry, elegant words, powerful, splendid images and provocative thoughts make them inspiring, but not necessarily divinely inspired.

PART II

THE CHRISTIAN SAGAS

Chapter 13.

THE MESSIAH NARRATIVES

Although contemporary references to Jesus are extremely rare, from the beginning there were many interpretations of him. Not all interpretations agreed, and quite soon the multitude of details, inconsistencies and contradictions would spawn a trajectory that lasts to this day, a trajectory that would result in more books (at least in the western world) about Jesus than any other topic. Initially, his own relatives thought he was crazy (Mark 3:21) and wanted to put him under house arrest. Herod saw him as a usurper, the Pharisees a heretic, the politicians a rebel and traitor, many of his fellow Jews thought him as too much and no longer walked with him, and some saw him as the Baptizer Returned. Others proclaimed him as "the Messiah, the Son of the living God" (Matthew 16:16) Moderns see a Personal Savior, Hellenistic Hero, Revolutionary, Wisdom Sage, Apocalyptic Prophet, Philosopher, Buddy, Superstar, Aquarian, the "soft, curled and hermaphroditic" (Melville), or the Aryan Jesus the Nazis concocted. Every age, it seems, projects itself into Jesus' identity – including our own which thrives on what George Carlin dubs, "Jesus Lite," a heck of a nice guy who judges no one and forgives everyone. The Gospel writers, on the other hand, saw him as the Messiah, and the Gospels they wrote are fundamentally highly edited and stylized interpretations of that particular belief.

I say stylized interpretations because right off we have to say that the Gospels, like the Old Testament books, are not history or biographies. Nor are they neutral, as John makes clear: "these things are written that you may believe" (20:31). They are what I call parabolic interpretations, drawing heavily on the already countless interpretations of the Old Testament. In other words, the Gospels not only tell the parables *of* Jesus, but are parables *about* Jesus. They are creative constructions that say, "This is how our community sees Jesus, describes Jesus. This or that incident or story – sometimes imaginatively created – tells what he is all about." As one writer puts it:

> "...the Gospels must not be regarded as mere collections of 'facts' about Jesus. They are not an assemblage of documents from a Jesus archive in the early Jerusalem community. Obviously, the authors of the Gospels had a multitude of traditions about Jesus at their disposal, but they used these traditions to *interpret* Jesus. They interpret his words, they interpret his deeds, they interpret his whole life. They interpret Jesus in every line, in every sentence."[1]

So what the evangelists wrote need not be objectively factual, although there are some factual traditions to draw upon, but biblical metaphors, fictional stories and contemporary symbols that explain Jesus. The evangelists sometimes invented stories and scenes, and they put words into Jesus' mouth as Jesus was "updated" to fit their times and their theologies. In short, we have parabolic interpretations of Jesus. Historian John C. Dwyer spells out the context:

> "The Gospels are not 'lives of Jesus.' Rather, they are records of early Christian preaching, beginning about a generation after Jesus' death; as such they are expressions of faith in Jesus, as this faith was experienced in a number of early communities. What the Gospels tell us, immediately and directly, is how these communities experienced Jesus from three to six decades after his death. The Gospel writers and those for whom they wrote were trying to live as Christians and to share their faith with others. They wrote Gospels to solve problems of *their* day and *their* time, and they tried to achieve this goal by telling stories of what Jesus *had done*, of what people *thought he had done*, of what he *might have done*, or perhaps

would have done, if he had had to confront the same problems they were facing in the years after his death. The Gospels, in other words, are not historical documents, at least as we understand this phrase today, and they are not biographies of Jesus. This does not mean that the Gospels are without value and it does not mean that they are not true, but it does mean that the question of the value and truth of the Gospels is not one that can be dealt with in a naive or simplistic way.... many of the Gospel narratives do not recount objective events; rather, they are stories, created by people whose imaginations and thought processes differed radically from our own. They intended, in writing these stories, to express their faith in a Jesus who really lived, and whose continued existence was vitally important to them at the time in which they lived...."

"Further, the fact that the Gospels are not historical docu-ments in the modern sense of the word means that much of the miracle tradition cannot be taken literally, but is a way of speaking about Jesus and about the fact that, in him, God entered into the brokenness of the human condition, and conquered that brokenness radically and in principle. Similarly, many of the words and sayings of Jesus in the Gospels are not a word for word record of his actual remarks, but probably found their way into the Gospel texts as a result of attempts of communities of later times to apply their faith in Jesus to problems of their own day."

"What all of this means is that the Gospels are excellent historical sources, not directly and immediately for the events of Jesus' life, but rather for events in the life of the church during the last four decades of the first century...."[2]

EXAMPLES

A case in point: In Matthew 10 Jesus appointed 72 disciples and sent them on a mission (another Jesus = the new Moses theme, cf. Num. 11:16). It's a truly momentous event. These 72 now clearly outnumber the Twelve Apostles – we might say today that these non-clerical, empowered people outnumbers the clerics – and, empowered they are. If Matthew shows us that Jesus gave extraordinary powers to the Twelve – heal the sick, raise the dead, cleanse the lepers, cast out demons – Luke (10:9) has Jesus give pretty much the same gifts to these 72.

If this is so, what is very strange is that, as foundational, significant, and dramatic as this appointment and these empowerments are, the 72 promptly disappear! How could this be? They are puzzlingly never mentioned again, causing scholars to suspect that the whole story, like so many in the Gospels, can't be taken literally. It is a Lucan invention, a parabolic narrative, a metaphor saying that evangelization is not limited to a few, much the same way as Matthew invented Magi, it shows that Jesus' message extends to all — Jew and Gentile, the ignorant and the learned.

Or, there is the Gospel passage in Mark (2:23-28) about the incident of Jesus and his disciples eating grain on the Sabbath. The Pharisees take issue with him, saying he is violating that sacred day. Jesus replies to them, "Have you never read the story of David and how, in the days of Abiathar the high priest, when he and his men were hungry and in need, David entered the House of God and ate some of the consecrated bread, which only the priests could lawfully do; and furthermore, he gave some to his companions? So, take note: the Sabbath was made for man, not man of Sabbath. The Son of Man is Lord, even of the Sabbath."

First of all, it was Abimelech who was high priest, not Abiather. Mark or Jesus got that wrong. Secondly, as given, Jesus' argument is specious and one can imagine a smart Pharisee retorting, "Hold it, Jesus! We're talking apples and oranges here! In the King David story he and his men are desperate and starving and in great need, and besides, the high priest gave them the bread. The Law allows for that. On the other hand, you and your friends are in no such emergency. You're just casually crossing a field and popping grain into your mouths which, as you know, is all right on any other day, but not on the Sabbath. The two incidents are in no way comparable, and you know it!"

So Jesus (Mark?) gets the high priest's name wrong and Jesus comes up with a weak non-sequitur argument. The scholars, of course, again sense that the whole incident is made up (that parabolic device again) and that the real point is, according to commentators, that decades after Jesus, by Mark's time, the followers of Jesus were drifting away from Sabbath worship and meeting on Sunday and they needed a justification for it, and Jesus declaring himself Lord, "even of the Sabbath," would provide it. The moral is that the biblical writer's agendas to justify current beliefs and practices must always be taken into account.

All this word play is not novel. In ancient times, and even today writers run the literary gamut using fictional characters in fictional stories (for example, C. S. Lewis' *The Chronicles of Narnia*) or factual characters in fictional settings (Evelyn Waugh's *Helena* or Arthur Koestler's *Darkness at Noon*), or fictional characters in factual settings (Jane Austen's *Pride and Prejudice,* or Margaret Mitchell's *Gone With the Wind*). In the Gospels themselves, we have Jesus using fictional characters in a factual setting in the story of the Good Samaritan (there is a Jericho and there is a road to it, but the characters are invented), and fictional characters in a fictional setting (The Prodigal Son), and a factual person (Jesus) in a fictional setting (the wedding feast at Cana). So, too, the Gospels, while they do convey what we call history, they also contain parabolic fiction about Jesus that is not historical but metaphorical. In short, written by people not present at the time or place of Jesus, the Gospels are handing down the expressive oral traditions of their outside-of-Palestine communities.

MORE EXAMPLES

From the beginning, for his Jewish audience Matthew presents Jesus as the new Moses, quickly sounding Mosaic themes in his infancy narrative: an endangered baby, a wicked king out to kill newborns, a flight to and from Egypt – just like the Moses saga. Jesus also delivers his 'Sermon on the Mount' just as Moses did his sermon on the mountain. The fact is, the historical Jesus did not have that harrowing beginning. He did not sit down Moses-like on a mountain (Luke has the sermon given in a valley) and deliver his chapters 5 to 7 on moral theology. Rather Matthew, borrowing from the genre of Hebrew wisdom literature, had simply collected the various sayings and teachings of Jesus, the wise sage, from his Greek sources and constructed a "Moses" scene to make his point. These are parabolic fictions to convey a great truth about who Jesus is and the truth of what he taught.

Other examples would be the story of the road to Emmaus, where the dispirited disciples do not recognize the Risen Jesus in the encounter or in the scripture he unfolded, but only in the breaking of the bread that Jesus took, broke and handed to them – just as at the Last Supper. The Road to Emmaus is not an actual historical account, but rather an extended Lucan parabolic interpretation saying that the Risen Jesus is to be found whenever true disciples gather to share bread, to care for one another. The Ascension does not mean that Jesus physically went up into the air, only that he returned to the Father. At Pentecost, those tongues of fire are meant to recall the burning bush of Sinai as well as the burning coal that touched Isaiah's lips. The gift of speaking in various languages means the commission to preach to all peoples. Then you have the birth narratives that are symbolic overtures to the presentation of a Great One. The temptations in the desert are hardly a factual account, where Satan hoists Jesus to the Temple parapet and they trade scripture verses. The episode is a creative story of the confrontation between good and evil, or how Jesus reverses the threefold failure of the Israelites in the desert. The Transfiguration on the mountain is a story fiction that portrays the slow revelation of who Jesus really was to the apostles. These are all symbolic stories about Jesus, not actual historical stories of Jesus, and they are true in their own way.

So at times the Gospels contain fictional parables about the historical person Jesus that are not always to be taken literally or historically. While there are the actual words and deeds of Jesus in the Gospels, some scholars say it's futile to try to extricate them from the narrators' creative stories. Yes, surely some of his words and deeds were saved in an oral society, where disciples assiduously preserved the sayings of a revered teacher and even wrote down some of his pithy sayings, but, as I said, it's hard to separate them from the total narrative. Besides, it really doesn't matter. We are to read the Gospels in the sense, not that Jesus always in each instance said this or did that, but rather in the sense that Jesus also did things *like* this and said things *like* that; or, were he here, this is how he might have acted or spoken.

THE HALF DOZEN ADMONITIONS

Here, then, are six things to keep in mind when we approach the New Testament. First, the New Testament we have today is several critical steps away from its original version. Jesus, after all, was a Jew in a Jewish milieu, heir to the (interpreted) writings we would call the Old Testament. He lived and died a Jew of Palestine. He came from Nazareth, a place so insignificant that it is never mentioned in the Old Testament. As we shall soon observe, no one called him simply "Jesus" but Yeshua bar-Joseph. He spoke and preached in Aramaic and possibly, as an artisan of some kind, likely knew some business Greek. None of what he said, except for a few occasional words in Mark's Gospel, survives in the original. He left no written record. Then, suddenly, his story and the comments on it are translated into Greek – not only into the Greek language but also into Greek thought categories. All but possibly one book (Second Peter) of the New Testament was written outside Palestine, and all translations, as the saying goes, betray to a certain extent. Further, none of the four evangelists themselves knew the historical Jesus and we have nothing written by anyone who accompanied Jesus on his journeys. Information was culled from whatever his earliest disciples preserved from him and later the writings of later Christians (like Paul) who did not know him personally. We have no idea if they misunderstood him or made factual errors, but the reality is our faith rests on their faith. In these accounts, Jesus becomes a Greco-Roman sage and savior. That Greek eventually gets translated into Latin and the world's other languages. Interpretations upon interpretations, some contradicting and competing with one another, are piled on, some winding up as strict orthodoxy with anathemas invoked on dissenters.

Second, as noted above, the Gospel texts were continually edited, redacted, added to, and corrected right up to their fixed canonical status in the 4th century C.E. All scholars, for example, admit that Mark's Gospel ended at chapter 16:8 and that the rest, from 16:9-20, cobbled from John 20 and Luke 24, was added later by another hand. In John's Gospel, some later editor added some 25 full verses to chapter 20, as is obvious from "the style that is not that of the evangelist" (Rudolf Schnackenburg). Among the four evangelists themselves there were varied viewpoints about Jesus and his work and mission, sometimes, as noted below, contradictory ones. Again, each evangelist had his own theological agenda. For example, the account of the multiplication of the loaves is the only miracle of Jesus recounted in all four, but John, with his different theology, adds all kinds of details peculiar to his understanding of Jesus (almost diametrically different from, say, that of Mark). He has Jesus go up on the mountain (the place of authority and revelation), not on the plain, and has the miracle occur close to the Passover. Only in John does Jesus take the initiative by testing Philip, thereby emphasizing his own knowledge of what to do. Like God of old, he will feed the people. Only in John is there the mention of barley loaves reminiscent of Elisha's miraculous feeding of a hundred people (2 Kings 4:42). Only in John does Jesus, always in charge, distribute the loaves himself, just as later he will have no Simon of Cyrene. He will carry the cross himself. Likewise, if St. Paul typically portrays God the Father as raising Jesus from the dead, John presents the Resurrection as the proof that Jesus himself has the power to lay down his life and take it up again (10:17).

Third, like the Old Testament, the New Testament definitely has its biases. Perhaps one of the most egregious is the de-Judahizing of Jesus. Jesus is, as Rabbi Shmuley Boteach remarks, one of the most famous Jews of all time, yet he's been stolen from the Jewish community, stripped of his Jewishness and made an enemy of his people.[3] The Gospels turn out to be a story of Jesus versus the Jews as if he were not one of them. In his Gospel we have John, for example, presenting Jesus like a gentile Greek Sage speaking to his fellow Jews about *"your* father Abraham (8:56) and "Is it not written in *your* law" (10:34) rather than *our* father Abraham or *our* law. In John, Jesus is a Roman-Greek Christian, not a Jewish rabbi. Reading the Gospels we have to ask, were the Pharisees really that bad? Were the Samaritans that good? Was Jesus a hypocrite? Were the Pharisee Jews the ones locked out of the king's supper? Were the Jewish purity laws that burdensome, Judaism misogynistic? Did Judaism really regard God as distant and Christians regard God as close, and was there really an antithesis between law and grace?[4] Even his parables, as we shall shortly see, are politicized by the evangelists into anti-Jewish sentiments. Sadly, it would be a short step into the Church's shameless anti-Semitism.

Fourth, there are contradictions. For example, Jesus is said to have baptized (John 3:22) and not baptized (John 4:2). Jesus said that David ate the consecrated bread in the time of the high priest Abitahar, while in fact Abimelech was high priest. Jesus carried the cross in one Gospel, and Simon of Cyrene did so in another. The Holy Spirit is given variously on Easter and Pentecost. In Matthew 5 (the Beatitudes chapter), among other things Jesus says, "But I say to you that if you are angry with a brother or sister, you will be liable to judgment and if you insult a brother or sister you will be liable to the hell of fire...You have heard it said, 'an eye for an eye and a tooth for at tooth.' But I say to you, 'Do not resist an evildoer...love your enemies.'" But in chapter 23, Matthew has Jesus spew the worst, most awful words at the Pharisees calling them hypocrites (about a half dozen times), blind guides, fools, snakes, a brood of vipers, and so on. Whatever happened to the anger and insult prohibition and the love of enemies of Matthew 3? More precisely, the Jew Matthew, pitting the Christian Jews against his opponents, the Pharisee Jews of his time, lets *his* mouth run off in the mouth of Jesus, heedless of the contradiction. In John 16:5, Jesus scolds the apostles saying, "But now I am going to him who sent me; yet none of you asks me, 'Where are you going?" But three chapters previously in John 13:36 we have this episode where someone *did* ask: Simon Peter said to him, "Lord, where are you going?" Jesus answers, "Where I am going, you cannot follow me now." No one has satisfactorily reconciled these contradictory texts. The best guess is that, true to what we have seen so far, they indicate the composite nature of John's Gospel. Then there's Mark's Jesus, who asserts that all foods are clean (7:19) abrogating thereby the Jewish dietary laws while Matthew's Jesus insists, "Do not think I have come to abolish the law and the prophets. I have come not to abolish but to fulfill" (5:17). The Jesus in Mark is markedly different from the Jesus in John. The birth stories in Matthew and Luke cannot be reconciled historically, but, like the Old Testament, it doesn't matter for the intent is faith, not history.

Fifth, it is obvious even on casual reading that the New Testament authors do not always agree with one another theologically. In other words, there are diverse and conflicting theologies in its pages, and we have to acknowledge that. Let's catalogue some of them. In Luke's Acts of the Apostles, he presents a highly idealized picture of the first Christian communities. He writes, for example, "They devoted themselves to the teaching of the apostles and the communal life, to the breaking of the bread and prayers...all who believed were together and had all things in common; they would sell their property and possessions and divide them among all according to each one's needs" (2:42-47). St. Paul, writing some 30-40 years earlier, gives a far different picture. In 1 Corinthians 11, he says he can't commend them. He criticizes their divisions and factions. He certainly makes no mention of anyone's dedication to the communal life. In fact he points out that there are some who are far from "dying to self" sufficiently to join the others in the breaking of the bread. In fact, Paul pointedly says that they are "eating the bread and drinking the cup of the Lord unworthily." He goes on: "for those who eat and drink without discerning the body eat and drink judgment on themselves." (A footnote, germane to the tenor of this book, from a scripture scholar: "It was only after I had been ordained for five or six years [with a licentiate in theology] did I discover in a doctoral course on 1 Corinthians that Paul wasn't speaking about discerning the Eucharistic bread as the Body of Christ; he was saying that the community was the Body of Christ.")[5]

Then there is the issue of the Holy Spirit. In his Acts of the Apostles, Luke presents a very careful, step-by-step trajectory, an unwavering path of the Holy Spirit moving the Church from a Jewish reform movement to one that combined both Jews and Gentiles into one Church whose non-Jewish members were not obliged to keep the Law of Moses. This completely contradicts the struggles, complexities, and conflicts Paul writes about in his letter to the Galatians. Luke further gives us a picture of the Holy Spirit operating only where there is communion, some connection, with the apostles. John's Gospel and epistles disagree. John has Jesus saying that anyone can receive the Holy Spirit. It blows where it will. Only love is required: "If you love me you will keep my commandments and I will ask the Father and he will give you another Advocate...the Spirit of truth..." There's no need for any in-between – any bureaucracy, as we would say. No need for apostles or the community. The Spirit was a free lancing agent. The love for God and neighbor is the only requirement. Certainly Luke, as well as Matthew and Mark, did not share this belief. Connection to the apostles was the standard. In other words, the Spirit operated within the organization. By the way, John's theory of a personal reception of the Holy Spirit didn't work out in practice and most scholars say that's why his community didn't last: too unstable, too idiosyncratic. In fact, John came around to that conclusion by correcting course. At the end of his Gospel, he rehabilitates Peter, the iconic leader of the community, by having charismatic John give way to Peter as the first to enter the empty tomb (20:4).

Mark's Jesus declares, "The one who believes and is baptized will be saved; but the one who does not believe will be condemned" (16:6).

And thus begins the conflict about whether others – billions as it turns out — can be saved. On the other hand, what about 1 Timothy 2:4 where Paul states that "God desires everyone to be saved and to come to the knowledge of the truth"? And what about John who declares that Jesus' sacrifice is for our sins, "and not ours only but also for the sins of the whole world" (1 John 2:2)? Then there's St. Paul's dismissal of the law of the Old Testament because it embodied the "letter" rather than the "spirit." He warns, "You who want to be justified by the law have cut yourselves off from Christ; you have fallen away from grace...the only thing that counts is faith working through love" (Galatians 5: 4-6). But Matthew's Jesus is quite clear: "Do not think I have come to abolish the Law and the Prophets; I have come not to abolish but to fulfill... so whoever annuls one of the least of these commandments and teaches people to do so will be called least in the kingdom of heaven..." (5:17-19). James also warns, "Whoever keeps the whole law but falls short in one detail has become guilty of breaking all of it" (8:10). Paul declares that if one believes in Jesus he will be saved and that faith in Jesus is the basis of salvation, not works (See Romans 4: 1-3,10-11). James counters that faith without works is dead: "You see that a man is justified by works and not by faith alone" (James 2: 20-24). The divinely inspired biblical authors had different and contradictory theologies.

Finally, the New Testament biases included the political realm. We must remember that the life of the Church in the last four decades of the 1st century involved not only seeking an internal identity but also externally coexisting with the Roman Empire. The Christians, therefore, were careful to distance themselves from any sign of resistance to the Romans such as the Jewish revolt of 66-70. Matthew, for example, creates the incident of Pilate's wife's dream declaring Jesus as innocent. He also, like Mark, famously makes sure that the Jews take the blame for Jesus' death. He was quick to quote Jesus as teaching the payment of taxes and even his phrase the "Kingdom of heaven" is meant to suggest an otherworldly kingdom, not a rival political one. This placating of the Romans is also strong in the Gospel of Luke. None of this equates to classic anti-Semitism as we know it, but we do get an unmistakable if unintentional inflation of the "exonerate the Romans, blame the Jews" motif. Here's a good a contemporary commentary as any. It's from a column by Karen Sue Smith:

> "At the Harvard Club recently I attended a lecture by Elaine Pagels, the well-known author of *The Gnostic Gospels* and winner of many prestigious awards including a MacArthur fellowship, a.k.a. 'the genius award'. Her presentation revolved around an important scriptural question: Why did the author of Mark's Gospel let the Romans off the hook so easily but come down so hard on the Jews as the people guilty of condemning Jesus to death? At the level of history Pontius Pilate appears to have been legally responsible for Jesus' death. Crucifixion was a punishment typically used by the Romans on political rebels and slaves. *It appears that Mark has deliberately exaggerated the power and responsibility of the Jewish leaders in Jerusalem and played down the legal responsibility of the Romans.* He presents Jesus as undergoing several 'trials' and as being condemned by Jewish leaders. Pilate seems reluctant to sentence Jesus at the hearing. When I asked Daniel Harrington S. J. about Mark he said that Pagels' view is plausible adding that '*Matthew and Luke go even further in exculpating the Romans and blaming the Jews for Jesus' death.*'"

> "Why? Pagels' answer, in a word, is that it was a matter of Christian survival. Jewish resistance to Rome boiled over into revolt in Israel (66-74 A.D.) about the time that Mark wrote his Gospel. 'In this context' Harrington says, 'it seemed to be in the best interests of early Christians to distance themselves from the Jewish leaders and their followers.' But what may be *understandable and even shrewd* in the first century can appear morally disappointing and even embarrassing in the twenty-first century."[6]

Admittedly, from a purely human point of view, the evangelists were absolutely right and politically savvy. They were trying to save their own necks. Who can blame them? Garry Wills, in his book on St. Paul, *What Paul Meant*, agrees with Krister Stendahl's argument that Luke, for example, omits material, misinterprets facts and rearranges the Pauline story for a purpose of his own, which was to cozy up to the Roman Empire. (This kind of revisionism recalls the Book of Chronicles reworking of the David story to further the author's agenda.) So Paul urges making peace with Rome: "Let every person be subject to the governing authorities; for there is no authority except from God, and the authorities that exist are appointed by God" (Romans 13:1).

EARTHLY JESUS, RISEN JESUS

We end this preamble with this provocative thought – that we have to take seriously the dramatic fact that, within two generations, Christianity dramatically shifted from being a Jewish to a Gentile Mission. The premier Catholic scripture scholar, Raymond Brown, contended that Jesus as a wandering preacher in Israel conceived of himself primarily as a reformer of Judaism. Again, Jesus was a Jew. His mother and relatives and all of his first followers were Jews, including the inner circle of Apostles. He was, as he said, sent only to the House of Israel, and it was assumed that only Jews would be interested in his prophetic message. As that reformer of Judaism, Jesus had, as many scholars believe, no intention whatsoever of founding a wider Church as we know it. His movement was 100% Jewish back in the 30s but, after his death, became almost 100% Gentile. Within a generation, non-Jews began to show an interest in what he said and taught, and that eventually forced the question as to whether these non-Jews, if they wanted to join the Jesus Movement, had to convert to Judaism before they could convert to Christianity. It would appear that initially the general feeling was that only Jews could be Jesus followers, and Gentiles had first to convert to Judaism, but radicals like Paul and his followers balked at that and began baptizing Gentiles. This reform movement within Judaism gradually, with much controversy, spun off to a separate religion.

By the end of the 1st century, the issue seems to be resolved so much so that, as we have noted, by the time of John's Gospel, Jesus appears almost as a Gentile with withering words for "you Jews." Brown notes this irony: instead of being just a reformer of Judaism, Jesus, the Jewish carpenter from Nazareth, is looked upon as the founder of Gentile Christianity. Quite a leap. Did he intend that? Did Jesus intend to found a worldwide Church? After all, Jesus protested that he was sent only to Jews, only to "the lost sheep of Israel," and he forbade his disciples from approaching gentiles or Samaritans (Matt 10:5, 15-24). Certainly at first, his immediate disciples continued as practicing Jews in their dietary behavior, Torah observation, and daily Temple attendance. It does seem clear, then, that Jesus did not intend to establish a new religion but to purify the one he knew and loved. Only later did the first outsiders appear to spark the eventual morphing of Judaism into a Gentile church ultimately opposed to the Jewish faith. The "Great Commission" found in Matthew (28:19) was added by later post-Resurrection hands.

The dividing line seems to be that Paul and the evangelists and those who thought like them basically made a distinction between the earthly Jesus and the Risen Jesus, the latter being a "new creation" who left behind the old restrictions. In effect, Paul taught, when the Jews rejected the earthly Jesus, the Risen Jesus reached out to the Gentiles. "It was necessary that the Word of God be spoken to you [Jews] first, but since you reject it and condemn yourselves as unworthy of eternal life, we now turn to the Gentiles" (Acts 13:14, 43-52). In no time did the Gentiles of the Risen Jesus shuck off the uniqueness of the Chosen Race, the Mosaic law, the Torah, dietary rules, circumcision, Temple worship, and, in certain circumstances, the divorce prohibition of the earthly Jesus the Jew, and go on eventually to embrace war ("Put up your sword"), wealth ("It's easier for a camel to go through the eye of a needle than for a rich man to enter heaven"), and power ("The one who would be the greatest must be the servant of all"), setting off the historical alternating conflicts of restriction and expansion, isolation and openness, exclusion and inclusion, papal claims and conciliarism, centralization and collaboration—or, in our terms, Vatican I and Vatican II.

This earthly–Risen Jesus dichotomy is evident in the Gospels. Since some felt, after the destruction of Jerusalem, that neither the revolutionary ways of the Zealots nor the Torah focus of the Pharisees were adequate to pick up the authentic tradition of biblical Judaism, they turned instead to Jesus. He was presented in the Gospels as the new interpreter and teacher: "You have one instructor, the Messiah" (Matt. 23:10). Mark, Matthew, and Luke (Matthew and Luke offering revised and expanded versions of Mark) frequently moved between the poles of earthly and Risen. Again, note that in chapter 10, Matthew has the earthly Jesus send his disciples on a mission only to Israel, and even prohibits any evangelizing in pagan or Samaritan territory, but in chapter 28 he has the Risen Jesus ordering the making of disciples of all nations. While Jesus encountered hostility in his earthly life, all those warnings of arrests, trials, and family division and so on (Matt 10:16-39) are clearly the experience of the early Christian community, the era of the Risen Christ. In short, many of the sayings of Jesus are post-Resurrection utterances designed to guide the community going through the painful process of separating from its traditional Judaism.

MODERN QUESTIONS

We jump the centuries to our times. Given this history we have just reviewed, as time went on and the scientific age dawned, people began to raise questions, namely, there may be the earthly Jesus, but is he also the Risen Christ? He may be the Risen Christ, but is he the earthly Jesus? These questions came to a head in the 19th century, when a full-scale reassessment of the Bible took place and the biblical narratives were assessed as national myths like any other national myths. David Friedrich Strauss, a Lutheran minister, wrote his *Life of Jesus* in 1835, portraying Jesus as a great teacher whose followers innocently retold his story in the only way they knew how, in the metaphors and images of the Old Testament. Thus, the New Testament was not historical fact, but symbolic narrative. The book was a shocking sensation then, but its premise, as we have noted in the previous chapter, has become cautiously acceptable today to mainstream biblical scholars. In 1863, Joseph Ernest Renan, who was studying for the priesthood, wrote *The Life of Jesus* that denied any divine character to Jesus. In 1906, Albert Schweitzer followed up with *The Quest for the Historical Jesus*. His Jesus was a deluded end-of-the-world-timer, whose death was to hasten the days of tribulation. Then, too, at that time, scientific discoveries, especially in archaeology, were beginning to show that many of the images, language, narratives, and ideas of the Bible were in fact borrowed from elsewhere. A disorientating sense of confusion and disillusionment was further heightened by the discoveries of Darwin, who seemed to offer a purposeless universe.

Closer to our own era, the questions about Jesus came to the fore once more with the German scholar Rudolf Bultmann, who wrote a watershed essay in 1941 that basically said that there was a 1st-century Jew named Jesus from Nazareth who, like an Abraham or a Joshua, started out as an historical person but who, thanks to the early Church, mythologized into a superhuman, a divine Messiah. In other words, the Jesus of history is quite distinct from the Christ of faith. Jesus of Nazareth, it is said, lived, taught, preached, healed, and was executed, and would be surprised to find himself an elevated divine figure, the Messiah of God, the world's redeemer and Savior. This identity of the Christ emerged from the believing community. What was remembered about Jesus was filtered through the perspective of those who were concerned with promoting this faith. There is no real internal connection with that man from Nazareth. After all, the facts are that the Gospels were written decades after the death of Jesus (and tinkered with long after); they were written in Greek, which was not the original Aramaic speech of Jesus, a type of Greek that Jesus and his disciples did not speak and could not write (presuming they could read and write at all) and must suffer from any translation's hazards when one crosses from one culture to another. Not to mention, again, that they were not biographies, but distinctly faith documents tailored to fit "prophecy."

Into this contentious mix comes the discovery in 1945 in Nag Hammadi, Egypt, of a trove of early Christian documents written in Coptic. This discovery was among some 75 other early Christian works unearthed in recent times. Collectively they are known as the Gnostic Gospels and have long been viewed as the works of Christian heretics. Recently, however, some scholars have dropped the term "gnostic," since it denotes heresy and began to view these works as examples of diversity of thought. For example, for some early Christian communities Jesus was married.[7] Some told the Jesus story from the point of view of women. Some recalculated the role of Mary Magdalene. It is clear that the Gospel of Thomas has close connections with the canonical Gospels. Other scholars properly keep the term "gnostic" because the books were written some three to four hundred years after Jesus. Hardly any of them tells a consecutive but alternate version of Jesus' life. They tend rather to be bizarre with a precocious Jesus, secret knowledge, weird and magical events and esoteric teachings – the stuff of popular novels and TV shows.

The controversies still rage, and it seems that as the research continues and discoveries surprise, the more one knows the less one knows. The stakes, of course, are high. If the Jesus of the Gospels is, as according to the prevailing revision, a fictionalized version of the man from Nazareth who lived in the 1st century then, of course, the historical reliability of the Gospels is doubtful. If we can't access the real Jesus, then obviously the Christian faith is undermined considerably. This is why there is no furor over the "historical" Moses (someone, as we saw, hard to verify), because as the later Israelite tradition developed, it wasn't dependent on one figure as Christianity is. So the question is important: did he exist and, if so, he is anything like the portrait in the Gospels? People like Bart Ehrman, Elaine Pagels, John Dominic Crossan, Marcus Borg, Burton Mack, Dan Brown, and an eager press sow the revisionist seeds and offer a cornucopia of Jesuses that displace the orthodox view. Other scholars more properly point out how their Jesuses look suspiciously like themselves. They claim that, on the contrary, the Gospels do reflect eyewitness testimony as refracted through the faith of the evangelists. They point out that if some say Jesus is the composite of current popular myths, why do Matthew and Luke follow so closely Mark, often using his identical phrasing – Mark who frequently offers precise local details? They are convinced that the Gospels are genuine testimonies to a larger and richer Jesus than the skeptics allow. The Jesus of history and the Jesus faith are the same person.

This conviction finds it expression in Sheldom Vanauken's book of forty years ago:

> "First of all, it appeared to us [his wife and himself, recent converts to Christianity] that these fellows [the German 'demythologisers'] were in the position of the man who couldn't see the wood for the trees, for one thing was absolutely certain: the personality of Jesus that emerged from all four Gospels and from St. Paul was so powerful, so individual, so remarkable that it was obvious that the New Testament writers knew him, perhaps through others, as we know Winston Churchill or Abraham Lincoln. They lived in the shadow of a Man so immense that his spirit and words burned in Christian minds. But our real 'salvation' from these wreckers came through our recognition of the quite unverifiable fundamental assumptions, in no way derived from the New Testament text that they brought *to* it."

> "If Oxford consistently teaches any one thing, it is that fundamental assumptions *must* be verified. But not the demythologisers: when they say that prophecy must have been inserted after the event, their unverified assumption is that true prophecy cannot occur. They assume – *merely assume* – that miracles cannot happen: no proof and, by the nature of the case, no proof possible....They argue that something could not have been said or written when it was supposed to have been said or written because its theology or ecclesiology is too advanced, assuming that no man could have been ahead of his times. If a New Testament is akin to an earlier myth, it cannot have happened, on the assumption that God could not have intended to turn anticipatory myth into fact. Moreover,

Christ's words were misunderstood by His followers and the early church though quite clear to critics. Assumption: the mind of the infinite God is not unlike that of a German critic... The emperors of demytyhologising has no clothes on; and they themselves required 'demythologising'"[8]

Bottom line is that, like the Bible itself, "there is no uninterrupted Jesus and that we are dependent on sources that historians find challenging."

Chapter 14.

SIR, WE WISH TO SEE JESUS

REPLACING MOSES

Before we consider Jesus, we must consider the political and theological context of the Gospel writers. First, a few pages back we wrote that, after the disastrous destruction of Jerusalem and the Temple in the year 70, the question arose about what was going to be the glue of Judaism. Who would preserve its traditions? With the Temple, priesthood, and sacrifice gone, the leaders turned more and more to the Torah, both written and oral. That, in turn, begged for official interpreters, and ultimately the Pharisees assumed that position. They gave rise to what we call rabbinical Judaism. For them Moses would be the authority, the lawgiver, the ultimate standard. Texts would be read through the eyes of Moses. Through him God speaks.

The new Christian Jews, however, seriously differed. For them, Jesus was now the official interpreter of the Scriptures. They were to be read through his eyes. Right off, in what we call the Sermon on the Mount, Matthew specifically has Jesus assume the role of another Moses: "You have heard it said, but *I* say to you..." (Matthew 5). Matthew 11 has Jesus say that all things have been handed over to him by his Father and "no one knows the Father except the Son and anyone to whom the Son chooses to reveal him" (v 27). Matthew 23 pointedly says, "You have one teacher" (v 8) and "one instructor, the

Messiah" (v10). In Luke's famous Emmaus story (24:13-35) Jesus explains the scripture: "And beginning with Moses and all the prophets he interpreted to them in all the scriptures the things concerning himself" and afterwards the two disciples exclaimed, "Did not our hearts burn within us while he talked to us on the road, while he opened to us the scriptures?"

So for the early Christians, Jesus was sole interpreter of the scriptures, the bearer of the true traditions of Judaism, and not just for them but also for all ages to come. "Where two or three are gathered in my name, there am I in the midst of them." This set up conflict with the Pharisees. This also explains the many New Testament references to the Old Testament, and Jesus as their fulfillment. We will note later how forced these midrash applications seem to us, how artificial and free-wheeling, way beyond the knowledge and intent of the original Old Testament authors, a kind of making scripture say whatever you want it to say. But we must see the references, not so much as proofs or precise prophesies from the Old Testament, as the connections of Jesus to it. The citations are metaphorical mantels that wrap Jesus in the ancient Hebrew traditions. Our discomfort comes from later interpreters who, as it were, made prose out of poetry, literalized the metaphorical auras and in turn used them as proofs to back up fixed dogmas that in turn became unassailable doctrines.

REPLACING CAESAR

Just as they had to choose between the old and new Moses, as it were, in the interpretation of scripture, so followers of Jesus had to choose between Caesar the emperor and Christ the King, in the interpretation of life. In recent decades, some noted scholars have called our attention to the strong political context of Jesus' and the early Church's existence, and how the early Church sought to subvert and mimic the Roman political narrative while tip-toeing around outright defiance. Take note: Julius Caesar was assassinated in 44 B.C.E. When four months later, a comet was visible in the sky, the emperor Augustus, adopted son and heir to Julius Caesar, saw it as a sign that Caesar was divine and was quick to add to his own title, that of "Son of God". The good news, the word "Gospel," was used to celebrate the establishment of the Roman kingdom of peace and security. People looked forward to the emperor's *parousia*, that is, his triumphal arrival to their cities, for he was indeed the Savior who brought salvation. Early Christianity, meeting in assemblies, reflected the Roman assemblies that honored Caesar. So the Christians adopted Roman language, symbols, and structures and became the subversive opposite of their claims. The Book of Revelation was really not an apocalypse, but a defiant contrasting mirror to Rome. The early Christians embraced the titles of "Son of God," Gospel, *parousia*, the "Kingdom of God" and turned them into a contest between Caesar and Christ. One had to choose.

The evangelists constantly play these catch words off one another and press the question of who is really King. This issue plays all throughout the Gospels and the rest of the New Testament. In Matthew, for example, from the first chapter to the last, the issue is in the forefront. From the Magi's search for the "King of the Jews" to Pilate's sign "King of the Jews" over Jesus' cross, the contrast is front and center. It's there in the birth narratives with its marvelous star as counterpoint to Caesar's comet. It's there in Pilate's grand military approach to Jerusalem, through one gate to Jesus' humble approach through another. It's there in John's exchange between Pilate and Jesus at his trial. All throughout the Gospels the question of allegiance arises: Caesar or Jesus, force or love, revenge or forgiveness, might or service? You cannot serve two masters. The Book of Revelation is even more emphatic. That's why Christianity early on was referred to as The Way. Which road does one take? Which master does one serve: Caesar or Christ? Conflict with Rome, both as reality and as symbol, was inevitable. Rome, ever alert to any political claims, probably killed Jesus as a political liability and that sign above Jesus' cross was a warning to others. But the point remains: Rome cast a long shadow over the early Christian movement even as Paul sought to placate it, by counseling obedience and tax payments to Rome, and Luke sought to excuse Pilate from Jesus' death.

SEEING JESUS

Those who saw Jesus as the new Moses and the true King did so because they saw him as the long awaited, long predicted, Messiah. Yet, recall that we have already noted in chapter ten, that in the Old Testament, it is impossible to make a case for a clearly annotated Messiah beyond the dedicated determination of the first Christians to see "fuller" senses in Old Testament passages. Recall, also, Leslie Hoppe's words from that chapter: "Early Christian writers sometimes projected the centrality of the Messianic idea in the New Testament into the theology of the Hebrew Scriptures..." So we may thrill to the glorious liturgies that resonate with the majestic cadences of the ancient prophets who "foretold" Jesus as the Word Made Flesh and Man of Sorrows but they're all the applied allegory not the literal descriptions of an earlier time. Can we see behind them? Let us look.

Our first narrative "seeing" of Jesus comes, of course, from the canonical Gospels. What do we see? First, there's his genealogy. All scholars admit that both the genealogies in Matthew and Luke are largely fictitious. The biblical names of the last third of Matthew's list, for example, can be found nowhere in the Bible. The genealogies are for polemical purposes, and we must now see them as functioning as a standard stylistic fanfare that introduces the pedigree of a hero, a quite common practice among the evangelists' secular contemporaries (and all eras for that matter). In fact, most scholars categorize the Gospels as a subset of ancient Greco-Roman biography with its mixture of fact and fiction. The King Arthur saga, for example, has scholars asking whether he existed at all but that did not stop many of England's Tudor monarchs from defending it as a means of tracing their genealogical lineage to him, and justifying their reign. Matthew includes four very shady ladies in the list: Tamar, who had incest with her brother in law, Rahab the Canaanite prostitute, Ruth, a Moabite and Bathsheba, adulterous wife of the hapless Uriah. Commentators often cite this inclusion of "outsiders" as an early indication of the universality of Jesus' mission. In point of fact it's also a subtle bit of apologetics. It was said that Jesus' mother was unmarried, and his contemporaries were quick to point this out. Matthew's point is "So what? Makes no difference. Look at the background of your favorite heroes – Judah, David, Solomon and the like. A shady background hasn't kept you from heaping legitimacy and high honor on them."

Bethlehem or Nazareth?

Jesus was born in Bethlehem. Was he? Some scholars question this, in spite of all those Christmas carols and the Christian Church that stands in that now destitute place. They hold that Jesus was born in Nazareth because Jesus is always identified in the Gospels as "Jesus of Nazareth," never as "Jesus of Bethlehem". His followers were initially known as the Nazarenes. The first Gospel, Mark's, does not specify Jesus' birthplace. The records show that there was no census held at the time of Jesus' birth (and even if one were held people would not have been forced to make long journeys to their places of origin). Still it is possible that Mary and Joseph had roots in Bethlehem, because, from a century or so before them, there had been a notable emigration of Judeans into Galilee, and one can't dismiss that Jesus' family could have been among them. Moreover, being of the lineage of David, Joseph and Mary's relatives were in Bethlehem, the relatives being the normal birthing crew in that society, and that's why he took his pregnant wife there. Jesus, then, was likely born in Bethlehem but we are also alert to the evangelists' need to connect Jesus to the Davidic promise, and that made it necessary that his birth be put in David's hometown.

Joseph, deliberately portrayed in Matthew's Gospel in terms that make us think of the patriarch Joseph, is a shadowy off-center character who, unlike the others in the infancy narratives, has no speaking parts. He does appear to be unmarried to Mary, for she asks the angel, "How can this be since I have no husband" (Luke 1:34). Pope Benedict, however, argued that, by this point, according to Matthew's version, Joseph and Mary *were* married, although not yet living in the same residence (Mathew 1:18). Joseph nevertheless persists, because elsewhere in the Gospels Jesus' disciple Philip identifies Jesus as Joseph's son (John 1:45), and the townspeople of Nazareth have the same understanding (Luke 4:22). For most people, Joseph is simply listed as a "righteous" person." Storytelling could never leave it at that, so about the year 400, after the New Testament canon was completed, someone wrote a book called "The History of Joseph the Carpenter." It was never accepted as inspired, but it did have tremendous influence on Christian lore. It said that Joseph was previously married, that he had four sons, that after his wife died, he, at the age of 90, took in Mary as his ward to care of her. Being 90, he died in the presence of Jesus and Mary, and thereby became the patron saint of a happy death.

INFANCY NARRATIVES

The Infancy Narratives are a good example of "theologically interpreted history." If they are taken literally, historical implausibility abounds. Both Luke's and Matthew's narratives, as we saw, place Jesus' birth in Bethlehem whereas, as we noted, everywhere in the texts Jesus is always referred to as a Nazarene. The astronomical records from the ancient world tell of no unusual star for this time period. One also has to ask whether it is plausible that Herod, with his vast network of spies and soldiers, would ask total strangers (the Magi) where Jesus was born (the first recorded interfaith gathering). After all, it's only five miles from Jerusalem to Bethlehem. Jesus is given royal heritage by having him go back to David in one case and Abraham himself in another. That's because Matthew is repeating an old tradition that Abraham himself was a king. He is relying on a translation of the word "king" found in the Septuagint version, but which is "prince" in the Hebrew version. So Abraham is a king, David is a king and so, therefore, Jesus is a king and this is precisely the tension in Matthew: the Jewish leaders keep on rejecting his kingship.

Consistent with the tradition of creative interpretation, Matthew does something that still stresses the modern mind: he deliberately alters a quotation from the prophet Micah (5:2). Micah originally wrote:

> But you, O Bethlehem, of Ephrathah
> Who are one of the little clans of Judah,
> From you shall come forth for me
> One who is to rule Israel.

Matthew's reworked version:

> And, you, Bethlehem, in the land of Judah
> *are by no means* least among the *rulers* of Judah;
> *for* from you shall come a ruler
> *who* will govern my people Israel.

Matthew takes Micah's description of Bethlehem as one of the little clans and turns it on its head to say that Bethlehem is in fact a very important and prestigious clan, far from the least of them. He also adds the word "for" and changes the word clans to "ruler," indicating that Jesus, who comes from a royal city of royal ancestry, is to be a ruler of Israel. Matthew also quotes a supposedly Old Testament saying, "He shall be called a Nazorean," but there is no such quotation in the Bible. Matthew is consistent. Later, in the passion account, he will relate Judas' death to the fulfillment of a prophecy from Jeremiah, while actually it is an adaptation from Zechariah (11:13), and in reality not fully from either. In short, the Matthew-Luke infancy narratives are just that: revelatory parables featuring stars, angels, dreams, mangers, Wise Men, shepherds, wicked kings, etc. to make the point so well captured by that elegant writer, Frederick Buechner:

"Let us assume that if we had been there that night when he was born we would have seen nothing untoward at all. Let us assume that the darkness would have looked very much like any darkness. Maybe there were a few stars, the same old stars, or the moon..."

"Maybe that is all we would have seen if we had been there because maybe that or something like that was all that really happened ... So a great many biblical scholars would agree with the skeptics that the great nativity stories of Luke and Matthew are simply the legendary accretions, the poetry, of a later generation, and that were we to have been present, we would have seen a birth no more or less marvelous than any other birth."

"But if that is the case, what do we do with the legends of the wise men and the star, the shepherds and the angels and the great hymn of joy that the angels sang? Do we dismiss them as fairy tales, the subject for pageants to sentimentalize over once a year come Christmas, the lovely dream that never came true? ..."

"Who knows what the facts of Jesus' birth actually were? As for myself, the longer I live, the more inclined I am to believe in miracle, the more I suspect that if we had been there at the birth, we might well have seen and heard things that would be hard to reconcile with modern science But of course that is not the point, because the Gospel writers are not really interested primarily in the facts of the birth but in the significance...Whether there were ten million angels there or just the woman herself and her husband, when that child was born the whole course of history was changed..."

"This is what Matthew and Luke were trying to say in the stories about how he was born, and this is the truth that no language seemed too miraculous to them to convey. This is the only truth that matters, and the wise men, the shepherds, the star are important only as ways of pointing to this truth."[1]

Indeed, the uniqueness of this child is the great truth wrapped in the parabolic birth story. It's a classic approach shared by the Greeks and Romans for their heroes. Yes, says the story, with all of its improbabilities, Jesus is special, indeed, unique, the very Son of God. This is why Pope Benedict said, echoing the great theologian Jean Danielou, that no essential faith would suffer if Matthew's Gospel was more a theological meditation (read: parabolic interpretation) than a statement of fact.[2] That much is settled for the believers for whom the birth story was written. It remains, of course, unsettled for those for whom it wasn't, but even they understand the message.

The family flees to Egypt. Ann Rice, in her book, *Christ the Lord* has the family stay in Alexandria, the most sophisticated city in the world at the time. There, she contends, Jesus received training in clear thinking from the great Jewish-Hellenistic scholar, Philo. That would explain his learning to those who wondered how a country boy could know so much. "They were astounded at his teaching because he spoke with authority" (Luke 4:32). Jesus comes back, is baptized and immediately goes to the desert to confront Satan. As we noted before, the usual Midrash on this episode is that Jesus is confronted with the same temptations as Israel, only he succeeds in overcoming them. The incident is full of folkloric elements, such as being whisked to the temple parapet and talking face to face with the devil. The temptation in the desert represented the cosmic struggle between God and Satan that, in Christian belief, was prophesied to occur at the end time during the ministry of Jesus.

MORE STORYTELLING

In his Gospels and Acts, Luke continues the parabolic narrative. He has, for example, calculated and obvious parallels between the apostles and Jesus. That is to say, that just as Jesus in Matthew was another Moses, so in Luke the apostles are another Jesus. Notice the parallels. The Holy Spirit descends on Jesus at his baptism, and the Holy Spirit descends on the apostles at Pentecost. Jesus stands before the crowd and preaches from Isaiah. Peter stands before the crowd and preaches Joel. Jesus calls disciples to join him; so do the apostles. Jesus heals the blind beggar. Peter and John heal the lame beggar. Jesus is arrested and questioned by the authorities, and so are the apostles. Jesus performs signs and wonders, and so do the apostles. The woman with the hemorrhage touches the hem of Jesus' cloak and is healed. The sick feel the shadow of Peter and are healed. The Jewish leaders want to kill Jesus because of his teaching, and they likewise want to kill the apostles for the same reason. Jesus raises up the widow's dead son, and Peter raises up Dorcus to life. Jesus heals the son of a faithful Roman centurion, and the apostles encounter a faithful Roman centurion. Stephen, called the first martyr, like Jesus, is also taken outside the city walls to be killed. Like Jesus, he hands over his spirit, and like Jesus he forgives his executioners. In short, just as the authentic Messiah is like Moses in Matthew, the authentic disciple is just like Jesus in Luke. It's all contrived "history," or invented extended parables to make a point for the inner circle of believers to embrace and the outer circle of non-believers to ponder. All this interpretation implies a growing consciousness of the Christian community as it continues its reflections on the promises of the Old and the fulfillment of the New Testaments in Jesus, "true God and true man."

A REFLECTIVE WORD

This much must be said and kept in mind: many believers have made a case for the connection between the earthly Jesus of Nazareth and Risen Cosmic Lord. Why else would his Crucifixion not be the last word? Why keep his memory alive if it were? Why would his closest followers who fled him, leaving him to his fate, return to Jerusalem, proclaim his Resurrection, call him LORD and die for that conviction? Indeed there must be the core of an extraordinary man who would warrant such an elevated connection in status in so brief a time. Jesus must have been a strong figure in his own right. Martin

Hengle was surely correct when he wrote, "The time between the death of Jesus and the fully developed Christology we find in the earliest Christian documents, the letters of Paul, is so short that the development that takes place within it can only be called amazing."[3] For example, the first Pauline letter, the first letter to the Thessalonians was written around 51 C.E. That's only some eighteen years between the death of Jesus in 33 and this epistle, and it describes Jesus as "LORD", "Messiah," and "Savior" (5:9). Not to mention again how quickly Jesus was worshipped in the early Church. This fact seems to have escaped those who, in our day, labor to deconstruct the Gospels and interpret Jesus in various secular or mythical categories. They completely ignore Paul, the first Christian canonical author writing decades before the first Gospel, who left no doubt that a divine Christ came before later speculations. Dipping into the primal tradition he received, Paul wrote confidently, "For I delivered to you as of first importance what I also received: that Christ died for our sins in accordance with the scriptures, that he was buried, that he was raised on the third day in accordance with the scriptures and that he appeared to Cephas, then to the Twelve." Paul did not attach the Godhead to Jesus. Remaining thoroughly Jewish, he radically rethought its central tenets in the light of Jesus, and he remained in continuity with Judaism. He just struggled with all kinds of gigantic metaphors to explain Jesus, simply noting that wherever Jesus was present so was God. Again, all this preceded the storytelling techniques of the four Gospel portraits of Jesus by people who lived outside Palestine, outside the traumatic destruction of its ruined capital, outside the Semitic world, outside its language and customs.

TEACHINGS AND PARABLE STORIES

Part of seeing Jesus is to ponder his teachings. One immediately thinks of Jesus on the mountain uttering the famous Beatitudes: "Blessed are the poor in spirit... the meek... the pure of heart." Once more, however, storytelling is going on. Even Catholic scholars are quick to say that Jesus never said these things all at once on the mountaintop – the traditional metaphorical locale (high up, touching heaven) for divine instruction. Rather, the Beatitudes are a collection of his sayings brought together by the authors in one place. Pier Paolo Pasolini, in his classic movie, *The Gospel According to St. Matthew*, has it right when he cuts in flashbacks different backgrounds as Jesus utters each Beatitude. But there's more. The discovery of the Dead Sea Scrolls possessed by the Qumran community, written roughly between 250 B.C.E. to 68 C.E., undermines somewhat the uniqueness of Jesus' teaching for in them we can find identical or similar teachings and rituals. The Scrolls reveal teachings very much like the Beatitudes in Jesus' Sermon on the Mount (or, in Luke's version, on the plain). As Catholic biblical scholar Joseph Fitzmyer, observes:

"The scrolls have shed a remarkable light, however, on many aspects of New Testament writings. Who would have thought 50 years ago that one would discover a Hebrew text with a collection of five beatitudes resembling somewhat the collection of eight in the Gospel of Matthew or the four in Luke? Or who would have thought of an Aramaic parallel to Gabriel's words to Mary in Luke, 'By his name shall he be named. He shall be hailed as son of God, and they shall call him son of the Most High?' Or of a Jewish text that has now come to light...bearing the phrase 'works of the law' used by Paul? ... Jesus' teaching on the poor, 'Blessed are the poor for yours is the kingdom of God' (Luke 6:20) reflects the Essene doctrine that valued poverty and the sharing of material wealth. The historian Josephus writes of these Essenes (thought to be the Qumran community), 'Riches they despise, and their community of goods is truly admirable; you will not find one among them distinguished by greater opulence than another. They have a law that new members on admission shall confiscate their property to the order.'"[4]

In the Dead Sea Scrolls, we also find these words, "When he had completed a year within the Community... his possessions and his earnings will also be joined at the hand of the Inspector."

One cannot help immediately think of Jesus saying, "For it is easier for a camel to pass through the eye of a needle than for a rich man to enter the Kingdom of God," (Luke 18:25) and the testimony of the Acts of the Apostles: "All who believed were together and had all things in common; they would sell their possessions and goods and distribute the proceeds to all, as any had need." (Acts 2:44-45). Jesus' teaching on wealth is not novel but the same as the Essenes', who uniquely in their time regarded poverty as a value.

Maybe, for all we know, Jesus was influenced by (and was a disciple of) John the Baptist, who may well have lived among the Essenes for a while. If there is any link with Jesus (and the Christian Movement) and the Qumran community, it certainly would have been through John. John baptized, and so did Jesus. Recall also John's words: "He who has two coats, let him share with one who has none and he who has food let him do likewise" (Luke 3:11). In short, as we noted, Jesus' teaching on poverty was not an innovation. Then, too, Jesus' teaching on divorce also seems to be a close echo to that of the Qumran community, who were out of step in this matter with mainstream Judaism. Except in rare cases, they also forbade divorce, even for the king, and they cite the very same passage in Genesis (1:27) that Jesus does in prohibiting divorce.[5] The Qumran community, like Jesus, also had an inner circle of the Twelve, who represented the twelve tribes of Israel. It also had a "guardian" of the camp, one equivalent to the Christian office of overseer or bishop.

A Qumran document describes a community meal that features bread and wine, with a character called the "Priest," who is the first to bless the bread and wine. Furthermore, the Qumran community was very much an apocalyptic one, awaiting the full manifestation of God's kingdom, very much akin to Jesus' preaching on the imminent coming of "the Kingdom of God." Add to this that it has been discovered that Jesus' use of calling God "Abba" or Father (in reality used only once in the four Gospels in Mark) – long regarded as unique to himself –was not and has parallels in the literature of Palestinian Judaism. Likewise, the title "Son of God" has been found in that literature, as well in the Qumran texts, one of which sounds very much like the words Gabriel spoke to Mary at the Annunciation: "He will be great and will be called the Son of the Most High, and the Lord God will give him the throne of his ancestor David" (Luke 1:32). A Qumran text, clearly referring to the Messiah, likewise speaks of someone as "The Son of God he will be proclaimed, and the Son of the Most High they will call him."[6] So the title "Son of God" was a Messianic title in Judaism a century before Jesus arrived on the scene.

We must be quick to point out that these parallels do not imply that any New Testament author knew of or used any of the sectarian material found at the Quram caves. What they do demonstrate is that the terminologies, the titles, the arguments over the interpretations of keeping the Sabbath, the meaning of miracles and other items that appear in the Gospels and in the scrolls are examples of the larger ongoing theological traditions and debates within Judaism itself. In a word, there are common strands shared among the sectarians and the early Christians. This means, significantly, that the more one knows about Judaism, the more one knows about the beginnings of Christianity.

Finally, Jesus famously taught the Golden Rule, but it is already found in Leviticus 19:18 and Deuteronomy 6:4 and the Book of Tobit: "Do not do to others what you would not want others to do to you" is a 6th century B.C.E. saying of Confucius. Some are quick to add that Jesus is the first one to join them together. This is not so. The pairing of the love of God and neighbor can be found in the non-canonical book, the Testimony of Issachar, where it states, "Love your Lord and love your neighbor," (5:2) and in the Testament of Dan, "Love the Lord all through your life and one another with a true heart." (5:30). As we have seen that the Ten Commandments reflect the common traditional wisdom of the Near East. So does Jesus' teaching.

INTERESTING PARALLELS

There is a five-hundred-year span between Buddha and Jesus, but their teachings are quite similar. Oxford scholar Burnett Hillman Streeter notes, "The moral teaching of Buddha has a remarkable resemblance to the Sermon on the Mount," which, in turn, as we have seen, has some of the identical teaching found at Qumran written a few hundred years before Jesus. Some examples:

> Buddha: Consider others as yourself.
> Jesus: "Do to others as you would have them do to you".

> Buddha: Abstain from killing and from taking what is not given. Abstain from unchastity and from speaking falsely. Do not accept gold and silver.
> Jesus: "You know the commandments: you shall not murder; you shall not commit adultery; you shall not steal; you shall not bear false witness; you shall not defraud; honor your father and mother."

> Buddha: The faults of others are easier to see than one's own.
> Jesus: "Why do you see the speck in your neighbor's eye, but do not notice the log in your own?"

> Buddha: Stealing, deceiving, adultery; this is defilement. Not the eating of meat.
> Jesus: "It is what comes out of a person that defiles, for it is from within, from the human heart, that evil intentions come forth."

> Buddha: For what reasons are these signs revealed? Is it that a god of great merit has been born? Or is it that a Buddha has emerged in the world? Never before have we seen such signs! We must trace them

together, crossing a myriad of lands, seeking the
glow and investigating it together.

Jesus: "In the time of King Herod, after Jesus was born
in Bethlehem of Judea, wise men from the East
came to Jerusalem asking, 'Where is the child who
has been born as King of the Jews? For we have
observed his star at its rising, and have come to
pay him homage.'"

Buddha: The long-haired sage looked at the baby, and with
great joy he picked him up. Now the Buddha was
in the arms of a man who had waited for him, a
man who could recognize all the signs on his body –
a man who now, filled with delight, raised his
voice to say these words: "There is nothing to
compare with this: this is the ultimate, this is the
perfect man." Just then, the hermit remembered
that he was going to die quite soon — and he felt so
sad at this that he began to cry.

Jesus: "Now there was a man in Jerusalem whose name
was Simeon; this man was righteous and devout,
looking forward to the consolation of Israel,
and the Holy Spirit rested on him. It had been
revealed to him by the Holy Spirit that he would
not see death before he had seen the Lord's
Messiah. Guided by the Spirit, Simeon came into
the temple; and when the parents brought in the
child Jesus, to do for him what was customary
under the law, Simeon took him in his arms and
praised God."

Scholars are aware of the strong resemblances between the infancy
stories in the Gospels and the Lalitavistara biography of Buddha and
the common sayings of Buddha and Jesus. That's why there has been
for a long time speculation that, as a young man, Jesus may have
visited India.[7]

THE GOSPEL PARABLES

Pick out any parable from the Gospels and read any one of them out loud. At most, the reading will take five or ten minutes. And right there, we're broadsided into a false stance. That's because we were raised in a text society, and that subverts our appreciation of the parables. Recall that Jesus lived, as did most of humanity until the 17th century of our era, in an oral society. That means that the mode of communication was storytelling, and the storyteller interacted with his audience. In fact, he was, more accurately, not merely a speaker, but a performer with gestures, facial expressions and voice changes providing critical nuances to the story. A parable like the Good Samaritan, for example, might take an hour or more with the give and take with the audience. And the meaning of the parable would have arisen from the total combined experience, with perhaps the main "aha" point only being made clear later on especially if the parable were a subversive or challenging one. There would not necessarily be only one meaning, for stories are open-ended and intolerant of just one interpretation. The danger of forever-fixed dogma is to canonize one meaning that inevitably proves too small.

So the scholars remind us that when the Jesus parables got passed around and eventually written down by the four evangelists, a lot of decades had gone by. The blunt point is that the evangelists, writing outside of Palestine, didn't always understand or like the Aramaic interpretation that came with the story. It didn't fit their times, their agenda, so they changed it. The result was twofold: 1) we never did learn Jesus' original point; and 2) the evangelists' interpretations, now written down and eventually canonized, became the only ones—and were sometimes erroneous, but we're stuck with them. In other words, when we now read Jesus' parables in the Gospels, we are getting them not necessarily as Jesus told them, but as the evangelists interpreted them, and sometimes they are not the same and we wind up interpreting the interpreters, because sometimes their interpretations rub us the wrong way.

As an example, we turn to the ever helpful and insightful John R. Donahue, S.J. who gives this commentary on Matthew 22:1-14. These verses tell the story of the king's wedding banquet for his son and the shocking indifference of the invited guests, some of whom beat up and killed the king's messengers. He, in turn sends out his hit men to take care of them and has his servants go to highways and alleys to invite others. Donahue (my emphasis in all quotations that follow):

> "Matthew, Luke and the second-century Gospel of Thomas recount this parable with *very different applications*. In Luke the substitute guests are 'the poor, the crippled, the blind and the lame,' an epitome of the Lukan Jesus' good news for the poor. In Thomas there is a simple dinner, and the guests refuse because the invitation conflicts with their business interests. Matthew is unique in *allegorizing* the punishment of the refusing guests into the destruction of Jerusalem, ("burnt their city") and adding the expulsion of the man without the wedding garment."

> "Matthew's interpretation of this parable has unfortunately *provided fuel for anti-Semitism*. The guests who refuse to come are equated with the Jewish people who first heard the invitation of Jesus but failed to respond. The consequence of this rejection was the destruction of the Jewish Temple. The guests who came to the feast in their place are taken to represent converts to Matthew's community, both Jews and Greeks. Such a view was unfortunately *part of the 'blame game,'* as it was played in the first century..."[8]

Another Catholic commentator, Arthur Dewey, offers his thoughts. He writes (emphasis ours):

> "In today's Gospel Matthew has taken over a parable from Mark 12:1-11. It should be pointed out that Matthew's source *had already been greatly reworked when it appeared in Mark.* The Markan passage is actually an allegory based on a more primitive version which fortunately can be found intact in the Gospel of Thomas, Saying 65.... Initially, the parable caused

both shock and puzzlement for Jesus' Galilean audience. To understand this, *we must forget what has been added by Mark* and imagine how the parable would have sounded to a Galilean...."

"*Thus, in the original parable, Jesus may well have compared the Kingdom of God to the situation of those tenants who seize a golden opportunity....* Today's reading goes well beyond the original parable. The passage is a twice-told tale. *Even in the Markan version*, it features additional scriptural interpretation (see Mark 12:1 – 9; Matthew 21:33- 40; Isaiah 5:2 – 5; see also Mark 12:10 and 11: Matthew 21:42; Psalm 118:22 and 23). Today's reading also features historical allusions to the prophets and Jesus (Matthew 21:35-39), and to the destruction of Jerusalem (Matthew 21:41). The text, *as it stands today*, is an extended allegory *placed on the lips of the Matthean Jesus* concerning the rejection by many Jews of God's design of love and the divine triumph despite apparent failure...."

All those italicized words are meant to ask: before Mark got hold of the original parable, was it the inerrant word of Jesus, the Revelation of the Father, with its distinct message? If so, did it "lose" its inerrancy and divine inspiration when Mark took it over and added his own interpretation (in fact a very bad *misinterpretation*, according to Dominic Crossan) and moved it into the official canon? When Matthew, in turn, took over Mark and, in his own personal extended allegory that he "placed on the lips of Jesus," added even more material never included nor intended in the original parable, did *that* become the inspired Word of God, and did it abrogate Mark's and especially the non-canonical Thomas? Does all this reworking, which strays considerably from the original meaning, come under new divine inspiration? Do we have a multiple choice of inspired interpretations? Did the original utterance of Jesus, now no longer known by ordinary people—or the scholars, for that matter—have nothing to say to them anymore? If it does, how will we ever hear this "word of God"? Did it lose its status as revelation?

The scholars chime in. The late Lawrence Boadt tries to explain:

"The Holy Spirit first directs the thought processes of the original contributors to the book, but as others add to it or edit it, the Holy Spirit guides them also through every step of the way until the book reaches its final form. This can continue for several centuries, as in the case of the book of Isaiah..."[9] Somehow the invocation of a busy Holy Spirit seems a bit too tidy, too self-serving to cover the changes and contradictions of scripture. And for several centuries? What happens if one reads scripture in the "in-between" times?" Do you get the genuine inspired words of God, or only partially inspired or on-the-way to final inspiration?"

Another scripture scholar unwittingly puts the whole issue in a nutshell:

"As stories became more fixed in written and edited traditions, applications would vary, and the final form of the story might *differ from the original*. The point of the story, in fact, might *dramatically change* in this process. Yet from a faith perspective, the stories of the Bible exist for the purpose of religious messages. Literal accuracy is less necessary than the assurance that God's Word is generally preserved in these sacred accounts."[10]

That indeed is a "faith perspective" assumption—that in the final filtered version, eschewing all those previous Words of God, we are assured that now at last we have God's Word. Apart from a "faith perspective," how does one know that this is "God's Word" if it "differs from the original," if it has been "dramatically changed," if it got lost because of less than "literary accuracy" of the transmitter? I repeat, if the words of Jesus, the very Son of God and the Revelation of the Father, have been trumped by the interpretations of the divinely inspired human evangelists and their redactors (is the Holy Spirit contradicting himself?) and the Divine Son's words have "dramatically changed in this process;" if a Jesus-told parable can become something entirely different in someone else's hands, then, to put it bluntly, why did the divine Jesus bother? If Jesus' original words and intent convey his spirit even though his original point languishes, that's all right? Literal accuracy is not necessary as long as we're assured that the end product is God's word, however modified or changed? Who does the assuring? Or is the inspired word of God so fluid that it, like any good story, can morph from century to century and, if so, is it (as we shall see) right in one century and wrong in another?

There are many scriptural applications of Jesus' parables, but one can, I suppose, be forgiven for asking, which "application" in Holy Scripture is the inerrant, infallible, living, eternal word of God? Is divine revelation in Thomas' non-canonical version, Luke's, or Matthew's "blame game" canonical version? Would Thomas recognize the denouement of Matthew's story? Would Luke? What is inspired: the original story as Jesus told it (do we have the original?), Luke's adaptation of, it or Matthew's adaptation? Would Luke even agree with Matthew's take on this story? Is Matthew's interpretation, which indeed has provided fuel for anti-Semitism, inspired? Are all versions equally the real, genuine Word of God, even though one has fallen into oblivion (Thomas')?

We do appreciate the insights of the Vatican Document, "On the Historicity of the Gospels," which gave us the three-stage process of Gospel formation: One, the Historical Jesus who lived between 6 B.C.E. and 30 C.E.; two, the Preached Jesus between 30 to 70 C.E. (would that we had tape recordings of these teachings!) and three, the written Gospels between 70 and 90 C.E. The second and third generation Christians who wrote these Gospels did not know the historical Jesus only the Risen Jesus. This is the Jesus they tapped, as it were, when faced with issues the historical Jesus never encountered. They couldn't access the historical Jesus so they zoned in on the Risen Jesus in their midst, his Spirit, the Spirit of truth, the One he promised to send. That was the warrant for altering his teachings and changing his stories. Still, for some it does become unsettlingly problematic when an ancient parable in Mark, already badly interpreted, becomes a seeding for anti-Semitism in Matthew.

As a parting shot, we should know that some of Jesus' teachings are found in earlier sources: for example, Jesus' words about taking the lowest place are found in Proverbs: "Do not put yourself forward in the king's presence or stand in the place of the great; for it is better to be told 'Come up here' than to be put lower in the presence of a noble. (25:6-7). That same book anticipates Jesus with its words, "If your enemies are hungry, give them bread to eat; and if they are thirsty, give them water to drink (25:21). Then there are parables Jesus told that bear striking resemblances to other rabbinic parables.[11] Jewish scholars have shown more than a thousand examples of parables preserved in rabbinic literature, many of which sound exactly like Jesus' famous teachings about kings, slaves, landowners, tenant farmers, and day laborers, raising the question of exactly what was unique about the Gospel parables other than the Christian spin put on them. Whatever the case, we have the Gospel parables, reworked or manufactured, and we're not always certain of their original context or meaning. Like all good stories, of course, they have more than one meaning. The problem comes when orthodoxy insists they don't.

Chapter 15.

KINGDOM AND DIVINITY

We come to the statement that Jesus came preaching the Kingdom of God, often saying it was imminent. He was God's unique messenger. The fact is that Jesus did preach an urgent coming but, as research shows, he was not unique. We now know that he was very much a part of his times, when end time scenarios and their messengers were all over the place. From the Dead Sea scrolls we know of a group (the Sadducees/Essenes?) that, about a hundred and fifty years before Jesus, had moved to the desert to escape the corruptions they saw in Jerusalem and formed an apocalyptic community to await the coming vengeance of the End Times. Interpreting the desert wanderings of the Israelites as a model, they, too, retreated to the desert (as Jesus would). Just as the Israelites had a charismatic figure, Moses, to save them, so too, they believed, a "Son of Man" figure would be the agent of God's salvation.

In the desert, this group rewrote and reinterpreted the Torah to fit their agenda (as the other Jews did and Christians would). They took Jeremiah and Isaiah (favorite books among the Jews) and interpreted their utterances solely in terms of contemporary events; that is, the prophets unknowingly were making predictions about the future, *their* future. They were preoccupied with the end of days and lived in a hierarchically structured community under a bishop, (the Greek word for overseer). As we have seen in the last chapter, they held property in common, organized care for the sick and elderly, went through an intensive catechumenate and shared table fellowship meals. They did not swear oaths and they rejected marriage (except for needed procreation) and embraced celibacy. Although there were differences, the similarities to the future Christians in Luke's account in the Acts of the Apostles are striking.

So, likewise did Jesus preach the imminent coming of the Kingdom of God, but, as we just saw, he was but part of a group of wandering prophets who did so. "The Kingdom of God is at hand" was his constant rallying theme. "Truly, I say to you there are some standing here who will not taste death before they see the kingdom of God has come with power" (Mark 9:1). "The time is fulfilled and the kingdom of God has come near; repent and believe in the good news" (Mark 1:15). "Truly I tell you, this generation will not pass away until all these things have taken place" (Matt 24: 34). There's no mistaking Jesus' end-time preaching and it seems that he expected the world to end soon. That would pose a difficulty when Jesus was considered human, but when he was declared divine it obviously had to be explained away. As we saw, St. Paul followed suit as he vigorously embraced this teaching. He, too, truly believed the end times were near: "the time is short" (1 Cor. 7:31; Phil 4:5; I Thess 5:2), and the "world in its present form is passing away" (1 Cor.7:31). Accordingly, Paul urged people not to marry or even act as married because all one's energy should go into the preparation for Jesus' return.

Scholars debate just how much this imminent expectation goes back to Jesus himself, and therefore whether Jesus' words are post-Easter convictions that Mark projected backwards. That would not be unsurprising if we recall that Mark had painfully and personally experienced the "end of the world" with the destruction of Jerusalem and the Temple, a cataclysm that well might have generated the hope that, from the physical and religious debris, something new might happen.

A CHANGE OF DIRECTIONS

Whatever the case, it does seem that Jesus, like Paul and, as we saw, the writers of Daniel and Revelation ("The time is near!", 1:3) had the calendar wrong in his urgent message of an imminent end time and the establishment of the earthly Kingdom. There does also seem to be some justification for the Jewish question about Jesus being that long-awaited Messiah to usher in that end time; namely, if Jesus the Messiah has truly come, where are the golden age and the peaceable kingdom that go with the territory? Look around you. It's still the same lousy mess, Jesus and all. In his book *Why the Jews Rejected Jesus*, David Klinghoffer points out precisely how Jesus is different from the expected Messiah. He writes, "The Messiah will change the world. There won't be any question about whether he's come," and he goes on to offer the analogy of seeing a woman who is clearly pregnant, and then later her stomach is flat. As he says, there's no need to ask, "Did you have the baby?" So, in the same way, this is the obvious answer to Christians who claim that Jesus who has come is the Messiah. Jesus, for example, didn't bring world peace, which is one of the main job descriptions of the Messiah. In short, in Jesus' time, the conventional hope was that God's covenant with his chosen people would prevail and there would be a collective restoration on earth, which meant that YHWH would deliver Israel from its foes. There would be a general Resurrection and judgment, the reestablishment of the Twelve Tribes, and perhaps even the restoration of the Temple. Jesus' urgent preaching of the coming of "the Kingdom God" seemed to promise this dramatic turnabout, this reversal of fortune. The thing is, none of this happened.

It is worth pausing to note here that more and more scholars, both on the right and left, remind us that this restoration, this "Kingdom of God", was something meant to happen here on earth; that, in fact, the concept of a fully restored, fully fulfilled afterlife has no basis whatsoever in the Bible. The emphasis, rather, was on *this* world and its transformation, a transformation that early Christians like

Paul thought would happen in their lifetimes. To be sure, it was an earthly transformation far from complete, and it required the active participation of God's people. But once it's complete, then the bodily Resurrection will follow with a fully completed creation here on earth, not in some afterlife in heaven. The concept of an afterlife (heaven, hell and purgatory) is a deduction of the Middle Ages and is not consistent with what we find in the New Testament. After a thousand years, when the concept took hold, it changed the focus of Christianity from changing the injustices of the earth to the personal striving "to be saved and get to heaven". "salvation" meant getting to heaven, not deliverance and transformation here. There is no doubt that for medieval Christians, for example, the main purpose of this life (for them short and brutish) was to secure salvation in the next, and a flourishing relic industry was meant to aid this quest. It is further noteworthy how dominant in Catholicism and other Christian religions are the liturgical prayers that emphasize that we do or believe certain things "so that we may rejoice with you in heaven."[1]

Remember, when Jesus read from the Isaiahan scroll at his hometown of Nazareth, those words: "The spirit of the Lord is upon me, because he has anointed me to bring good news to the poor. He has sent me to proclaim release to the captives and recovery of sight to the blind, to let the oppressed go free, to proclaim the year of the lord's favor." He pointedly said, *Today*, this scripture has been fulfilled in your hearing." The Messianic Kingdom is here. To return to our initial point, even if we entertain the notion that this "Messianic Kingdom" is here but incomplete, it's hard for some people, pointing to empirical evidence, to believe that such a kingdom exists at all.

Christians respond by insisting that these promised days have indeed been fulfilled – "already but not yet." It's an eschatology that is present yet not fully complete. That is to say, the Messiah, Jesus, has already come, but the stunning fruits of his coming – judgment, victory, prosperity and peace – are not yet apparent. Apologists like C. S. Lewis and Anders Nyren make the comparison between the situation of World War II and this "already but not yet" explanation. They say that the victory won over sin through the death of Jesus is like the liberation of an occupied country by Nazi rule. For example, there comes the startling news of a far off battle that has turned the tide of the war. The result is that the occupying power is in utter disarray and its backbone broken. It's only a matter of time before the Nazis are driven out of every corner of Europe, but for the time being they are still present in the occupied country. So it is with Christ's victory. He has conquered sin and death and inaugurated the Messianic Kingdom, but it will take time to be complete, to be obvious.

Somehow, two thousand years after the arrival of Jesus' Messianic Kingdom and several genocides, holocausts, global wars, religious wars, inquisitions, plagues, epidemics and earthquakes later; after Hiroshima, Dresden, Rwanda, Zimbabwe, Bosnia, Cambodia, Iraq, Afghanistan, Libya, Syria, Chernobyl, Treblinka, Newtown, Connecticut, 9/11, terrorism, Agent Orange, drones, mass graves, disappearing forests and water, global warming, and pollution; after slavery (even among the ancient Hebrews), colonialism, Manifest Destiny, ethnic cleansing; after Wall Street meltdown, disproportionate wealth, the growing chasm between the super-rich and the poor – the litany is never ending – after all of these, Lewis' comparison gets thinner and thinner, and it challenges the mind to think that, if we are living in the time of Jesus' Messianic Kingdom, how could it possibly be worse without it? Besides, if Elijah tells the drought-stricken widow of Zaraphath that YHWH promises no longer to withhold the rain (1 Kings 17:7-16), and Matthew says that God is always working behind the impersonal forces of nature – "For he makes his sun rise on the evil and the good and sends rain on the just and unjust" (Matthew 5:45) – should not God be accountable for nature's horrors as well, even in Messianic times? (Think tsunamis, and the 20,000 people who died in the 2005 one.) Two prominent Protestant preachers weigh in on the conundrum: Lewis Smedes wrote, "Sometimes I hang on to my faith by my fingernails: when the dream of a new world of Jesus' peace and love is more than two thousand years old and still shows no sign of coming true, anybody's faith is bound to turn to doubt."[2] Fred Craddock has pointed out that there is always enough suffering in the world to make the idea of a Messiah a powerful one. On the other hand, he adds, there is always enough pain in the world to render ridiculous the statement "The Messiah has come."

To expand on the theodicy issue raised in chapter 8, the question of how a good, loving, all-knowing, all-powerful God could allow suffering in the "good" world he created (Genesis 1:10, 18, 21, 25) a world further redeemed by the blood of his Messianic Son, who sent a life-giving Spirit, remains for many the greatest barrier to belief. This unsolvable mystery, moreover, puts a special strain on biblical believers because although YHWH could be quite erratic, petulant, bloodthirsty and revengeful, there are passages extolling his mercy and forgiveness and his declaration that he has loved his people "with an everlasting love." In the New Testament, the Incarnate God tells us that the hairs of our heads are numbered, that we are no longer slaves but friends, that we are worth more than the birds of the air, and, if we strive for his Kingdom of God and his righteousness, God will give us food and clothing; that if we ask, what we ask for will be given us. For, after all, if we know how to give good things to *our* children, "how much more will the Father in heaven give good things to *his*" (Matt 7:11)? Moreover, he did say that he came, not only to give us life, but to give it abundantly. Not only that, but wherever his followers are gathered in his name, he is there – the one who "was moved with compassion" (Luke 11:13), the one who wept over his friend Lazarus' death (John 11:35) – in their midst. His disciple John sums it all up by declaring that God so loved the world that he sent Jesus so that in fact we may not perish. Truly, "God is love." How could such a biblically engaged Love-God allow the classic case of the torture of children and not do anything about it? If the Messiah and his kingdom had not come, would things be any different? Such is the ongoing tension between claim and reality, between atheists and believers and among believers themselves.

Exorcisms, healings and miracles

Then there are those exorcisms and healings. The scholars admit that there is no doubt that Jesus was noted for his exorcisms and healings. But so were many others. (As to those controversial stories about Jesus healing on the Sabbath, John Meier holds that they have little or no grounding in history.) The Bible in general, and the Gospels in particular, mention others who performed these same deeds, so they were not unique to Jesus. Jesus even used certain ritual actions known to have been used by both Greek and Jewish healers (cf. Mark 7:31-37). Besides, in those days, what we would call common ailments—for example, seizures or epilepsy—were thought of as demonic possession. We see this kind of transitional interpretation in Mark 1:31, where Jesus heals Peter's mother-in-law: "He came and took her by the hand and lifted her up. Then the fever left her." By the time we get to Luke, the incident reads, "Then he stood over her and rebuked the fever, and it left her." Notice here Jesus "rebukes" the evil force. The healing in Mark has been transformed into an exorcism in Luke. The fact is, as mentioned above, mental, physical, and psychosomatic diseases were often attributed to demonic possession, and Jesus would have seen himself called to do battle against them. It would be quite natural for him to see his mission in terms of exorcism. As one Catholic scholar observes, "An obvious corollary is that a twenty-first century Jesus would view the situation very differently; he would not be an exorcist."[3] That's a provocative thought.

A quick postscript on a famous exorcism, not only notes that the Jesus-sent demons into the swine near Gadara need not bring criticism of Jesus' indifference to the swineherds who saw their livelihood suddenly drown in a body of water, (of which, incidentally, there is none near that town, much less a body of water large enough to engulf 2,000 pigs.) But that the exorcism incident is not factual. It is parabolic.

As for miracles, belief in them has supposedly long been subverted by the rationalists of the Enlightenment, with people like Voltaire calling miracles "a violation of mathematical, divine, immutable, eternal laws," and David Hume called belief in miracles "a superstitious delusion." Lately, however, thanks to popular television shows like Oprah Winfrey and bestselling books, miracles are in, with some 42% of Americans, even those with no religious affiliation, believing in them. The premier miracle in the Gospel is the feeding of the thousands and all four Gospels relate it. Yet this incident has all the dynamics of the famous folktale "Stone Soup," wherein hungry soldiers con the local villagers into ferreting out their hidden root veggies and tossing them into the pot to enhance the cooking stones. So some commentators hold that Jesus, in like manner, simply got the crowd to share what they already had stowed away, and that was the real miracle, the moral miracle: people learned to share. This interpretation may be clever but it is a letdown for the average person to learn that there was no "real" miracle, no "new creation" of molecules and atoms to make new bread and fish, only a psychological miracle. It's not quite the same thing. Nevertheless, one biblical scholar reminds us:

> "A problem that some Christians have in reading Old Testament stories as bearers of religious truth is what they regard as a denial of the miraculous by the rationalism of the modern era. Because we do not think "miracles" happen, they do not happen. There are events that defy explanation in the lives of individuals and nations. When such events happen, we thank God for them, but we are always ready to accept a scientific explanation. Such an explanation ought not to diminish a believer's gratitude. The 'miraculous' are elements in biblical stories by which the storyteller underscores God's presence in Israel's life and God's activity on Israel's behalf. The story of a miracle, then, is not so much a report of what happened as much as it is an affirmation of faith and gratitude..."[4]

For some Jesus' miracles are important because they prove he was God. But that doesn't work because many other holy men and women were reputed to perform miracles. Tacitus and Suetonius, for example, recount the healing of two men by the emperor Vespasian around the year 70 C.E. He spread his saliva on the eyes of a blind man and cured him. Josephus tells of a certain Eleazar whom he himself witnessed expel a demon from a man. There are, in short, well-attested accounts of healers and miracle workers in the time of Jesus and none were considered proofs of divinity. Miracles, rather, had to do with power, or more precisely, the source of power behind the wonderful work. In Jesus' case, some defended his miracles as displaying "the power of God among us" and others defamed them as displaying the power of Satan because he did miracles on the Sabbath. Thus the miracles of Jesus had a meaning beyond the deed and were to be understood theologically and spiritually, not historically and factually. That is, his miracles, very much rooted in Old Testament imagery, connect Jesus to God's plan of salvation and validate his mission.

DIVINITY CLAIMS

The Catechism of the Catholic Church admits that, both in scripture and early Christian writings, the notion of the man Jesus as God has an extremely ambiguous history. "During the first centuries, the Church had to defend and clarify this truth of faith against the heresies that falsified it" (#464). The thing is that nowhere does any scripture writer indicate that Jesus explicitly claimed to be God. Moreover, in the Old Testament, the term "God" could only refer to YHWH, the God of Israel, and it was absolutely impossible for the Palestinian mind to accept the idea of a second god. Thus the Pauline epistle states, "For there is one God. There is also one mediator between God and the human race, Christ Jesus, *himself human...*" (1Tim 2:5-6). Indeed, Jesus is often presented as inferior to God. He is initially presented as completely human, but one specially chosen and gifted by God. The synoptic Gospels show a human Jesus as having heavenly powers, but also a human Jesus (in Mark) who affirms that God alone is to be called good and prays, "not my will but yours be done." When Jesus cried out, "My God, My God, why have you forsaken me?," he was clearly not talking to himself. "I can do nothing on my own authority," Jesus told his disciples. To Magdalene he said, "I am ascending to my Father and your Father, to my God and your God". At his Baptism, the Holy Spirit is said to enter Jesus, and in that sense he was possessed by God. Only later, after 80 C.E. is Jesus called God but in a very broad sense, as one who is a mediator of God's presence, an external manifestation of God or the image of God who personifies God's wisdom. Jesus is one who makes God's felt presence visible.

John's so very different Gospel flirts dangerously close to Docetism (Jesus was really God in a make-believe body) by giving us a genuine human Jesus but with an awesome superhuman consciousness. John 1:14 give us the famous verse, "And the Word became flesh and dwelt among us." According to James W. Kinn, this quote "means that the Word dwells in Jesus in the sense that the word of revelation becomes part of human existence in the person of the human Jesus... in John's Gospel Jesus, the Son of God, is presented as the unique, historical being who expresses God present in history, who has the authority and power to lead people to salvation, and in whom people see and hear God the Father."[5]

Not quite the same as saying Jesus is God. John offers sentences like, "I and the Father are one" (John 10:30) alongside "The Father is greater than I" (John 14:28). The 4th century Arian heresy appealed to this latter quote in rejecting the divinity of Jesus. Some Church Fathers countered, saying that it means that Jesus was simply recognizing that he proceeded from the Father, others that he was saying that he came in the form of a servant and therefore the Father was greater, others that he was expressing divine humility. No one's really happy with any of these explanations, and the interpretation remains unsettled. Then there's, "Believe in God, believe also in me," as though Jesus and God were somehow separate. Perhaps, too, "Father and I are one" meant that "we are in agreement," since Jesus claimed always to do the Father's will. Although notions of preexistence begin to surface, yet Jesus also continues to appear subordinate to the Father who actively raises him up and he sits at the Father's right hand. Jesus, in some traditions, is the Wisdom figure of the Old Testament and said to have a role in creation.

Still, there are those Gospel titles of "Son of God" and "Son of Man" (this latter we noted before), which ought to clinch it. Yet John Meier, in the *New Jerome Biblical Commentary*, reminds us that the title, the "Son of God" meant something different in Jesus' time from what it does in ours. It meant, as we shall see in the case of the centurion at Jesus' death, someone close to God, a righteous person, a good man. The great scholar Bernard Lonergan used to tell his students, "Just because Jesus or others spoke of him as Son of God, it doesn't mean he's made of the same 'stuff' as God. It could simply mean he's a child of God in the same way you and I are children of God." As for that "Son of Man" title, which (as we noted previously) no one calls Jesus except himself, scholars used to think it referred to Daniel's mysterious apocalyptic figure, because this person comes upon "the clouds of heaven", YHWH's usual mode of transportation. So, it was held, Jesus was stressing his divine nature when he used it. Today, more and more scholars think that is not so. Rather, Jesus' reference to the Son of Man matches the sense used by the prophet Ezekiel, who wrote, "Son of Man, what do you see?... Son of Man, say this to the people..." In this case, as we have already noted, the title simply means "human being" (as the New Revised Standard Version translates it). Which means that Jesus called himself the Son of Man in order to contradict some of the overloaded titles others were laying on him. The same dynamic is operating in Jesus' resistance to taking on the title of king. He never calls himself a king (that would be political suicide). Only his enemies do, at his trial, and whenever they do he strongly rejects it. (Therein lies the irony: the three Gospel passages Christians celebrate on the feast of Christ the King tell us not to celebrate it!) No divinity is necessarily implied in either New Testament title, "Son of God" or "Son of Man." Finally, although Jesus is called "Lord" early on, the word in Greek does not necessarily carry with it religious significance. It was merely a term of respect, akin to our word "Sir." It did not carry connotations of divinity.

As to clear proof of Jesus' divinity most people turn to Paul's famous words in Philippians 2:6-11, the early (maybe late 30s or early 40s) classic kenosis hymn (translation, *The New Oxford Annotated Bible*):

> Let the same mind be in you that was in Christ Jesus
> who, though he was in the form of God
> did not consider equality with God
> as something to be exploited,
> but he emptied himself
> taking the form of a slave
> being born in human likeness,
> he humbled himself
> even to the point of death on a cross
> and became obedient to the
> extremes of death.

Here, the footnote to 2:6 explains, "In the form of God, that is, preexistent and divine." The Jerusalem Bible went further and translated the verse, "who, in the form of God" as, "who, though he was divine." And that seems to clinch it: the Bible hymn affirms that Jesus was divine long before the 4th century Council of Nicaea, but in its new edition, the New Jerusalem Bible changed its translation from "though he was divine" back to "being in the form of God." What happened? The answer is a dispute over other legitimate interpretations. The phrase "being in the form of God" may also simply mean being made, like Adam and Eve, in God's image (Genesis 1:27). As to that grasping metaphor, Raymond Brown asks, was Christ *already* equal to God but did not grasp at it, or was he offered the possibility to become equal to God and did not grasp at it? In short, the whole text is quite ambiguous and cannot be used to prove the divinity of Jesus.

Some point to Romans 9:2-6 where Paul says he could even wish himself accused and separated from Christ for the sake of his own people. In one translation he goes on: "They are Israelites and to them belong the adoption, the glory...the promises...and from them, according to the flesh, comes the Messiah, *who is God over all...*" The New Oxford Annotated Bible, however, translates that passage this way: "*... comes the Messiah, who is over all. God blessed forever. Amen.*" It offers the footnote variant, "*Or Messiah who is God over all, blessed forever*" or: "*Messiah. May he who is God over all be blessed forever.*" The issue of alternate readings lies in the lack of punctuation in the ancient manuscripts. Bottom line: Romans 9:2-6 can't be used to prove the divinity of Christ.

The point is, that for some four hundred years after Jesus' death, Christianity was not entirely united about the divinity of Jesus, with Church Fathers on either side of the issue – for example, the influential Athanasius on the pro side and the great Origen on the con side. There's a lot more to be said, but we conclude by saying that the centuries-long evolution of Jesus from God-favored, the visible image of God and exalted man and mediator to ontological God reached its end in the 5th century Council of Chalcedon which affirmed 4th century Council of Nicaea's statement that Jesus is "True God from true God...of one substance with the Father, in two natures..." That is to say, Jesus is always fully human and fully divine. James Martin S.J. explains:

> "Jesus is not human during one event and divine in another, no matter how it might seem in any particular episode in his life. He is divine when he is sawing a plank of wood, and he is human when he is raising Lazarus from the dead. In our reading of various Gospel passages, we may feel we are seeing his humanity more in some, his divinity more in others. And in this book, some chapters highlight parts of Jesus' life that readers may associate with his human nature (for example, his work as a carpenter); others focus on events some may associate with his divine nature (his healing a paralyzed man). But even speaking in those terms is misleading, for Jesus is always human and divine, whether he is building or healing the sick. His two natures are inseparable, united in one person at all times."[6]

Or, as the *Catholic Catechism* puts it, "Everything that Christ is and does in this [human] nature derives from 'one of the Trinity.'" [#470]

We may puzzle over what was transpiring when the inseparably fully YHWH'd human Jesus was praying to the Divinity, YHWH. It's a deep mystery, and no attempt was made to explain how this paradox was possible. Impatient with mystery, some modern scholars take the position that Jesus was indeed specially approved of and exalted by God, who used by him for the purpose of salvation but any notion of Jesus' divinity as the Second Person of the Blessed Trinity is a "theological statement," a metaphorical way of expressing Jesus' indelible significance for the human race. This, of course, is heresy according to standard Christianity, but it shows how scholars deal differently with parabolic scripture that is always open to interpretation. None of this speculation detracts from the central and majestic doctrine of the Jesus' divinity, but it does suggest that perhaps we need replacements for the outmoded Greek concepts of nature, person, hypostatic, consubstantial and so on that no longer carry meaning for us. Anyway, as James Carroll astutely remarks, "A scientifically minded believer wants to discard that notion [of divinity], but before he does, he should remember that if Jesus were not regarded as somehow divine almost from the start of his movement, we would never have heard of him. And if faith in the divinity of Jesus is left behind because it fails the test of contemporary thought, Jesus will ultimately be forgotten."[7] To this, Luke Timothy Johnson astutely adds that all the scripture interpretations designed to extract the divinity of Jesus, all the wrangling over the Resurrection extrapolations about the empty tomb, and so on, really count for nothing. The divinity of Jesus rests not on the written word, but on the direct lived experience and witness of those first apostles and followers of Jesus. They came to realize that when they encountered Jesus, they encountered God. That's the bedrock "proof."

All this speculation also raises the issue of Jesus' self-consciousness. We know that this "the Father-and-I-are-one" Jesus nevertheless "increased in wisdom," at least according to Luke. Mark has Jesus say that not even he knows the hour of the last days. Jesus seems to change his mind in the healing incident of the Syrophoenician woman's daughter. In fact he appears to grow into his self-understanding, so much so that theologian Elizabeth Johnson suggests that he was surprised when his "ultimate identity burst upon him with all clarity" on Easter Sunday.[8] In dealing with divine matters, we must expect mystery.

Chapter 16.

THE LAST DAYS

An Introduction

Holy Week presents many challenges. There are as many timelines as there are commentators. For instance, was Jesus' cleansing of the Temple at the beginning of his ministry as John writes, or at the end of his ministry as the other Evangelists write? The latter certainly fits better at the end by escalating the tensions between Jesus and the authorities. Did Jesus make one or four journeys to Jerusalem? Did he make one or two visits to the Temple? Did he die at 9 a.m. on a Friday as Mark would indicate or at noon as John indicates? When, actually was the Last Supper? Did Jesus celebrate the Passover on Thursday or, more likely, according to some scholars, on Wednesday? Was it, in fact, a Passover meal or, as John Meir suggests, was it a Passover-*like* meal? Why did John, who was so eloquent about Jesus' discourse about being "the Bread that came down from heaven," his Body being food and his Blood being drink (Chapter 6), have no words of institution, words which would have dramatically and logically fleshed out his earlier account? Who added some 25 verses to John's already long Gospel discourse he put in the mouth of Jesus?

Why are what we call 'the words of institution' different in each Gospel account as well as St. Paul's account (1 Cor. 11:27-29)? Was the consecration of the cup during or after the supper? The Evangelists differ. What calendar was Jesus using? (There were several in his time.) We take note that Jesus' betrayal by his friend, Judas, took place in a garden, calling up the original fall in the Garden of Eden and his later Resurrection in a garden, not to mention the garden's significance as precisely the spot where King David was betrayed by *his* friend, Ahitophel. Ahitophel later hanged himself. Did he becomes the storyline for Judas? Did Jesus actually sweat blood or, as Luke says, "his sweat became *like* great drops of blood?" How do we square Jesus' admonition to Peter who sliced a servant's ear in the garden with the sword, with his admonition (Luke 22:36) when sending out his disciple on a mission, "The one who has no sword must sell his cloak and buy one." Who was Mark's lightly covered man who fled naked? Was he the same one who reappeared as Mark's "young man wrapped in a linen cloth" at the empty tomb? Or was he a neophyte, clad in his baptismal robe, who apostatized. Or was he a symbol that all human decency had been left behind? Were the conversations with Caiaphas, Herod, Pilate and Peter's tormentors "recorded" or "dramatized? Were there really seven distinct "last words on the cross" or words that reflected the theologies of the evangelists? Did Simon carry Jesus' cross or did he carry his own? Did Jesus die in distress as in Mark, or in dignity and in control, as in John?

All these issues in no way detract from the great and holy drama of Jesus' death. I cite them simply because they point out once more, as scholar Raymond Brown has reminded us, that, in dealing with the scriptures, we are always in the realm of theological symbolism, rather than historical description.

HOLY WEEK

Because the disciples of Jesus are portrayed as despondent over their leader's sudden and horrific public death, because their movement was at an apparent end, they fled (Luke 24:13-25). Jesus' tragedy was theirs and they wanted to put it all behind them. Certainly, they were not inclined to report their failed enterprise, much less chronicle it. Far from it. So, ask scholars, where did the Passion narratives come from? Some answer, from Jesus himself. The clue is in the Gospels. Their Easter accounts tell us that the Risen and wound-bearing Jesus appeared to his disciples in the Upper Room, showing them his hands and side. Later that day he appeared to the depressed disciples on the road to Emmaus and interpreted for them the Old Testament scriptures in reference to himself and how it was necessary for him to die. The first Jewish Jesus Movement communities told and retold this revelation of the Risen Christ, and that's how the Passion narratives got started. Whether these scholars' theory is correct or not, it is clear that, somehow, gradually, from these early communities' retellings and interpretations, from their seeking meaning in Jesus' suffering and death and triumph over death, the passion narrative took shape. The original Passion story that would have an influence on Mark, the first apostolic witness to record it, likely arose in various communities' liturgical celebrations, during their time of prayer and reflection and against the background of their interpretations of the Jewish scriptures. Over time these reflections became stereotyped in the four Gospel accounts that wound up climaxing the story of Jesus in all four.

Because the Passion narrative arose from various communities' reflections, it is not surprising that they present different emphases and do not always agree. Chronology differs between the Synoptics and John. Some well-known details, and even whole episodes, are found in only one of the four Gospels. While all four Gospels, for example, tell the story of an anonymous woman who anoints Jesus' feet during a meal, Mark and Matthew put the incident two days before Passover, in the house of Simon the leper in Bethany, while John places it six days before Passover, in the house of Martha, Mary and Lazarus, and gives the woman a name: Mary of Bethany. While Judas agrees to betray Jesus, only Matthew specifies that it was for 30 pieces of silver while Luke and John mention the influence of Satan (though John never says Judas met with the high priests). Only John has the washing of the feet and does not mention the agony in the garden, and only he names Peter as the one who cut off the high priest's slave's ear. Only Luke introduces Herod Antipas in the trial before Pilate. So it goes. Such are the by-now-expected adjustments we have come to know. But there are the other issues we must now look at.

THE LAST SUPPER AND THE PRIESTHOOD

Jesus, before his Passion and death, ate a Last Supper with his Twelve Apostles, during which he ordained them the first priests when he ordered them, "Do this in memory of me."

Concerning such an "ordination," here is the official statement found in the *Catechism of the Catholic Church* (1337), which reads:

> "The Lord, having loved those who were his own, loved them to the end. Knowing that the hour had come to leave the world and return to the Father, in the course of a meal, he washed their feet and gave them the commandment of love. In order to leave them a pledge of this love, in order never to depart from his own and to make them sharers in his Passover, he instituted the Eucharist as the memorial of his death and Resurrection and commanded his apostles to celebrate it until his return; thereby he constituted them priests of the New Testament."

This, of course, is a long-standing interpretation, but (no surprise) some scholars are asking is if this could be accurate, that Jesus established the priesthood at the Last Supper – this Jesus who himself was not a priest? One Catholic scripture scholar, Francis J. Maloney, says that, on the contrary, the only references to the term priest (*hiereus*) in the New Testament is that in Hebrews 9:6-22, a work which was, significantly, written after the destruction of Jerusalem and the Temple and even then it was used analogically comparing Jesus' perfect sacrifice of himself to the sacrifices of the Temple. This allusion to the Temple is significant because the Jews were suddenly deprived of their Temple, cultic sacrifice and priests. What to do? What the Jews did was to turn to the portable Torah as the focal point of their religion. The scriptures were now central and, as we have seen, this focus spawned a whole industry of interpreters. The Jewish Christians, on the other hand, took the occasion to point to Jesus as the fulfillment and perfection of all that had merely been a sign (namely, the cultic sacrifice and priesthood). That, they said, was the meaning of the reference in Hebrews 9. Christ was the mediator. He came "as high priest of the good things that have come." With such language it wasn't long before this attitude began to suggest the association of the Temple, sacrifice, and priesthood with the Christian Eucharistic gatherings. The notion of the Eucharist as a replacement of the Temple sacrifices, the link to Temple talk and vocabulary, were eventually brought to bear on the Christian gatherings where they broke bread at the Lord's Supper.

From the 2nd century on we see a development of these Eucharistic gatherings and, increasingly, note the sacrificial language beginning to attach to them. We also get a hint from the 2nd century document, called the *Didache*, that wandering charismatic prophets were called high priests, and this may suggest that they were designated individuals who presided over the celebration of the Eucharist (male? female? married? celibate?). St. Cyprian of the third century was a strong proponent of priestly terminology being attached to Church leaders. He is the first to apply the term priest to the bishop presiding at the Eucharist. Soon, the analogy between the sacrifice of the Temple and that of the Eucharist became stronger and with that development comes the concept of Christian priests. But this came later because nowhere in the New Testament is there any mention of a particular individual being a priest who presided over the Eucharist. It surely did not happen at the Last Supper in 33 C.E. As Mahoney writes:

> "Over the centuries, the Roman Catholic tradition has looked back to the New Testament accounts of the Last Supper as the moment when Jesus 'constitutes' the Twelve Apostles 'priests of the New Testament.' There is no literary or historical

evidence for this tradition...a historical link between the Last Supper and priestly ordination is unlikely...the earliest literature we have from the emerging Church provides no evidence of any individual who functioned as a 'priest,' a person set apart by God to preside over the cult of the Christian community, or to act as an intermediary between God and the believers."

We may also note that the offices of overseers, elders, and deacons (in modern terms, bishops, priests and deacons) do appear early in Christianity, but when these offices appear in the Christian community and clearly they "...are not associated with a cultic ministry. They are never associated with the celebration of the Eucharist, and are almost always described or instructed in a way that suggests they were the senior administrators of a single community ... [so] while there may have been some sense of hierarchy there does not appear to be any *hiereus* ('priest') in the early Church."[1]

As expected, some disagree with this thesis and would seek to make a case for apostolic priesthood by citing John's use of the word "consecrate" three times in chapter 17 of his Gospel, maintaining that it reflects the ancient ritual of ordination for the Levitical priests. Still it remains true that the Gospel writers, quite familiar with the concept of priesthood, never apply it to Jesus or the apostles. Whatever the case – and it will continue to be debated – the critique is one more challenge in the effort to come to terms with the biblical interpretation.

PASSION AND DEATH

Before the Last Supper, Jesus had made a triumphal entrance into Jerusalem. Even here, Matthew makes a minor gaffe. In 21:6-7 of his Gospel, he cites an Old Testament text, completely misunderstanding the use of Hebrew poetic parallelism. In the Gospel text, he cites the prophet Zechariah's words:

Look, your king is coming to you, humble and mounted
   on a donkey
and on a colt, the foal of a donkey" (9:9).

The second line, following Hebrew usage, merely repeats the thought of the first verse. There's only one animal. It's like us saying:

Through the red door the Chieftain came
Yes, through that stretched window he came

– meaning, simply that the Chieftain came through only one door and in using both lines to say the same thing, we simply express the event in an emphatic poetic way. There weren't two doors. But Matthew didn't grasp this, and so had Jesus riding in on two animals, "sitting on *them*" – quite a balancing act.

We also have a mistranslation used for Christian apologetics. The prophet Ezekiel, in the MT Hebrew text in 17:22-23 writes,

Thus says the Lord God:
I myself will take a sprig
From the lofty top of a cedar;
I will break off a tender one
From the topmost of its young twigs;
I myself will plant it
On a high and lofty mountain.
On the mountain height of Israel
I will plant it.

However, the Greek version (the Septuagint) translates the last sentence as, "and I will plant on a high mountain, and I will hang *him* (not it) on a mountain top of Israel." Eager Christians, reading this version, took this as a foreshadowing the Crucified Jesus. One can see an early instance of this in Luke's Acts of the Apostles, where he writes, "they put him to death by hanging him on a tree" (10:39).

At Jesus' death, Mark (writing some forty years later) has the Roman centurion exclaim, "Truly this man was the Son of God!" (15:39). But once more the Greek does not say that. It says, "Truly this man was *a* son of God" (lower case), which simply means that the centurion had seen many men die, but this one was extraordinary, a veritable god-like figure in his endurance. It was a common expression. Yet one thinks of the commentaries on how a gentile recognized Jesus' divinity – with the implication that his own people did not ("he come to his own and his own received him not" (John 1:11) – and how remarkable was his act of faith. No such faith was given or intended, only admiration. That's why in Luke, ever sensitive to placating the Romans, as we have seen, we get very different words in the mouth of the centurion: "The centurion who witnessed what had happened glorified God and said, 'This man was innocent beyond doubt'" (23:47). That centurion was only confirming, in Luke's scheme of things, what Pilate and Herod had declared much as, later on, Luke would have the Roman officials who encounter the apostles come to the same conclusions (Acts 16:35; 18-15; 23:29; 25:18-19).

JESUS DIED FOR OUR SINS AND SAVES US

"Jesus suffered and died for our sins." This basic and ubiquitous affirmation of Christianity appalled devout Unitarian, John Adams: "An eternal, self-existent omnipresent omniscient Author of this stupendous universe suffering on a cross!!! My soul starts with horror at the idea." He wasn't the only one perplexed at the idea of atonement. After all these centuries, while many fervently believe in the atonement, no one knows for sure how it "works." One theory after another has come under scrutiny and been found wanting. C.S. Lewis struggled with it and finally came to consider the dying and rising of Jesus as "a true myth". He wrote:

> "We are told that Christ was killed for us, that His death has
>   washed out our sins, and that by dying He disabled death

itself. That is the formula. That is Christianity. That is what has to be believed. Any theories we build up as to how Christ' death did this are, in my view, quite secondary: mere plans or diagrams to be left alone if they do not help us, and even if they do help us, not to be confused with the thing itself."[2]

So Lewis emphasizes the *what* but not the how and the why. People want to know. Even *TIME Magazine* presented a cover article asking, "Why Did Jesus Have to Die?" (April 12, 2004). The New Testament writers gave various explanations to help their communities understand what Jesus' criminal death meant. Was Jesus' individual death a sacrifice for us, a "sacrifice of atonement' as Paul wrote (Romans 3:24)? Was Jesus the biblical scapegoat onto whom the sins of the people were transferred? Was he "a ransom for many" as St. Mark has Jesus say (10:45) – but a ransom paid to whom – the devil? (Gregory of Nyssa, among others) God? Is God really a cosmic pawn broker demanding his blood money, a Shylock demanding blood? (Some call this "divine child abuse.") Certainly everything we have seen about the character of YHWH would support this view. Was our guilt really transferred to Jesus? If so, what about moral responsibility? Is violence redemptive? St. Paul does teach that we are all under the wrath of God (Romans 3), and that Jesus' blood shedding turns it away: "Since we have been justified by his blood, how much more shall we be saved from God's wrath through him" (cf 1 Thess 1:10). Is the "substitutionary atonement" theory right, namely, that our sins leave us owning God a debt we cannot pay but Christ came along and suffered and died for our sins, doing on our behalf what we cannot do? Is St. Anselm right who said that the dignity of the Offended must be matched by the dignity of the Apologist, and so the Son was the only sufficient candidate to appease the Father? Was Jesus' death the result of his steadfast fidelity to the principles of his Father, or was his love so cosmic and deep that it canceled all the world's cumulative hate? Are we talking retributive justice or restorative justice? Did Jesus, going meekly and silently to his Passion and death, become an inadvertent model of passivity before injustice? Did the Father really send him to die like the son in one of Jesus' parables whom the Master sent into his vineyard hoping that the vineyard workers who had manhandled his servants would respect his son? Is Jesus Luke's forgiving victim (23:34)?

Whatever the questions, there is no doubt that there is a strong Christian sense that God is deeply involved here, that he is the ultimate reason why Jesus had to die on the cross. ("Not my will but thine be done.") His death was according to God's plan. Yes, Jesus was sent into the world to die for our sins. This is the doctrine of sub-stitutionary atonement, but modern folk are impatient with notion that Jesus' death was something demanded by God.

William O'Malley, S.J. is one of them:

> "Note well: I do not deny the centuries-old teaching on atonement. I just no longer pretend I understand it. Not even a fool could deny the effects of original sin. But I balk at the economic metaphor – an almost irreparable debt to explain what caused human inconstancy. If the degradation God endured for us has not been deadened by repetition, I wonder if we could find a depth beyond atonement. In his forthright confrontation with evil and suffering, Christ did indeed free us from fear that our sins might defy forgiveness, fear that our sufferings have no meaning, fear that only a few loved ones really care."[3]

Expanding on this theme, Catholic scripture scholar Roger Vermalen Karban says that Jesus' words about his coming not to be served but to serve "and give his life as a ransom for many" has nothing to do with vicarious suffering, but everything to do with being a paradigm. That is to say, he was totally a "man for others," and would not com-promise that stance. His suffering and death were potent signs that he would not back down, not compromise his message, no matter what the pressures. His disciples, buoyed by that extreme example, would thereby be compelled to live the same way. In this way, Jesus "ransomed" them from the spiritual ennui of the unexamined life. In this sense, he died for these "many," for these people and all future people who would accept his teaching. He didn't die for all, as the former Catholic Mass told it, but for "many," as the current Mass text says, the "many" being his contemporaries, whatever their number (about two dozen, according to Fr. Jerome Murphy-O'Connor), and those who, through the ages, were inspired by a message that was so dramatically backed up by the ultimate sacrifice of giving one's life. Karban explains it this way:

> "The historical Jesus died because it was the only way he could be faithful to that small handful of women and men who actually dared follow him. If he ran away or 'turned state's evidence,' he wouldn't have kept faith with those who had committed themselves to his dream of surfacing God's kingdom among them.

> "Those two dozen soon multiplied. And each new disciple – even those who never came into contact with the historical Jesus – eventually began to understand he also died for her or him..."[4]

It would seem in this view that the axiom "Jesus died for our sins" is basically didactic and invitational. Who wouldn't follow someone who so believed in his message that he dare not compromise it, even the point of death, "death on a cross"? Who would refuse to be rescued from a life lived solely for oneself? Many, of course, did refuse, but for those who accepted, they knew they were "ransomed" from spiritual death, saved by what Christ did on Calvary. Meanwhile other theologians are also working on the issue of atonement from radically different perspectives (for example, the work of James Alison). The truth of Jesus' atonement definitely remains, but so do the questions and the search for better answers.

OTHER TENSIONS

Then we have to deal with the tension that if Jesus saves us from our sins, as Gabriel told Mary (Matt 1:21), we also have in scripture the mention of salvation quite apart from faith in Jesus. In Matthew 25, that famous judgment scene where Jesus lays out the criterion for salvation – when did we give you to drink when you were thirsty, give you food when you were hungry, or visit you when you were in in prison – the response is that if you didn't do these things, these good works, to the least of my brethren you did not do them to me and *therefore* you are doomed. If you did, *therefore* you are saved. Good works are the sole criterion. Luke's Good Samaritan Gospel has Jesus tell the man who has listed his good deeds, "Do this and you shall live" (10:28). The Epistle of James, recall, pointedly states (as against Paul) that faith without works is dead. The Book of Revelation also passes judgment according to people's works. All this is thorough-going traditional Judaism and it makes one wonder what Jesus is needed for in the matter of salvation. And as for undoing Adam's ("original") sin, we have already seen in the chapter on Genesis that a first-parent-transmitted fault is evolutionarily problematic.

Yet, slowly but early on, the notion that salvation could come only through Jesus developed as his death began to be seen as having cosmic, salvific significance. It was vicarious. It happened "for us," and the Old Testament was mined to come up with an atoning death of the Messiah on behalf of the people. Yes, he died for us, for our sins, in the same way that a martyr gave his/her life that others might live. Paul speaks for that view: "If you confess with your lips that Jesus is Lord and believe in your hearts that God raised him from the dead, you will be saved" (Rom. 10:9). Yet the fact is that God's grace was available long, long before Jesus came. Not to mention that common sense question to the Adam and Eve case: why didn't God just forgive them on the spot? Since God did not cease to be merciful, for what purpose was Jesus needed in the matter of salvation? One scholar summarizes these conundrums:

> "What is the relationship between human effort and divine grace? What is the real significance of Jesus? Apart from Paul's more polemical statements, the all-but unanimous answer to the first question is that God's mercy and grace are

the indisputable basis for salvation, but without the consent and cooperation of humans this grace remains ineffective. What Rosemary Ruether wrote about 'ordinary Christianity' in general applies fully to early Christianity: it 'assumes the view that we are already loved by God, and yet must also do something to become what we are supposed to be... In practice, Christianity constantly tends to boil down to a religion of grace and good deeds structurally identical to Judaism.' But then the question arises, for such an ethic, does one need a Messiah? It would seem that creation, Covenant, and commandments would suffice."[5]

"Jesus died for our sins" is a powerful Christian truth but explaining it is challenging. The people who wrote the New Testament firmly believed that Jesus was uniquely the one who reconciled human beings with God. With that conviction in mind they interpreted the Old Testament in their own special way to come up with the notion of vicarious suffering and atonement. They put a whole new spin on concept of the Messiah and the "necessity" of a suffering Messiah who would die and rise "on the third day" and, true to story's intent, that was sufficient for them.

THE RESURRECTION OF THE MESSIAH

We recall that St. Paul, our earliest witness, wrote:

> "For I handed on to you as of first importance what I in turn had received: that Christ died for our sins in accordance with the scriptures, and that he was buried, and that he was raised on the third day in accordance with the scriptures... and that he appeared to Cephas, then to the Twelve. Then he appeared to more than five hundred brothers and sisters...then he appeared to James, then to all the apostles" (1 Cor 15:3-7).

What strikes one as astonishing is that there is no extant accounts of such foundational experiences, not even those of Peter and

James, undisputed leaders. It's hard to imagine how such pivotal occurrences, how the experiences of such primary and powerful witnesses like Peter and James, could be left out of the community's first recorded (even constructed) stories. But, more than that, we note that Paul, although he twice mentions "in accordance with the scriptures", does not cite any particular passages probably because, as scripture scholar Gerald O' Collins reminds us, there's not much to be found in the Old Testament. Only the late books of Daniel and Wisdom offer suggestions, and these had to be interpreted to come up with the notion of Resurrection.

Paul's account is very early, and doesn't match the stories in the Gospels. It seems the two accounts eventually got melded into one. In any case, it is strange that, unlike so many other instances in the canonical Gospels (and in Paul also for that matter), there is singularly lacking any Old Testament quotes or references in the Gospel Resurrection narratives. This seems to indicate a very old oral tradition. Then, as mentioned above, if there are no Peter, Paul, and James accounts of the appearances of the Risen Jesus – powerful and credible witnesses because of their privileged positions – it is remarkable that the witnesses whom the evangelists *did* cite were by their nature not powerful or credible but quite invalid, namely women. This suggests that the Resurrection story must have been true, for no first century male would have mentioned them otherwise. Finally, as N.T. Wright points out[6], the Risen Jesus is no overpowering shining presence, just Jesus with a recognizable human body – transformed but quite human.

It is commonplace to note that the evangelists, writing much later after the event, interpret and pass on traditions they had inherited and, as the late Walter Wink wrote, "Although no two Resurrection accounts in the four Gospels are alike, all seem to be late additions to the tradition."[7] Indeed, they do differ: was it one young man who greeted the women (Mark 16:5) or two men (Luke 24:4); or was it an angel? One angel in Matthew (28:2), two in John (20:12)? When Jesus dies the Temple curtain is torn and the Roman centurion identifies Jesus as the Son of God or, as we have seen, *a* son of God. Three women come to Jesus' tomb, and they find the stone rolled back and the tomb occupied by a young man in festive garb. He tells them not to be alarmed, that Jesus has been raised, and points to the empty tomb and the women are ordered to tell the apostles that Jesus will rendezvous with them in Galilee. Since they were too afraid to say anything, they departed, and here Mark's account breaks off in mid-sentence. As a result other future editors of Mark had to finish the story with a series of alternative endings that they modified from the other evangelists whose accounts they apparently knew. The only trouble is that their efforts raise more questions than they resolve. Regardless, the Church recognized the interpolated words as also inspired.

Matthew includes the story of the women and the empty tomb and adds some post-Resurrection appearances of Jesus. Although, true to his style, Matthew more elaborately turns, for example, the young man at the tomb into an angel who descends from heaven during an earthquake and whose clothing is as white as snow – a kind of Mt. Sinai theophany. Recall that Matthew has the earthquake at Jesus' death and a bunch of mini Resurrections as graves are opened. The women also receive a command to tell the others ("brothers," in this case in contrast to Mark's "disciples"), but before they can start out to do so, they encounter Jesus himself. Then follows the great commission from the Jewish rabbi who declared that he was sent only to Israel to evangelize the whole world.

In his Gospel account, Luke has the women find two men "in dazzling clothes" instead of Mark's single young man or Matthew's angel. Luke finds a hint of the Resurrection in the psalmist's cry to God, "You will not abandon my soul to the netherworld, nor will you suffer to your holy one to see corruption (Acts 2:27). Luke has the women find two men "in dazzling clothes" instead of Mark's single young man or Matthew's angel. Luke, remember, also gives us the famed story (parable) of the encounter of two disciples and Jesus on the road to Emmaus. There, the Risen but hidden LORD opens up scripture to them and utters those words we have seen before in connection with Isaiah: "Did not the Messiah have to suffer and so enter into his glory?" and, as we saw, creatively redefines the exalted title of Messiah as the Suffering Servant. To recall our remarks on Isaiah in Chapter 9, we observe again that the notion of a suffering Messiah was triggered by the unassailable fact that Jesus of Nazareth, believed by his followers to be the Messiah, died a shameful criminal death. His early followers had to come up with reasons why. Old Testament resonances of a "fuller sense" were not long in coming: Jesus was in the line of the rejected prophet like, say, Jeremiah. He was the innocent sufferer. Like Isaac, he was destined to die in accordance with the Father's will. His death was a sign of his total obedience. He bore the sins of all and paid for them. And so on. Out of all of this speculation emerged the notion of a suffering Messiah. The term "Christ" or Messiah soon got transformed from its traditional images of royal power and privilege to weakness and death, just as the title "Son of Man" also moved from the notion of exultation and glory to suffering and death. "The Son of Man must undergo great suffering" (Mark 8:31).

> "Luke in particular promotes this development of a Christian doctrine of the Messiah. It is precisely in his capacity of "Christ" that Jesus has suffered. 'The Christ must suffer' the Risen Jesus instructs his followers, going through whole scripture from Moses to all the prophets to prove his case (Luke 24:26-27). Luke wisely refrains from specifying the alleged predictions. He simply assumes that so central a fact must have been announced by the holy writers; the suffering of the Messiah emerges (ex post facto, of course) as a necessity imposed by the divine order of salvation history. This claim that the 'Messiah must suffer' (as prophesied) seems to be a Lukan innovation."[8]

We may also note that Luke, in his Gospel sequel, the Acts of the Apostles, when most of the original witnesses are dead, finds a hint of the Resurrection in the Psalmist's cry to God, "You will not abandon my soul to the netherworld, nor will you suffer your holy one to see corruption" (Acts 2:27 quoting Psalm 16:10). Then he adds for good measure, "You have made known to me the paths of life (Acts 2:28, Psalm 16:11). Clearly, in lieu of definitive literal texts, Luke is creatively interpreting these Old Testament references as predictions of Jesus' Resurrection.

The notion of a suffering Messiah – nowhere, recall, found in the Old Testament – was a concept that befuddled Luke's sophisticated Greek believers (after all, God was impassible and immortal) and puzzled his Jewish ones (where is that in scripture?). At that Emmaus supper, by the way, the disciples recognize Jesus in the breaking of the bread – the same sequence of taking, blessing and giving thanks that is found in all three evangelists' accounts of the Last Supper – and Jesus disappears. Luke has done his job, which is to reassure his community that Jesus walks with them still and indeed can be known in the breaking of the bread.

In modern times, those uncomfortable with the traditional doctrine of the Resurrection, even some Catholic writers, resort to psychological interpretations:

> "Whatever happened after the crucifixion, his followers came to know with an assurance called faith that Jesus was still with them. In some mysterious way he had risen – risen in their hearts, risen in their lives, and was now closer to them than their heartbeat, nearer than their breath. He lived in them. As they shared their new experiences of him with one another, their conviction of his continuing presence grew. Private spiritually burst forth in shared Easter faith. Yes, they had all seen him. He had risen as he said. They were sure of it."[9]

But faith, of course, insists on going further than a psychological explanation. Faith says that the Risen Christ *is* the Jesus of history. Even though some doubted on seeing him (Matthew 28:17), and the Emmaus disciples' eyes "were kept from recognizing him" (Luke 24:13) and the other disciples were "startled and terrified and thought they were seeing a ghost" (Luke 36:37), and Mary Magdalene at first "did not know it was Jesus when she first saw him (John 20:14) and his disciples "did not know it was Jesus on the beach" (John 21:4) – those who knew him during his earthly life ultimately recognized him and made the connection for the simple reason that they had known him before, heard him before, saw him before. And this faith is buoyed by realization that in a society where Crucifixion was a most shameful way to die, reserved for the lowest of the lowest criminals, scoundrels, and those guilty of treason, who in his right mind would concoct a story about embracing a man crucified and risen, betrayed and abandoned by his own disciples, with disqualified women being the chief witnesses, unless it were true? Whatever happened, our earliest witness, Paul, could declare that "If Christ has not been raised" then his whole evangelization effort had been in vain as well as the people's faith. (1 Cor. 15:14) Whatever limits we have, however, the metaphors played out. Those witnesses believed the presence of a Risen Jesus was real enough to die for.

PAGAN RESONANCES

Christian themes of death and Resurrection were not novel. For example, by 3000 B.C.E. Egypt had developed a theological understanding of reality orientated around a dying and rising sun. Further, Luke Timothy Johnson's learnedly informs us that after-death stories were not unknown in Hellenistic culture whose understanding of the world made the passage between the human and the divine more accessible and common. Stories of heroes becoming immortal or ascending to the heavens were common. Even the Torah contained accounts of heaven bound heroes like Enoch (Gen 5:24) and Elijah (2 Kings 2:9-12), with the understanding they were available for future revelations and visitations.[10]

Indeed, the notion of risen heroes was not the only concept present in the Mystery religions and the Roman culture that found its way into Christianity. First century Rome had many immigrants and visitors who brought with them exotic religions, religions replete with signs, omens, ghosts and divinations. Those mysteries:

> "...included sacramental or symbolic actions: sacred meals; weddings; fertility and birth rites; baptisms; investitures with sacred garments; rites of death and Resurrection in the form of symbolic journeys. Roman rites and mysteries were presided over by priests and mystagogues.

> "Christian rituals gradually incorporated cultural elements into them reinterpreting them for Christian usage. Rites of anointing entered the Roman Liturgy as the practice had been long established within the Greco-Roman culture. Footwashing of the newly baptized along with the kissing of the feet was another practice that came from non-Christian traditions of the day but was gradually incorporated into the Rites of Initiation. Acts of renunciation and acclamation were also graphically portrayed in the Baptismal rites and clearly related to similar symbolic gestures in ancient Roman religions... Baptism was called 'Enlightenment'. But that same term was used simultaneously in the mystery cults of Isis and Mithra. Indeed, as we study the initiation process within Roman Christianity and the mystery religions, we find a common vocabulary: washing; initiation; illumination... the water bath by immersion, the putting on of the white garment; the meal of initiation; the post-baptismal period of mystagogy...

> "Other liturgical elements were borrowed from Roman practice. Kissing the altar and sacred images...prostrations, processions and the use of incense and candles. Likewise, the vesting of Roman clergy exhibits the same cultural borrowings as distinguishing clothing of Roman state officials was borrowed and reinterpreted."[11]

Like ancient Israel in its long history, Christianity also absorbed and explicated its mysteries within the metaphors of the local culture. Sometimes what was revealed and what was borrowed is hard to distinguish.

A REFLECTION

As we close this section on Jesus, it is evident that for many, who and what Jesus was seems to depend on which books they read. After two millennia, there is still no consensus about Jesus, and it is confusing. Indeed each year more books keep appearing, pushing back and forth on the issue.[12] For the minimalist authors, the Gospel stories of Jesus are recycled Old Testament or common mythological tales. The miracles of Jesus are from the Elijah –Elisha cycle. The teaching Jesus is Moses redux. The Passion of Jesus is appropriated Isaiah and Jeremiah and Psalm 22. The betrayal of Jesus by an intimate in the Garden of Olives, for example, reflects David's betrayal by an intimate in that same garden (2 Samuel 15:30-31). Jesus takes his place among other celebrated rabbinic wonder-workers. And so it goes. The story of Jesus of the New Testament – his life, events, parables, and miracles – simply rewrites the Old Testament paradigms and their commentaries. Paul, it is maintained, is the chief architect of the "Jesus Myth," the Cosmic Christ. He made up the whole passion-atonement-glorification mystery. He, along with the evangelist John, created the Christ of faith and transitioned the Jesus Movement to the Gentile world. There's a straight line, it is argued, from Paul to the Council of Nicaea.

Others disagree. These people range from evangelical literalists to the historical-critical scholars. They see Paul's metaphor-heavy writings not as inventing but as reflecting the life of a real historical person, Jesus, the one who was indeed a charismatic interpreter of YHWH's will. Again, Paul's epistles were written some fifteen to twenty years after the crucifixion. As a popular author puts it:

> "They [Paul's epistles] don't have the whole elaborated theological vocabulary for describing him that came later – partly because they themselves are helping invent that vocabulary... but they, the letters, do have an absolutely definite set of convictions about him that are casting around for adequate words to express. That Jesus's actions in the world were

God's own actions in the world; that where Jesus was present, God was directly present too; that his death and return from death were an initiative by God to take from humanity the weight of guilt and shame and disgust, and to show us a life larger than law. This cluster of propositions is Christianity's first layer of organized words and understandings. It, not the biographies, is the foundation. Which mean that the strange God/man mixture is there *in* the foundation. It may not be true, it may still be a piece of the after-the event fabrication or misunderstanding, but it is not an addition to the story. It is, itself, the thing the story is struggling to report."[13]

Scholars also caution us about how much we are influenced by Paul's writings, both his own and those of his forgers, and the Acts of the Apostles, giving the impression that Paul was the only Christian missionary and source of the early Church. We underestimate the countless and nameless missionaries who brought the story of Jesus to the Near East and the West. We pay little attention to the very venerable and ancient Christian communities of Syria, Egypt, Africa and elsewhere. These communities' witnesses to Jesus, their preaching, teaching and liturgies, as well as many apocryphal writings, reveal a wide variety of beliefs and practices about Jesus, who he was and what he meant for them. They were important conduits to early Church traditions about Jesus. In short, the road to Nicaea is not a monolithic path emanating solely from Paul (and John), but a rich tributary of many ancient streams that nourished the understanding and concept of Jesus as orthodox Christianity understands him to this day.

Chapter 17.

SIR, WE WISH TO SEE MARY

C entral to Jesus' birth is Mary, the "Woman Wrapped in Silence." We begin with the Annunciation scene in Matthew's Gospel:

"Now this is how the birth of Jesus Christ came about. When his mother Mary was betrothed to Joseph, but before they lived to-gether, she was found with child through the Holy Spirit, Joseph... decided to divorce her quietly. Such was his intention when, behold, the angel of the Lord appeared to him in a dream and said, Joseph, son of David, do not be afraid to take Mary your wife into your home. For it is through the Holy Spirit that this child has been conceived in her...." (1:18-23).

As written in our Bible, the word Spirit is capitalized (and sometimes the adjective "holy," as well) and the article before the Spirit is the definite one. The capitalization is a subtle faith statement (as is the adjective "Holy" attached to the word Bible). In the original Greek, the article is indefinite. "... it is through *a* holy spirit (lower case) that this child has been conceived in her." Observe the explanation that follows:

> "Realizing how shocking this story [of Mary's pregnancy] might be to his readers, Matthew inserts a reassuring comment to the report. Mary was pregnant through a holy spirit (the Greek lacks a definite article here and in v. 20). Our ancestors in the

faith did not have a concept of personal causality. Hebrew has no expression like 'it rained.' Rather, God sent the rain. Some person is always responsible. If no human person can be identified, then it must be an other-than-human person, namely a spirit. In this instance, Matthew tells the readers it was a holy (rather than a capricious or malicious) spirit."[1]

So the Greek text does not say that Mary was pregnant by the Holy Spirit, the Third Person of the Holy Trinity – a concept that the first century Matthew could hardly conceive of – but merely that her pregnancy can only be explained, lacking any human agent, by a benevolent spirit, or, at best, by God's creative power present and active in all creation. That *The Catechism of the Catholic Church* (#484), in particular, and Christianity in general, hold to the use of capital letters is, like the word "virgin" for "maiden", an interpretation.

We also observe here that it was not unusual in the ancient world for notables to have dual paternity, a human and divine parent. Miraculous births in the Bible included Hanna, Samuel's mother, and, of course, Abraham's wife, Sarah, who conceived Isaac at the age of 90. In Jewish tradition, Sarah is described by Philo of Alexandria as a virgin at the time she conceived. In the extra-biblical world, miraculous conceptions included the pharaohs, Alexander, Augustus, and others. If one checks out images of Isis on the internet, one will find a Madonna and Child statue that seems identical to the typical images of Mary we know. That would be the Egyptian goddess Isis, who was known as the Divine Mother or Queen of Heaven. As a virgin, she gave birth to Horus, the sun god. Horus killed Seth, the Egyptian version of the devil, and it was claimed that Isis remained a virgin forever. Then there's the Persian birth story of the first Zarathustra. His virgin mother walks into the waters of a sacred lake, and when the water reaches the level of her abdomen, she is impregnated by a holy spirit and later gives birth as a virgin. Stories of the Greek gods as having human mothers and divine fathers were commonplace. All this means is that the Virgin Mary of Christianity has literary antecedents and counterparts beyond the Bible. It also means that, if one is seeking to establish the credentials of Jesus as someone above the normal and even as divine, the infancy narratives of a virgin birth, with Mary as the human and the Holy Spirit as the divine cause, would be the perfect symbol at hand. Both statements demonstrate, as we have amply seen, that there existed creative links between the culture of the day and the religion of the early Church. Both imply that Mary's virginity is more metaphorical than literal. Both evoke the notion that interpretation of an interpretation is at work.

MARY'S PERPETUAL VIRGINITY

Concerning Mary's perpetual virginity, the first evangelist, Mark, knows nothing about it. Nor does John, the last evangelist. Nor does Paul. In fact, Mark ("Then his mother and his brothers came... 3:31) and Luke ("All these devoted themselves...to prayer, together with...Mary, the mother of Jesus and his brothers" Acts 1:14) speak several times about Jesus' brothers and sisters. (Still, we must take into account that in Jesus' time, the close communal living styles of conclaves of related clans, members were often referred to as brother and sister.) As we saw in chapter 8, the great prophecy of Isaiah about "a virgin shall bear a son" was in the Hebrew text, "a young woman [married or unmarried] shall bear a son," the son being King Ahaz's anticipated child or Isaiah's son. The Greeks, however, translated "young woman" as "virgin" and that's what Matthew quoted and what St. Jerome passed on in his translation, "Behold a virgin shall conceive and bear a son (Matt.1:18-25). Matthew chose to cite the Septuagint version rather than the Hebrew version because he had a point to make, namely, that the virgin birth of Jesus had a legitimization in the biblical prophetic tradition. But it's not so simple:

> "One of the problems in Matthew's narrative is the use of
> Is. 7:14 as a prophecy of the virginal conception. Modern

opinion tends to the view that Matthew saw the true meaning of the prophecy *only in the light of its fulfillment.* The rabbinic interpretation of the prophecy in the era immediately before Christ gives no evidence that a virginal conception of the Messiah was expected, even though the Septuagint had rendered the Hebrew [word maiden] by the technical word in Greek for virgin. Recent exegesis of the strictly literal sense of the text and comparison with Ugaric writing tend to *confirm this view.* It is also confirmed by the fact that much of the early Jewish opposition to Christianity centered on the Virgin Birth. When Matthew sees here the fulfillment of the prophecy, this might possibly be explained on the basis of the *somewhat loose rabbinic usage of the term fulfillment;* but the insistence of the patristic tradition from Justin onward, in seeing the fulfillment of the prophecy in the birth of Christ, seems to *oblige* the Catholic exegete to see, *as the ultimate meaning of the text intended by God,* the mother of the Messiah and the virginal conception of her Son."[2] (My emphasis).

That says it all. Recall that the original Hebrew text in Isaiah speaks of a maiden giving birth, a word that might also mean virgin, but Matthew uses the narrow Greek translation, which opted for the term "virgin" and consequently "opted for a somewhat loose usage of fulfillment." That usage legitimizes the conclusion that all along, this was *really* the "ultimate meaning" intended by God Himself (as if we knew). A footnote in the *New American Bible* reminds us that Isaiah himself need not have known the full force of and complete fulfillment of his words. It is worth adding that those early Jewish Christians known in history as the Ebionites were rejected by other Christians precisely because, unlike their Gentile, Greek-speaking Christian counterparts, they knew that the growing belief in Mary's virginity was based on a misreading of Isaiah.

Where then did the notion, not only of Mary's virginity but her *perpetual* virginity, come from? Likely from the apocryphal Gospel of Peter, where there is a very elaborate and colorful story of Mary's pregnancy and the miraculous birth of Jesus, who just passed through the womb leaving it intact. Mary was a virgin before, during and after the birth of Jesus. Also, in a consistent reading of scripture that baffles the modern mind, ancient commentators turned to Ezekiel 44:2 which talks about the shutting of a gate which only the Lord could enter. "Obviously" this refers to Mary's perpetual virginity. So, with the translation of Matthew's "young women" to "virgin," the popularity of the apocryphal Gospels, and pious commentary, Mary's perpetual virginity slipped into "tradition" and then solidified into doctrine. As part of the overall imaginative or Midrashic character of the infancy narratives (which we saw), Mary's virginity may serve more as a theological statement than an objective fact. That may be startling to some, but recently one of Catholicism's most prestigious scripture scholars, John Meier, openly said so, calling Mary's virginity precisely that: "a theological concept." That is to say, Mary's virginity, like the whole infancy narrative, is a metaphor. It has one point in mind: This is all God's doing. God has kept his promises of deliverance. God remains ever the central Actor. The point is never Herod or the Magi or Mary. The point (which is continuously subverted by our sentimentality and the impulse to make doctrines out of metaphors) is always God. Luke's song put into Mary's mouth is right on target: "He who is mighty has done great things for me and holy is *his* name."

Some modern scholars, especially feminist ones, also have ideological problems with Mary's perpetual virginity. Does it, they ask, reflect a negative theology of sex? Does it denigrate sexual love, making Mary remote from the travails and joys of ordinary childbearing? Can Mary be a Woman for All Seasons and our Mother ever tender and close, and yet not identify with the average woman in this most elemental reality? Would a God who "became like us in all things except sin" exempt his mother from this primal experience? In short, some hold, depriving Mary of all sexual and sensual realities takes something away from the mystery of the incarnation. In Elizabeth Johnson's words, Mary's perpetual virginity should rather be seen a metaphor for her readiness to face whatever is asked of her. Further, we might add that there is a slight irony in the concept of Mary's perpetual virginity. Matthew and Luke, in their fictional genealogies of Jesus, press hard to make Jesus a descendant of David, and therefore of the Messianic line by having him born in Bethlehem. However, by having Joseph only the putative father of Jesus, the evangelists instantly disconnected Jesus from the Davidic line. That is why Matthew hastened to add that, prompted by the angel, Joseph adopts Jesus as his legal son, and that ploy restores Jesus to David's family.

A parenthetical gloss on this paragraph also has some wondering that the God who indeed would "become like us in all things except sin," the God who proclaimed that "It is not good that the man should be alone; I will make him a helper and a partner" (Genesis 2:18) and elicited the biblical editor's commentary that therefore "a man leaves his father and mother and clings to his wife, and they become one flesh" (2:24) – why would that same creative God become incarnate by entering into the fullness of our human condition as a minority celibate and forgo the two-in-one-flesh that is the norm? A footnote on Genesis 2:18 in the New Oxford Annotated Bible says, "To be fully human one needs to be in relation to others who corresponds to oneself." True, this does not exclude celibate friendship, but as a footnote to Genesis 2:18 it clearly has marriage in mind.

Speaking of family

Jesus actually had a large extended family that we tend to overlook. Luke, in his Gospel, speaks of John the Baptist as a cousin of Jesus. But Mark, the first Gospel writer, speaks of many siblings. "His mother and his brothers arrived and, as they stood outside, they sent word to him to come out" (3:31). Later, Mark tells us that their names are James and Jude, Simon and Joses. Sisters are also mentioned. They were concerned about Jesus' eccentric behavior and at one point, Mark writes, "His family came after him when he was in Capernaum and suggested that he be locked up" (3:21). (Matthew, who copied so much from Mark, omits this embarrassing episode in his Gospel.) There also appears to be some tension between Jesus' brothers and his disciples: "But when the Jewish feast of Tabernacles was near, Jesus' brothers said to him, 'You ought to leave here and go to Judea, so that your disciples may see the miracles that you do. No one who wants to become a public figure acts in secret. Since you are doing these things, show yourself to the world.' For even his own brothers did not believe in him" (John 7:2-5).

St. Paul tells us that Jesus appeared to his brother James after the Resurrection, and Jesus' brothers are present at Pentecost. The presence of James, the powerful leader of the Jerusalem community, as the brother of Jesus (or at least a cousin of Jesus) raises the auxiliary issue inherent in the life of any extraordinary leader: Who is in charge of that leader's legacy when he dies: his blood relatives or this non-blood loyal followers? Where does authority reside? It seems it at first resided with James who wound up presiding at the first Christian council and sending delegates to Antioch, a community in Gentile territory. When he dies, who inherited the mantle? Not, apparently, anyone in the blood line. We know that Mark, writing a decade after James, significantly gives us these words, "Who are my mother and my brothers? And looking at those who sat around him, he said, 'Here are my mother and my brothers. Whoever does the will of God is my brother and sister and mother'" (3:33-35). That seems to have settled it.

The early Church historian, Eusebius, says that a large number of Jesus' relatives gathered around James in Jerusalem. James soon became a major figure in the early Church, though, for most of the Church's history, it has ignored him and the intractable Jewish character of Christianity's beginnings. He was eventually martyred. It is reputed, though challenged, that Jesus' brother Jude wrote the epistle attributed to him. He, too, was likely an important figure in the early Church. Eusebius says that, after the Jewish Wars, many of Jesus' family fled Jerusalem and among those who survived were grandsons of Jude.

We seldom think of Jesus having a family, probably because Catholic tradition has insisted that Mary was a virgin all her life. It was

4th century St. Jerome who came up with the explanation that Jesus' brothers were really his cousins, since it was not unusual in the Middle East to refer to a whole clan who grew up together as brothers and sisters. The Orthodox tradition proposed that these brothers and sisters were the children of Joseph by a previous marriage. Protestant tradition holds that Mary was a virgin at the time of Jesus' birth but not afterward. Whatever the case, Jesus apparently grew up in a lively household, not as he is often pictured in art, as an only child of the Holy Family triad. It was *Cheaper by the Dozen*, not Bill, Hillary and Chelsea.

THE IMMACULATE CONCEPTION

The misunderstandings continue. There is no biblical account for Mary's immaculate conception. It was only in the 8th and 9th centuries that the idea that Mary was sinless took hold – in spite of Paul's words that "all have sinned and are deprived of the glory of God" (Rom 3:23) – and that soon led to the conclusion that she was sinless from the moment of conception. So it was no surprise that, some twelve hundred years later, on December 8, 1854, Pope Pius IX proclaimed the doctrine of the Immaculate Conception, which stated that "In the first instance of her conception, by a singular privilege and grace granted by God, in view of the merits of Jesus Christ, the Savior of the human race, [Mary] was preserved exempt from all stain of original sin." That is to say, Mary, who should have been born subject to sin in consequence of her origin from Adam, was, by the anticipated merits of her son, born free of original sin. How do we know this? It's right there in scripture and tradition.

True, admitted the proponents of the doctrine, there is no direct and unassailable scriptural proof, but there is that suggestive reference in Genesis 3:15 cited as a prophecy text by Pius IX which reads, "I will put enmity between you [the snake] and the woman and her seed; she shall crush your head and you shall wait for her heel." (This ancient text reflects the usual relationship between humans and the snakes they feared. Vertical humans would strike at the snake's head to kill it with one blow. The horizontal snake in the grass would be apt to strike at a person's heel.) But, as the Catholic Encyclopedia tells us, "The translation 'she' of the Vulgate is thus interpretive. It originated after the 4th century, and cannot be defended critically". That's because the correct pronoun in the Hebrew is "he", not "she"; that is, the woman's seed – Christ if you want – shall do the crushing. Victory is his. So the biblical translation, which so strongly affected the traditional representation of Mary and this doctrine, is generally recognized today to be a mistake. (Think of all those millions of statues of Mary, dressed in white and blue, with her outstretched arms standing there with her foot on the serpent.)

Well, add the proponents, there is always Luke's phrase, "Hail, full of grace," (1:28). Grace is a loaded word. It is taken to mean the later medieval concept of sanctifying grace, so obviously Mary is being proclaimed "full" of sanctifying grace, that is, so full that it's from the very beginning, from conception. But the word in Greek for grace does not mean that. The word simply means "to be favored" and that's why the modern translations used in church reads 'Hail, highly favored one" or, as the New Oxford Annotated Bible puts it, "Greetings, favored one!" – something of a shock to the annual Christmas Mass-goers who suspect political correctness is lurking around somewhere – and not quite proof of an immaculate conception. We should point out here that in the Mass for the Feast of the Immaculate Conception on December 8th, the first reading is Genesis 3:15, and the translation used is the erroneous "she" not "he." The mistranslated pronoun is still being used metaphorically at public worship to "prove" a point.

With scripture suspect, the Church turns to tradition. These traditions not only come three to four hundred years later after, the Gospels, but are not unanimous. For example, the church father Origin thought that Mary indeed did sin when, at Jesus' passion, a sword of disbelief pierced her soul and she was struck by doubt. He also taught that Jesus died for Mary's sins as well. St. Basil also speaks of the sword of doubt that pierced Mary's soul, and St. John

Chrysostom accused Mary of ambition and being pushy when she tried to speak to Jesus at Capernaum (Matthew 12:46). St. Bernard of Clairvaux objects to this belief. St. Thomas Aquinas wrote that Mary was indeed conceived in original sin but was sanctified in her mother's womb. However, enough other early Church Fathers compared Mary to Eve and extolled her purity to swing the vote. St. John Damascene went so far as to include Mary's parents who, by association, were filled with the Holy Spirit and made free of all sexual concupiscence. In short, Mary came from spiritually pristine material.

Finally, "reason" capped the grounds for the Immaculate Conception. After all, it would be totally incongruous that the flesh from which the divine Messiah was to be formed should ever belong to one who had ever been a slave of sin. (One would have thought that, on the contrary, a genealogy that included those shady foreign ladies would lead the evangelist to make the point again of Jesus' identity with sinners and those outside the law. "I have come to call, not the just but sinners.") Besides, it was reasoned, if God would give Jeremiah and John the Baptist in-the-womb sanctification privileges, how much more Mary? Still, the official stance of the Church has been to maintain that the definition of the Immaculate Conception is in organic unity with the Church's beginnings and simply matured without interruption over the years. From 54 C.E. to 1854 C.E. there has been a steady development. The historical fact is you can't find this teaching anywhere in the early centuries, especially before St. Augustine's theory of original sin in the 5th century. An honest look at history of the doctrine cannot produce a narrative of continuous and unswerving development.

Yet, in spite of that, the misunderstandings piled up, and in time you wound up with "tradition" which, in circular fashion, really was little more than canonized misinterpreted scripture. We see the full expression of this "tradition" in Pope John Paul II's encyclical *Redemptoris Mater*:

"The divine plan of salvation...according to the teaching contained in [the letter to the Ephesians] and other Pauline letters... is also eternally linked to Christ. It includes everyone but it reserves a special place for the "woman" who is the Mother of him to whom the Father has entrusted the work of salvation. As the Second Vatican Council says, 'she is already prophetically foreshadowed in that promise made to our first parents after their fall in to sin' – according to the Book of Genesis (see 3:15). Likewise she is the Virgin who is to conceive and bear a son, whose name will be called Emmanuel" – according to the words of Isaiah (see 7:14). In this way the Old Testament prepares for that 'fullness of time' when God 'sent forth his son, born of a woman...so that we might receive adoption as sons.'"

There it is. The average person knows that the Church holds and teaches these things but sees that they are not based on scriptural grounds, but like infant baptism (which even Protestants practice) based on tradition. Now tradition is critically important but he can't help but wonder about a tradition, cast as dogma, that is based on a faulty or 'creative' reading of scripture even if Cardinal Joseph Ratzinger did write, "Dogma is by definition none other than an interpretation of Scripture" with Scott Hahn adding, "Dogmas are the Church's *infallible* interpretation of Scripture."[3]

THE PRESENTATION

The Catholic Church celebrates the feast of Mary's Presentation in the Temple at three years old (an instance of her mother fulfilling her vow), a feast that should have been discarded in the 1969 revisions of the Church's liturgical calendar. It was not only kept, but made an obligatory memorial. It should have been discarded, because there is no historical basis for it. Its origin is found in the apocryphal Gospel, the *Protoevangelium of James*, a 2nd century work. (It supplies the names of Mary's parents as well: Joachim and Anne.) The feast moved into liturgical use in the 6th century dedication of a church in Jerusalem and later in the 8th century in Constantinople. It made its way westward to England in the 12th century, the papal court in the 14th century, was suppressed for a while, and then finally reappeared in the Universal Church Calendar in 1585. As history it has no foundation (no female would be allowed to live in the Temple, especially when she reached puberty). Like so much in the Bible, however, it functions as a metaphor (which is why I mention it). The angel Gabriel called her "full of grace" or "highly favored" of God. She was indeed the first believer, the first disciple and remained so to Calvary's end. She was present at the birth of the Messiah and present on Pentecost at the birth of the Church. So, from the very beginning, she was God's person. The Presentation story functions as an interpretative parable of that never-changing status.

As a final comment, we might mention that what was lost in Mary's exaltation was an appreciation of her historic role precisely as that "first disciple." Which is to say, as Robin Fox and Peter Brown point out, building on Mary's and other New Testament women's critical role in the life, death and resurrection of Jesus, women would become the majority members in the Church of the 3rd century. Indeed, Christianity would become known as a woman's religion (in contrast, say, to Islam), and Richard Rubenstein gives the reasons why:

> "There were several reasons for this. Christianity was not a feminist movement in the modern sense, but the community's yearning for sexual purity operated to the advantage of those long relegated to the status of sexual playthings or childbearing 'vessels'. Although the Church shared the strong patriarchal bias of Roman society, it protected widows (a large group because of girls' early marriages to older men), cherished virgins, considered adultery by either spouse a serious sin, opposed prostitution, and tried to prevent men from 'putting off' their wives. It enabled women to play leading roles in the Christian community and perhaps most important, considered them no less capable than men of winning eternal life."[4]

Indeed, the first Christian communities were sympathetic to women. St. Paul (or his imitators) did have negative words to say about women, but nevertheless spoke of there being "no male or female for you are all one in Christ Jesus." Before Christianity, women in fact had already been attracted to the synagogues outside Palestine and were generous benefactors. They simply continued this influence when Christianity came. They were certainly attracted to Jesus and he responded. We think of the Samaritan woman at the well, Mary of Bethany, good friends Martha and Mary, Mary Magdalene (the "apostle to the Apostles"), Peter's mother-in-law, the poor widow who donated her mite, the woman caught in adultery, those who ministered to Jesus.

After Jesus, women shared in the Eucharist and were quite active. Priscilla, for example, sponsored Apollos, the Jewish intellectual who rivaled Paul. She's mentioned half a dozen times in the New Testament, and it's possible that she and her husband founded the church at Corinth. They sailed with Paul on a missionary journey. The four unmarried daughters of Philip were said to be prophets, and Paul stayed at their house. Paul mentions Prisca and Junia (praised as a prominent apostle in Romans 16:3, 7, 15). Julia, Euodia and Syntyche are called his fellow workers (Philippians 4:2-3). Paul cites Prisca, Lydia and Nympha as house church leaders. Women were deacons and financial supporters. In fact, women were so active in the early Church that the pagan philosopher Porphyry, around 300 C.E., complained that they were hurting Christianity.

Feminists today tend to see Mary as part of this trajectory. In any case, Mary's prerogatives function well as "myths," as interpreted metaphors honoring her deservedly high place in the early and medieval Church. Working through these stories, we can arrive at what "He Who is mighty" did for her and, indeed, holy is his name. They function, however, less well as objective doctrines.

PART III

TENSIONS

Chapter 18.

INTERPRETATION TENSIONS

These days, disbelief is dramatically on the rise. Ironically, in those countries traditionally Catholic Christian, atheism reigns. Among the young the "nones" [no religion] continue to grow at record numbers. Many today, conditioned by an intractable secular media and an aggressively secular educational system, can't reconcile the discoveries of the natural sciences with religion. They are heirs to the bestselling skepticisms of popular authors and the "tsunami of secularism" (Cardinal Donald Wuerl's phrase) that defines the culture. A glance at the history of Christianity, as one critic put it "is the best school for atheism."[1] In addition, the public is not immune to the scriptural developments heralded in the media or the tensions concerning the Bible that we have examined in the first two sections of this book.

Today's people, carrying the unconscious assumptions of society, look at the complex development of the Bible, note its use and misuse, its partisan and competing methods of interpretation, its fluidity, its many authors politically and religiously motivated, and wonder where its truth, its authority, resides. The fact is, to believe in the Bible one must be armed with certain *a priori* assumptions. One puts on the faith glasses, and everything is read through them. Therefore, where there are contradictions and errors, the believer must assume the text is not wrong, but coded to express a different, hidden meaning. We turn to James Kugel as he carefully sums up the four assumptions that the ancient interpreters brought to the Bible (and many do today).[2]

In summary, they are these:

1. The ancient interpreters assumed that the Bible was basically cryptic, full of words that said one thing but really meant something else, something deeper, something hidden. They had to unlock the meaning. To the modern mind, the only trouble with this is that everything is in free fall. There's no criterion, which is why we come up with different theologies in the Bible and conflicting biblical religions. A full-page ad in the *New York Times* (October 19, 2010) pushing *The Bible Code II* reads in large letters above a large display of the book:

> In May 2008 Oprah Winfrey sent Barack Obama
> Three predictions from "The Bible Code"
> The first has already come true.
> (On Sale Today)

Such claims to deciphering may be clever, cunning and captivating (and computer driven) but is it the word of God or the word of some very creative and committed interpreters whether ancient or modern? The Bible is constantly in flux.

2. The ancient interpreters assumed that the Bible was a how-to book for all times; that is, a book of instructions on what to do, how to live, how to please God. All those ancient stories, they were convinced, had relevance for their time, and they were willing and ready to sift the text to make them so. We still do this, as we shall see, using our sense of "growing consciousness" to reverse former teachings derived from the Bible to make them fit us today.

3. The ancient interpreters assumed that the Bible contained no error or contradictions. If any were apparently found, they were just that, apparent, and were soon interpreted to conform to the belief of inerrancy. Allegory was a favorite way to neutralize any seeming contradictions.

4. Finally, the ancient interpreters assumed that the Bible was a divinely given text. You have those familiar phrases all over the place to prove it: "And the Lord spoke to Moses..." or one of the patriarchs or prophets. To them the Bible is of divine origin in the same way that the Muslims insist that the Qur'an is of divine origin and the Mormons The Book of Mormon – three competing "divine" books.

The early Christians, being Jews like their founder, worked from the same four assumptions. The later Christians, being Greeks, resorted to allegory in their method of interpretation to preserve these assumptions. The bottom line is that these four assumptions – and they *are* assumptions – have guided Bible reading ever since. The problem comes when, as in modern times, these assumptions are called into question. That's always happened to some degree throughout history, but no era has ever had the evidence, the research, and the physical and linguistic material as to make a credible and sustained critique. To stand outside those assumptions today may be an honest, not necessarily hostile, stance.

An interpreted Bible

It is abundantly clear by now that the Bible we have is a highly interpreted work. We can't stress this too much: the Bible is, from top to bottom, from the beginning to now, an interpreted work. To quote Kugel at length (his emphases):

> " ...Gradually, as the centuries passed, these traditional understandings come to be the meaning. The historical circumstances in which a particular biblical passage might have originally been uttered were eventually forgotten or, in any case, considered irrelevant. What was important by, say, the third or second century B.C.E. (and quite possibly, even somewhat earlier) was what was thought to be the text's deeper significance, that is, how it was explained by the traditional

interpretations that now accompanied it. And this traditional interpreted Bible — the Bible itself plus the traditions about what it really meant — was what was taught to successive generations of students, expounded in public assemblies and, ultimately, canonized by Judaism and Christianity as their sacred book."

"The way in which these traditions of interpretation came to cling to the biblical text may be difficult for people today to comprehend. We like to think that the Bible, or any other text, means 'just what it says.' And we act on that assumption: we simply open up a book—including the Bible—and try to make sense of it on our own. In ancient Israel and for centuries afterward, on the contrary, people looked to special interpreters to explain the meaning of a biblical text. For that reason, the explanations passed along by such interpreters quickly acquired an authority of their own. In studying this or that biblical law or prophecy or story, students would do more than simply learn the words; they would be told what the text meant—not only the peculiar way in which this or that term was to be interpreted, but how one biblical text related to another far removed from it, or the particular moral lesson that a text embodied, or how a certain passage was to be applied in everyday life. And the people who learned these things about the Bible from their teachers in turn passed on the same information to the next generation of students."

"And so, it was this *interpreted Bible*—not just the stories, prophecies, and laws themselves, but these texts as they had, by now, been interpreted and explained for centuries— that came to stand at the very center of Judaism and Christianity. This was what people in both religions meant by 'the Bible.' Of course, Judaism and Christianity themselves differed on a great many questions, including the interpretation of some crucial scriptural passages, as well as on just what books were to be included in the Bible. Nevertheless, both religions had begun with basically the same interpreted Bible. For both inherited an earlier, common set of traditions, general principles regarding how one ought to go about reading and interpreting the Bible as well as specific traditions concerning the meaning of individual passages, verses, and words. As a result, even when later Jews or Christians added on new interpretations— sometimes directed against each other or against other groups or ideologies within the world in which they lived—the new interpretations frequently built on, and only modified, what had been the accepted wisdom until then."[3]

That's an insightful and challenging quotation, and worth mulling over. It means that we are not really consciously reading the sacred authors directly. We are subconsciously reading multiple *interpretations* of the original sacred authors' oral or scripted works, interpretations which began well within the biblical period itself and which we interject into the text as "natural revelation," but which are actually someone else's later thoughts. It is quite accurate to say that the only Bible we know is the interpreted Bible and it is this interpreted Bible, and not the original writings of different authors of different periods, that is the real Bible for us. The Bible is not as a single united corpus that has been passed down through the ages, but a rich tapestry of many colors of many, many hands of many centuries. In short, the collection we call the Bible is a two-thousand-year-old community project, a composite enterprise of continually expanded, revised and sometimes conflicting and opaque texts and, as a result, its authority is still up for grabs.

And, like ancient writing in general, the Bible is full of challenge. It twice mentions the Books of Jasher in Joshua and 2 Samuel. It cites the Books of the Wars of the Lord, the Books of the Chronicles of the Kings of Israel, the Books of the Chronicles of the Kings of Judah, and others that we do not possess. So we do not have a full picture. Worth noting, too, is that copyists of the Torah are obliged to copy not just every letter but every character, every mark – but over the years fallible copyists have inscribed enlarged or shrunken characters, backward, upside-down or fractured letters and yet all these must, by law, be faithfully included in order for the Torah to be considered kosher and usable. Like a virus, these notations and subsequent ones keep replicating themselves over the centuries.

GOD-INSPIRED OR JUST INSPIRED?

In all this complexity, the question arises: Are the transcribers and first interpreters of the Bible inspired? It's a legitimate question. There are difficulties in our copies of the text. Remember, we have no original manuscripts — some scholars wonder if there is such a thing as an original manuscript; but instead, more likely, there are just bits and pieces of oral stories, eventually written on papyrus, animal hide, or etched in stone and, as just mentioned above, the copies we do have are not always consistent with one another. The earliest complete Bible we have dates to the 900s C.E. and the earliest complete New Testament dates to the 300s C.E. and a lot of altering went on in all that time. That stunning discovery of the Dead Sea Scrolls in 1948, for example, revealed several versions of the Great Isaiah Scroll. As the editors of the volume *Discoveries in the Judean Desert* (2011) put it, "the biblical text was pluriform and still developing prior to the Jewish Revolts [in 66 C.E. and 132. C.E.... It is] full of isolated interpretive insertions." Right up almost to the Christian era, interpreters were tinkering with the books of Isaiah leaving us multiple versions. How do we know which one is valid, which one is *God's* Word?

Moreover, to this day, some of these copies are still impossible to read with certainty. They are opaque, full of contradictions and puzzling and unexplained statements. Understandably, there is always the natural tendency for words, clear at one time or in one social context, to become puzzling to a later generation. There are the shifting meanings of words that render the text no longer clear. Then there are the *hapax* words: that is, words that occur only once in the entire Bible or elsewhere so there's no other places to make comparisons with to detect their real meaning. The Book of Job is full of them. Also, given the fact that Hebrew has no capital letters, periods, commas or spaces (letters run together), it is difficult to know where one sentence begins and the other ends and meanings can change dramatically depending on how one punctuates it. Recall the famous definition of a panda as a passive vegetarian: an animal who eats shoots and leaves; or, a panda as a cold hearted killer: an animal who eats, shoots and leaves. Depends where one puts the commas. Also, Hebrew has no vowels. Those little signs that indicate them were added much, much later. Which means that the adders of the vowels had to make choices as to which vowel they chose and where they put them. So, for example, if you had just the consonants "l" and "v" you could add the vowels of your choice and come up with "love", "alive", "olive", "lava" and others and so alter the meaning.

Then, too, the ancient biblical texts differ from one another and scholars are not sure which ones are accurate. Formerly there were two standard texts of the Bible – the Masoretic Text, finalized only around the year 1000 of our era and the Septuagint Text from the beginning of the third century B.C.E. With the discovery of the Dead Sea Scrolls, texts were found that play against these standard texts and sometimes tip the translation or interpretation one way or another. For example, there's YHWH's rest after creation. Most Bibles rely on the Hebrew text and say, "And on the seventh day God finished the world he had done and he rested." But this "finishing" raises the question that therefore YHWH must have done *some* work, but how can this be reconciled with the tradition that people are not permitted *any* work on the Sabbath? So the Samaritan Pentateuch gets around it by saying, "On the *sixth* day God finished..." So which text to believe? This verse is altogether omitted in the Dead Sea Scrolls. Another example: in Samuel 1:24, Samuel's mother Hannah came to Shiloh to make a sacrifice. The Hebrew Text says she brought three bulls; the Septuagint says one bull. In Jeremiah (10:3-10), the prophet rants against idolatry and in the Hebrew text of these words there are inserted persistent refrains praising YHWH. These refrains are absent in the Septuagint text, indicating that such verses were added later. Finally there is the Great Isaiah Scroll, the most famous of the Dead Sea Scrolls, handsomely displayed in the museum in Jerusalem. It's by far the oldest and best-preserved copy of any book of the Hebrew Bible, dating to around 100 B.C.E. But, as the scholars note, "with its numerous mistakes and omissions, contextual changes, unusual spelling system and bad handwriting,"[4] it does not provide much help in deciphering or standardizing today's Bible.

It is no wonder that the great contemporary Hebrew scholar Robert Alter openly admits how little of the Hebrew Bible we can translate with confidence. For all these reasons the Bible was necessarily interpreted by its transcribers from the very beginning. They faced a daunting challenge, but the fact is that, in their efforts, they frequently wound up changing the text, changes which found their way into subsequent books of the Bible. As James L. Kugel remarks, "Carried to an extreme, the freedom of interpreters to read a single word in different ways or to break up a block of text into various syntactic combinations could at times allow them to make a text out to be saying exactly the opposite of its apparent meaning."[5]

And that's the disturbing truth. So the question is, which is the inspired word of God: the original text, which we no longer possess, or the interpreted texts of copies of copies of copies? Translations of these copies complicate the issue. At latest count the Old and New Testaments, whole or in part, have been translated into 2,010 different languages. Conceding that every language has a host of profound cultural assumptions embedded in its history and beliefs, the margin for error and misunderstanding is large. In our own culture, the history of the Bible in English is famously one of constant controversy and theological warfare. As Marilyn Chandler McEntyre writes in her splendid book, *Caring for Words in a Culture of Lies*:

> "The history of the Bible in English offers a fascinating study of how highly politicized, fraught with special interest, and riddled with ambiguities is the business of translation, and how consequential...The mere fact that there are over seventy-five translations still available in English invites comparison and some reflection on what difference the differences make."[6]

The very fact of complex and multiple translations of variant copies of copies of the Bible invites the inevitability of "infelicities and inaccuracies," and raises the question whether such infelicities and inaccuracies can be the Word of God.

STANDARDIZING THE RELATIVE

The issue is that the interpreters, in struggling with meanings not clear to them, came up with interpretations that gradually became the standard ones, but ones not necessarily meant by the original inspired authors. Often the *interpreters'* interpretations became standard text and leached into the canonical books of the Bible. The petulant question is, did inspiration leak from one to another? For example, the story of Adam and Eve presented many problems. There was the case of the talking serpent. So maybe, concluded some interpreters, at that time *all* animals had the gift of speech, which they lost (an old Christmas legend says they got it back for one night: to announce the birth of Jesus). If the text says that the snake was condemned to slither on his belly, that obviously meant that at one time he had legs, and maybe arms, too. More importantly, for some he became identified as Satan or his agent. As we saw, this is the interpretation that caught on and became dominant. Thus, many, many centuries later: "Through the devil's envy death entered the world and those who are on his side suffer it" (Wisdom, 2:24). A speculation, fluid storytelling, an interpretation of an interpretation, became fixed scripture.

God had said to Adam concerning the fruit, "for on the day you eat it you shall die," but, after eating it, Adam not only stayed living, but went right on living to the ripe old age of 930 years. We should all be condemned to death like that! Stymied by this apparent contradiction, the interpreters had to come up with redefining the word "day," which, in God's typology, could be a thousand years. Better, they said Adam didn't die in the sense of expiring, but, created to be immortal, he died in the sense that he lost immortality. That was his real punishment, not working by the sweat of his brow. His descendants also lost immortality because, even though it seemed unfair to get penalized for someone else's sin, they, too, inherited the very condition of sinfulness.

If Enoch is said to have "walked with God" (Gen. 5:21-24), interpreters suggested this meant that he was, like Elijah, taken up to heaven. Others disagreed, saying God killed him because he was wicked. The latter speculation faded, and the former speculation found its way into sacred scripture of the New Testament Book of Hebrews, which says, "By faith was Enoch taken up so that he should not see death" (11:5). Now we have a speculation that has crossed over to "truth." What was it before that?

BLEACHED TEXTS

There are many more examples of this sort of thing, but the point is, none of these scenarios are in the text itself, but, through the speculations of commentators over the centuries, some interpretations became the dominant ones. Whether they were right or wrong, they got into later books of the Bible. They are now official canonical scripture, even though they are inherited interpretations. They are not in the original texts themselves. What does this say about divine inspiration? Does it mean that possibly erroneous interpretations have now become official and get the seal of approval? Were they uninspired when free-floating, but acquired inspiration when a naive author took a long-standing speculation as fact? What happened to the original word of God as it came from the hands of the first authors now that it is overlaid, radically changed, or even lost by new interpretations? What about those speculative interpretations that, displacing the original inspired text, were adopted into scripture? Did they, formerly uninspired and concocted by men, now suddenly become inspired, the very word of God? Did other interpretations become declassified? Did the original text lose something? Does inspiration "move" with each new layer? The extraordinary document of the Catholic Church called "The Interpretation of the Bible in the Church" admits that such "re-readings"(*relectures*) of the Bible are unique to the Bible itself, but nevertheless such re-readings "develop new aspects of meaning, sometimes quite *different* from the original sense" (90). If one applied that assessment to any other writing (the Qur'an, the Book of Mormon, Russian history) we could justify every latest revisionism. Why is the Bible uniquely excused from this charge?

This excerpt from Margaret Barker highlights the same point. Speaking of Isaiah she writes:

> "Another variant is at Isaiah 53: 11 where both the Old Greek and the Qur'an text include the word 'light' which is absent from the MT [Masoretic Text]. After his suffering the servant sees the light (of God's glory). It must have been this version of Isaiah which Luke had in mind when he told the story of the walk to Emmaus. Jesus explained to the two disciples that it was necessary for the Anointed One (the Christ) to suffer and enter into his glory (Luke 24-26). There is no prophecy in the MT which says this, but there is the verse in the Isaiah Scroll. As important Messianic proof text, which Luke says was used by Jesus, is thus from a 'variant' Hebrew text, a clear indication that the Hebrew Scriptures which Jesus knew were not the Masoretic Text."[7]

Note once more: there is no prophecy of a suffering Messiah, yet this belief is all over our doctrinal catechetical, doctrinal and liturgical texts.

Let's go further and point out what scripture scholar Raymond Brown has reminded us: that the Bible we hold in our hands today is brand new, around only about a dozen years. It quite frankly contains some editor's decisions. Manuscripts have variant readings, with some things left out, others obviously inserted by scribes. Modern scholarship and discovery have led to many of them. The editor of your current Bible had to choose among the variants and the almost inexplicable texts, and the resulting version of the Bible is his or her choices that may be quite different from the Bible St. Jerome gave us.

Speaking of Jerome, his translation of the Bible in 384 became the official translation of the Church for a thousand years. In the 16th century, Erasmus, the great Dutch humanist (and the illegitimate son of a priest), dared to find mistakes in Jerome's work. One of the most famous of these is found in Matthew 3:2, where Jerome translates John the Baptist's cry, "*Metanoeite!*" as "Do penance," which, as a proof text, fitted in nicely with the medieval Catholic system of confession and penance. Erasmus (and Luther) correctly pointed out that the word actually meant "Repent!" and had nothing to do with confession. With that one correction, Erasmus overturned Jerome's translation and the whole traditional understanding of the Bible.

We're not through with this sort of thing. Because of the wars in Iraq and Afghanistan and elsewhere in the East, the cradle of Christianity, many manuscripts and artifacts have been destroyed. Alarmed, 21st-century scientists, armed with highly sophisticated digital technology, have fanned out across the nations, feverishly digitizing literary treasures. They are currently working on the 30,000 endangered manuscripts from the Eastern Christian traditions. They are digitizing the 5,000 scrolls and manuscripts at St. Catherine's, the oldest functioning monastery in Egypt (330 C.E.). More to our concerns, so far they have discovered 75 New Testament manuscripts, many with unique commentaries, formerly unknown to scholars. What effect will they have on the inspired texts?[8] Will they "correct" what we know now, and wind up de-inspiring the current inspired text?

METHODS

The ancient biblical interpreters worked hard and loyally to make sense of the Bible, but their methods confound the modern mind. The interpreters either resorted to a literal reading of the texts or they freely took the words of the prophets and bent them to fit this or that person or situation. We moderns tend to be put off by this. We would never use such "forced" methods. It's a challenge for us to grasp that it was an acceptable and honorable procedure in the ancient world, one quite prevalent in Greek allegorical and typological literary schools, particularly in the Platonic schools—and these schools, of course, heavily influenced the biblical writers. We have seen, for example, how Matthew severely changes the wording, tenses, and emphasis in Micah's comments about Bethlehem and turns them on their head to fit Jesus. He wasn't being conniving or dishonest. He was only doing what was common in his time. There's the category called *midrash*, which ingeniously relates texts of similar expressions into new formulations. In the Christian canon, the infancy narratives of Matthew and Luke are considered *midrash*; that is, not historical, but a pastiche of like-sounding texts reformulated to make a theological point. This pattern of superimposing past words and events onto current stories is a stock device in the Bible. It's as if the sacred writers, in talking about a mountain, hit the 'search button' for all times the word "mountain" was mentioned and then they made their findinsg apply to a current text, no matter how alien. It's like they took a Disney cel image and superimposed it on a basic drawing, producing a final product of detail, color, and images, not previously there on the master template.

As I said, this kind of interpretation (*Pesher. Midrash, Haggadahm, Halakhahm, Mishnah, Targum*, etc.) was common. It was a stylized commonplace in the ancient world of interpretation, and we have to immerse ourselves in that world to understand the scriptures, because to our modern minds this kind of reworking of words seems a dangerous blank check. You can make the words say what you want them to say, and when they don't fit anymore, another biblical writer will come up with a new version.

It is the same with the early Church Fathers with their instinctive Christological interpretations of the Old Testament. They were only following the New Testament authors. Think, for example, of the Gospel parallel between the Jonah story and the Resurrection, or how St. Paul sees the passage of the Israelites through the Red Sea as a type of baptism and in his parallel between the first and second

Adams in Romans 5, 17-19, about sin coming into the world through one man and with it death, but "just as one man's trespass led to condemnation for all, so one man's act of righteousness leads to justification and life for all. For just as by the one man's disobedience the many were made sinners, so by the one man's obedience the many will be made righteous."

One modern commentator, Joe Nolan, says (emphasis mine), says, "For many, Paul's account needs updating, but he wrote in his own time, and considered the Genesis account of the Fall *as factual*, a record of what happened, even though figurative language was obviously employed." So Paul was wrong to believe Genesis as a literal account (what would he have said if he knew of evolution?), and he built a theology on this literal reading, but we have allowed that "metaphorically" he can be right. *His* interpretation has become Christian doctrine, not the original words of the text.

THE CHURCH FATHERS

To return to the Church Fathers. They were, remember, highly sophisticated and educated men who were raised in the Greek philosophical tradition, which was highly abstract. Many of them could not read Hebrew or Aramaic—a decided handicap. They had little resonance with the direct, earthy, inelegant, concrete writings of the Hebrews (What in the world did "circumcise your hearts" mean? And how do you come to terms with the odd, sensuous, sexual language of the Song of Songs?) but they knew the Bible, which had been used extensively in the liturgies they attended from childhood, and they grew up reading and chanting the biblical texts. Therefore, when they came to their commentaries, they approached the Bible with one inexorable framework: the so-called Rule of Faith, thought to have originated in the times of the apostles themselves. That is to say, everything was necessarily seen through the lens of some basic, fundamental beliefs about Jesus, especially his Resurrection. In short, when the first Christian commentators read the ancient scriptures, they fully expected to find Christ in every verse, and some quite openly said so. This deep faith approach has given us some beautiful and powerful insights, and we would be unspeakably poorer without the exegetical writings of the early Church Fathers, but to us it is rose-colored glasses reading.

Here's some samples from Barnabas: when Moses broke the tablets in anger, that was a sign that the old Covenant with Israel had been broken (see Chapter 21); the biblical prohibition against eating pork means to avoid people who only pray when they're in trouble, just as pigs only snort when they are hungry. The prohibition against eating rabbits, hyenas and weasels really warns against deviant sexual practices. When Abraham circumcised 318 men, it really is a symbol of Jesus' redemptive work, for the number 318 in Greek is the first two letters of Jesus' name which represents the cross.

Origen, the first Christian scripture scholar, simply followed the lead of 2 Corinthians, 3, where Paul writes that the Jews have a veil before their faces. This means that they, the Jews, cannot see the true meaning of scripture, and so they are limited to the letter of the text, which kills. Only when Jesus explains scripture, as he did to the disciples on the road to Emmaus, can the true meaning be revealed. He also says that the five kings who attack Gibeon in the Book of Joshua and end up hiding in a cave after the Lord had famously lengthened the 24 hour day are really symbols of the five senses, and through one of these each person falls into sin; that when Abraham stood under the tree of Mamre (Genesis 18), "Mamre" (by a rather torturous etymology) means "sharpness of sight" or "insight" and therefore this means that Abraham, being pure of heart, was able to see God. These are typical of Origen's moralistic interpretations. Moderns find these allegorical stretches more comical than enlightening.

Then there's Irenaeus, the one who really gave us the first official canon of the New Testament. He not only saw Christ as the subject of scripture, but also its ultimate author. So Irenaeus takes Jesus' statement in John 5:46, "Moses wrote of me," to mean that the writings of Moses are actually his (Jesus') words and likewise so are the words of the other prophets as well. This kind of Christological interpretation of the Old Testament goes back to the beginning, but to us it has its limits. Take, for example, the epistle to the Hebrews with its vast number of Old Testament quotations. One noted scholar, Felix Just, SJ., tells us (emphasis mine), "Many of the biblical quotations found here in Hebrews are fairly short and they are used *without much regard for the historical or literary context they were originally in*. Most of the texts, we might have to say, are *taken out of context* because they're interpreted almost exclusively as speaking about or referring to Jesus ..." This 'Disney cel' process, this bold wrenching out of context by an advocate bent on showing the superiority of Christianity over Judaism is both offensive and disturbing to the average person and strains credulity. Yes, he realizes that this kind of allegorical argument is foreign to his modern mentality, though it made sense in an age more attuned to symbol and metaphor. Still, to him it's an application that undermines the authority of the Bible or at least taints it as unreliable and fickle.

HOLY PROPAGANDA

Finally, concerning this whole issue of esoteric (to us) interpretation, the problem becomes more acute when we find unmistakable signs of outright propaganda and political chicanery in the biblical writings. We have already seen instances of tortured and distorted texts and bold fabrications that push an agenda. For example, the whole story of David and Saul and the murder of Saul's sons by David is a mishmash of lies and deceit that whitewashes David, the ideal king. Scholars hold that much of 1 and 2 Samuel is one long propaganda sound bite on behalf of David's administration. A passage in Isaiah would not only trigger a compatible metaphor about Jesus, but also, the fathers insisted, the 800-year old author, although he didn't know it, was penning all the while, under the inspiration of the Holy Spirit, a deeper meaning about the Jesus Christ of the future. In both cases, of course, each commentator could claim the presence of the author's unconscious deeper meaning meant by God, and that's one of those statements you can't prove one way or another. The truth is that the Bible does not aim to be a disinterested reporting of events. It is deliberately, and, at times, ferociously quite partisan. It is an out-and-out partisan collection that has been written, copied and redacted (many, many times) and edited by people who had a firm faith who interpreted reality through that faith. YHWH's relationship to Israel is in, under, above and behind it, all of which is why we must always remember that the Bible is a faith-based interpretation of events. The situation is akin to what the curator of the British Museum wrote about the Aztecs: "... how much can we actually know about the Aztecs...? Virtually all the accounts of the Aztec Empire were written by the Spaniards who overthrew it, so they have to be read with considerable skepticism."[9] True, as we noted previously, sometimes the Bible narrates things that have actually happened, but as Northrope Frye famously said, "If there is any history in the Bible it is there by accident." We have to remember these facts in reading the Bible. (It might be noted that the other two books that aver that they are divinely inspired, the Qur'an and the Book of Mormon, have the same restrictions).

Historically, there has always been a massive re-reading and reinterpretation of the Bible. It is, for example, a long way from the declaration of the first Catholic Biblical Commission that everything in Genesis must be taken literally to these revisionist words:

> ".... the stories in the New Testament as well as the Old are also fictionalized works of art, written imaginatively by authors for certain purposes. These authors drew from historically based traditions that had been handed down to them, but they created 'history' by drawing on symbols, metaphors, myths, fables, and legends that were part of their culture at the time. They filled in the historical gap, supplying dialogue and narrative interpretation out of their own rich imaginations to convey some revelatory truth as they saw it."[10]

That statement from the Commission is a landmine of issues: the biblical books are fictionalized works of art...written for certain purposes (propaganda, agenda) ... created "history"...supplied dialogue out of their rich imaginations... the "truth" as *they* saw it... It's hard to imagine saying that about any literary work and then insisting that "of course" this is the revelation of YHWH. Take my word for it. To do so is to submit to the mysterious subconscious complexities of nature and grace.

The Christians re-read the Bible in the light of their belief of Jesus as the Messiah, giving them the New Testament. The Jews, after the fall of the Second Temple, reread the Bible in the light of accumulated interpretations and traditions, giving them the Oral Torah. Modern scholars read the Bible in the light of historical-critical criticism, giving them doubts. All read the Bible "as they saw it." Ancient and modern biblical scholars are often at odds, and some say their views are irreconcilable. How does one confront modern scholarship and not lose the Bible as sacred scripture? Is reconciliation possible? In any case, one thing is clear: one's assumptions in approaching the Bible are everything. The Talmud is right: you don't see things as they are. You see things as *you* are, and that's not necessarily the strongest foundation for a universal religion.

Chapter 19.

THEORY TENSIONS

S o the Bible, it is clear by now, is an eclectic collection, with contradictions abounding and points of view differing. It simply does contain a single, unified set of teachings, but offers rather a synthesis of various schools of thought about YHWH and the people who claim him as their God. It is also clear that it generates its varied traditions from the different Jewish and Christian communities that settled in Babylon, Persia, Egypt, Judea, and scattered Mediterranean communities. Therefore, it reflects a wide diversity while at the same time necessarily provoking diverse interpretations. And that's the problem: how do you integrate that diversity of thought and interpretation into a coherent unified message? If, as the saying goes, fiction is the lie that tells the truth, how does one take the Bible's historical "lies" and ferret out the truth? One approach is this: if one holds fast to Kugel's four assumptions (Chapter 19) – the Bible is full of cryptic messages, it is a book valid for all times and places, it contains no errors, and it is divinely given – then you have an interpretative place to stand on. The following authors clearly belong here:

> "Many explanations have been given for the Red Sea event. Some scholars try to explain it as natural phenomenon, reducing the story to science. Others explain that the setting for the event is not actually the Red Sea but the Reed Sea, a marshy area to the east of the Nile where people could walk through the shallow sea but where heavy chariots would become bogged down. This reduces the story to a geography lesson. Both

lines of argument miss the real point: against all odds, Yahweh conquered. Against all odds, it paid to follow Moses."[1]

Scripture scholar, Father William J. Parker adds:

"The teaching on biblical inerrancy does not mean the Bible has no errors. What it does mean is that when the Bible is teaching truths about our salvation, then it is without error. Once again, the *Dogmatic Constitution on Divine Revelation* says it best: 'The books of Scripture must be acknowledged as teaching firmly, faithfully, and without error that truth which God wanted put into the sacred writings for the sake of our salvation.' (11) Whether Darius or Cyrus succeeded Belshazzar does not matter [the sacred writer said that Darius did but he was wrong. It was Cyrus]; what does matter is the truth contained in the story of Daniel and Belshazzar, that is, that God is working behind the scenes for the salvation of those who remain faithful, even when it means standing up against the strongest of earthly powers."[2]

Finally, Margaret Ralph's book, *And God Said What?*, explains the incident of Moses and his rod, which drove back the Red Sea:

"A modern reader might well ask, 'Well, which was it? Was this a natural event, a wind, or a supernatural event? Moses and his rod?' The question ignores the intent of the authors. The distinction between natural and supernatural is irrelevant. In both accounts we are dealing with an event in which God's presence was experienced. The difference between the methods through which God acted—through the wind or through the more dramatic and marvelous action in which Moses raised his rod illustrates the exaggeration that is characteristic of legend. In the later version the author has embellished the story using exaggeration to make Moses' role more dramatic.

"Remember that the legends were told and retold not merely to recall the past but to affect a present audience. To embellish a legend with marvelous details is to make it all the more interesting and inspiring to the next generation. In most legends, exaggeration is used to build up a human hero. In these legends, however, the religious purpose of the author is always present. It is not really Moses, but God acting through Moses, who is being glorified. The author wishes to inspire his audience with the marvelous nature of God's intervention in the history of God's people. Their God is a God who saves."[3]

All these metaphorically interpreted quotations are clear and most helpful, but we have to notice that they rest on our prior four underlying assumptions. The bottom line is assumed, taken for granted; namely, that God is working "behind the scenes" and they are determined to mine that. This is the direct faith approach to interpretation. The Bible is true because it says so. One just has to dig out the revelation.

MORE VIEWPOINTS

Others, seeking to expand the narrative style of the Bible and to anchor its truthfulness, opt for its social context. The reason for that is that we don't know who most of the authors are. They are anonymous (including Matthew, Mark, Luke, and John), and furthermore there's so many of them. As we have seen, by the time you got the interpreters, the rewriters, redactors, translators, compilers, pseudographers, etc, into the act, you may be talking literally about thousands of unknown people who had a hand in the Bible we have today. So, many say, forget the piecemeal authors and think in terms of the wider community. It's the life of the community—the way it accepted certain books, and especially the way it used them in their liturgies—that counts and that validates the Bible's meaning. The Spirit breathed, as it were, on the whole community in the formation of the final written text. After all, as it pointed out, Jesus wrote nothing, nor did he order his followers to do so. He didn't leave a written text. He did leave a community and let it take it from there, so why not the Old Testament community? Follow their interpretative beliefs, even though they disagree and contradict each other, and you're safe. This is appealing but not completely convincing, especially since so many biblical "communities" are at variance with one another.

In a similar vein, others also say to forget the individual conflicting parts but to check out the Bible as a whole, as a completed project, and you'll get the voice of God. It's the "Scripture interprets Scripture" dictum. The long-synthesized overview will provide the correct interpretation of the Bible. In other words, the very establishment and existence of a canon—*somebody* had to make it authoritative—presumes many commentators and traditions, and so the Bible is both the product *of* tradition and is best interpreted *by* tradition. Scripture and tradition are the yin and yang of the Bible, and its divine message is revealed in that interplay. The Bible critiques tradition and tradition critiques the Bible.

The problem with this is that sometimes (often?) what we call tradition appears to be, as I stated previously, scripture misinterpreted and hardened into doctrine. There's a distinct circular process that goes on here. Take an example we've used before: It is Catholic doctrine that Mary conceived Jesus by divine intervention and that she was a virgin before, during, and after his birth—although such a virgin birth was unknown to Paul and Mark, the earliest New Testament writers. Mary is "ever" Virgin. Protestant doctrine is that indeed Mary conceived Jesus by the power of the Holy Spirit, but she had other children in the normal way, as the several passages referring to Jesus' siblings testify. It seems that some early Church Fathers read the pertinent New Testament passages erroneously, ignoring the fact is that there is no Old Testament evidence of a virginal conception of the Messiah. The angelic "full of grace" did not refer to the later medieval notion of supernatural grace. "A virgin shall conceived a child" was an incorrect translation of the word for a young (married or unmarried) woman. Genesis 3:15 was mistranslated to yield a sinless Mary. Add to this the apocryphal Gospel Peter, which absorbed all these strains and used them in turn to interpret scripture, and you come up with Mary's perpetual virginity. It doesn't quite add up, but now, thanks to the back and forth osmosis between scripture and tradition, we have a "divinely revealed" doctrine. As we have noted, this has not prevented a prominent Catholic scripture scholar from publicly saying that Mary's virginity is "a theological" concept, not a physical one. In short, the tradition does not pass scriptural muster.

Interpreted scripture plus tradition doesn't always work out either. Recall the famous Galileo case. Here you had both scripture and tradition wrong. Some say that God, in the Book of Joshua, commanding the sun to stand still was only accommodating (see below) himself to the people's knowledge at the time. Back then, they could hardly understand the science we have. Tradition, not to mention common sense—after all, everyone saw the sun rise and set—guaranteed the Bible's word and its interpretation, and this was pressed as a convincing argument against Galileo. Yet, with all of this, an outside force, science, trumped both. So now this means we have to consider another agent in trying to interpret the Bible and, so to speak, be more cautious in our certainties, prudently hedging them while awaiting the next scientific discovery. There seems never to be a last word in the interpretation of the Bible. The "word of God" is always a provisional word. It is something of a puzzlement that we did misinterpret and misunderstand the Joshua story for some 1,600 years and made a hard case out of it. That's a long time, especially when we thought we were under Jesus' promise: "If you love me, you will keep my commandments. And I will give you another Advocate to be with you forever. This is the Spirit of truth ... he abides with you..." (John 14: 15:17).

REVERSING SCRIPTURE

We often forget that it's always been so, that is, people have changed or ignored the scripture to fit new insights and needs. After all, Jewish Christians had no trouble ignoring Genesis' command to keep holy

Saturday as they freely changed it to Sunday. Nothing is more clear in scripture than that in order to keep God's Covenant all males shall be circumcised. Yes, circumcision is divinely commanded *in perpetuity*, "for generations to come" (Genesis 17:9). But the early Church, after much debate, did not hesitate to reject this divine command, even though the Old Testament case for circumcision is fairly ironbound.[4] There is nothing even remotely suggesting that it could be changed in the case of gentile converts. When the first Jewish followers of Jesus – himself and his apostles all circumcised – argued that circumcision was as a matter of fact always too burdensome and that, besides, the uncircumcised gentiles *did* receive the Spirit – then those twin arguments, both outside the precise and unambiguous directives of the Bible, overcame the scripture and a tradition of a thousand years. Those who favor the ordination of women in the Roman Catholic Church pick up on this. They logically ask that if a distinct command from God, if a millennium worth of practice-become-tradition can change, why not the prohibition against the ordination of women? This same argument, as we shall see shortly, is being applied to homosexuality: exclusion and rejection are too burdensome and, look around, have you ever seen such kind, good and loving gay people devoted to social justice and good causes? Think of the former archbishop of Milwaukee, Rembert Weakland, the first Catholic bishop to out himself, Ground Zero's hero, Father Mychal Judge, or famed spiritual writer Henri Nouwen. They, like the Gentiles, certainly had the Spirit.

THE TRAJECTORY OR PROGRESSIVE REVELATION

Within this concept of considering the Bible as a whole to get the genuine divine voice, we have what we might call the "trajectory," or progressive revelation theory. Vatican II held to such a progressive revelation, to a "specific divine pedagogy: God communicates himself to man gradually" (DV, no. 53). Revelation in short, goes in stages. For example, slavery was a social system unerringly held by and morally approved by the Bible for some three thousand years. True, here and there, over the long run, items in the Bible provided a "trajectory" for eventually reversing this moral inequity and dubbing it as an "intrinsic" evil. A word here about being made to the image and likeness of God, a phrase there about there being no longer male or female, slave or free, and so on, and sooner or later these tiny dissonant voices would coalesce to provide a larger context and hermeneutic for the entire Bible and wind up reversing what was acceptable. In short, revelation progresses to meet the growing consciousness of the people. (Or is it the other way around, the growing consciousness of the people critiquing and subverting standard "revelation"?)

As an example, one thinks of the centuries-old teaching of the Catholic Church that there is no salvation beyond its borders. Citing the scriptures, several councils and popes have insisted as much—Innocent III in 1206, Boniface VIII in 1302, the Council of Florence in 1442, Pius IV in 1564, Pius IX in 1854, and so on. Only in the 20th century, at Vatican II, was this modified. As one writer put it:

> "Prompted by the Spirit, Paul VI and the participants at the Second Vatican Council acknowledged that all Christians 'are joined with us in the Holy Spirit for to them also the Spirit gives gifts and graces and is operative among them with sanctifying power.'".... (*Lumen Gentium*, #12) Further prompted by the Spirit, the council also acknowledged that two thirds of the world population who are not Christian 'are most dear to God' and that therefore 'we ought to believe that the Holy Spirit, in a manner known only to God, offers to every human being the grace of being blessed by the paschal mystery... For it is God...as Savior, [who] calls that all be saved.'"[5]

God's ways are indeed mysterious, and the Holy Spirit, the Busy Prompter, delayed his advocacy of non-Catholics, the world's vast majority, for some eight hundred years until, at last, in the 1960s, in an act of progressive revelation, he prompted in a latter-day pope and the bishops to reverse course by discovering in scripture and tradition reasons for doing so.

It would be like this for several changes of heart, as, for example, the move from polygamy to monogamy, or the move from slavery to freedom. This progressive or trajectory theory has value and embraces the reality of growing human consciousness and we may be seeing this process at work in the current case of homosexuality. What all this means is that the climate of interpretation has changed not the texts themselves. Or, as Peter Gomes expresses it, "It is not scripture that has changed, but rather the moral imagination by which we see ourselves, and see and read scripture."

PROGRESS

This appeal to the moral imagination affirms our placing the Bible into the category of narrative or storytelling. This means that, as a storytelling narrative, the Bible, in telling us what happened, doesn't mean that it should always happen, or that it should have happened at all. The narrative is relaying just what happened at the time, perhaps regrettably, but what happened was a step towards a fuller revelation. At the moment, the text is just narrating the urgency of the here and now. The "here and now" is part of an unfolding story, and no ethical or moral imperatives need be immediately drawn from it, because the narrative, since it is a narrative, is not over. So, in this context, as regards to our former example of the God-directed extermination of the Canaanites, attend to Brian D. McLaren:

> "The violence of the Jews in entering Canaan in 1400 B.C. was
> not extraordinary; it was typical of their day. And so we ask:
> In that context was God commanding the people to do, not
> what ideal or ethically desirable for all time, but what was
> necessary to survive in that world at that point? Was there a
> viable alternative at the time for a group of wandering, home-
> less, liberated slaves seeking as homeland? In other words,

assuming history is real and not a simulation, not a chess game in which God plays both sides, not a video game moving to the pressure of God's thumbs on a controller – if God is going to enter into a relationship with people, then God has to work with them as they are in their individual and cultural moral development. And back in those days, that meant that any group of people, if they were to survive, had to fight.... According to the Torah, while God is commanding the destruction of Canaan, God simultaneously commands that once it was subdued, the Jews should treat their neighbors and aliens with respect and kindness."[6]

That last short sentence is exploring the link in the narrative trajectory towards Jesus' "love your enemies." This explanation has great appeal. Still, perhaps ungraciously, it leaves us to wonder about those who, officially and unofficially, for three millennia, took the story as an end, a revealed doctrine carved in stone, and made it unchangeable dogma and not a progressive means to further enlightenment. Moreover, that our moral imagination finally "got it right" seems a small comfort for the abusive horrors that women have suffered as the property of men. Cutting their bodies down from tree limbs is small comfort to the slaves who hung there for three thousand biblically approved years. Being declared as "separated brethren" is small comfort for those infidels who had to be eliminated in the name of orthodoxy. Then too, some might ask, is there really a narrative progression, or does it depend on how one looks at it?

ACCOMMODATION

Then there's the accommodation theory, and this too offers helpful insights. It says that God accommodated his words to the people's development and cultural understanding and social beliefs of the time. We all do this. We speak very differently to the college class than to the third grade class. It's adult talk versus baby talk. In retelling the story of an accident we witnessed, we pass over whether it occurred at Maple or Market Street—who cares if *we* get it wrong? We want to get to the main point. So Luke had to make sense of Mark's story of the friends letting their friend down through the roof thatches, because his sophisticated Greek audience wouldn't know a thatch if they fell over one, so he changed it to tiles, something they understood because that's the way their houses were built. So, too, in a similar way, God does not correct mistaken human viewpoints but lets them ride as long as he gets his point across. After all, people can hardly see reality the way God sees it.

For example, God let the old comprehensions of cosmology stand in the creation stories as long as the point of divine intervention was made. From both plain human sense experience plus the Bible's clear statement that the sun stood still at Joshua's command, the ancients held that the earth is clearly the center of the universe and sun revolves around it. Rather than give the Copernican explanation of the universe, which the ancients would hardly comprehend, God allowed the biblical author to say the sun stood still, the point all the while being that God is in charge. YHWH is fighting on the side of his people. The point was not science but theology. ("The Bible shows how to go to heaven, not how the heavens go.")

Once more there's the representative problem of God commanding genocide in Joshua. Accommodation theory says that God accommodated himself to the people's level of understanding at the time, i.e. that the whole event is really saying that, in their eyes, as a way of preserving themselves as God's Chosen People, perpetuating their sense of ethnic identity and and extolling YHWH's supremacy, the need for warfare was necessary. In short, their hearts were in the right place – God's promise and God's honor – and that's what we should take away from this horrific incident. When YHWH callously ordered lepers to be expelled from the community and segregated into pitiless ghettos, it was because he accommodated himself to a people who did not understand Hansen's disease or modern sanitation or had no notions of antibiotics, and it was the best they could do to contain the disease. So he allowed this heartless solution. The trajectory of "Love your enemy" was still far off. You really have to understand the context of the times.

We see the same thing when Jesus said, in contention with the Pharisees, that God allowed divorce in the old days because of "the hardness of their hearts." In other words, they weren't at a critical or moral understanding of God's original intent of one man and one woman in a stable marriage, and God accommodated himself to where they were. Now it's different. Jesus was setting the record straight (even though in a few decades Paul would override him). In other words, this theory says we have to pay attention not only to what God says here and there in separate instances but whether he is, as it were, still saying it today. Marcus Borg puts it this way:

> "Passages in the New Testament that affirm slavery and patriarchy and condemn same-sex marriages tell us how some of our spiritual ancestors saw things, not necessarily how we should see things. Of course, what they thought in their then matters – but it may or may not be normative for our now."[7]

Context, then, is everything, but look where that puts us: so much depends on what century we were born in. Gay couples who celebrate marriage today were stoned yesterday. Patriarchs considered blessed yesterday by YHWH because of the vast numbers of slaves they owned are cursed today by the Church for the same reason. This then-and-now context may be valid, but we can't help coming back to three thousand years of slaves as property. I think of a similar case in history, when Christianity came to Iceland in 999 where the leaders there readily accepted baptism, but in an accommodation to their long-standing custom, the bishops allowed the people to continue the practice of infanticide by leaving unwanted babies out in the cold exposed to the animals. Presumably this intrinsic evil was allowed until such time as a trajectory of morality could be recognized and established. The concept of accommodation is a genuine consideration but somehow, though, it doesn't seem quite right. A lot of people were enslaved and a lot of babies died as "then" moved to "now". Still, the point of accommodation is a consideration.

THE BIBLE AS IDEAL APPROACH

Finally, there are those who hold that the proper approach to the Bible is to behold and read it as a metaphorical "peaceable kingdom," an ideal to challenge us. We'll see this approach more concretely in the next chapter, when a pervasive nostalgia transforms all the conflicting texts about Abraham. Here we explore its claims. An example of this approach is used by the distinguished scripture scholar Luke Timothy Johnson. In an article in *Commonweal* (May 22, 2009) aptly entitled "How Is the Bible True?" he reminds us that we do not read the Bible texts to seek out information about the ancients and their times, places, and adventures, but read them because they have some truths to tell us on how to live as human beings. The Bible, therefore, is not true in the sense of historical accuracy or its proffered prophecies, but rather in its ability to help us "imagine the world scripture images." So readers should always ask, "Are we encountering the world that the Bible imagines, living in a manner consistent with its vision?" He sums up his approach thusly: "To read the Bible truly, one must be in the process of being transformed by the world that scripture imagines; to speak truly about Jesus, one must be in the process of being transformed into his image."

This approach has the merit of co-opting biblical literalism and absolving all of the scholarly challenges that throw into sharp relief the contradictions and errors of the Bible. It offers us instead a spiritual reading, a spiritual template, against which we measure our spiritual strivings. It offers us a paradigm of the possible. Read as one long *lectio divina*, it offers us, in more modern language, truths to live by, ideals to strive for. Transformation is the name of the biblical game, and it is an appealing game.

The trouble with this, it seems, is that it is too generic and too dangerous. After all, Isaiah did envisage a peaceable kingdom as well, as we have seen, a vision of all nations coming to YHWH, the one true God. But, he implies, they had better, and they had better come in fawning subjection. The Bible preaches that peace and harmony and brotherly love are ideals to be grasped – on its terms. More than this, to anticipate the chapter on pluralism, the emphasis on the Bible as transformative has to be understood, of course, as referring to its own devotees (as I presume Johnson intends it to be) and to that extent it is, as I said, appealing and helpful. However, still in a critical frame of mind, we just have to remember that the Bible isn't the only work to offer an ideal and transformative vision. From Mitch Albom to Marianne Williamson (to name two influential contemporary Jewish figures), from Norman Vincent Peale to Rick Warren (to name two influential gentile figures), from Buddha to Thich Nhat Hanh (to name two influential Buddhist figures), from the utopian fantasies of Thomas More to the *Chronicles of Narnia* of C.S. Lewis (to name two influential literary figures), from Chairman Mao to Karl Marx (to name two influential political figures), we have no lack of ideal visions of life and images to challenge us to make the ideal real. The Bible is only one of many cosmic visions and ideals. It indeed does offers its challenging vision to live up to, but only a gratuitous faith can claim that it, among all the others, is unique and privileged – and better.

DIFFICULTIES

The difficulty with all these quite valuable allegorical, analogical, and metaphorical readings of the Bible is the stubborn fact that in reality, everybody in the Synagogue and Church for centuries and centuries, hierarchy and laity alike (creating a real *sensus fidelium*), firmly believed that the biblical narratives were literally and historically true, officially pronounced them to be so, and wrote them into their official creeds and liturgies. It's undeniable that synagogues and churches have built faith systems and doctrines on such putative literal history. The biblical writers themselves often believed they were true (when they were not creating fictions themselves) and that in them, as they stood, revelation was to be found. That belief still persists today. In any case, figuring out which is legend, saga, and allegory and separating the two "voices," the voice of the culture bound writer and the voice of the eternal God revealing eternal truth, is daunting and the danger of subjectivism – amply testified to by the endless variations of Christianity – is a challenge.

THE INSPIRATION MANTRA

When it comes to the Bible as the inspired word of God, most people, unconvinced by these theories, usually, it seems, opt for a kind of fideism: "The Bible's authority stems from the Church's belief that while we do not know how biblical inspiration works, the Bible, under the guidance of the Holy Spirit, can guide our lives in areas of faith and morals."[8]

Vatican II weighs in with [the] same act of assumed faith:

> "Since, therefore, all that the inspired authors, or sacred writers, affirm should be regarded as affirmed by the Holy Spirit, we must acknowledge that the books of scripture, firmly and faithfully and without error, teach that truth which God, *for the sake of salvation*, wished to see confided to the sacred scriptures" (DV, #11).

In one way, this seems like a kind of a whimpish definition. That "for the sake of salvation" phrase underscores not so much the text but divine intention; that is, inspiration must be seen in terms of salvation, not in terms of historical or scientific accuracy. But immediately you have to ask, how does anybody know what God wanted to put into scripture "for the sake of salvation?" There's no criterion. One Catholic writer explains inspiration this way,

"Inspiration is a mysterious process. It's not as if God dictated, and the authors wrote what they heard. Instead God instilled in human beings divine insights which they described in their own words using images from their own culture to help the readers understand the message."[9]

That's a good description as any but, in the last analysis, we have to ask how this works.

Who, for example, can forget the internecine warfare among the Jews of the New Testament that morphed into anti-Semitism? It's hard to see that "His blood be upon us and our children" is for the sake of salvation, or what the "divine insight" is behind these cultural words. The claim is that there is a "behind the scenes" truth here, but do we really know what it is? What we do know has been horrific. Many other examples could be given that make you wonder how this or that could relate to salvation. The bottom line is that if we insist on some divine influence on the writings of anonymous authors who wrote some pretty terrible things, as we try to ferret out some "religious message" or even listen to our Church's often contradictory interpretations, we still have to reconcile the tensions of opposing theories. Again, it comes down to reading the Bible through the lens of faith or reading it as literature. Which one you choose is left, it seems, to the vagaries of fate and culture.

A CATHOLIC EXCURSUS

We close our discussion of the interpretation theories in this chapter by concluding that apparently one thing is quite clear: with all of the solid scholarly investigations, with all of the recent discoveries of the cultures and records of the Near East, no one can read the Bible quite the same way anymore. Outside of rigid conservatives, no one can take it literally anymore. Religions and denominations, as we have seen in this chapter, have dealt with this tension differently, offering various theories that seek to reconcile the old interpretations and traditions with new insights. Here we reflect on the Catholic Church's dilemma.

Before 1943, when Pope Pius XII gave permission to read the Bible differently, the Catholic Church for the most part offered its literal reading of the Bible wrapped in its unique traditions. But with Pius XII, the Church switched to what we might call a contextualist approach. This is to say that, Catholics could now consider a particular biblical passage within its context – its idioms, its literary form and conventions, and its allusions – and not simply take what is says literally. If, for example, there is a talking snake, we can admit that we're in folklore, not history. If God is walking and chatting with Abraham we know the conversation is the author's invention, not an overheard conversation. If an author wanted to show God's creative power, he looked to the world he knew and saw and had God work on canopies that separate the waters, and built up posts on the four corners of a flat earth. His point was not accurate cosmology that he did not know. It was God's creative power and his relation to the world. We could consider that the story of Adam and Eve and the trees and apple and snake as not historical. It's a story about suffering, relationships to God and the planet and sin. When Paul told slaves to be obedient to their masters, he wasn't condoning slavery only commenting on the social order as he knew it and simply insisting that, no matter what is was, people should treat each other with love. When Matthew kept on saying that this or that took place in accordance with the prophets, he didn't mean that the prophets actually consciously foretold future events, but rather that current events were injected back into the scriptures as a way of understanding the prophets' words more fully and on a new level. In other words, for example, Jesus' virgin birth was not a literal fulfillment of Isaiah but a read-back suggestion that, you know, the prophet was saying more than he realized. He left us tantalizing language we can apply to Jesus.

The point is that, in all these examples, we are taught to read the context in which the biblical words were written down and not project our understandings and times into them. We are to seek to understand the story's point, not its faulty science or unlikelihoods. We need to separate the core truth from the context of its genre, time and place and not transplant the context to our times as literal realities. In short, "A symbolic story cannot be the basis for biological or historical claims."[11]

THE AMBIGUOUS SNAKE

But, to use the metaphor from Genesis, there is a theological snake in this garden of contexualism. Tensions persist. For example, if Pius XII gave Catholics the freedom to re-read the Bible in a new context, he was not above regressing when later he insisted in his encyclical *Humani Generis* (1950) that Adam and Eve were indeed the actual biological parents of the whole human race and the whole issue of Original Sin was a literal one. (Later, Pope John Paul II would correct this.) But this is the problem that remains and vexes Catholics today. The Catholic Church sometimes holds on to or reverts to fundamentalism by presenting some of its teachings as though the biblical authors supported them, when in fact they do not. The agitation of current issues like church authority (especially papal authority), the ordination of women, contraception, annulments, ecumenism, abortion, the conversion of the Jews, and gay marriage each center on scripture-based traditions that are hotly debated. Today's Church's move from Rock of Ages to Pilgrim Church is a contentious one.

The last three issues I mentioned – abortion, Jews, and gay marriage – we turn to in the next two chapters, where not only are traditional teachings about them being challenged, but where the whole issue of the Catholic Church actually changing its teachings is exposed, as well as the angst that this causes Catholics who feel doctrinal certainties slipping out from beneath them.

Chapter 20.

THREE MODERN TENSIONS

Three particular tensions trouble the modern person of faith, the three hot-button polarities of tradition and abortion, evangelization and the Jews, and scripture and the gays. In the context of this book, they readily become a microcosm of the pivotal issue of the Bible's authority.

TRADITION AND ABORTION

First tension: abortion. Abortion still divides the country – and the synagogues and churches. The appeal to scripture to settle this case is futile. Jeremiah 20:15-18 clearly speaks of human life in the womb but pro-life people tend to use two quotes. One is Genesis 30:19, "Choose life" and is a logo on much of pro-life literature. This directive, however, is a rhetorical flourish. Moses has set before the people "life and prosperity, death and adversity" (30:15) He is urging his people to choose the right path, to choose the way he has laid out before them. To refuse to do so is to court death. Don't do this, he says. Choose life. The other biblical quotation is Exodus 20:13, "Thou shalt not kill." The correct translation is, "Thou shalt do no murder." That is, you must not take the life of someone *already* born. However, absent any explicit biblical prohibition against abortion, there is the whole tenor of scripture and tradition and, until recently, the consistent stance of Christians.

The Talmud taught that life begins once "the greater part of the child was already born," that is, halfway through birth, and allowed abortion when medically necessary. The famous 1st century Jewish philosopher, Philo, roundly condemned gentiles for practicing abortion and infanticide. The Church Fathers also weighed in condemning abortion, for example from the *Didache* written during the New Testament period: "Commit no murder, adultery, sodomy, fornication, or theft. Practice no magic, sorcery, abortion or infanticide." The early 2nd century Epistle of Barnabas: "You shall not kill either the fetus by abortion or the new born." The early 2nd century Apocalypse of Peter: "Those who slew the unborn children will be tortured forever, for God wills it to be so." Clement of Alexandria, Tertullian, Hippolytus, Basil the Great, Ambrose, Jerome and a whole host of Church Fathers, plus early Church synods condemned abortion. The prohibition of abortion was fairly unanimous and was considered to be based on the teachings of the Bible.

So at one time the Christian consensus, in contrast to the Greek and Roman state religions and the various Mystery religions, was fairly unanimous: abortion was morally wrong. There was, however, some debate as to whether there was a real human being in the womb for the first 40 (males) or 90 (females) days – there was as yet no "ensoulment" – but after the first trimester, it definitely was murder to kill the unborn child. Jews also were opposed to abortion and infanticide, making exception only if the pregnancy posed a risk to the life of the mother. Augustine was different in that he felt that early first trimester abortion was not murder because there is no ensoulment yet, but after that ensoulment, it was morally wrong but his view did not prevail. Besides he condemned abortion, not because of the status of the fetus, but because it meant that sex was used for reasons other than procreation, which he thought was always wrong. Later, Thomas Aquinas would feel the same.

Later centuries found the Catholic Church teaching that this ensoulment was present from the moment of conception. In answer to the modern question, "When does a person become a person?"

The Church answered the moment when the egg and sperm meet. That's when God breathes in the soul. The deduction, then, is obvious: to destroy this simple organism, this impregnated egg, devoid of context, is thus to commit murder. But some ask if this can be true. Can a soul reside in just a primitive single sperm-egg combination and not in some kind of a body, without a womb to animate it? Augustine wondered about this. So did Aquinas and so did Pope Gregory XIV. They all felt that just the simple sperm-egg combination without a formative or forming body could not be considered a person. It was not a fully animated fetus. It was still in the process of becoming a person. This meant a woman who followed a well-formed conscience could justify terminating that early "pre-person." That opinion might have prevailed were it not for Pius IX who in the nineteenth century closed off this possibility. He pronounced excommunication for *any* stage of pregnancy even the first moment of sperm-egg contact regardless of any further context or implantation in the womb. But then, some ask further, how does one respond to the fact that modern science has shown that many eggs are fertilized but never get implanted in the womb and they die? Are these really "persons"? Science also shows us that sometimes a fertilized egg can divide and eventually become more than one person just as two fertilized eggs can merge and eventually become one person. Do the "souls" of these people similarly multiply or subtract? Some would argue that it would seem that early on, before the impregnated egg attaches to the womb, there is some leeway for a termination.

But, notwithstanding these considerations, the Christian tradition was unanimous that, from the start, abortion, at least after the first trimester, was morally wrong, intrinsically evil. The tradition never envisaged that in our day the horror of abortion on demand at *any* stage of pregnancy right up to the moment of birth for whatever reason, however frivolous, could or would ever be, considered socially and morally acceptable, and become a woman's enshrined sole absolute right. The "sole" is unique. The community is entirely left out of the discussion. Individualism has reached its apex.

The acceptance of abortion, by some forms of biblical Judaism and Christianity, is equally stunning. At this writing, the Roman Catholic Church, the Church of England, and some evangelical churches still absolutely oppose abortion. The Eastern Orthodox Church is opposed, except in cases of danger to the mother's health. Other denominations, such as the United Methodist Church, Evangelical Lutheran Church in America and many other mainline Protestant churches hold a weak pro-choice position. Others, like Unitarians, the United Church of Christ, and the Episcopal Church in the U.S., are strong pro-choice churches. We should note that with the advance of technology today, which enables doctors to extract early DNA that can map the genes and reveal the fetus' genetic characteristics along with the ability to detect its gender, parents more than ever have the incentive to choose abortion for gender preference[1] – India, for example, has 37 million more men than women —-or ensuring "healthy" babies or even designer babies with desired traits. In any case, if you want an example of an extreme reversal of the ancient Christian tradition attend to the words of Katherine Ragsdale, the dean and president of the Episcopal Divinity School of Cambridge, who calls abortion, not a sin, not a necessary yet regrettable choice, but a positive blessing! Speaking to NARAL in Texas in 2007, she said:

> "And when a woman becomes pregnant within a loving, supportive, respectful relationship, has every option open to her [and] decides she does not wish to bear a child; and has access to a safe, affordable abortion – there is not a tragedy in sight – only a blessing. The ability to enjoy God's good gift of sexuality without compromising one's education, life's work or ability to put to use God's gifts and call is simply blessing.

> "There are two things I want you, please, to remember – abortion is a blessing and our work is not done... I want to thank all who protect this blessing – who do this work every day: the healthcare providers, doctors, nurses, technician, receptionists, who put their lives on the line to care for others you are heroes – in my eyes, you are saints..."

This message of a Christian dean of a Christian divinity school is clear. It gives the woman a total, complete autonomous power over human life. She is to enjoy sex and if, by chance, she gets pregnant and it threatens her lifestyle (education, career, self-expression) then she should avail herself at any time during the pregnancy of the wonderful God-given blessing of a safe and affordable abortion by handing herself over to the heroic saints of the industry. It's hard to think of a more extreme example by a Christian of turning scripture and tradition on their heads and consequently making them both obsolete, irrelevant, to the times.

CONVERT THE JEWS?

Second tension: converting the Jews. On this subject, there has been a radical reversal in the matter of the treatment of Jews and their conversion. We always thought (and were taught) that, although the Jews gave us the Old Testament, they were a perverse people whose revelation had been superseded by Christianity. Their only hope of salvation was conversion. That attitude prevailed for 2000 years. Then came Vatican II and its document, *Nostra Aetate*, and the other, *The Jewish People and Their Sacred Scriptures in the Christian Bible* issued by the Pontifical Biblical Commission in 2002. They both say that Catholics should not evangelize Jews. It is forbidden to do so. It is "no longer theologically acceptable." Why? Because the original Hebrew Covenant remains binding and valid. Among the scriptural sources given for this novel stance are passages from the Epistle to the Hebrews (#82) that clearly underscore the enduring validity of Israel's Covenant. Then there are the words of Pope Benedict XVI in his 2011 book, *Jesus of Nazareth: Holy Week: From the Entrance Into Jerusalem to the Resurrection*. In this book, he firmly and unequivocally stated that Christians should not seek the conversion of the Jews. "Israel is in the hands of God, who will save it 'as a whole' at the proper time when the number of gentiles is full" – whenever that "proper time" comes. No one knows the answer to that, but there is the sequence: gentiles first, Jews second. Benedict does not endorse a kind of "two Covenant" theory meaning that Judaism and Christianity represent two parallel paths to salvation so that Jews are saved without Christ. But his statement stands: the Church has no program to convert the Jews, nor *should* it have. That's a completely radical reversal of Church teaching and, ironically, it is based on scripture.

For some scholars, however, it's not that simple. They note that the statements of the Council and the Pope turn out to be based on a very selective reading of the New Testament, especially the Epistle to the Hebrews. Father Joseph Fitzmyer, S.J., for one, points out that the Church document conveniently omits other strong passages in Hebrews that completely contradict the thesis. He cites Hebrews 8:6-13 which reads: "In speaking of a new Covenant, he [Christ] treats the first as obsolete. And what is becoming obsolete and growing old is ready to vanish away." That's quite clear. He also cites Hebrews 10:9 which reads, "Then he added, 'Lo, I have come to do thy will.' He abolished the first order to establish the second." The words "abolish," obsolete" – nothing can be clearer than that. Yes, the Jewish Covenant has given way to the New Covenant, and for millennia, therefore, starting with Peter's (Luke's) words in the Book of Acts urging his fellow Jews to be baptized and accept the Lord Jesus, the conversion of the Jews was a given. It was then, and remained till recently, quite proper to try to convert the Jews, whether by force or persuasion. Now, in our times, some 2,000 years later, it is improper. Scripture is cited to support either stand as the Church document selects one set of quotations, leaving others that say the opposite unmentioned. In an exchange with Father Fitzmyer, Fr. John T. Pawlikowski makes this mind-teasing reply to his criticism:

> "Joseph A. Fitzmyer is correct about the apparent contradic-
> tion between several texts in Hebrews and *Nostra Aetate's*
> proclamation of continued Jewish covenantal inclusion after
> Christ. The answer to this dilemma can only come from a
> theological understanding of the authority of an ecumenical

council to make an interpretation in such a situation. And the Second Vatican Council decided by an overwhelming vote to make Romans 9:11, with its strong affirmation of covenantal continuity for the Jewish people, the prevailing biblical text for understanding the church's relationship to the Jewish people. According to Catholic theology, the council had every right to make such a decision."[2]

CARDINAL DULLES

Another Jesuit, the late Cardinal Avery Dulles, also cried, "Wait a minute!". He wondered how the Church could finesse Scripture so.[3] He points out that the document is in fact quite contrary to, and not consistent with, papal pronouncement and scripture. He cites Pope Paul VI's encyclical *Evangelii Nuntiandi,* which forthrightly states "that there is no true evangelization if the name, teaching, the life, the promises, the Kingdom and the mystery of Jesus of Nazareth, the Son of God, are not proclaimed." And he notes that Pope John Paul II backs up these words. Dulles notes that the Gospel is to be proclaimed to all the world, no exceptions. He cites Peter's sermon in Acts (2:38) that everyone listening to him should be baptized. He points out St. Paul's constant preaching to his fellow Jews. Paul explicitly looked forward to the day when all will be grafted into Christ, and he also looked forward to the day when all of Israel will recognize Christ and be saved (Rom. 11:26). Dulles also cites the verses above, (Hebrews 7:12, 8:13 and 10:9), which boldly declare that the "first Covenant" is obsolete, abolished by Christ himself. He summarizes forcefully: "Once we grant that there are some persons for whom it is not important to acknowledge Christ, to be baptized and to receive the sacraments, we raise questions about our own religious life."

The Cardinal also noted that an ecumenical council, the Council of Constance (1414-1418), insisted that Jews could be saved only through conversion and baptism. *The Catechism of the Catholic Church,* while acknowledging the Church's "link with the Jewish people," and maintaining that the "Jewish faith, unlike other non-Christian religions, is already a response to God's revelation in the Old Testament," nevertheless still proclaims, " Having been divinely sent to the nations that she might be 'the universal sacrament of salvation', the Church, in obedience to the command of her founder and because it is demanded by her own essential universality, strives to preach the Gospel to all men. Go, therefore, and make disciples of *all* men, baptizing them..." (849)

A DIFFERENT TAKE

So we seem to have a contradiction about the Jews, an inexplicable reversal. But once more, and surprising (to most lay people) is an answer put forth with its challenging hermeneutic:

> "Much of Cardinal Dulles's critique of these concepts in *Reflections* flows from his reading of the New Testament. It is not enough, however, to cite Scripture without recognizing that the Bible is the church's book and that, therefore, the church continuously interprets those texts. In the words of the Pontifical Biblical Commission, '...[I]nterpretation of Scripture involves a work of sifting and setting aside...it stands in continuity with earlier exegetical traditions, many elements of which it preserves and makes its own; but in other matters it will go its own way, seeking to make further progress'(*The Interpretation of the Bible in the Church*, 1993).

> "Thus, we are troubled by Cardinal Dulles's assertion that the Letter to the Hebrews offers 'the most formal statement of the status of the Sinai Covenant under Christianity.' Without further analysis, he quotes Hebrews: The first covenant is 'obsolete' and 'ready to vanish away' (Heb. 8:13). Christ 'abolishes the first covenant' in order to establish the second' (Heb. 10:9).

> "Cardinal Dulles implies that Catholics believe that God's covenant with the people of Israel is obsolete. In contrast,

we argue that official Catholic teaching today has, in the Biblical Commission's 1993 formulation, 'gone its own way' and 'set aside' the opinion of the author of Hebrews about Israel's covenant. As Reflections notes, Pope John Paul II has on many occasions declared that Jews are 'the people of God of the Old Covenant never revoked by God,' 'the present-day people of the covenant concluded with Moses,' and 'partners in a covenant of eternal love which was never revoked.'

"The magisterium can explicitly contradict an idea of an individual New Testament author because the Catholic tradition is one of commentary, not of *sola scriptura* (Scripture alone). The author of Hebrews, convinced that he was living in the final stages of human history, could argue that the Old Covenant had yielded to the New. Two millennia later, however, in a church whose pope has prayed for God's forgiveness for the sins of Christians against Jews, such an assertion is unacceptable. The constant disparagement of postbiblical Judaism through the ages and general ignorance of its character encouraged European Christians to marginalize and even at times demonize Jews, thus providing a fertile seedbed for the Shoah."[4]

These words are perplexing to most people. They seem to present such an uneven hermeneutic and undermine a very unstable Bible. Anyway, take a good look again at how others might understand them.

THE TENSIONS

We have scripture, a long and consistent tradition, an ecumenical council, papal encyclicals and a universal catechism – all unerringly and consistently proclaiming that the Gospel must be preached to all, even the Jews. This belief has been hallowed by a two-thousand-year tradition (which sometimes included a nasty anti-Semitism). Now it seems that, after twenty centuries of scripture interpretation and tradition, all has been reduced to a culture bound biblical writer's mere "opinion" and tradition's unachieved consciousness that has only lately arrived to reverse the position. The Catholic Church now officially states that it no longer seeks the conversion of the Jews. It declares that the Jewish expectation of a coming Messiah is valid and the Jewish covenant with YHWH has not been abrogated but continues even after the coming of Jesus.

The Jewish Covenant, in other words, is not outdated after the coming of the Anointed Messiah, Christ – a concept that will not only force some changes in the Advent liturgy with its strong stress on the fulfillment of the Messianic prophecies in Jesus, but leaves us all faced with a seeming contradiction.

It is the principle that, though legitimate, perplexes. The appeal to "new consciousness" or a leap of the moral imagination confuses most. That principle says we can set aside scripture, tradition, papal encyclicals, and a Church council, completely reverse them all, and declare that what was divinely mandated, allowed and taught for millennia is now prohibited or discouraged. This is no development of doctrine, but a reversal of doctrine. The whole issue seems to make scripture totally provisional, and time- and culture-bound, full of words of command and restriction waiting to be liberated by a new age. Who knows when another era will reverse another century's teaching? The criterion has been set: at any time in the future, arriving at a new consciousness, we can "sift," "set aside," "go our own way," and "explicitly contradict an idea of an individual biblical author." The logical result seems to be that the best we can say of any scripture passage is "yes, this is what it means – for now." As for those Christians who wholeheartedly took the Church's official teaching seriously for the last two thousand years, they are excused because of invincible ignorance. As for the harassed and proselytized Jews (often under force), they just happened to be in the wrong millennia.

Realizing the tensions we have mentioned, in 2008 the U.S. bishops decided to delete the reference to the Covenant between God and the Jews from the U. S. Edition of the Catechism. They said too many Catholics misunderstood the words, "Thus the Covenant that God made with the Jewish people through Moses remains eternally valid for them." The bishops felt that it sounded too much like Jews do not need Jesus to be saved. The statement, they said, was not necessarily wrong, but rather too ambiguous. So the bishops issued this statement: "While the Catholic Church does not proselytize the Jewish people neither does she fail to witness to them her faith in Christ, to welcome them to share in that same faith whenever appropriate." This seeming backpedaling rankled several Jewish groups, who said that their relationship with the Roman Catholic Church is at risk. They feel that the new interpretation means that interfaith dialogue implies a covert form of inviting Jews to become Catholic.

CONTEXT

Let's go back to our context of scripture. Here, we agree, tradition can deepen and explicate a previous passage, but to outright contradict an inspired writer? Make the sacred writer's views, embraced for centuries, "unacceptable," reduce his conviction to an "opinion?" What it seems to come down to, as we stated, is that it all depends what time frame you live in. At one epoch, the word of God means one thing. At another epoch, it is not only obsolete but also untrue and even harmful, and must be vehemently disregarded. "Obsolete" is acceptable. "Untrue" and "harmful" are stumbling blocks. As one Catholic commentator on a similar situation, namely Paul's infamous passage on women keeping their place, writes:

> "There is one advantage in the lectionary shift: you don't have to read that passage from Paul on that day. It shouldn't be read unless it is used as an example of how things have changed, and rightly so. As we say elsewhere, his views on women, sex, marriage, and virginity, compressed in one paragraph, cannot now be defended. But who are we to update or censor the lectionary choices and to cast out a passage of holy writ? Who are we? People for whom biblical scholarship has enabled us to understand and sometimes to correct or omit the biblical texts we employ."[5]

We are indeed such a people who are free to "correct" or "omit" those biblical texts we find out of date. After all, the Church is a living tradition, and every fixed canon needs its Supreme Court to contextualize scripture. The Church has in fact, as we shall see, changed it teachings several times. It's just that it's difficult to find some stability and credibility in such a wealth of corrections, and reversals and it's difficult for most people to accept a malleable Bible as the eternal, much less inerrant word of God. Ongoing, ever new consciousness renders the biblical word quite relative. That time lapse is bothersome. Once more, what about the people who lived in former times whom in conscience adhered to former teaching? What about the mavericks who can claim, say, that late-term abortion is not only right but can be found in scripture, and that they are prophets simply ahead of their time awaiting the vindication of a future "sifting"?

ACCEPT THE GAYS? A CELEBRATED CASE

The third tension: gay marriage. "Rising consciousness" criteria have found another hot-button issue: homosexuality. Scholars today argue that the scriptural prohibitions against homosexuality are as obsolete as the other dietary laws and ritual taboos that we no longer follow. So it's no surprise that the newly elected Lutheran bishop of Stockholm, the Rev. Eva Brunne, is the first openly lesbian bishop in the world and the first who lives in a registered homosexual partnership (with another lesbian priest), and has received her church's blessing. Let's turn closer to home to a celebrated case, with no judgment implied. In August of 2003, the Episcopalians confirmed Gene Robinson as their first openly gay (and divorced) bishop and approved same sex unions. On November 2nd of that year, he was officially installed. He received the miter from his two daughters, from his previous marriage, and his male companion. Then, in July of 2009, the bishops of the Episcopal Church, by a large majority, voted to give latitude to its bishops to bless homosexual unions, indicating that an official ritual is not far off. (In this they joined the Unitarian Universalist Association, the United Church of Christ, the reform movements in Judaism, the Quakers, and the Evangelical Lutheran Church, the largest Lutheran denomination in the U.S. Others are in the wings, for example, in June of 2014, the Presbyterian Church, U.S.A. changed its constitution's definition of marriage from "a man and a woman" to "two people" – although "two" is already being challenged by polygamists. Immediately, the more conservative Episcopalians and other Christians asked the expected biblical questions: What about those verses in both the Old and New testaments that clearly pronounce homosexual acts to be immoral and against the will of God?

Besides, one would have thought that the issue of gay marriage had been definitively settled by no less a person than Jesus: "Have you not read that he who made them at the beginning made them male and female, and for this reason, a man shall leave his father and mother and be joined to his wife, and the two shall become one flesh?" (Matthew 19:4-5) YHWH is the origin of the male-female arrangement, and the male, by divine will, is joined to his wife not his husband. But, even here, such fundamental foundational words can be set aside as belonging to a different context. Elsewhere there are these witnesses:

"You shall not lie with a male as with a woman; it is an abomination." And "If a man lies with a male as he lies with a woman, both of them have committed an abomination. They shall surely be put to death. Their blood shall be upon them." So says the word of God in Leviticus 18:22 and 20:13.

St. Paul weighs in: "For this reason God gave them up to degrading passions. Their women exchanged natural intercourse for unnatural; and in the same way also the men, giving up natural intercourse with women, were consumed with passion for one another. Men committed shameless acts with men and received in their own persons the due penalty for their error." (Romans 1: 26-27) "Do not be deceived! Fornicators, idolaters, adulterers, male prostitutes, sodomites, thieves, the greedy, drunkards, revilers, robbers – none of these will inherit the Kingdom of God!" (1 Cor. 6:9-10).

The tradition of the Church Fathers piled on:

The Didache: "You shall not commit murder, you shall not commit adultery, you shall not commit pederasty" (2).

The Letter to Barnabas: "You shall not be a corrupter of youth" (10).

Clement: "It is not, then without reason that the poets call him [Hercules] a cruel wretch and a nefarious scoundrel. It were tedious to recount his adulteries of all sorts, and a debauching of boys. Or your gods did not even abstain from boys" (Exhortation to the Greeks, 2).

Cyprian: "Turn your looks to the abominations not less to be deplored, of another kind of spectacle ...Men are emasculated, and all the pride and vigor of their sex is effeminate in the disgrace of their enervated body; and he is more pleasing there who had most completely broken down the man into a woman" (Letters 1:8).

John Chrysostom: "The pagans were addicted to the love of boys, and one of their wise men made a law that pederasty should not be allowed to slaves as if it were an honorable thing...As for their passion for boys, whom they called their *paedica*, it is not fit to be named" (Homilies on Titus. 5).

Augustine: "Those shameful acts against nature such as were committed in Sodom ought everywhere and always to be detested" (Confessions 3:8:15).

The Catechism of the Catholic Church sums it all up by declaring that homosexual acts are sinful, a conclusion solidly based on scripture – for example, Genesis 19:1-29 (the Sodom episode), 1 Corinthians 6:10, and 1 Tim 1:10. The Catechism also makes reference the teachings of the Congregation for the Doctrine of Faith, *Persona humana* 8 (#2357): "Basing itself on Sacred Scriptures, which represent homosexual acts as acts of great depravity, tradition has always declared that homosexual acts are intrinsically disordered."

EXPERIENCE RULES

On the Anglican side, the Rev. David P. Jones, a co-chairmen of the search committee that confirmed the bishop, well aware of such verses and well aware of the centuries-old church tradition, nevertheless said these remarkable words (emphasis mine): "Ten years ago I would not have been happy about this because I would have felt it's clearly *contrary to the Bible, contrary to the traditions of the church*. It's all because I've experienced the ministry of this man and a couple of others that I think I was mistaken." In 2013, the Mormons helped pass a bill in the U.S. Senate banning workplace discrimination because of gender identity and sexual orientation. Senate Majority Leader Harry Reid, a Mormon, helped push it through. Senator Orin Hatch, also a Mormon, joined him. For the Mormons that's a complete turnabout. (Like the Catholics,, the Mormons now say that homosexuality is all right, but acting out on it is not.) Interestingly, Senator Hatch (he has a niece who is lesbian) also cited experience, saying that he changed his mind when he realized that orientation was not a choice.

All this would seem to be a simon-pure example of experience negating the written word of scripture and long-standing tradition. Not all are happy with this. N.T Wright remarks:

> "If 'experience' is itself a source of authority, we can no longer be addressed by a word which comes from the beyond ourselves. At this point, theology and Christian living cease to be rooted in God himself, and are rooted instead in own selves..."[6]

Nevertheless, the Rev. Jones, enlightened with the new consciousness and experiencing the niceness and graciousness of the newly appointed bishop, insists that these have superseded the tradition of three millennia and rendered null and void words "clearly contrary to the Bible." Canadian columnist David Warren has also noted that Gene Robin, the gay Episcopal bishop of New Hampshire, has boldly declared, "Just because Scripture and tradition say something is wrong that doesn't necessarily mean it's wrong." This indeed may be so, but to many he's seemingly just vacated the authority of both and that's what bothers people.

Chapter 21.

THE TENSIONS CONTINUE

There is this howler from a liberal Baptist minister (at one time that description would have been an oxymoron) who supports gay marriage by quoting scripture from the Book of Ecclesiastes: "If two lie down together, they will keep warm. But how can one keep warm alone?" That's it? Yes, not quite the same as Leviticus 20:13, but the verse, in his eyes, is clearly a biblical support of gay marriage. I think we can do better by turning to the Catholic Scripture scholar, Luke Timothy Johnson [Disclosure: he has a lesbian daughter]. He admits that the scriptural texts are clear and they are straightforward: they *do* condemn homosexuality – *but*, he adds, there are grounds for standing in tension with [scholarly jargon for disagreement with] the commands of "the-Word-of-God" scripture. He writes (emphasis mine):

> "I think it important to state clearly that we do in fact, reject the straightforward commands of Scripture, and appeal instead to another authority when we declare that same sex-unions can be holy and good. And what exactly is that authority? We appeal explicitly to the weight of our own experience and the experience of thousands of others have witnessed to, which tells us that to claim our own sexual orientation is in fact to accept the way in which God has created us. By so doing, we explicitly reject as well the premises of the scriptural statements condemning homosexuality – namely that it is a vice freely chosen, a symptom of human corruption and disobedience to God's created order..."

"Implicit in an appeal to experience is also an appeal to the living God whose creative work never ceases, who continues to shape humans in his image ever day in ways that can surprise and even shock us. ...Our situation vis-à-vis the authority of Scripture is not unlike that of abolitionists in nineteenth-century America. During the 1850s, arguments raged over the morality of slaveholding, and the exegesis of Scripture played a key role in those debates. The exegetical battles were one-sided: all abolitionists could point to was Galatians 3:28 and the Letter of Philemon, while slave owners had the rest of the Old and New Testaments, which gave every indication that slaveholding was a legitimate, indeed God-ordained social arrangement, one which neither Moses or Jesus or Paul raised a fundamental objection. So how is it that now, in the early 21st century, the authority of the scriptural texts on slavery and the argument made on their basis appear to all of us, without exception, as completely beside the point and deeply wrong? The answer is that over time the *human experience* of slavery and its horrors came home to the popular conscience..."

"Many of us who stand for the full recognition of gay and lesbian persons within the Christian communion find ourselves in a position similar to that of the early abolitionists...*We are fully aware of the weight of scriptural evidence pointing away from our position*, yet we place our trust in the power of the loving God to reveal as powerfully through personal experience and testimony as through written texts."[1]

As we have noted at the end of the last chapter, the prolific Anglican bishop of Durham, N.T. Wright, strongly criticizes this tendency to add "experience" to the traditional three-legged Anglican stool of Scripture, tradition and reason.[2] Perhaps the bishop also has in mind one of those embarrassments common to all religions; in their liturgy the Anglicans celebrate the heroic and fiery deaths of a set of martyrs in Uganda for refusing the orders of their king to commit sodomy. This has left the Ugandan Anglican Church a bit uneasy as the American Anglican church ordains a practicing homosexual as a bishop, and the American Anglican Church a bit sheepishly looks the other way.

Anyway, our point here is that a noted Catholic scripture scholar, like the Anglican clergyman quoted above, has a "set-aside" and "sifting" card to trump scripture and tradition: the growth of human consciousness, which puts things in an entirely different context and negates the written word: "God can reveal as much through personal experience as through the biblical texts." He may indeed be right, but it leaves open the question of criterion: who decides between them? Who decides between them when personal experience [new consciousness] and the official traditional views bump into each other? How many times are we told that we no longer need to follow the "God-given" laws found written in the Bible: laws about diet, dress, sacrifice, etc. They don't make sense anymore. They are culture bound. The same argument is now being made on behalf of homosexuality. The explicit words of scripture are apparently not the last word; that over time, they lose their force and that more and more they are seen as very contextualized pronouncements of a primitive people, not the unchangeable, enduring "Words of an eternal God" or "God's Word in human words." That's why, as we have seen, we discarded the Sabbath observance and circumcision.

We see the same thing happen in the issue of divorce. Lost in all the discussion about Bishop Gene Robinson's homosexuality is the issue of his divorces. The bishop divorced his wife in the late 1980s in order to marry a man in 2011. Three years later, in 2014, he also divorced his new husband. One heterosexual and one homosexual marriage and two divorces of a gay Episcopal bishop – all quite legitimate in his church which honors scripture. Again, what about that scripture? "Now a bishop must be above reproach, married only once." (1 Tim. 3: 2), and "I left you behind in Crete for this reason that you should put in order what remained to be done and should appoint elders in every town as I directed you: someone who is blameless, married only once..." (Titus 1:5) Do we apply, "Just because the divinely inspired Paul said a bishop must be married only once doesn't mean that he's right?" "Human experience" and "growing consciousness" have declared the biblical words obsolete. If it's a process that's legitimate, it still confuses.

INTERPRETATIONS

To go back to the Rev. Jones: to give the reverend his postmodern due, maybe in those ten years he has embraced these twin assessments, namely that the words of scripture are as culturally time-conditioned as its dietary laws, and all those obsolete ritual purification laws of Leviticus we mentioned above really came from the priestly caste some eight hundred years before and were put into the mouth of God. So they don't apply. There is some truth here. The fact is that over time, we have simply ignored some aspects of scripture and tradition that didn't fit anymore. It can be similarly argued, for example, that when St. Paul spoke of homosexual acts as an abomination, he presumed that people had a choice; that they were heterosexual people being freely dissolute and perverse in turning something natural into something unnatural. Paul had no notion of homosexual orientation, whether genetically or socially induced, and no notion that, therefore, no homosexual person experienced homosexual acts as an evil, objective disorder the way he did. In short, St. Paul's notion of homosexuality was miles apart from what we understand today. It is clear in this context that his concept of homosexuality was male pederasty and male prostitution practiced by the Romans, and he wanted Christians to have none of that. Thus, Paul focused – as did generations after him – on the act itself and not on the larger moral or psychological context. Then, too, the Bible, in assuming that marriage is between a man and a woman, does so within a political and social context we no longer share. Seldom in the Bible, it seems, is marriage described as a result of mutual love, but as a matter of practicality. The Hebrews were an under populated people, so they allowed a man to marry several women, although not women from outside the faith. A man had to marry his

brother's widow, and female slaves could be forced to serve as surro-
gate mothers. Paul's opinion was that it was better not to marry at all.

The same social context pervades Genesis 1 and 2, where God made
Adam and Eve and gave them the mandate to procreate and fill
the earth. The situation here was the need to have more Hebrews,
because from them would come the Messiah and the biblical authors
didn't want to jeopardize that. This needed heterosexual paring did
not necessarily imply that male-female is the *only* form of sexuality,
just a practical one. The same context exists with the Holiness Code,
where Leviticus forbids the men to lie with a man as with a woman.
The situation here is that is what those "pagans" do and you're not
to be like them. It's in the same category as saying that the Hebrews
are not to worship Ba'al or follow any of those pagan national
behaviors. You're different. Thus, these prohibitions, in a word, are
all identity-builders not universal standards of conduct, and just
as we have jettisoned all of the Holiness Code as irrelevant to our
situation today – who today among Christians follows its dress and
dietary laws "from YHWH"? – so we can set aside what was meant
for another time.

The retired Anglican Archbishop of York, John Habgood, offers
his thoughts:

> "The apparently divisive text, Leviticus 18:22, 'you must not
> lie with a man as with a woman: that it is an abomination,'
> is a prime example of how such failure, [to take the Bible's
> ultimate message], together with the assumption that actions
> always carry the same meaning, can lead unwary readers in
> the wrong direction. What in our day might seem to be an
> unequivocal reference to homosexuality did not originally
> refer to a kind of sexuality at all. When Leviticus was written,
> the real offense in the idea of 'a man lying with a man' was
> that it entailed a violation of male superiority. It was seen as
> shameful for a man to be treated as a substitute woman. In
> short, it was more about gender relationships than sexual
> relationships."[3]

The same kind of social interpretation is put on the Sodom story. The men who wanted Lot's male friends to have sex with him were not guilty of homosexual acts – although such acts clearly were on their minds: "Bring them out to us so that we may know them" (v. 5), and Lot pleaded with them, "I beg you, brothers, do not act so wickedly" (v. 6). No, the moral point wasn't about sex. It was about etiquette. The Sodomite men were guilty of breaching the Near Eastern code of hospitality. That interpretation appears a bit strained to some, but there it is: no condemnation of homosexuality in this scriptural citation. Anyway, the impression seems to be that contemporary consciousness, born of experience, is the real *de facto* biblical hermeneutic. (Whose consciousness will prevail is an unanswered question in these days of relativism.) Reason is the final arbiter of scripture and tradition. It really determines faith and morals, accepts and makes legitimate what the Bible and tradition formerly forbade. Sooner or later official religion catches up and embraces the new position. An excerpt from an editorial by Tom Roberts of the *National Catholic Reporter* makes the point:

> "I'm tired of having the Bible dragged into this discussion' my friend and occasional lunch partner wrote in an email. He was adding a postscript to a discussion we had over lunch recently about homosexuality and same-sex unions, having gathered up more thoughts on the ride home. 'One side quotes scripture, while the other side tries to render the quoted passages harmless. As if somehow it all hinged on scripture; as if scripture decided the question for us.'"

> "I think he makes an important point, especially since few other questions in the public square, except perhaps abortion, attract as much religious language and conviction. So I'll let him speak for himself: 'What's really going on is that scripture is being used to justify preexisting prejudice. Look at it this way: No one cares what scripture has to say about slavery. No one cares what Jesus said, or didn't say, about slavery. Still more noteworthy is the fact that no one cares that when scripture touches upon slavery it's either neutral

toward slavery as a societal institution or actually approving of it. Indeed, there was a time when slaveholders used scripture to prove their point. Not anymore."

"Not even the most diehard literalist pays attention to what the Bible says about slavery. Why? Largely because nonbelievers, allied with a handful of believers who ignored what the Bible had to say on the subject, decided that slavery was unacceptable. That's worth bearing in mind when both sides on the issue of sexual orientation rush to their Bibles. The Bible doesn't change popular opinion. It follows it.'"[4]

This reflects the cover story in *Newsweek* magazine published (just in time, of course, for Christmas) December 15, 2008, whose cover title is, "The Religious Case for Gay Marriage." It's not just that the editors use the irrelevant standard argument that gay marriage is about civil rights and belongs to the same category as racial segregation, but that even *thinking* of resorting to the Bible to prove otherwise "is the worst kind of fundamentalism" and, furthermore, that "To argue that something is so because it is in the Bible is more than intellectually bankrupt – it is unserious, and unworthy of the great Judeo-Christian tradition." On the contrary, the authors argue, the loving acceptance of gay marriage is actually mandated by the Bible. There's also a documentary making the rounds at films festivals called *For the Bible Tells Me So* that seeks to make the case that the Bible does not condemn homosexuality. All this may be true, but let's admit it, that's a long, long way from what the Judeo-Christian world held a hundred or a thousand or two thousand years ago, and that puts the strain on the discussion today.[5]

THE PROVISIONAL BIBLE

Let us assume that all these critiques are correct: that homosexuality is morally all right, that Leviticus is speaking of male shame, Genesis is nothing more than finger wagging at a serious lapse of etiquette, and Paul's epistles reflect a woeful ignorance of the meaning of sexual orientation in their focus on homosexual acts. Let's concede that the Bible, in reality, is condemning sexual activity that is rooted in violence or power regardless of gender and that the Bible in fact remains silent on whether or not sex between two homosexual people who love each other and are committed need not be sinful. Let us concede that sex need not be only procreative because the Church allows marriage for the infertile, the postmenopausal and those with a hysterectomy. Let us concede that, in fact, a sexual relationship in these instances, although not open to conceiving new life, is open to the expression of mutual love.

Let's grant all this, but once again, the fact is that these scriptures, literally understood and embraced, *have* found their way into tradition and *have* been fixed into the centuries-old official teachings of the synagogue and church (Catholic and Protestant). Thus they are Spirit-guaranteed, "infallible" teachings. You can see how confusing it is to the ordinary person as the scholars systematically reinterpret those scripture texts to reverse (not simply "develop") those long held teachings. Fifty years ago no one in his wildest dreams would find in the Bible sanctions for gay marriage, (today a done deal) divorce, abortion (a "blessed" event) and female rabbis, priests and bishops. There is no reason why, fifty years hence, another generation, free of our culture bound restrictions, cannot discover, in principle, biblically approved polygamy which was common in ancient Israel and endured into the early rabbinical period, the restoration of concubinage, the killing of defective babies, the freedom of assisted suicide (noted Catholic theologian, Hans Kung, afflicted with age and Parkinson's, has opted for assisted suicide) and the need to cancel the restrictive patriarchal arrangement of marriage and marriage itself altogether. All these are already here. They're just awaiting biblical certification. The Bible appears to be radically provisional work and those words, "The Bible doesn't change popular opinion. It follows it," appear more and more accurate. The result of this long trajectory is that it leaves us all quite wary about the binding force of scripture – at least as it has been authoritatively and officially interpreted – and at least hesitant about clinging too firmly to it as the last word. Not when the real last word may be situationally down the pike a hundred years from now.

THE PILLAR OF TRUTH

The bottom line is that we are talking about the authority of the Bible, and it's not easy to identify it, especially, as we shall see in another chapter, in the context of another one of our cherished presuppositions – pluralism, where more than one book claims to be the Word of God and where it is considered the height of arrogance to claim one is better, "more true," than the other. The other bottom line is the authority of the Authority; that is, the credibility of the synagogue or church that embraced the text as literal, derived "eternal truths" from it, and spun doctrines. We ordinary people depended on the Church as a safeguard, the church that sees itself as "the pillar and bulwark of the truth." *The Catechism of the Catholic Church*, for example, is quite confident of being that. Expressing itself in the terms of the documents of Vatican II it says:

> "To the Church belongs the right always and everywhere to announce moral principles...(2032 ...The Roman Pontiff and the bishops are authentic teachers. That is, Teachers endowed with the authority of Christ (2034)... The law of God entrusted to the Church is taught to the faithful as the way of life and truth. (2037)..."

As we shall see in the following chapter, this claim of being pillar and bulwark of truth doesn't always hold up. They've crumbled here and there. Meanwhile, we are left to ponder how to sift the culture-bound from true revelation, how to handle a Bible chastened, if not bowdlerized, by experience and, most of all, how a living Tradition credibly works.

Chapter 22.

THE TENSION BREAKER

I have no way of knowing, but I'm guessing that a thousand years ago everyone considered the Bible 20% metaphor and 80% literal. Today, the ratios, I dare say, are reversed. We moderns, chastened by current biblical criticism, now say some stories in the Bible are true – but others that once we thought were literally true, are not, but rather they "tell a truth." Once we thought that Jesus really did walk on water. Now we know he didn't, but say that the account is a post-Resurrection retrojection heralding that he, the Lord, has triumphed over the watery grave and the beasts of the seas.

Who decides which interpretation, literal or metaphorical, is true? Who does the sorting? Who breaks the tensions? The answer (for partisans) proudly is, "the Church," meaning the Catholic Church. Everybody can tell that's why Protestantism split into thousands of sects and why each evangelical minister is his own pope: there is no central, authoritarian referee. That's precisely why some ministers convert to Catholicism: to find an authoritative, unchanging voice of scriptural interpretation. At the Council of Trent, in fact, the Church insisted on its right to alone interpret the Bible, and the Vatican II document on *Revelation* repeated the claim by saying, "The task of giving an authentic interpretation of the Word of God, whether in its written form or in the form of Tradition, had been entrusted to the living teaching office of the Church alone." Yes, just as secular disciplines have taught us to distinguish the meanings of Dante's *Divine Comedy*, the *Harry Potter* series, Bill O'Reiley's *Killing Lincoln*, and the poems of W. H. Auden, so the multiplex community called the

Church for over twenty centuries has helped us navigate the literal-metaphorical pathways of the Bible.

The fact is, however, that the record of the Central Authority, the Church, is not perfect here, and history shows that at times its official interpretation of scripture was wrong – or was quite fluid to say the least. For example, in its early stages (say, from 1902 to 1915), the Catholic Pontifical Biblical Commission issued a number of decrees that strongly defended the literal historicity of the Bible, affirmed that Moses was the primary author of the Pentateuch, insisted on the accuracy of the Genesis account of creation, held that Mark's was indeed the second Gospel to be written, and taught that Paul himself wrote the Pastoral epistles. Woe to the scholars who suggested differently. The Church had spoken. After World War II and Pius XII's encyclical, *Divino Afflante Spiritu* in 1943, Catholic biblical scholarship was given more latitude, and all of the above was eventually reversed. If you lived in the in-between period and were a loyal Catholic, you had to read the Bible in a certain restricted way and later had to accommodate yourself to the changes of the Church's unchanging teaching authority with the lingering questions as to what other reversals would lay in the future. It's disingenuous to claim that technically this was not infallible teaching. It was beyond a doubt authentic magisterial teaching that had to be followed in and out of the classroom and in and out of the pulpit.

The Church was off the mark in other matters. Think of Pius XI's 1930 encyclical, *Casti Connubii*, where he taught that contraception was sinful because scripture forbade it. He specifically cites Genesis 38:9, where Onan "spilled his seed on the ground" and was punished by God for preventing conception and birth. No scholar accepts this interpretation anymore. The real interpretation is that the incident refers to levirate marriage duties. The Vatican now agrees with this interpretation. Think of the Galileo affair, with an apology four centuries down the road. Think of how Church tradition has changed on the issues of human rights, the fate of unbaptized infants, the morality of capital punishment, the moral status of homosexuals and the conversion of the Jews. None of these come under the heading of "development of doctrine." "Development" is hardly the word that fits some cases. Some changes are radically discontinuous from the past, and the notion of a Church that is *semper eadem* – always the same – has been a bit of institutional self-deception. As Charles E. Curran wrote in his introduction to *Change in Official Catholic Moral Teachings*: "Commentators have pointed out that Catholic theology has paid little attention to the issue of change in moral theology in comparison with the very abundant literature of the development of doctrine... others claim that the discontinuity is so great that one cannot properly speak of development."[1]

And in his essay in that book, John Noonan opens his remarks with these words, "That the moral teachings of the Catholic Church have changed over time will, I suppose, be denied by almost no one today. To refresh memories and confirm the point, I will describe four large examples of such change in the areas of usury, marriage, slavery and religious freedom..."[2]

First, there is no question but most passages of the Bible support slavery. Right in the Book of Exodus, Israel, ironically born of liberation from slavery, has one of its laws start off with, "When you buy a Hebrew slave..." Slavery is taken for granted in the Bible from beginning to end. Neither in the Old or New Testaments is there any instance of the demand for the general freeing of slaves or the assertion that it is wrong. On the contrary we read, "Slaves, obey your early masters with fear and trembling." (Ephesians 6:5); "Let all who are under the yoke of slavery regard their masters as worthy of honor." (1 Timothy 6:1); "Tell slaves to be submissive to their masters and to give satisfaction in every respect." (Titus 2:9); and "Slaves, accept the authority of your masters, not only those who are kind and gentle, but also those who are harsh" (1 Peter 2:18). Protestant divines used Paul's words, "Each one should remain in the condition in which he was called" as a biblical expression that the stratification of society was part of God's plan. Slavery was biblically sanctioned. There is no dispute about that.

So the roots of slavery are deep and consistent, from the Church Fathers to Aquinas, Luther, Calvin, and the Puritans. Then along comes Vatican II and Pope John Paul II in 1993, and they declare that slavery is among those matters that are "intrinsically evil" – something a hundred years earlier Cardinal Newman balked at because, as he said, if slavery were in fact intrinsically evil then St. Paul would have had to order Philemon, "liberate all your slaves at once." (In fairness, slavery meant something quite different in Paul's time.)

"Intrinsically evil" is what the Council and Pope John Paul II said. "Intrinsically evil" is theological jargon meaning something that of its very nature is prohibited everywhere, always and forever, without any exception. It is a violation of a universal, immutable norm. Yet, as we saw, the historical fact is that slavery – this intrinsic evil – in some form or another, was accepted both in Hebrew and Christian scriptures and in Christian theology and teaching and in practice. It was only from pressure from Protestant Britain that in 1839 the papacy condemned the slave trade, and finally 1888, after every other Christian nation had done so, that the papacy endorsed the abolition of slavery with, of course, the usual reference that the church has "always" taught this. There is no question that there has been a complete moral turnaround on the morality of slavery and that in the 21st century what is considered intrinsically evil, in the 5th or 10th or 13th or 16th centuries, was considered morally defensible with numerous and explicit scriptural citations to back up this position.

PROGRESSIVE MORALITY

Some come to the Church's defense and recall what we have noted in a previous chapter, namely, that in the New Testament we have what is called the 'trajectory motif" or "progressive truth" process operating. That is to say, you remember, a text doesn't outright say such and such is wrong, but it provides a "direction" where that conclusion might be reached another day. Again, St. Paul freely accepted the common practice of slavery in his day and did not condemn it outright, but he did provide a direction, when he told slaves that their servitude was not really to their human masters but to Christ, and when he charged Philemon to accept his escaped slave as a brother in the faith. This would be the start of a trajectory that would lead to a condemnation of slavery. But twenty centuries later? The presiding bishop of the Episcopal Church, writing in the *New Yorker*, wrestles with the problem:

> "I'm struck by the fact that in the Gospel of John Jesus says, 'I have many more things to say to you, but you cannot bear them now. However, when the Spirit of truth comes, the Spirit will draw from what is mine and reveal it to you.' Now when we look at how we have come to understand the cosmos over the centuries, how we have come to understand the complexities of our physicality, and have seen advances in surgery and medicine and all the rest of it, we can say to ourselves, 'Why didn't God plant the fullness of knowledge in us at the beginning? Why has it taken us centuries to be able to cure fatal diseases that existed in the Middle Ages? How unkind and thoughtless of God not to give us all the information at the outset.' And yet, we've been structured in a universe in such a way that truth is progressive."[3]

USURY AND REMARRIAGE

Noonan turns to usury, making a profit from a loan, and reminds us that the Church once condemned it as unnatural and considered that money-making money is intrinsically evil. When society changed, capitalism grew, and a money economy emerged, the Church officials found a way to work around any moral prohibitions, and usury simply dropped from the Church vocabulary and the Church's concern. Noonan also mentions that religious freedom, or the freedom of conscience, were prohibited for "error has no rights." It took about 1,500 years for the Church to realize that persecution does not foster faith.

Finally, take Noonan's words on marriage. He notes that monogamy without divorce is a Gospel imperative attributed to Jesus himself. After Jesus, a radical change takes place. St. Paul teaches that, in the case of two married unbelievers, if one converts and the other does not and deserts, the convert is free (1Cor. 7:10-16) and the Church Fathers, using this citation, allow that convert to divorce and remarry. This exception to Jesus' teaching remained the sole exception until the 16th century, when African slaves, who wanted to convert but had been torn from their spouses and shipped to South America, were allowed by Pope Gregory XIII to remarry after he dissolved the previous marriage. Noonan continues:

> "The next step in this direction was taken under the impetus of the great canonist Cardinal Pietro Gasparri in the 1920s. In a case from Helena, Montana, Gerard G. Marsh, unbaptized, had married Frances R. Groom, an Anglican. They divorced: Groom remarried. Two years later Marsh sought to marry a Catholic, Lulu La Hood; Pius XI dissolved Marsh's marriage to Groom "in favor of the faith" of Miss La Hood. Apparently exercising jurisdiction over the marriage of two non-Catholics (Groom and Marsh), the pope authorized Marsh to marry a Catholic under circumstances that, but for the papal action, would (morally, not civilly) have constituted bigamy for Marsh and adultery for La Hood. Prior to 1924 the teaching of the church, expressly grounded both on the commandment of the Lord and on the natural law, was that marriage was indissoluble except in the special case of the conversion of an unbeliever. The teaching was unanimously expressed by papal encyclicals and by the body of bishops in their universal ordinary teaching. Then, in 1924, by the exercise of papal authority, the meaning of the commandment against adultery was altered: what was bigamy was revised; and a substantial gloss was written on the Lord's words 'What God has joined together let no man put asunder.'"[4]

As these words show, this was no mere development. It was radical reversal.

Then there's St. Augustine, who in the 4th century taught that spouses had to intend procreation when they had marital relations. Any exclusion of that was morally wrong. Move some 1600 years later and we have two popes, Pius XI and Pius XII, who accepted the rhythm system of controlling births, a system, by definition, which was intended by the spouses to precisely avoid procreation. Likewise, the procreation and education of children was long taught to be the sole primary end of marriage, but recent Church teaching has included the unitive aspect of marriage as on an equal par. The Revised Canon Law of the Church (1055.1) states:

> "The marriage covenant, by which a man and a woman es-
> tablished between themselves a partnership of their whole
> life, and which of its own very nature is ordered to the
> well-being of the spouses and to the procreation of children,
> has, between the baptized, been raised by Christ the Lord to
> the dignity of a sacrament."

Vatican II in its document *Gaudium et Spes* set off a controversy by seemingly giving priority to the unitive over the procreative (thus justifying limiting or having no children at all) and although subsequent popes, like Paul VI and John Paul II, insisted on the "inseparable connection between the unitive significance and pro-creative significance of the marriage act," controversy continues.

When asked about such changing interpretations, Raymond Brown once replied, "And if you object, 'Were my ancestors in Christianity misinformed when they read the Bible with the views of their time?', the answer is that presumably they did the best they could with the information then available and therefore fulfilled all their respon-sibilities."[5] This seems a little too pat, because, remember, we're dealing here with eternal salvation or damnation. Why did it take a pope twenty centuries to reverse such a terrible fate? The claim that the Church is the final, eternal, unchangeable arbiter of scripture is, from the record, subject to challenge.

FROM THE START

From the beginning of Christianity, there has been change. Examples abound.[6] We have already seen St. Paul's conviction that the world was ending soon, and even that he himself would be alive to see it (1 Thess. 4) strategically undermined by the author of Second Peter who, recognizing that the end wasn't going to happen any time soon, said, well, now, let's consider that in God's eyes a day may be a thousand years. There was the world-changing movement from Jesus' intent to reform the faith of Judaism to bringing the faith to the Gentiles, a truly radical development. Certainly, the "orthodoxy" of Peter and the Apostles disappeared when Gentiles did not have to go to the Temple, be circumcised, embrace the Torah, or observe dietary laws. What could be a more radical change than that? Think, too, of the early Christians including in the canon of their accepted books four Gospels that clearly show a very definite Christological development, with Matthew and Luke revising Mark and John giving us a Jesus that none of the other two evangelists would fully recognize.

Think of the underappreciated question of authority in the early Church and the issue of where exactly it resided. Initially it rested with the Twelve, then Jesus' relatives (especially, as we have seen, James), and then, when they all passed on, with some local leaders, overseers and prophets – a question, not, we might add, without a lot of bickering and arguing, and a lot more if we are to believe Paul's first Epistle to the Corinthians. The issue of authority basically came down to the question of the Spirit-charged charismatics versus stable ministers like the eventual overseers, deacons, and presbyters. Would one prevail over the other? Could they work in harmony? Even though the prophets, speaking under the influence of the Holy Spirit, had history on their side, they lost out.

As to be expected, the tensions between the Spirit inspired prophets and local community leaders grew and went on for a long time, perhaps best symbolized by the centuries-long running feud with the Montanists (a loose community of prophets). But, in the long run, there *was* the long run. That is to say, prophets were basically too destabilizing to be practical as the urgent needs of organization grew. By definition, the Spirit could not be controlled. Prophets upend continuity, and people can't handle new visions and revelations all the time. Then, too, like the Old Testament prophets, no one could be sure how to separate the genuine ones from the false ones. Anyway it's just plain hard to figure out just how the Holy Spirit speaks to the Church. Rational decrees are safer and solid.

Finally, not too far beneath the surface was that undeniable fact of female prophets. Women were part of the Jesus Movement from the beginning. St. Luke tells us about the women who travelled with Jesus. Paul himself, in his epistles, testified that women in his communities had prophetic gifts, and the Acts of the Apostles tells us of the deacon Philip's daughters, who were Spirit-speaking prophets. How would such authority make itself felt? Would these charismatic females remain involved as sources of authority?

The answer was no, as Christians eventually moved back to their Jewish roots and accepted the Greek mode of thinking about women. For the Jews, a good woman was one who married the man her parents choose and begot sons (not daughters) for him so his name would endure. Sterile women were disgraced. As for the Greeks, Plato had wondered why women existed at all, except that sex and procreation were needed. Aristotle called women "misbegotten males." The upshot was that Greek Christian leaders could not endure uncontrollable charismatics in general, and could not accept the reality that women could prophesy in particular, and so the stable triad of overseer (bishop), deacon, and presbyter emerged to guide the growing Church. Women were sidelined. A development bordering on change had been breached.[7] There was, in short, no "golden age" when the Jewish Apostles smoothly handed on in unbroken succession the baton of leadership to Greek bishops who oversaw their harmonious communities that shared everything in common. There was radical change all the way.

SUMMARY VOICES

Let's hear from two scholars on the "unchanging" Church. First, Peter Steinfels weighs in (emphasis mine):

> "Historically Catholicism solved the problem of change simply by denying it. Understandings of the Trinity, the priesthood, the papacy, the Mass and the sacraments that emerged over a long time were *projected back into New Testament texts.* Theologians joked that when a pope or other official circuitously introduced a modification of church teaching, he would begin, 'As the church has always taught...' Such denial, still widespread, means that examining change in official teaching...poses two challenges: first, to establish that alterations – some more than minor – have unquestionably occurred; and second, to show how they can be reconciled with the church's claim to preach the same essential message Jesus and his disciples did 2,000 years ago..."[8]

A recent instance of the ahistorical attitude is Archbishop William Lori's pointing out in 2013 how the Church has always championed religious freedom. He goes on to cite the forthright words of the U.S. Bishops' Conference, Vatican II's decree on religious liberty and the encyclicals of Popes John Paul II, Benedict XVI and Francis. They indeed celebrate the Catholic "tradition" of championing religious freedom, but, as Dennis O'Brien would rightly observe, this would be a classic instance where the Catholic Church has a strong sense of tradition, but no sense of history. The Archbishop demonstrates this because he completely ignores the earlier historical encyclicals of Gregory XVI, Pius IX, Leo XII, Pius X, and Pius XI which were vigorously hostile to religious freedom, and the long, long history of suppression of religious liberty that goes back to the early Church Fathers.[9]

Anyway, we know that change is in the air when a noted Catholic moral theologian, Richard A. McCormick, S.J. writes an article significantly titled, "Changing My Mind About the Changeable Church" in which he relates how he discarded his formerly held view of a pyramidal Church that held certain and infallible authority, an authority that trickled down to the people below, immune from challenge, accountability, and consultation ("Why is it that Rome generally consults only those who already agree with it?") and, further, demanding of total and unquestioned obedience. All this, he says, was upended by Vatican II when it defined the Church in terms of mystery, justice, collegiality, a Pilgrim Church, and a people of God wherein the laity also had its distinctive role and voice. It recognized the ecclesial reality of other Christian churches stating explicitly that "whatever is wrought by the grace of the Holy Spirit in the hearts of our separated brethren can contribute to our own edification." With such concepts, the absolutist monopoly was broken and the unchangeable "certainties" of eternal truths or rather, their official "divinely instituted" (to use a favorite phrase of the Catechism of the Catholic Church) doctrinal formulations were called into question.

These remarks sum up the arguments of this chapter. The truth is that everyone is more or less trapped in his or her limitations of their eras and their assumptions about the morality of this or that. It does make us ask, to what extent we are similarly bound. What has escaped our attention and understanding? What doctrinal and moral revisions lie in the future? No wonder that one of the main points that John O'Malley makes in his book, *What Happened at Vatican II*, is that the Catholic bishops had to acknowledge the possibility and the actuality of development or evolution in official Church teachings and how to deal with them.[10]

Secondly, a provocative summary-quotation from Catholic theologian, Richard R. Gaillardetz ends this short chapter on a challenging note:

> "What happens when the Church ceases to affirm an insight, belief or practice that had commonly been affirmed in the past? Tradition is not always the story of enduring or developing beliefs or practices; sometimes it is the story of beliefs

and practices that have been abandoned or rejected over time. Tradition involves not only the recognition of continuities with the past, but sometimes the recognition of dramatic discontinuity and even the reversal of positions. Some beliefs and practices simply lose their authority over time. We mentioned earlier the sad truth that slavery was long viewed as an institutionally in accord with both natural law and divine revelation. The grudging rejection of this viewpoint in the consciousness of the Church can only be viewed as a communal recognition of dramatic discontinuity with its past. In a similar way the Church has found it necessary to repudiate longstanding beliefs about the immorality of charging interest when lending money, the inherent inferiority of women in the natural order and the denial of religious liberty to non-believers."

"What distinguishes this sense of tradition from the previous two is that it is acknowledging not a sense of stability or continuity of belief and practice over time but rather a sense of dramatic discontinuity. Some theories have tried to gloss over such discontinuities by claiming that, if one looks deeply enough, there is a consistent affirmation evident underneath the appearance of change and repudiation. Efforts have been made, for example, to see in the Second Vatican Council's teaching on religious liberty and the universal outreach of God's saving power nothing more than new formulations of past insights. These insights may have been expressed imperfectly or in an underdeveloped manner, it is held, but they can be found in the tradition."

"One senses a kind of historical dishonesty in such attempts, however. Perhaps it is more honest simply to recognize the general fallibility of the Church as a pilgrim people (regarding that which does not pertain directly to God's saving offer) that is moving toward 'the fullness of truth,' but is not protected from wrong turns along the way."[11]

When, a long time ago, I was a child in parochial school, I was taught that, added to the four marks of the Church – one, holy, Catholic and apostolic – was indefectibility. That is, the Church could not make a mistake or ever be wrong, doctrinally or morally. It's been a long way from that proudly chauvinistic attribute to the more humble words (notwithstanding its caveat about the deposit of faith) of Vatican II:

> "Thus, if, in various times and circumstances, there have been deficiencies in moral conduct or in church discipline, or even in the way that church teaching has been formulated – to be carefully distinguished from the deposit of faith – these can and should be set right at the opportune moment" (*Decree on Ecumenism*).

Translation: "We are a Pilgrim Church and at times we lose our way."

ANATHEMA SIT

At this logical point – the Church migrating from the immutable teacher of immutable truth to the Pilgrim Church of adaptation and reinterpretation – I need to add a postscript that colors and contextualizes the arguments of this book.

Except for the most inflexible, most middle-of-the-road, most believing scholars, most defenders of the Bible all admit that in the past we were taught wrong in certain matters. We interpreted wrong. We believed wrong. We know also that from the beginning we have changed theological positions and ignored former biblical commands. Today we are very aware of that. We know we do not have to shun pork or rebuild the Temple, offer animal sacrifice, keep the Sabbath or circumcise our male children. We readily recall the about face when the earthly Jesus, at one point, allowed preaching only to the Israelites (Matthew 10 5-6), and the Risen Jesus commanded preaching to everyone (Matthew 28:19). Then there's the litany of doctrinal reversals we have mentioned all throughout or will: from no divorce to Pauline and Petrine exceptions, from sinning by participation in a Protestant service to ecumenism, from error has no rights to freedom of conscience, from converting the Jews to forbidding such attempts, from marriage only of man and woman to same sex marriage, from acceptance of slavery to its prohibition and so on. Over the ages we have actually reformed and changed biblically based doctrines and need to change more.

Yes, some of today's finest scholars are earnestly at work "sifting," "setting side," and "going their own way," and are creatively recasting weighty issues such as original sin, the Kingdom of God, revelation, the atonement, tradition, transubstantiation, eschatology and the like into new and different categories and contexts correcting, deepening, bypassing and sometimes contradicting the old ones. I have noted, at times cynically, the dilemma this has caused, and this brings us to a point I have made before. The point is, that such theological renewal is not in the same category as adding amendments to the Constitution, discontinuing using leeches to draw blood, restraining the rod to beat children, subjugating women or imprisoning the Japanese during World War II. These things caused harm to human dignity and health. But in religion – at least for most of the two millennia of Christianity – we are in the high stakes of eternal life or eternal damnation.

In the Catholic Church's history, for example, there are those canons forthrightly proclaiming that if one does not believe and accept this or that doctrine, if one rejects that or that doctrine, *Anathema sit*, let him be damned! God, of course, was under no obligation to comply but the people could not comprehend that back then. In the people's minds, the Church was the Voice of God. They risked bad conscience in following theirs. Firm and deeply cultural believers in heaven, hell and purgatory, they, as everyone knew, invited excommunication, denial of Christian burial and the punishment of eternal hell fire. The current reversals, the new creativity, welcome as they are, have come too late to soothe the troubled souls and restore the tortured bodies of the victims of ecclesiastical anathema. I am just pointing out that that's a heavy legacy at the other end of the renewal arc, and one ponders the mystery of why it endured so long, so many centuries. We ask why the Jesus-promised and Truth-Guided Spirit allowed error so early and truth so late and such suffering in the in-between time.

Chapter 23.

THE TENSION OF PLURALISM

Not everyone has the time or opportunity to compare religious assumptions. Up to now, there were few opportunities for such reexamination of one's own religious system for comparisons with other religions. Now that pluralism and diversity have become the politically correct standard, and globalization via the internet and smart phones is a reality, the relationship between Christianity and the world's other religions is dominating the theological scene as never before. The field of examination has expanded and assumptions are challenged more openly and seriously.

Theologians struggle with the question of similarity, commonality and exclusivist stances. One of them, Jacques Dupuis, S.J., a Catholic theologian, was in the forefront. He wrote a book whose title, *Christianity and the Religions: From Confrontation to Dialogue* argues that the plurality of religions ought to be seen as an integral element of God's universal will to save all and not merely an accident of history or an obstacle to be overcome by Christian missionaries. In a review of his book in *The Tablet*[1], Terrence Merrigan comments:

> "Dupuis' theology of religions is inspired by a quintessentially Catholic concern: the question of precisely how God's saving presence is mediated to the world. The concern for mediation explains the Church's understanding of itself as an essentially sacramental reality, that is to say, a visible and historical

body by means of which God's saving presence is offered to humanity, especially through its Eucharistic life. Since Vatican II, the Church regards this presence as universal, able to operate outside the confines of Christianity in the hearts and minds of all, even avowed atheists. The fundamental question that Dupuis asks is precisely how this presence is mediated to the practitioners of non-Christian religions.

"His answer is that the most likely means is their religious traditions as such. This does not mean that Dupuis regards other religions as equal partners with Christianity in God's plan of salvation. Whatever value they possess, they owe to their 'participation' in the saving work of the one mediator, Jesus Christ. In making this claim Dupuis places himself squarely within the camp of the so-called 'inclusivist' theology of religions elaborated by Vatican II. He ventures beyond the traditional position, however, by ascribing to non-Christian religions a real mediatory role on behalf of their members. Dupuis finds inspiration for this view in the thought of Pope John Paul II who spoke of the possibility of 'participated mediation' in the work of Christ without, however, extending this to non-Christian religions."

So Dupuis seems to embrace the so-called pluralist theology of religions – many religions represent independently valid paths to salvation – but with a link to Jesus, adding that, while Jesus is an essential or constitutive element of this history, God's saving work is above all a work of the Trinity in its entirety working in the hearts of individual men and women and no less in their religious traditions. Which means, for him, that the triune God is at work in non-Christian traditions, and so it is possible that their sacred books also might expose aspects of divine mystery that have not been not highlighted with equal force in Christianity. For him, though not equal to Christianity, their saving figures may also be enlightened by the Word or inspired by the Spirit and so become pointers to salvation for their followers. It's a cautious approach and Dupuis, who died in 2004, was investigated by the Congregation for the Doctrine of the Faith regarding his orthodoxy. Still, it appears that for some, he doesn't go far enough. Dr. Joseph C, Hough Jr., president of Union Theological Seminary, goes further:

> "Religion, our rituals, our music, even our theology, is a human attempt to express what we have experienced. Since we have only our human language and symbols to use in expressing our faith, religions differ as much as cultures differ. Therefore, we want to be careful about claiming that one religious form is the only one that is authentic or real....What is essential for Christian faith is that we know we have seen the face of God in the face of Jesus Christ. It is not essential to believe that no one else has seen God or experienced redemption in another place or time."[2]

We cite again American Rabbi Michael Kogan, who echoes the same thought and speaks for a segment of Judaism when he says in true postmodernist fashion, "I believe God choose the Jewish people. But who said God can only make one choice?" He goes on to remark that the Jewish people are *a* chosen people not *the* Chosen People.[3]

Interestingly, the revered former Jesuit General Father Pedro Arrupe would agree. He saw a world in which the various religions had to stop fighting over religion. Besides, he said, few people could change the faith they were raised in anyway and that the important thing was how deeply they understood and loved that faith and how they made it work in their lives. In other words, choose your brand and stick with it. One religion is not more privileged than another. Each one's assumptions are "true" for its adherents, and they should stay with them. Everyone's sacred scripture deserves a hearing. It was Jacques Derrida who taught that the alternative to blind belief is not simply unbelief, but a different kind of belief – one that embraces uncertainty and enables us to respect others whom we do not understand.

In other words, some scholars aver, those scriptural stalwarts, "I am the way and the truth and the life. No one comes to the Father except through me" (John 14:6) and "There is salvation in no one else, for there is no other name [but Jesus] under heaven given among mortals by which we must be saved" (Acts 4:12) are really not exclusive claims, but rather the language of faith, discourses intended to highlight the significance of Jesus for this particular faith community and not necessarily having any bearing for those outside it. Such an understanding is stunning for those who always took these words as universal truths and terrifically undermining to the centuries of unilateral proselytizing, but it sheds light on ecumenism and the Bible's status as a sterling faith document for the faithful and not as an exclusive blueprint for the "unfaithful." Which is to say that the Christian mission is no longer understood as bringing everybody into the one unified, "true" religion of Christianity, but rather a dialoguing, partnering, and cooperating religion in a democratic way with others. This may provoke what Pope Benedict XVI called the "dictatorship of relativism," but the International Theological Commission of his church had already opened the door when it stated that "the possibility of salvation for those outside of the Church who live in accordance with their conscience is no longer in question." And this raises precisely the issue of what role the different religions and their sacred scriptures do have in the plan of God.

This may be helpful. In his remarkable book, *When Religion Becomes Evil* Charles Kimball quotes Wesley Ariarajah, a United Methodist Minister from Sri Lanka who argues that it is possible to embrace and affirm religious truth without defining truth for others. He suggests we can find our way forward by untangling absolute truth from confessional statements. He illustrates the distinction:

> "When my daughter tells me I'm the best daddy in the world and there can be no other father like me, she is speaking the truth, for this comes out of her experience. She is honest about it; she knows no other person in the role of her father. But of course it is not true in another sense. For one thing, I myself know friends who, I think, are better fathers than I am. Even more importantly, one should be aware that in the next house there is another little girl who also thinks her daddy is the best father in the world. And she too is right. In fact at the level of the way the two children relate to their two fathers,

no one can compare the truth content of the statements of the two girls. For here we are not dealing with the absolute truths, but with the language of faith and love.... The language of the Bible is also the language of faith.... The problem begins when we take these confessions in the language of faith and love and turn them into absolute truths. It becomes much more serious when we turn them into truths on the basis of which we begin to measure the truth or otherwise of other faith claims. My daughter cannot say to her little friend in the next house that there is no way she can have the best father, for the best one is right there in her house. If she does, we'll have to dismiss it as child-talk!"[4]

I think he is saying that the Bible is not so much the bearer of absolute truth as it is the bearer of faith. Its faith claims are valuable and are to be pondered, prayed over, and embraced, but it is not a standard of truth that measures, much less condemns, other faith bearing books that claim to be the word of God. The Bible is a valuable voice in the human dialogue and inclusive dialogue there must be if the world is to be healed.

TENSIONS

The fundamentalist slogan is, "The Bible says it, I believe it, that settles it." Mormons, like Catholics, think that while Christians merely "have a portion of the truth, what God revealed to Joseph Smith is the fullness of truth." Peter Berger and Anton Zijderveld in their book *In Praise of Doubt: How to Have Convictions Without Becoming a Fanatic,*[5] have second thoughts. They maintain that such fundamentalism enforces a consensus about ultimate ends without accounting for difference, while relativism makes sharing common values impossible. This conclusion is obviously a challenge for us who live in an atmosphere of politically correct pluralism and diversity, elements that totally upend the recorded isolation hectored by the biblical prophets (one thinks of Ezra) or the persistent exclusive claims of the Catholic Church. (And the Church has reacted strongly against pluralism in its September 2000 document, *Dominus Jesus*.) Nevertheless, as the world shrinks and western Christianity breaks down, its book, the Bible, downgrades to one privileged text among many, and Christianity's status as a religion is one among many others (9,900 of them and growing each day); and, as the plausibility structures of Christianity in general and Catholicism in particular continue to erode, then using the Bible in any sense as the definitive, unique, true, revelatory, and exclusive word of the one and only God becomes problematic without examining our assumptions about the book and its Author and examining, as Dupuis put it, "others' sacred books which might expose aspects of the divine mystery."

Then there is the purely theoretical question: can we revise the Bible to include some of these other books? After all, the canon wasn't fully formed until the year 90 (for Jews) and 312 (for Christians) of this era and not fully accepted and ratified until the Council of Trent in the 16th century. This was the end of a long and torturous journey after much disputing (and much politicking) about which books should be included. Clement of Alexandria (150-215), for example, cited the *Didache* as Scripture and regarded *1 Clement, Barnabas, Shepherd of Hermas, the Preaching of Peter* and *the Apocalypse of Peter* as inspired. Even after the canons were fixed, the actual texts of both testaments were fluid until the invention of printing in the 15th century. Before 1000, only four manuscripts contained solely the books of the current New Testament. To this day the Protestant canon has fewer books than the Catholic canon (they are minus Tobit, Wisdom, the two books of Maccabees, and parts of Daniel), the ancient Syriac Orthodox Church includes the Apocalypse of Ezra and the short Psalm, 151, and the venerable church of Ethiopia contains 81 books (against the 72 of the Roman Catholic canon) including the influential Book of Enoch and the Book of Jubilees. (The Catholic canonical Book of Jude quotes Enoch's writings as inspired prophecy.) The fact is that, historically, the biblical collection has been more fluid than stable and there were all kinds of Jewish texts still circulating until after the time of Jesus. The centuries-long persistence and popularity (and sometimes preference) of these Jewish and Christian extra-canonical books testify to the basic instability of the Bible and even, speculatively, raises that question of whether some books could be deleted or added today. Mormons have been known to suggest that some of their writings, such as the *Book of Mormon, The Doctrine and the Covenants* and *The Pearl of Great Price* might be included in the Christian biblical canon. That, of course, will never happen because in no way could everyone reach an agreement on which to delete or add. They had a hard enough time with the original process.

EXCLUSIVISM

We battle daily the claims of those who feel their particular version of religion, their particular interpretation of scripture, is the "true" way, and everything else, by definition, is false and, by extension, should be contained, confronted, or exterminated (one thinks of Elijah). This is somewhat bold in this country, where we are the most religiously diverse nation in the world, not to mention that with the current world being in such dire danger today, there is no room for religious tensions among the three Abrahamic religions of Christians, Muslims, and Jews to fester. The fact is that it's hard for some to believe that their understanding of and experience of God does not exhaust all the possibilities. That's why some, like Joseph Campbell, argue for a far more inclusive understanding of religion. He maintains that religious denominations are all variations on the same theme – namely, the meaning of life, the mystery of life, how to live individually and communally. Each religion has its sacred stories, steeped in symbol and imagery, that plumb the overarching myth of how to understand and live human life. Each religion has its sacred texts, symbols, and metaphors that circle the same myth. Most religions, for example, have stories about a final cataclysmic war (reflected in pop culture such as the *Star Wars* trilogy, the *Chronicles of Narnia*, the *Harry Potter* series), savior figures, personified evil, a golden age, etc. Therefore, no one sacred text is the last word. One's sacred text is a helpful word, a valuable one, a sustaining one, but no amount of words can fully capture the mystery of the Deity. To make inflexible absolute truth claims for any sacred text like the Bible, to read it literally, is to court an unwarranted arrogance, to make the boast to know the mind of God. Perhaps that's why the Dalai Lama said, "I've found that Buddhism is the best. But that does not mean that Buddhism is best for everyone." Diana Butler Bass sums up the average person's dilemma:

> "A popular contemporary answer to the question, 'Where is God?' is that God is found in all denominations and all religions, a kind of universal light shining through the varieties of faith. Critics often treat this answer with contempt, depicting it as 'cafeteria Christianity,' with uneducated masses simply picking and choosing what they like from a variety of faiths to construct a truth that fits their own longings. To me, this answer is less a matter of sloppy thinking and more often a response to the problem of religious diversity. How can it be that so many different religions claim to be true? And how can human beings, limited as we are, commit to any one form of faith?"[6]

CAUTIONS

All this seems to mean that we have to be careful when we claim that the Bible alone is the exclusive word of God, or that it is God's words in human words. We have already seen how this gets us into embarrassing verbal sleight of hand, whereby we see-saw between what is "culturally bound" (we can't accept this today; it doesn't make sense) and what is the firm, sure, unmistakable voice of the Lord, with no certain criteria to go by except an ever expanding consciousness. Modern exegesis' continuing "declassification" of literal and time-honored interpretations is evidence of this dilemma. What, then, to do with the Bible? An answer can be derived from the attitude of Vatican II, where the Catholic Church officially embraced an inclusivist theology and gave special praise to Muslims and Jews, the other Abrahamic religions. As we saw, in a reversal, the Catholic Church proclaimed the teaching that salvation is possible for people outside the Church. It's a kind of moving away from Christianity as the center to God as the center and all religions revolving around him. This stance need not water down one's own faith tradition, but enrich it. As Diana Eck, the premier observer of the religious land-scape in the United States, puts it:

> "Through the years I have found my own faith not threatened, but broadened and deepened by the study of Hindu, Buddhist, Muslim and Sikh traditions of faith. And I have found that only as a Christian pluralist could I be faithful to the mys-tery and the presence of the one I call God. Being a Christian pluralist means daring to encounter people of different faith traditions and defining my faith not by its borders but by its roots."[7]

This would also apply to the non-Abrahamic faiths including paganism, the choice of many young people today. Knowing other faiths can open up new appreciation and depths for one's own faith. This is not to cover over disagreements, but to offer a means to work together while dialogue goes on. It beats the Inquisition.

It is worth noting that currently Oxford University is trying to come to terms with the truth claims of the various religions by concentrating on engaging all of the authoritative texts and their significance for faith today, whether it be the Qu'ran, the Old Testament, the New Testament, Hindu or Buddhist writings. In short, the theology department is taking an interfaith approach by reading the various scriptures even while being apprehensive with the dangers of a "pick-and-choose" style of teaching theology in a pluralistic setting. Interfaith study of each other's sacred writings can be indeed be fruitful, but obviously it is also challenging to any one "scripture" that claims truth beyond the others.

IT'S IN THE AIR

This drive to seek unity in pluralism is in the air. About a half dozen years ago, for example, a religious survey reported that 70% of Americans – among them strong majorities of Protestants and Catholics – believe that "many religions can lead to eternal life." It's the global thing that brought it about. Through travel, immigration, supra national corporations, television, and (of course) the internet, not to mention your lovely Hindu neighbors and the Muslim children your kid plays with, polyglot realities have leveled exclusive religious claims. Our ancestors who send dissenters to the rack would be amazed. Yes, denominations had flirted with religious pluralism before, holding meetings and conventions as far back as two centuries ago, but they never dreamed that, after the death of optimistic modernism with the explosion of the first atomic bomb, this kind of everyday pragmatic ecumenism would happen.

But more than the traumas of social and political upheaval, people become wary of the acrimonious divisions and high ideological walls separating liberal and conservative, modernist and fundamental Jews, Muslims and Christians. In Christianity, these divisions have given way to the suspicion that its dogmatic forms of religion and especially its whole legal structure is dying, that maybe Bonhoeffer's "religionless Christianity" (whatever that means) is about to take place. It is obvious that there is a search for more personal, committed, vital forms of following Christ through prayer, forgiveness, and most of all, the kind of open, non-discriminate hospitality that brings all to Jesus' table-fellowship meals. It's the "spiritual not religious" mantra in play today.

As Christianity disappears in the West and expands in the southwest and East, as legal, top-heavy clericalism dies in a Catholicism that has lost its monopoly on salvation, as alternate voices are heard and new patterns emerge, new ways of being Church, new ground-level, democratic spiritualties more and more draw on pluralistic sources. Diana Butler Bass sees the pattern in:

"Dorothy Day, an American convert to Roman Catholicism, who dedicated her life to social justice for the oppressed; Dietrich Bonhoeffer, a German Lutheran theologian, who argued for 'costly grace' and was executed by the Nazis; C. S. Lewis, a British university professor who offered a simple and unifying description of Christian doctrine; Howard Thurman, an African American theologian whose vision of the 'beloved community' shaped Martin Luther King, Jr.; Thomas Merton, a Roman Catholic monk, who renewed interest in the practice of contemplation; Oscar Romero, a Latin American archbishop, who embodied God's love for the poor and was martyred while celebrating the Eucharist; Verna Dozier, an African American Episcopal laywoman, whose theology of 'the dream of God' inspired new interest in the church as an agent of God's reign; Madeleine L'Engle, an American writer, whose poetry and fiction sparked the Christian artistic imagination; and, of course, Henri Nouwen. "These Christians pushed away obstacles that constricted the flow of faith, creating wide channels for God's spirit."[8]

Where does all this put the Bible? The stance of pluralism can help us appreciate what scholars have amply shown us and we have noted in this book, namely, that the Bible itself is a loan collection: its concepts and names for God, its laws and rituals, its songs and vocabulary, its stories and heroes, are all borrowed from the Near East matrix of civilization, where, like people everywhere, they struggled to make sense of life and death – and God. We can fruitfully parse the Bible as one people's unique spiritual journey and as a template for our own. We can enter into its stories, not as history, but precisely as story – as parables, as a literary means of circling over and over again the mystery of God and humanity. We can embrace its lessons and reject its limitations and distortions and even at times its perverse theology. It's our book, but we have to free it of its literalism and its exclusivist status. It's a book to be used for unity, not division. It must be in dialogue with other sacred writings. As Alice Laffey says, "By and large, however, the biblical teacher of the near future will tolerate multiple readings and interpretations of a single biblical text."[9]

This approach is consistent with the rabbis, who were willing to see a multitude of possible meanings to a biblical passage in contrast to any single "authentic" meaning. The Babylonia Talmud said, "In the School of Rabbi Ishmael it is taught: 'See, My word is like fire, an oracle of the Eternal and like a hammer that shatters a rock' (Jeremiah 23:29). Just as a hammer divides into several sparks, so too every scriptural verse yields several meanings." The Christians adopted the same approach. Both Jews and Christian had to, because some of the biblical texts are ambiguous and allow for various translations, and interpreters still argue over them. As we have seen this is not novel. If we characterize the Bible as story, then the process of multiple readings is consistent with the rules of storytelling. So this means reexamining those texts which have caused harm to others: slavery, sexism, anti-Semitism, war. It means, as someone put it, that we should live by the commandments but not die by their observance. Or, as Jesus spun it, the Sabbath was made for people not the other way around (Mark 2:27).

MORE THAN ONE BLESSING

In this whole issue of pluralism, what we have is not only the viability of other "endings" to shared biblical stories but even the legitimacy of other, non-biblical stories to begin with. All this, as true as it might be, leaves uneasy intellectual problems we've touched on before. If traditional interpretations are not always the final meaning, what about (a) The synagogues and churches that froze them into one interpretation and deduced "everlasting" doctrines from them, creedal propositions which we are bound to believe? (b) Why did a single "negative" reading last so long, for centuries and centuries, putting people in bad faith? (c) What about those who gave their lives for the traditional meanings? (d) Can the doctrinally oppressed today hope for a future reading that is more compatible to them?

It seems that, in reference to the Bible, we need multiple readings to salvage meaning. We have to come terms with the Old Testament and the "cut and paste" literary architecture, say, of the New Testament – for example, the stories of Jesus' birth and Passion. We have to keep in mind myth-making, decipher symbolic "miracles," sort out partisan distorting propaganda, and so on. We need to resort to metaphor and storytelling (as we should) to understand it all, and, as always, we must solemnly nod to that mysterious Spirit who cleverly and subtly is really revealing hidden truths – only we haven't figured them all out yet, and even when we think we have and have constructed our doctrines, a new consciousness comes along and we have to reverse ourselves. It's all more complex than we think.

To add to the complexity, we haven't even mentioned an insider's diversity problem among believers – namely, the sheer multiplicity of translations. Yes, the Bible is the perennial best seller and copies run into the billions (as do profits), but the very assortment of translations, including "niche" Bibles (The Bible Code I & II or The Stock Car Racing Edition) continue to sow confusion. biblical pluralism has undermined a common voice. With so many translations (at least 200 English translations published since 1900) that don't always agree, the Bible winds up dividing rather than unifying.

We end this chapter with a quotation from the famed Vietnamese monk, Thich Nhat Hanh. A Christian asked him if it was all right to meditate. He answered:

> "I think it is possible to profit from many traditions at one time. If you love oranges, you are welcomed to eat them, but nothing prevents you from enjoying kiwis or mangoes as well. Why commit yourself to only one kind of fruit when the whole spiritual heritage of humankind is available to you? It is possible to have Buddhist roots a well as Christian or Jewish roots. We grow very strong that way."

This may be nothing more than the practical advice to appreciate truth and beauty wherever one finds them. His advice, however, can't escape the inclination and legitimization of today's wide-open tolerance and pluralism to presume that the scriptures belonging to those roots are equal – one not better, more revelatory, or more true than the other. Not since the Vietnam War and the revolution of mass media and communication, both of which opened up a large, vastly complex world of customs, beliefs, practices, and worldviews, can people easily accept the truth claims of the elite Western world and not opt for the "One God, many paths" slogan.

There is a book by Mary C. Boys titled, *Has God Only One Blessing?*[10] It's a book about the equal validity of the Church and Synagogue and an argument against supersessionism. The book's title is a play on the words an anguished Esau spoke to his father Jacob after his brother Jacob stole his birthright: "Have you only one blessing, Father?" (Genesis 27:38). Has God only one book?

PART IV

THE SEARCHERS

Chapter 24.

NOSTALGIC SEARCHING

There are several reasons why believers give special treatment to the Bible. One is tradition which is to say that the Bible, carried on and exploited by a triumphant Christianity, became a part of Western civilization, as did Christianity itself. It was the Book, the reference, the anchor, the great mega-story, the binding narrative, and its allusions, stories, characters and plots became the fabric of Christian and western society in buildings, art, literary works; in a word, the whole culture. So there is a deep emotional attachment to and investment in the Bible and the God it presents, even if there are suspicions as to its accuracy.

As one author, writing an introduction to the New Testament, expresses it:

> "Biblical texts bear all the marks of human composition: historical conditioning, prejudice, factual error and moral limitation, as well as deep theological and religious insight into the mystery of God's relationship with humanity... in sum, the Gospels are not literal records of the ministry of Jesus. Decades of developing and adapting the Jesus tradition had intervened. For some, this calls the truth of the Gospels into question. Truth, however, must be evaluated in terms of the intended purpose. The Gospels might be judged untrue if their goal was strict reporting or exact biography; but if the goal was to bring readers/hearers to a faith in Jesus that opens them to God's activity, then adaptations that make the Gospels less than literal—adding dimensions of faith,

adjusting to new audiences—were made precisely to facilitate this goal and thus to make the Gospels true."[1]

A worthy and accurate description, but still, one wonders that if truth is not to be deterred by cultural conditioning, prejudice, error, or moral limitation, but found rather (and most determiningly) in terms of the intended purpose of the author bent on "adding dimensions of faith" (where these extra dimensions come from is another matter), then, of course, one could say the same thing about any book in the world – say, for example, the Qur'an. Muslims believe that their sacred book was revealed in one language (Arabic) to the prophet Mohammed over a period of 20 (adapting) years. Perhaps, too, some Muslims might not accept the Qur'an with its "historical conditioning, prejudice, factual error, and moral limitation" as a literally true work, but rather will evaluate its truth from its "intended purpose" which is to open them up to Allah's activity. In other words, if the Muslims bypass the awkward literalisms and limitations of the human author(s) and re-read the Qur'an as a metaphor and embrace the author's purpose to open his readers to Allah, then that book, no matter how erroneous, is true and evaluated as the "Word of God."

The Bible. The Qur'an. The Book of Mormon. Using the same canons for all three, you have three "true" books from God.

As long as you're sincere

This seems to be the prevailing sentiment: even though the Bible can be shown to have false, contradictory statements, anachronisms, and claims disproved by archaeology, causing more than reasonable doubts whether, for example, any of the patriarchs existed, and painting a horrific portrait of YHWH that is the worst reflection of Ba'al, people have an emotional attachment that makes them overlook the errors and the pagan antecedents and declare that, regardless, they see the Bible either as being "true" in a metaphorical sense, as fascinating literature, or as a faith document, a record of their awareness of God (not anyone else's). Listen to Bruce Feiler as he mines the same sentiment. Of his mentor, a man named Gabi, he writes:

> "How does proving the Bible help faith?" I said. 'I'm a local Jew," he said, 'I don't care whether this or that detail is incorrect in the Bible. It doesn't change my attitude toward the Bible, toward religion, toward God. Or toward myself.' …'Look', Gabi said, 'Serious people know that some parts of the Bible go well with archaeology, others do not. So what? I'm not going to find in archaeology, ever, a business card that says 'Abraham, son of Terah'. But it doesn't matter. It's not a book of history. It's a book of faith."[2]

Ah, yes, faith. Again and again, this sentiment occurs: the biblical stories may or may not be literally true, but what counts is the message, the feeling one gets from them, the inspiration one takes from them, the faith one brings to them. This comes very close to the old bromide that it doesn't matter what you believe as long as you're sincere. More: "What is vital is only that what happened [in the Bible] was experienced, while it happened, as the act of God." Thus claims Martin Buber. You could say the same about Mormon founder Joseph Smith and his purported visions from the archangel Gabriel that were experienced by him "as an act of God."

Again, Feiler quoting a conversation:

> "From my point of view, there are three possibilities about the stories in the Bible", Doron said. It was late afternoon now and we were sitting on the edge of the sentry post with our feet dangling over the side. The bright white heat of midday had diminished. Our conversation had grown more personal. These were the moments I once avoided; now they were the ones I most craved.
>
> 'First, things happened as they are told in the stories. Second, some things happened as they are told; others were made up. And third, a very, very clever man made the stories up. So which one do you believe?' I asked."

'In some ways it's my personality to believe the religious way of thinking. In other ways it's my personality to believe that someone made it up. I don't have a concrete opinion. And that's the nice thing about the Bible. You can take it however you want. What really matters are the clues within the stories about how to believe.'

'So, one two or three, in the end they're all the same.'

'The basic message is the same. It's solid truth."

"Arriving back to the campsite I thought about Doron's comments. Here was a man as dry and scientific as any I had met who viewed the Bible as offering him some higher meaning. In many ways Doron's attachment meant more to me now than that of the people I had met during our earlier stops in Israel. It seemed to confirm my own evolution, my embracing the story for its emotional resonance regardless of its factuality. I could accept the story for its moral code even as I struggled to identify its grounding in reality."[3]

These last two sentences surely express what most believers feel about the Bible, although "emotional resonance *regardless of factuality*" may or may not cut it with rationalists. Still, it's an honest comment but one that leaves us squarely in the land of fideism.

Feiler again:

"As with many places in the Sinai, the absence of evidence hardly matters, as modern visitors have decided these sites are the ones mentioned in the text. As we were sitting, a tour bus rolled up and fifty South Koreans disembarked, said a quick prayer by the spring, and prepared to re-embark. 'This is the site of Marah,' the minister explained, when I asked why he had come. Moments later a car full of American college students appeared and repeated the ritual. Their professor was less confident, 'I don't worry about assigning places,' he said, 'In the end it doesn't matter whether they took the northern route, the central route or the southern route. What matters is that they were here.' Minutes later, a carload of Frenchwomen arrived. 'Who cares if the Israelites were actually here?' one woman said. 'We're here because it's biblical!'"[4]

Once again, it doesn't matter what you believe, as long as you're sincere. This aphorism is apparently good enough for fundamentalists, but increasingly less so, I suspect, for the average person.

In a *National Geographic* article, "Abraham: Journey of Faith"), the author, Tad Szulc, writes:

> "...when I asked scholars the question, 'Was there ever a man called Abraham?' as often as not they were respectful (we can't disprove it) but convinced of the futility of trying to find a flesh-and-blood individual. 'Abraham is beyond recovery,' said Israel Finkelstein, a biblical archaeologist at Tel Aviv University. Without any proof of the patriarch's existence, the search for a historical Abraham is even more difficult than the search for a historical Jesus."

> "The important thing, we are told, is to assess the meaning and legacy of the ideas Abraham came to embody. He is most famously thought of as the founder of monotheism, although Genesis never credits him with this. The stories do, however, describe his hospitality and peaceableness and, most important, his faith and obedience to God."[5]

And he goes on:

> "Why is Abraham so vividly alive today? Faith – Judaic, Christian, and Islamic – and his majestic yet elusive presence provide one answer. But the most eloquent explanation I've heard originated with Rabbi Menahem Froman, who lives near Hebron. He said, 'For me Abraham is philosophy, Abraham is culture. Abraham may or may not be historical. Abraham is a message of loving kindness. Abraham is an idea. Abraham is everything. I don't need flesh and blood.'"

Philosophy, culture, loving message, an unhistorical idea...so we're back to metaphor, projection, emotion, nostalgia, psychological need, faith. Are these enough for the less than emotionally attached people to accept the Bible as the Word of God? Can we not apply this sentimental canon to any book, holy or not?

In a similar vein, in his book, *The Good Book*,[6] Peter Gomes recalls the New York Times article (December 15, 1995) in which the then Israeli foreign minister Shimon Peres, said that he disapproved of some of the activities of King David meaning his brutality, his slaughter of Saul's kin, his affair with Bathsheba, the murder of her husband, and so on. The speech provoked a storm of controversy. One rabbi told Peres in no uncertain terms to "shut up!" Another shouted, "You will not give out grades to King David!" The rabbis vehemently declared that David was holy, and that was that. One rabbi summed it up by warning that "whoever says that King David sinned does nothing but err." The reaction was predictable: do not slur an icon or challenge a myth. People prefer to hold onto the myth, which is far more nourishing than the facts that diminish the ideal that gives them hope and identity. Abraham, the Exodus, the Promised Land, the flawless monarchy of the Golden Age, Masada, the Six Day War, all are needed and necessary myths – a "philosophy, a message, a culture" – for the insiders who invented them, but they need not be necessarily compelling or true for those on the outside.

Perhaps no one put this emotional fideism better that the Mormon speaker and apologist Clifton Jolley. When he was challenged by religious reporters about the DNA test that showed that American Indians are not descendants of the Hebrew tribes as held by Mormon doctrine, Jolley replied, "After we have been defeated and all our stories have proven untrue we will perhaps come to know the more important reason and the only question that ever is – not whether the stories are true, but whether we are true to our stories." These attitudes characterize most religions (and politics). Perhaps Harold Kushner spoke for all religions when he wrote in his book *To Life!*, "Judaism is less about believing and more about belonging." He may be right for he and all the others I have mentioned have chosen myth over reason, something we shall explore in the next chapter. That choice is sufficient for the heart but not the head and maybe for some it doesn't matter.

FOUNDATIONS OF BELIEF

Apropos to our discussion are the words of the noted biblical scholar Raymond Brown, who frames the argument this way:

> "Let me be precise about the limits of this discussion of the Bible as the word of God, lest I arouse misunderstanding or false expectations. First, I fully accept the Roman Catholic doctrine of the Bible as the word of God, and the whole discussion assumes that fact. This may disappoint those who think proof is needed that the Bible is the word of God – no such proof is possible beyond biblical self-claim and Church doctrine; it is a matter of faith."[7]

A matter of faith. Whose faith? The modern searcher teasingly suggests that we replace the terms:

> Mary Mormon: "I fully accept the Mormon doctrine of the Book of Mormon as the word of God...This may disappoint those who think proof is needed that the Book of Mormon is the word of God – no such proof is possible beyond the Mormon self-claim and imams doctrine; it is a matter of faith."

> Mohammed Muslim: "I fully accept the Muslim doctrine of the Qur'an as the word of Allah...This may disappoint those who think proof is need that the Qur'an is the word of Allah –no such proof is possible beyond Muslim self-claim and church doctrine. It is a matter of faith."

> Josiah Jew: "I fully accept the Hebrew doctrine of the Torah as the word of God...This may disappoint those who think proof is needed that the Torah is the word of God. No such proof is

possible, beyond biblical self-claim and synagogue doctrine. It is a matter of faith."

This is what gives post-modernism a good name! Each of the above holds different and quite contradictory doctrines, e.g. Jesus is the Messiah, the Son of God vs. Jesus is not the Messiah nor Son of God vs. Jesus is a human being and God has a material body. All three rely on freely accepted assumptions (assumed not proven; indeed such assumptions cannot be proven) and self-validating claims that cut off questions and ultimately limit dialogue. The issue is not what makes one religion better than another but what compels such a faith stance to begin with?

UNBELIEVERS

Then too, we ask again, can the divinely ungifted be blamed if he or she, for whatever mysterious reasons known only to God, has not been chosen to receive the free gift of faith? Some don't want it, some do, and some, like physician-author Richard Selzer, lament the fact:

> "My entire life has been one long search for faith. I haven't found it. I do not believe in God. Having said that, which should lift an eyebrow or two, I want you to know that I love the idea of God. I love piety. Without it, you lead your life un-moored, in a state of isolation. You are a tiny speck in a vast universe. I'm jealous, frankly. I feel as though I've missed out on the greatest thing that can happen to a person – faith in God. It must be wonderful."

Innocent unbelievers obviously bring a different understanding to the Bible. Graced believers just as obviously bring susceptibility, a preordered faith, to it. Attend to the apologetic in these words:

> "The human dimension of the Bible is easily understood as an-tagonistic to its revelatory character: either scripture is God's

word or it is a human product...[These days] biblical scholarship is accused of occupying itself too much with scripture's human side while forgetting about its divine author.
Theologically, this alternative is nonsense. If we maintain the
belief in God's self-revelation in Jesus, then the human Jesus
is the locus of revelation....the same obtains for scripture,
which is the human witness of divine revelation; whoever
attempts to know this witness must also attempt to know the
human text..."[8]

Notice how the author resorts to fideism: yes, the Bible does have all
the human origins and limitations listed in this book, but that's okay
"if we maintain the belief in God's self-revelation..." That's Kugel's
fourth principal of interpretation, "The ancient interpreters assumed
that the Bible was a divinely given text." Yes, if we maintain this belief, this assumption, we will make it work. The fact is, embracing the
Bible as truly and uniquely revelatory of God is something to cherish,
but these impulses, prior to the book, are not everyone's spiritual gift
nor intellectual inclination, and, in the last analysis, the gap between
the findings of the scholars and the trustful nostalgia of the believers
might be too large to cross. Those Christians who have made the
leap have to account for their Mormon and Muslim counterparts. It
seems that Cardinal Newman was right after all: "Religion has never
been a deduction from what we know; it has ever been an assertion
of what we are to believe."

PASCAL'S WAGER

Newman is on to something, and he prompts me to spotlight my
ambiguity by ending this chapter with a subversive thought. Blasé
Pascal famously said that we really can't be sure about God, that he
exists, that he cares for the world. But since we really don't know, it's
probably better to err on the side of belief than disbelief, because if
you're wrong, it doesn't matter, but if you're right, you're ahead of the
game. Some people, as we have amply seen in this book, have reason

to doubt God's existence, his love and concern for the world (the theodicy question) and the collection (Bible) that purports to reveal him and contain his instructions for the human race. Yet many people, it seems, still opt for Pascal's wager: they know about the scholarly findings but what prevails is the "Abraham is an idea. Abraham is everything. I don't need flesh and blood sort of thing." Belief for them, in other words, is larger than the intellectual acceptance of doctrinal propositions. Religion and belief are tied into meaning and a sense of community. To believe really means to hold dear, to trust, to pledge oneself to something larger, something more than oneself, because life is experienced as awesome. Whatever the findings of modern biblical scholarship, one's sense of Something More, Someone More, is greater than their conclusions. People don't act because they first believe. People believe because they first act. They ponder the mystery of life. They experience mystery and joy first, and then believe later. Whether the official statements are literal or not is not of primary importance. Faith is more about the questions one focuses on than the propositions one must hold. Faith is more than the "Nostalgia Searching" of this chapter's title. Faith is not just fideism, but assent to the mystery behind it.

It's hard for secularists to make the distinction between faith as belief and faith as hope and love. Educated in a narrow scientific and rationalist mindset, they automatically feel that if Adam and Eve are disproved, they have won the case against a faith defined only in its official doctrines. They can't seem to react to awe and its consequences.

Here's an interesting parallel to ponder: The atheists in this book's title are the believers in an indifferent world, one run by the neutral, mechanical, evolutionary forces of nature. Nothing exists beyond that. They are hostile to religion because it posits a deity that not only deceives humanity with false promises of an afterlife but also constricts it with dogmas here on earth. The Bible, as they have rightly pointed out, is Exhibit A of scientific error and ignorance. Both religion and the Bible must therefore be deconstructed and removed from public life as hostile to human freedom and advancement. Many of these atheists are nihilists.

But not all. There are, paradoxically, "religious atheists." They do not believe in God, certainly not a personal God and even more certainly not in the God of the Bible, who is concocted from Middle Eastern mythology and is, erratic, crude, bloodthirsty, and discriminatory against women, slavery, heretics, enemies de jour, and so on. But in common with believers they do believe in mystery, in something greater than themselves, a "force" that is behind the universe and binds it together. They sense such a "force" in the incredible beauty of the universe, the overwhelming power of Grand Canyon, in those stunning, breathtaking Hubble photographs from outer space. Such beauty, such macro and micro wonders, evoke awe and provoke a moral response to life, a generous and caring heart. This "religion without God" is best summed up by perhaps the world's most famous atheist, Albert Einstein:

> "To know that what is impenetrable to us really exists, maintaining itself as the highest wisdom and the most radiant beauty which our dull faculties can comprehend only in their most elementary forms—this knowledge, this feeling, is at the center of true religiousness. In this sense, and in this sense only, I belong in the ranks of devoutly religious men."

In other words, for "religious" atheists, the overwhelming complexity, beauty and sublimity of nature are indications of something transcendental, something that permeates the universe, something truly super-natural, but not God. Whatever it is, it endorses a religious attitude towards life and generates compassion, kindness, and a sense of justice. Why it does so is not made clear. Theirs is an "irrational" faith as much as religious faith is, but without God.[9] There does seem to be some unfairness here, as it appears that such "religious" atheists will allow believers to share their natural faith, but they need not sympathize with believers' supernatural faith, let alone accommodate them.

Default faith

Nevertheless, they represent a new paradigm that is taking hold, what we might call a default faith. This kind of default faith is flourishing today as more and more people are declaring themselves "spiritual but not religious," which is to say people who have spiritual or mystical experiences, perhaps brought on by meditation, exercise, music, or awe-inspiring nature, but can't find satisfactory expression for these experiences in organized religion, heavily freighted as it is with dogma and hierarchy. They are keen to the spiritual, but searching for other language than what organized religion provides.

A case in point is atheist Sam Harris. He is famous for his book, The End of Faith. Recently he had a "religious" or spiritual experience when walking in Jesus' footsteps on the shore of the Sea of Galilee, but he would and could not explain it in terms that have anything to do with religion. Rather, he notes that the transcendence he experienced is common to all times, places and people. It's built into the human psyche and is prior to, and has nothing to do, with creed or religion. The transcendent experience can be simply the natural chemical rhythms of altered consciousness, just like people on drugs can experience a high, a euphoria, a sense of power, otherness and so on. It's just that organized religion has coopted such narratives and left no other viable way of explaining such experiences. As Harris says, "There's truly no secular or rational alternative for talking about questions of meaning and existential hopes and fears." Religion, in short, has wound up being a default language. Today, however, as it evident from all the polls, people are struggling to come up with expressing transcendence and awesome experiences in terms not related to the lexicon of religion.

These thoughts are an apt introduction to the next chapter on reason and myth.

Chapter 25.

SEARCHING THROUGH THE LENS OF REASON AND MYTH

It may seem counterproductive to travel through 24 chapters of rational arguments only to seemingly upend them all with a chapter on myth. It will not be that simple, as we shall see, but we do have to examine this critical category, and perhaps the best introduction is to observe that atheists have a hard time grasping Karen Armstrong's words:

> "Most cultures believed that there were two recognized ways of arriving at truth. The Greeks called them mythos and logos. Both were essential and neither was superior to the other; they were not in conflict but complementary, each with its own sphere of competence. Logos (reason) was the pragmatic mode of thought that enabled us to function effectively in the world and had therefore to correspond accurately to external reality. But it could not assuage human grief or find ultimate meaning in life's struggle. For that people turned to mythos, stories that made no pretense to historical accuracy but should rather be seen as an early form of psychology; if translated into ritual or ethical action, a good myth showed you how to cope with mortality, discover an inner source of strength, and endure pain and sorrow with serenity."[1]

Because the atheists and critics are alert to *logos* and deaf to *mythos*, they unleash a one-sided criticism of a book they consider literal history, ignoring the fact the biblical authors, like all the ancients, wrote in stories. They little appreciate that they are western Greek thinkers trying to understand Mid-Eastern Semitic thinkers, that they analyze while Semites synthesize, that they seek history while the Semites are writing theology more concerned with the meaning of what happened than in narrating the facts of what happened. So the Bible becomes an easy target, a mere repository of "bronze-age myths" (Christopher Hitchens). They don't realize that today more and more modern scholars do appreciate the Bible as a collected book of stories, with perhaps some pretense (but little claim) to historical accuracy. They are beginning once more to recognize the Bible as an ongoing imaginative narrative hostile to stopping at one sentence or paragraph or episode as if it were the final word. Its stories deliberately have lots of gaps and leave much unsaid in order to bypass judgment or make a point. This means that the Bible circles and circles the imponderables of God and human life in exotic, poetic language. Its stories are ever evolving, ever expanding to fit new circumstances, and not in the sense of adding more technical or historical information or literary flair but in the sense of taking another dive into the mystery. The Bible and its symbols (*mythos*) are not meant to compete with reason (*logos*), and to judge it by the latter is not fully fitting. In the Bible we are dealing with a different dimension of search and meaning. If, as someone said, the best theology is akin to art and poetry, the best reading of the Bible is akin to story. As such, it follows the rules of oral storytelling and not the rules of written grammar, logic, and composition. If we don't apply oral rules to the Bible, but rather apply the literary canons of the later written text, then we're not far from the literalism and fundamentalism that furiously hugs facts, not meaning, and makes best sellers of atheistic shortsightedness.

READING THE BIBLE AS STORY

Because "truth in story" is fundamentally true, let me turn quite rhapsodic in this section and declare that, as unlikely as it is, were

I ever to teach a course on the Bible, I would first require a whole semester on the study of the imagination and storytelling. I would have my students study storytelling's dynamic and rules, read poems, novels, and fairy tales, attend plays and dissect and discuss some of the great films of our time. I would repeat to them this story from Gregory Bateson's book, *Mind in Nature*. Bateson tells about the scientists who recently found a way to design a software program that makes computers function like the human mind. After installing the software, the programmers type in this question: "How does the human mind work?" The computer replied, "Well, let me tell you a story..." This insight echoes the words of storytellers John and Mary Harrell who said, "Storytelling is so natural to human beings it suggests a definition: we are creatures who think in stories," and Joseph Campbell's dictum that myth is a story whose truth is too large to be contained by mere facts.

Literary critic Terry Eagleton gives us a modern expression of this axiom when he writes:

> "Fiction does not primarily mean a piece of writing is not true. Truman Capote's *In Cold Blood*, Norman Mailer's *The Executioner's Song* and Frank McCourt's *Angela's Ashes* are all offered to us as true, yet they translate the truths they convey into a kind of imaginative fiction. Works of fiction can be full of factual information. You could run a farm on the basis of what Virgil's *Georgics* has to say about agriculture, though it is doubtful that it would survive for very long. Yet texts we call literary are not written primarily to give us facts. Instead, the reader is invited to 'imagine' those facts, in the sense of constructing an imaginary world out of them. A work can thus be true and imagined, factual and fictional, at the same time. ...There is a difference between being true to the facts and being true to life."[2]

The Bible is like that: imaginative fiction that conveys a truth. Yet the fact is, we moderns have lost the taste, perhaps even the ability, to think in stories. When it comes to the Bible, we seem to think we have only two choices – skepticism or fundamentalism, facts or truth. The figurative sense of story is foreign to us, and so we have relegated stories to the children's domain and have equated telling stories with telling lies. We have learned to distrust and distain the imagination. It is not hard to figure why. Our whole educational system is in service to the practical needs of the corporations, the efficient, the predictable digital. Which is why universities shortsightedly dismantle the humanities and build science labs. Scientism is equated with truth, and the modern mindset is that only science is the path to it. Everything else is merely entertaining. "Real" knowledge is that which is observed, measured, and capable of being plugged into a database.

So, there's the story of the little lost boy in the police station and the police are asking him to describe his mother. His response is that she is the most wonderful, beautiful lady in the world. When the police do locate her, she turns out to be a rather small, mousy looking woman and they enter her statistics and photo into the national database. They have her weight, height, photo, blood type, address, and email. The boy only knows that when he was sick she took care of him, that she made his lunches, read to him at night and gave him lots of hugs. Who has the "truth" about this woman, the poetic boy or the literal database, the neuropsychologists seeking the mechanical gene for "compassion" or a rabbi's fictional story about a good Samaritan?

The one-dimensional "objective" conviction of today is closed to the insight of Ursula Le Guin, the author of the wonderful fantasy series, EarthSea, who writes words that should be on the frontispiece of every Bible:

> "The great fantasies, myths and tales ...speak from the unconscious to the unconscious, in the language of the unconscious – symbol and archetype. Though they use words, they work the way music does: they short-circuit verbal reasoning, and go straight to the thoughts that lie too deep to utter. They cannot be translated fully into the language of reason, but

only a Logical Positivist, who also finds Beethoven's Ninth Symphony meaningless, would claim that they are therefore meaningless. They are profoundly meaningful, and usable – practical – in terms of ethics, of insight, of growth."

The weight of this statement is to underscore that if we think in propositions and the ancients thought in stories, the ancients' concept of truth was simply not like ours. We do not live in the enchanted world of the ancients, but in a world of natural processes that we seek to describe scientifically. We do live in a digital, truth-as-objective-statement culture. So we issue briefs. The ancients lived in the world of imagination and told stories, and for them faith consisted in knowing those stories rather than agreeing with certain theological propositions. Our sense of history is, "Just the facts, Ma'am. What do they say?" The ancients' sense of history is, "What do the facts mean?" We stop at phenomenon. The ancients look behind the phenomenon, where other powers are at work. The biblical writers were not writing history, but story. The formidable literary figure Harold Bloom, Sterling Professor of Humanities at Yale University, reviewed an illustrated Book of Genesis. Responding to anyone who might possibly comment, "This is what they looked like back then," he replied, "There was no 'back then.' Genesis, like Exodus and Numbers after it, is fabulous tale-telling, and not historical fact. You can call it myth if you want or whatever you think best fits the tale of the tribe."[3] So, there it is: the Bible is essentially a particular people's epic, and therefore basically a people's anthology of national stories with a mercurial YHWH as its main character. We should take it as coded, in the sense that, through its stories, behind its metaphors and fictions, its parabolic interpretations, one finds truth as they saw it, one finds out how to live, or at least so its devotees believe. Karl Barth was right when he said, "I take the Bible far too seriously to take it literally."

So the bottom line is that people of the pre-scientific age thought and wrote (those who could write) and told stories rich in allegory, metaphor, and symbolism. This was not only because they were superstitious and ignorant of our scientific knowledge and our great power of manipulating nature (which would have stunned their minds) but because, free of our resulting hubris, they innately sensed that reality could not be fully grasped by the human mind or categorized by human systems however "scientific." They felt and respected the power of mystery and could only resort to mumbling about it in indirect ways, the ways of story and metaphor (what we call myth). Above all, they had a highly developed sense of God (under any title) as awesome, as ungraspable, and anything they had to say about him had to be unsaid almost immediately or quickly cast in opposing and contradictory ways. (YHWH is forgiving. YHWH is cruel.) There was a transcendence whose existence could not be proved, but only intuited. When it came to God and life's mysteries, the Greek philosophical terms we've inherited, like "omnipotent," "omnipresent," and "omniscient" made no sense. Story and poetry, tale and folklore were the only adequate terms. In a word, where we today are resigned to a meaningless universe and have embraced the palliative technical marvels and entertainments of the digital here and now, the ancients wrestled to find human meaning through the poetries and contradictions of allegory and metaphor. The Semitic ancients preferred *mythos* over reason, although, in a twist of history, reason via the Greeks eventually triumphed. Alas, the Church also came down on the side of reason.

THE MYSTERIES OF LIFE

Because the reason-*mythos* point is so important, allow me to present it another way. Scientists and philosophers, from the beginning, have tried to define human life and what makes it worth living, or whether it's basically different from animal or plant life. For some (especially among the vocal atheistic ones), modern science reduces us to primal evolutionary urges, the end product of the development of DNA, the march of physics, growing complexity, relentless mathematics, and the activities of "selfish genes." We appeared just when all natural phenomena were in a unique proper alignment that promoted the development of self-consciousness. We are sophisticated processing machines. We are and remain capable of being explained in material terms. That is to say, we are to be understood in terms of science alone. Somehow, however, in spite of the awesomeness of nature, the fantastic grace and power of evolution and the overwhelming splendor of the universe, science still fails at the basic level of meaning, which is why Einstein said that science is not possible without a spiritual sensibility: "Behind all the discernible laws and connections, there remains something subtle, intangible and inexplicable. Veneration for this force beyond anything that we can comprehend is my religion." And he suggested that the greatest achievement of science is not to explain it all, but to point more clearly to that which is beyond its scope. Science does explain much but fails to tell us how to live. That's why, as far back as the Greeks who pondered these questions, Aristotle, quite conscious of our animal nature, felt we always had the capacity to transcend the limits of our biology and could not be totally explained in terms of nature.

All this, again, brings us to the subject of story and storytelling. It's the stories and their evolving interpretations we tell and pass on, not the scientific discoveries that speak to human life and how it is to be lived that stir our moral imagination. That's why we covet our moral heroes and morality tales. Such stories mirror our own struggles and come closest to plumbing the hard-to-name nuances of life, the "something more" perfume that hangs in the air even in laboratories. Stories, as befits the complexities of life, are ambivalent, multi-leveled, and, in one sense, never finished. Stories exist because we have learned that there are simply moments too precious, deep, mysterious, and unspeakable to be explained fully by science. How often we say or hear said, "Words fail me," or "There are no words to express this bounty" or "this horror" or whatever. Normal, rational categories *do* fail us, so we turn to poetry and story. We struggle to make sense of human experience, and stories are really the only venue to express the messiness and ambiguities of life. They move beyond any simple, reductive, scientific answer. Their range is wide.

They supply the language, metaphors, poetry, allegories, and paradoxes that come nearest to expressing our fears, joys, and desires for fulfillment. In a word, human beings cannot understand themselves or the world without resorting to stories and myths. To this day, the great movies, novels, and even TV shows captivate us. We are a storytelling people, because science has its limits.

The Bible, like other great sagas, fits in here. It is a story anthology, one not meant to be taken literally, not meant to be consistent or logical or historical or the last word. It is a mythos that challenges us and helps us, through its stories, to define ourselves and our place in this universe.

We must also remember that all stories reflect the mindset and worldview of the storytellers. We must honor the native metaphors and symbols that they draw upon, the ones they rework and reconfigure in order to lay out the truths they wish to convey. The challenge is to go back and try to understand that mindset, that worldview of the writers. How did the ancient Egyptians, Chinese, Incas, Greeks and Jews see the world? How did they express and record what they saw? How did the medieval mind interpret reality? Scholars expose the mentalities of this or that people, this or that historical time era, so that we do not impose our own current instinctive reflective understandings on concepts and words that have no relation to what previous peoples meant. In other words, we can't understand Pliny or Shakespeare, what and how they wrote, without understanding their times and assumed allusions and metaphors. So, too, concerning the biblical stories, scholars expose the ways the ancients regularly took and recycled old myths to capture new truths. For example, the biblical writer comfortably took the centuries-old Elijah story of bringing back the widow's son to life (1 Kings 17:17-24), and moved it forward to interpret Jesus' raising of the widow's son at Naim (Luke 7:11-17). This was his way of explaining who Jesus is, the tradition he stood in, what he was about. So we don't necessarily have to literally parse the Jesus version with modern one-dimensional scientific minds to "prove" Jesus raised someone from the dead. We have to parse the story in its contextual recycled metaphors to discover what the story is trying to tell us about Jesus.

Unfortunately, in modern times, dismissive of any "reality" prior to the 18th century Enlightenment, there has been a loss of appreciation of the power of ancient myth. The rise of science as the sole arbiter of truth and reality have pressured religion to explain itself in scientific categories, offer rational explanations of doctrines and evidence of its truth and concoct dogma and creeds that "clinch" religion's rationality. The catechism becomes a proof text taming the utter mystery of God and the Gospel. The following are examples.

EXCERPTS FROM THE BIBLICAL STORYBOOK

Catholic nun Fran Ferder:

> "An angel visits a young girl and tells her she will bear the son of God. An entire host of heavenly beings announce the child's birth to shepherds in the night. An ordinary jug of water becomes fine wine. A blind man begins to see, and a silent one finds his voice. A little girl awakens from the dead. A rotting corpse walks out of a tomb. A few loaves of bread and a little fish feed everyone who is hungry. A stranger on the road makes the hearts of fearful people burn with passion again. So did things in the Bible really happen this way? From the perspective of historical fact, probably not. From the perspective of faith, absolutely."[4]

"Probably not." Shocking as this is to the average person, all those stories she alludes to really did not happen. They are metaphors, allegories, parables. They are the ancient writers' way of portraying, in a most memorable manner, someone they want you to believe in and hard to put into prose. They are stories, culled from the symbols of Near Eastern lore and the stories of the Old Testament, designed to inspire belief in YHWH or Moses or Jesus. You have to believe in them and through them to get to their truth. You have to have a "faith perspective." (Where have we heard that before?) The biblical stories are, in the words of scholar Raymond Brown, "imaginative retellings," inventive fiction, narrative parables. As such, the Bible is best presented as a compendium of wonderfully creative stories sacred to a particular people struggling to make sense of the world. If read literally, of course, the atheists and skeptics *will* have a field day, but why should we concede the day to them? If read metaphorically, believers will have something to ponder.

GENESIS REVISITED

Let us take a second storybook look at Genesis. It contains all kinds of cosmological myths, or "myths of origin": like all ancient and modern peoples, the Hebrews wanted to know, how did the world get started? Why are we here? Who is the god that created the world? What are we supposed to be doing with our lives? This world of ours is in a sorry state. It couldn't have come that way from God, so we need an explanation of how it got that way. These are urgent and time-less questions, and myths like Genesis try to deal with them in round about, imaginative language within their time and culture. Israel's myths, for example, are clearly written in dialogue with and some-times in competition with the other Near Eastern myths of Babylon, Assyria, Egypt, etc., and so it tries to define itself in relation to its neighbors and over and against its neighbors. So, Genesis chapter 1 is not, as it appears, a factual story of creation, much less a literal scientific explanation of the origins of the universe – like the world being made in seven days in opposition to the findings of geology. Rather, it is a myth; that is, it is an identity story, a meaning story, a community story, and an ethical story. It is, as we indicated, specifi-cally a response over and against the Babylonian creation myth. It's a response written by Jews in exile in the 6th century in Babylon when they had no place or space, and the story told them not to worry: they could make time sacred wherever they were. They could keep the Sabbath, circumcise, mark the days, honor the week in a foreign land or anywhere. So the Genesis story becomes an identity story, a vested-interest story: a story of how the Israelite people defined themselves as different in the midst of an alien land and culture.

The whole intent of the Adam and Eve Fall account, in no way historically true, may simply be an etiological story to answer the everyday questions of why childbirth hurts, why we have to work to eat, why we fear snakes, why we wear clothes, and so on. And, in the process, that "desire for your husband" becomes a great story metaphor if we read it as a gloss on Plato's *Symposium* where Aristophanes says that human beings were originally whole and complete in themselves until Zeus cut them in half. Love, then, is the desire to find one's other half and become whole again, and *that* existential plot is replayed one way or another in almost every piece of literature.

The Exodus story is the great human metaphor of a journey, a theme found everywhere, from Abraham's and Odysseus' wanderings to those of Sinbad, Dante, Robinson Crusoe, and the characters of Grimm's Fairy Tales. The Exodus utterly fails as history, but as narrative it is replete with adventure, danger, backsliding, and doubt: "Is God among us or not?" is the great human question endlessly asked in time of collective pain and loss. The stories found in Joshua, Judges, the monarchy, the Exile, and the Gospels resonate with humanity and form a vast template against which we can work out our human lives and from which we can extract metaphors to live by. We are invited to enter into the Bible's folklores and legends, its Hamlet-like plays within plays. We are asked to resonate with duplicitous Jacob as Uriah Heep, Joshua as Roland, David's Madame Bovary escapades, Solomon's Arabian Nights fantasies, unsubtle propaganda, esoteric poetry, the simplistic theology of the Deuteronomists, the lonely voices who said they were nuts, the fantastical overtures of Jesus' birth, the power plays of his arrest and death, the apocalyptic wishful thinking, the artists who kept on reworking, manipulating and coloring the stories to make them politically correct. It's all there, reflecting common human themes and aspirations, just as the Egyptians, Assyrians, Babylonians, Persians, Greeks, and so on did, but with a large difference. There is, ever and at all times, irritatingly present, like a giant oak standing in the middle of a desert, YHWH. YHWH is the insistent, mercurial, unifying thread of these stories, the Main Character the people couldn't live with and couldn't live without and, from all accounts, vice versa.

The great tragedy has been to take all these stories and make them literal history, and this book has exposed scholars who have picked this history apart, and fundamentalists who, like the Ice Queen of C.S. Lewis' *Narnia*, have embraced the stories and frozen them into prose and moral absolutes. The churches got into the act and found doctrines in metaphors and dogmas in allegories. We hasten to add that doctrines and dogmas are desirable and necessary to keep the story within its deepest limits and its profoundest meanings, but they should be used as sparingly and broadly as possible, lest commentators, holding the moonbeam in a too-firm hand, snuff out the light altogether. Catechisms and anthologies are not quite the same thing, although both serve a purpose, and it's a shame that preachers tend to preach the former and not the latter. All should heed the words of William Sloan Coffin: "I read the Bible because the Bible reads me. I see myself reflected in Adam's excuses, in Saul's envy of David, in promise-making, promise-breaking Peter... I find God who not only answers our questions, but equally important, questions our answers...If you take the Bible seriously, you can't take it literally – not all of it."[5]

And it's a shame that scholars themselves have also tended to compartmentalize their disciplines into unnecessary hostilities. As Richard Holmes writes at the end of his fascinating book *The Age of Wonder*:

> "We need to understand how science is actually made, how scientists themselves think and feel and speculate. We need to explore what makes scientists creative, as well as poets or painters, or musicians...The old rigid debates and boundaries – science versus religion, science versus the arts, science versus traditional ethics – are no longer enough. We should

be impatient with them. We need a wider, more generous, more imaginative perspective."[6]

Or as our literary critic Terry Eagleton so succinctly put it, "Part of what we mean by a 'literary' work is one in which *what* is said is to be taken in terms of *how* it is said."[7] That's the Bible: the *what* and the *how* are intrinsically linked.

Chapter 26.

A SEARCHER'S EPILOGUE

The metaphorical approach to the Bible of the previous chapter is an honorable, ancient approach. Third century Origen thought it was self-evident that the biblical stories "are figural tales, communicating spiritual mysteries, and certainly not historical records." Seventh century St. Isidore spoke for his time when he wrote that the Bible is to be understood in a triple way: historically, tropologically, and mystically. Still, for all of the compelling richness of this approach, for all of the renewed appreciation of the ancient way of pondering truth, there are, like the proverbial biblical snake in the grass, problems. They center on one main one we have alluded to many times, the issue of criteria. To ask a pre-postmodern question, whose parabolic interpretation is right? Many commentaries on biblical passages are pleasing, profound, moving, insightful—and sometimes, weird. They can get quite inventive, if not strained. For some feminists, for example, Mary is every unmarried pregnant teenager, a prototype feminist, every woman who has lost a child. Elizabeth, who insists on naming her baby John instead of Zachary, is a primitive Betty Friedman striking a blow against male supremacy. Joseph is every male who doesn't have a clue. The dove at Jesus' baptism is a symbol indicating the presence of the Spirit, and the voice from heaven is everyone's inner voice calling him or her to his or her full potential. The temptations in the desert never literally happened. The whole scene is a metaphor for the struggle between good and evil, a sign of the daily enticements we all face. The devil, whose existence we owe more to Milton's *Paradise Lost* than to the Bible, is a symbol of our inner wicked impulses. The storm at sea represents the many trials the early Church had to face. The Transfiguration is an inventive story indicating the gradual understanding of Jesus by his followers and their growing conviction of his closeness to God.

The cleansing of the temple is a symbolic wiping away of every vestige of racism, sexism, and ageism. The encounter with the foreign woman pleading with Jesus to heal her troubled daughter is really a symbol of the breaking of the boundaries of exclusivism. Jesus' healing of Jairus' daughter with his command "Little girl, get up!" (Mark 5:41-42) is not only a cure, but a distinct call for all females to get up and stand up and claim the power within them. Lazarus is everyone "dead," bereft of hope and meaning. The rending of the temple veil at Jesus' death is a metaphor for the presence of God no longer confined to the elite (clergy, religious), but given to all. Luke's one-of-a-kind Pentecost story (only he has it; no one else has the story of the tongues or outpouring of the Spirit) is an empowerment story, the empowerment of everyone now bound by rules and society. It's a Spirit who reminds us that, just as we gradually got rid of dietary laws and circumcision, so there remains other Pentecost-inspired freedoms to achieve: the marriage of homosexuals, the ordination of women, the blessings of abortion, the salvation of Muslims and Buddhists. The Exodus is the universal symbol for the flight from slavery to freedom. Job is every decent person treated unfairly. Peter is the paradigm of the second chance. Finally, the Watergate scandal during the presidency of Richard Nixon was clearly predicted in the Bible, because Nehemiah 3:26; 8:1 mentions the "water gate."

Such free-floating exegeses, even those that are uplifting and insightful, with seemingly no criterion, are the fundamental problem we have to face with this renewed emphasis on the contextual, the allegorical and the metaphorical in reading the Bible. Well, yes, there is that "rule of faith" and there is tradition. Raymond Brown was right to call Tradition, the divinely guided reflection of the Christian community on the mystery of Jesus (which is why we accept Mark,

Luke, Matthew and John but not the Gospels of Thomas or Peter) but, as we have seen, tradition is hard to pin down and it has been so dramatically challenged under the rubric of "human experience" that it is equally hard to identify its consistency.

CATHOLIC DILEMMAS

Catholics who say that, in matters biblical, they have the Church with its guaranteed Spirit of Truth and unchangeable doctrines to guide them, have to confront a litany of contradictions and reversals. They have to recall the mistranslation of Paul's words affirming that it is in Adam "in whom" we have all sinned, St. Jerome changing the word maiden to virgin, the ahistorical, oversimplified use of scripture to prove that Jesus himself was foretold, the doubtful ordination of the apostles as priests, the gradual and complex development of offices that were often based on Roman and Jewish models, a Messiah who suffered, died, and rose on the third day "according to scripture" when scripture, except as interpreted by Christians, has no such scenario. Then there's Boniface VIII's declaration that every human being must submit to the Roman Pontiff as an absolute necessity for salvation (later reversed by Vatican II), Pius IX misusing the story of Onan to condemn contraception (wisely omitted by Pope Paul VI in *Humane Vitae*), insisting that human life begins at the precise moment of conception and using a faulty translation of Genesis 3:15 to prove the Immaculate Conception, and along with Pope Gregory XVI citing the absurdities of calling for the freedom of conscience. There is Pope Nicholas's *Romana Pontifex* (1455) authorizing the King of Portugal to enslave pagans. All these doctrines were claimed to be Bible based. Then there is the reversal in the Church's beliefs and teachings about and treatment of the Jews, the reversal of the condemnation of usury (Council of Vienne in 1311 and Benedict XIV's encyclical in 1745) to acceptance, from discrimination against women to equality (in theory), from its nearly millennial acceptance and defense of slavery to its condemnation. Finally, there is the Church's attitude towards the Bible itself with its radical trajectory, as it were, from Pius X to Pius XII signaling the change (not development) from reading the Bible fundamentally to reading it contextually (though this has not been consistent).

Catholics (and Protestants) have had to come to terms with the biblical contradictions where, say, the Book of Deuteronomy permits divorce, while the prophet Malachi says that God detests it. And what are both to make of Paul's urgent expectations of the second coming of Christ and his free-wheeling exegesis, as when he introduces the Adam = Christ paradigm, or where in Romans 10:5-8, he takes Deuteronomy 30:1-4 and mangles it to apply to Christ? As the Protestant commentator, Clayton J. Schmit, remarks on this latter: "This sleight of hand is not to be imitated by preachers today, for it could lead to the advancement of any kind of theology or belief... While scholars may debate over Paul's motives for such sloppy exegesis, we can read with confidence what he clearly intends for us to know."[1] — because, he adds, Paul's an inspired author and it's a matter of faith. So Paul gets a pass but historically over the centuries, motivated by change in politics, knowledge and attitudes, biblical interpretations *have* led to "any kind of theology or belief." In this regard the following quotation surely sums up the underlying rationale of all the biblical writings, why they were written, edited and saved to begin with:

> "What does a great empire do when faced with imminent invasion and destruction? It can rearm at home and seek allies abroad; but more cunningly it can revisit its history to forge a myth that will unite the people and carry them through to victory, a myth that will demonstrate to everyone that their county has been specially chosen by history to uphold justice and righteousness... history reimagined can be a very powerful weapon."[2]

This is our modern take on the Bible, what we consider the Bible to be all about. The Bible is constantly revisited history constantly reimagined as times and circumstances warrant change. Since this strategy, used by many people throughout the ages including our own, is so apparent why would anyone give the Bible special credence? With such a natural explanation at hand, why should we believe that God had anything to do with it, that he is somehow its author? Why did we and do we take the Bible as literal, free of the agendas and purposes of propaganda and survival? Why the "Word of God" when the consistently and motivated reimagined word of man is so obvious and traceable? And, as far as the doctrines deduced from the biblical canon go, to quote Cardinal Newman, we "find ourselves unable to fix an historical point at which the growth of doctrine ceased, and the rule of faith was once and for all settled."

OTHER QUESTIONS

Let's press on: we know that the biblical authors did take the old oral sacred legends and folklore common to the Near East and weave them into stories to suit their purposes. They were even hesitant, as we saw, to dismiss any revered source in their own tradition, including contradictory stories, and conflicting plots such was their reverence. All was grist for the grand narrative of their interpretative affair with YHWH, but – and here is the rub – as noted in this book, we are quite aware that the sacred authors, by nature of being "sacred", had agendas. That's why they were writing in the first place. We saw that. They were not neutral, and we need not be surprised at that – we expect that – but their partisanship often led them, in telling and reimaging their mythical stories, to distort facts, sour attitudes, promote prejudice, invite revenge, demonize enemies and leave us a legacy justifying terrible injustice and cruelty. One biblical scholar offers pertinent comments we should read very carefully:

> "Every historical narrative is composed of two basic dimensions: details of the events and a viewpoint from which those details are delivered. In the case of the Bible story, our right to survey the details of the events, to listen to whom we wish to

listen, to see what we wish to see has been usurped. The storyteller acting through the narrator in the story makes those decisions for us. Those decisions are not made thoughtlessly but strategically in a bid to influence our adoption of a specific ideological point of view. If we follow the leading of the narrator, we do not get to cheer for Goliath, even though we may have been able to find some things in his real life to celebrate. Ultimately, we are not permitted to side with King Saul. Rather we are cajoled into celebrating the rise of David at the expense of both Goliath and Saul. The narrator is leading us to adopt this point of view."

"In contrast to what some may call 'fair and honest reporting' the narrator typically directs the camera and the microphone so that the reader meets only those actions and words that ultimately reinforce the intended perspective of the narrator. Thus the goal of the divine storyteller is not merely to inform about the past but to transform the future by impacting the reader's values and attitudes. It is the 're-presentation of past events for the purpose of instruction.'"[3]

This comment is not easily dismissed and calls up David Brooks' observation in an Op Ed piece in *The New York Times* concerning data. Data "is never raw; it's always structured to somebody's predispositions and values. The end result looks disinterested, but, in reality, there are value choices all the way through, from construction to interpretation."[4]

These words apply to all written material, including the Bible. Which is to say, concerning the Bible, no matter how you slice it, no matter how much more congenial the new interpretations are to the modern mind, all this is simply a soft way of saying that it is a matter of "value choices." We shouldn't be surprised at that any more than we would be in reading the official version of Russian history. The storyteller interprets events and bends them to his ideology "for the sake of instruction," and, even though we are told (on faith) that this is the work of a divine storyteller, his ideology has left at times a legacy of considerable mischief, the mischief of racism, xenophobia, sexism, superstition, and so on, and we're stuck with it since this is, after all, "the word of God." While some "metaphorical" parabolic biblical stories do leave a legacy of inspiration, challenge, comfort, and awe, others leave a bitter ideological aftertaste that, as religious history has amply shown, has spat out war, racism, witch hunts, colonialism, exploitation and persecution. Even at best, nervous modern interpreters leave us their faith convictions. Yes, as one scholar has said, the Bible is all "foreground," leaving subsequent authors to fill in the background but often the background they filled in from their imaginations became foreground.

ONE MORE THING

Then, too, what about the common hermeneutic of lifting older biblical words and relocating them to make them say something different? Recall our Jesuit commentator on the Epistle to the Hebrews (which we discussed in Chapter 19) who wrote that many of the Old Testament quotations it cites were used "without much regard for the historical or literary context they were originally in. Most of the texts, we might have to say, are taken out of context..." We mentioned previously, that such citations were really not meant to be taken literally, but merely to underscore Old Testament connections, latch onto its literary empathies, and use its provocative language. But, as we also mentioned, in time they were in fact taken and applied literally. One thinks of Augustine using the Gospel parable admonition, "Compel them to come in" as a justification for war against heretics (he advocated the violent suppression of the Donatists) or the Christian fundamentalists' interpretation of Ezekiel's Gog and Megog as none other than Russia, or the Catholic Church finding in the words of the Last Supper the institution of the priesthood. Whatever justification the ancients had for context wrenching, some find it all too convenient, too capricious.

Moreover, even when scholars sensed that they were dealing with stories that were enveloping larger truths, they still held onto select stories as literal and went all over the mountaintops searching for Noah's ark or the Mount of the Transfiguration as if they were factual and not an old common folkloric fictions that had a truth to tell. They might as well try to locate the Hogwarts School from the *Harry Potter* series or Middle Earth from the *Lord of the Rings* series. In short, the Bible's critics, like some of the scholars mentioned in this book, as well as the Bible's interpreters and theologians, read the stories literally, the former to point out the obvious contradictions between text and historical or archaeological fact and the latter to concoct concrete doctrines and moral absolutes out of fluid metaphors. *Logos* and *mythos* have been at loggerheads, and we have suffered from that.

This is as good a point as any to pause and offer a summary citation of the problems associated with the Bible. As you read it slowly and carefully, keep in mind all that has been written in this chapter and all the others preceding it. It is from the conservative Catholic magazine, *First Things*:

> "The long history of defective scriptural exegesis occasioned by problematic translations is a luxuriant one, and its riches are too numerous and exquisitely various adequately to classify. But I think one can arrange most of them along a single continuum in four broad divisions: some misreadings are caused by a translator's error, others by merely questionable renderings of certain words, other by the unfamiliarity of the original author's (historically specific) idiom, and still others by the untranslatable remoteness of the author's own (culturally specific) theological concerns. And each kind comes with its own special perils and consequences."

But let me illustrate. Take for example, Augustine's magisterial reading of the Letter to the Romans, as unfolded in realms of his writings, and ever thereafter by his theological heirs: perhaps the most sublime 'strong misreading' in the history of Christian thought and one that compromises specimens of all our classes of misprision. Of the first, for instance: the notoriously misreading Latin rendering of Romans 5:12 that deceived Augustine to think of original sin – bondage to death, mental and moral debility estrangement from God – even more insistently in terms of an inherited guilt (a concept as logically coherent as that of a square circle), and which prompted him to assert with such sinewy vigor the justly eternal torment of babes who died unbaptized. And of the second: the way, for instance, Augustine's misunderstanding of Paul's theology of election was abetted by the simply contingency of a verb as weak as the Greek *proorizein* ('sketching out beforehand,' 'planning,' etc.) being rendered as *praedestinare* – etymologically defensible, but connotatively impossible. And of the third: Augustine's frequent failure to appreciate the degree to which, for Paul the 'works' (*erga, opera*) he contradistinguishes from faith are works of the Mosaic law, 'observances' circumcision, kosher regulations and so on). And of the fourth – well, the evidence abound: ...his entire [mis]reading of Romans 9-11..."

"...regarding that part of his [Augustine's] patrimony that has had the widest effect – his understanding of sin, grace, and election [predestination teaching] not only do I share the Eastern distaste for (or, frankly, horror at) his conclusion; I am even something of an extremist in that respect. In the whole, long, rich history of Christian misreading of Scripture, none I think, has ever been more consequential, more invincibly perennial, or more disastrous."[5]

This timely quotation encapsulates the issues: a massive misreading of an inherently unstable Bible by a foundational theologian that got firmly fixed into Christian theology, doctrine and practice to burden it for almost two millennia. Today, as the quiet dismantling of Augustine's legacy in this regard goes on, one has to question the authority of the Bible and the official far reaching teaching of a Church that claims the infallibility of the Holy Spirit.

Finally, I suppose while we are at it, we should also take time to give nod to today's colophony of other voices, feminist voices, socially constructed gendered advocates' voices, and so on. We are never sure that we have captured the right voice, caught the Bible's real meaning. As a result we have become adept at routinely offering revisions in the light of the latest social, textual, psychological and anthropological or archaeological discoveries, and a stream of endless books, article and monographs about the Bible continue to pour out century after century testifying either to the Bible's inexhaustible richness or its bottomless opaqueness, depending on how one looks at it.

The Biblical enterprise

With all this being said, we have to admit that for some the whole biblical enterprise seems to come down to this: the Bible, in its most fundamental identity, is a certain people's national (self-serving) epic, one that, unlike others, caught on in the West because of the triumph of Christianity. It is one people's mythology among other people's mythologies. As such, it serves, as it is supposed to, the noble purposes of meaning, identity, and community. "Why is this night different from any other night?" The story that is the response reinforces the national epic, the national identity and ethnic cohesion. No matter what scholars say about the Passover's origins or the blatant historical difficulties of the Exodus stories, the mythology holds fast. The myths persist despite contradictory evidence because the story, regardless of the facts, embodies a deeper truth that people need. So what if Marie Antoinette didn't say "let them eat cake" – the story captured a regime that showed little concern for the public welfare. So what if George Washington didn't confess to chopping down the non-existent cherry tree – the story captured his reputation as a man of integrity. So what if St. Francis didn't write the "Canticle of the Sun" – the story captured his environmental spirit. This mingling of myth and memory suffuses every epic, every saga, and the Bible is no exception.

Nobody said it better than anthropologist Bronislaw Malinowski, who over a century ago argued:

> "Myth fulfills in primitive culture an indispensable function:
> it expresses, enhances, and codifies belief, it safeguards and
> enforces morality, it vouches for the efficiency of ritual and
> contains practical rules for the guidance of man...Myth is thus
> a vital ingredient of human civilization; it is not an idle tale,
> but a hard-worked active force; it is not a intellectual expla-
> nation or an artistic imagery, but a pragmatic charter of prim-
> itive faith and moral wisdom"[6]

That's the Bible and its validity, even for those who see it as a merely
human work. It is precisely in its stories and the core truths those
parabolic stories contain. Its worth lies in its claim to call kings to
order, undermine conventional thinking, castigate injustice, and sit
in judgment on capitalism and sovereign self-interest in a time when
people no longer know how to describe what they are doing without
the language of individualism and when unrestrained greed undermines society and the ideals it offers. In short, the Bible gives shape
to history, provides a narrative, a sweep of events, a communitarian
ethos (in contrast to "debauched libertarianism"[7]), community, a morality for people whose tendency is to be selfish and shortsighted.
Its deconstruction is a loss for today where our nation is soul-sick,
where everyone just goes his or her separate ways making individual
choices.

It is within this context that some seek to preserve the Bible by offering a conciliatory stance, a spiritual flavoring:

> "Instead of getting bogged down by debates regarding the his-
> torical accuracy of the patriarchal narratives, of the Exodus...
> can we focus rather on what it means to be called, to be
> saved, to be a covenanted people (Genesis through Kings).
> Can we learn from the prophets the importance of loyalty to
> God (Hosea, Jeremiah) and of living in justice (Amos, Isaiah,
> Micah)? Can we learn from Israel how to pray in joy and
> sorrow, in need and in thanksgiving (Psalms), and how to find
> God reflected in the world (Israel's wisdom tradition)? Can
> we move beyond the simplistic notion of suffering and sin as

the author of Job did and as Jesus did in the New Testament?...
Can we learn what it means to say God is love?...prayer from
psalms, loyalty from the prophets, God's presence from the
wisdom tradition, what it means to be human from Jesus' life,
death and Resurrection?"[8]

The generous answer, of course, is yes to all of these questions, but at
the same time we can't forget the disagreements and a long history
of orthodoxy-inspired persecutions and punishments that attend the
Bible. We can't forget the doctrinal difference, the contradictory and
mutually hostile interpretations that still exist. Mostly, even as we
adopt a live-and-let-live attitude, we can't forget that consistently
the biblical text still escapes us, that it has become and remains history's perennial Rorschach test.

What about the Bible's authority? By the same logic, it is secure
and valid but only for its adherents. It's the charter statement for
the Jews and Christians in the same sense that the Loyal Order of
Moose or the Chamber of Commerce have charter statements or
mission statements or the United States has its Constitution. These
are identity, cohesive, defining ideals that are authoritative sources
for its members, its adherents, its citizens, not necessarily outsiders,
though its claims are universal. Further, in regard to the Bible, we
are reminded that it is a compendium that reflects how the ancients
viewed reality and not necessarily how God did. The Bible, like all
sacred writings, is a particular response to the ancient Israelites' and
early Christians' experience of God in the particular culture in which
they lived. If the Bible is sacred scripture to Jews and Christians it's
only because they themselves declared it to be so and in that sense it
is, authoritative but not exclusive, not "the only way." In addition, we
must keep remembering that there are two other claimants to being
God-revealed books out there that are sacred for their adherents.
Like Bible believers, they too can rightly claim them as authoritative
but not necessarily, vis-à-vis the Bible, as the only word of God.

My own Catholic Church for the past half century has, in the shadow
of the Vatican II document *Dei Verbum* that insists that the Bible

reproduces "firmly, faithfully, and without error that truth which God wanted to put into the sacred writing for the sake of our salvation," has been tireless in promoting Bible studies. But, as we observed previously, the big issue is, what precisely is that truth "for the sake of salvation?" There's just too many conflicting, God-inspired "truths" in the pages of the Bible. There are too many tensions between, say, the "truths" of Proverbs and Job, between Paul and James, between the punishments of Deuteronomy (for example, 22:24) and John (for example, 8:1-11). So we all (officials and non-officials) tease out our answers depending on our faith predilections and our time and place in history. We make judgments as to the right answer, sometimes coming up with literal ones, and more often these days, via the historical-critical method, resorting to metaphor and allegory. That doesn't always go over well. The people in the Bible study sessions I have attended over the years, no matter how educated and enlightened, cling to a fundamentalist reading and resist the historical-critical method as too disturbing, even though for them the commonsense questions of this book keep kicking in. This fundamentalist attitude perseveres everywhere. For example, in June 2014, a Gallup poll reported that 42% of Americans believe that "God created humans in their present form 10,000 years ago." A third of the respondents believe that the Bible "is the actual word of God and it is to be taken literally, word for word" and half believe that it is the "the inspired Word of God, but not everything in it should be taken literally" (no mention is made of how to distinguish).

AN AMBIVALENT ENDING

Is the Bible anointed especially because it is God's Word, or is it special because it contains very human stories about the human struggle to find meaning and purpose? Other sources do that. Or is it special, as we suggested before, because it provides a template from which we get our language, metaphors, and stories to ponder life? But, again, other sources do that. Have we finally moved from a primitive literalism, "this is what God says," to a more nuanced "this is what people have said that God says, but we know better" to our modern liberating individualism of "what do *you* say?" Who decides? Whatever the answer, perhaps we should really end a biblical reading not with the "Word *of* God," as if it were a direct communiqué, but the "Word *about* God." We should introduce the Gospel not as "The Gospel according to Matthew" but as "The Gospel *tradition* according to Matthew." That leaves room for development and diversity. Think of proclaiming a horrid passage from Joshua where YHWH commands genocide and ending it with "The Word of the Lord!" Barring a long and convoluted exegesis, we, of course, never read that kind of inerrant scripture because we know that the resource phrase "Word of the Lord" connotes a literal meaning, a divinely literal validation of what was read. We have to substitute another phrase that suggests open-endedness and nuance, something that pays respect to the fact that the Bible is the repository of stories, legends, and myths by a people at various stages trying to come to terms with life, death, meaning, and God. Its authors obviously thought it was worthwhile to tell the story, warts and all, of a stiff-necked people from God's point of view. Why? Because fundamentally, just telling the story is itself a sign of hope, precisely because it is a story of a forbearing God. That is no small thing.

Perhaps it is true that in today's climate of disbelief, skeptical scholars and the rude presence of the new atheist crowd "with its peculiar mix of overconfident reductionism and crowing self-righteousness about morality and politics"[9], the Bible's "crude" conservatism is unappealing. What people have historically done and still do with it is at times appalling ("God hates gays"). Still, the Bible, for all of its carefully crafted collection of improbable stories and interpretations, offers a coherent world picture that transcends the current understanding of the world as a cold, indifferent and empty cosmos. Perhaps Augustine's biblically inspired restless heart seeking ultimate rest in God is truer to the social and psychological indispensability of human belief and that the Bible, in its own way, is true after all, truer to reality. There indisputably does remain a large, silent majority who do experience a biblical faith that motivates spiritual and corporal works of mercy, a faith that rests deep in hearts that accept doubt along with fervor and confusion along with clarity. This majority accepts the truth of the Bible and endorses the creeds that derive from it. They distance themselves from the easygoing, adaptable "spiritual not religious" crowd and have no resonance with the purely horizontal secular world picture of the intellectuals for whom the center of a godless evolutionary world is solely the human being imbued with rights and with obligations only to oneself and yet who, for some illogical reason, insist on moral absolutes.[10] The Bible deserves a second thought that, if for some it is not accepted as the self-revelation of a God who aches for us and with us, it nevertheless deserves respect and a place of honor.

Anyway, all this wishy-washy, playing-both-sides-of-the-fence rhetoric is not to undermine the 400+ previous pages but to suggest that, while we owe the scholars much, theirs is not necessarily the last word.

So I end as I began: as long as fundamentalist atheists read the Bible as literal history and fundamentalist Jews and Christians insist that it must be read so; as long as parabolic interpretations conflict, cancel, contradict, and condemn one another and as long as interpreters' interpretations of interpretations produce objective doctrines and moral absolutes out of fluid metaphors then the Bible will remain the atheists' best friend and its authority will be questioned.

Endnotes

Foreword

1. See *The New Experience of God: Being, Consciousness. Bliss*, David Bentley Hart. Yale University Press and Stephen Bullivant's *Faith and Unbelief*. Canterbury Press.

2. Evangelical Christian colleges are especially caught in the crossfire of literalism and science. See "Byran College Is Torn: Can Darwin and Eden Coexist?" by Alan Blinder. *New York Times*. May 20, 2014.

Chapter 1: The Hebrew Genesis

1. Darwin, Erasmus. *The Botanic Garden*. 1791.

2. Sparks, Kenton L. *God's Word in Human Words*. Baker Academic. 2008, p. 98.

3. Horowitz, Victor. "The Genesis of Genesis." *Bible Review*. Anniversary Issue. p. 37ff.

4. *The Old Testament*. Oxford University Press. 2006. p. 16.

5. Jossey-Bass. *Falling Upward*. 2012. p. xxii. italics mine.

6. Mahoney, Jack. "Humanity's Destiny." *The Tablet*. 14, January, 2012. p. 7.

7. "The Search for the Historical Adam." *Christianity Today*. June 6, 2011.

8. Finkel, Irving. *The Ark Before Noah*. Doubleday. 2014.

Chapter 2: The Sagas of the Patriarchs

1. Coogan, Michael D. *The Old Testament: A Historical and Literary Introduction to the Hebrew Scriptures.* Oxford. 2006. p. 79.

2. *Inheriting Abraham: The Legacy of the Patriarch of Judaism, Christianity and Islam.* Princeton University Press. 2012.

3. Bray, Warwick. *Everyday Life of the Aztecs.* Peter Bedrick Books. 1991.

4. Gitline, Todd & Leibovitz, Liel. *The Chosen Peoples: America, Israel and the Ordeals of Divine Election.* Simon & Shuster. 2011.

5. *National Catholic Reporter.* September 19, 2003. p. 4.

Chapter 3: The Sagas of the Grandsons

1. *New Interpreter's Study Bible.* Abingdon. 2003. p. 81. italics mine.

2. Zakovich, Yair. *Jacob: Unexpected Patriarch.* Yale University Press. 2013.

3. *A Short Introduction to the Hebrew Bible.* Fortress Press. 2007. p. 40.

Chapter 4: The Exodus Saga

1. April 3, 2003.

2. *The Bible Today.* March/April 2009. pp. 126-131.

3. Shanks, Hershel. "Where is Mount Sinai?" *Biblical Archaeology Review/ BAR.* (hereafter, BAR) March/April, 2014. pp. 30 ff.

4. Hendel, Ronald S. "The Pharaoh, the Bible and Liberation Square." *BAR.* May/June, 2012. p. 31.

5. For an interesting insight see: Gabriel, Richard A. *The Military History of Ancient Israel.* Praege. 2003.

6. Coogan, Michael D. *The Ten Commandments.* Yale University Press. 2014. p.114.

7. See Burton, (O.F.M.) William L. "The Passover." *The Bible Today.* March/April, 2009. p. 101ff.

Chapter 5: The Sagas of Joshua and Judges

1. "Did All This Really Happen? Archaeology, the Bible and History." *The Bible Today*. March/April, 2007. pp. 1113, 114.

2. Westminster, John Knox. *Joshua, a Commentary*. 1997. pp. 80, 82.

Chapter 6: The Saga of YHWH

1. Feiler, Bruce. *Walking the Bible*. William Morrow. 2001. p. 281. italics mine.

2. For example, Smith, Mark & et al. *Ugaritic Narrative Poetry*. and Coogan, Michael D. *Stories from Ancient Canaan*.

3. Greenstein, Edward L. "Texts from Ugarit Solve Biblical Puzzles." *BAR*. November/December, 2010. p. 48.

4. *God, a Biography*. Vintage. 1966. pp. 21, 21, 72.

5. MacGregor, Neil. *A History of the World in 100 Objects*. Penquin Books. 2010. p. 441.

6. *New York Times*. September 1, 2009. p. A22.

Chapter 7: YHWH in a Bad Mood

1. Orn, Barbara. pp. 148, 149.

2. *America*. September 29, 2008. p. 16.

3. See Hawk, L. Daniel. "The God of the Conquest: The Theological Problem in the Book of Joshua." *The Bible Today*. p. 141ff.

4. *Laying Down the Sword: Why We Can't Ignore the Bible's Violent Verses*. HarperOne. 2011.

5. Collins, Paul. *The Birth of the West*. BBS Publications. NY. 2013. p. 135.

6. MacGregor, Neil. *op. cit.* p. 519.

7. *Forward*. February 20, 2001.

Chapter 8: The Sagas of the Prophets

1. Collins, John. *op. cit.* p. 154.

2. Miles, Jack. *op. cit.* p. 268.

3. Kugler, Robert and Hartin, Patrick. *An Introduction to the Bible.* Eerdmans. 2009. p. 237.

4. Quoted by Langenbrunner, Norman. "Weekly Homily Helps." Franciscan Media. August 14, 2014. He is also the commentator on the Zedekiah story.

Chapter 9. The Sagas of the Monarchy and the Messiah

1. See the excellent study and Collins, Adela Yarbro and Collins, John J. *King and Messiah as Son of God.* Grand Rapids. Eerdmans. 2008.

2. Kugler, Robert and Hartin, Patrick. *op. cit.* p.151.

3. *Sacred Pagina: The Gospel of Matthew.* The Liturgical Press. 1991. p. 367. italics mine.

4. *Messianic Expectations in the Old Testament.* p. 50.

5. Fitzmyer, S.J., Joseph. *The One Who Is To Come.* William Eerdmans. 2007. p. 16.

6. Fitzmyer, S.J., Joseph. *op. cit.*

7. Ryan, Stephen. *The Bible Today.* November/December, 2010. p. 20.

8. Hoppe, O.F.M., Leslie J. "The Significance of Messianism." *The Bible Today.* May/June. p. 152. italics mine.

9. *New York Times.* January 7, 2011. p. A6.

Chapter 10. The Saga of Solomon and the Divided Kingdom

1. Miller, Maxwell. "History or Legend? Digging into Israel's Origin." *Christian Century.* February 24, 2004. p. 43.

2. *The Bible Today*. June/July, 2010. p. 228.

3. The best book on the subject is Benite, Zvi Ben-Dor. *The Ten Lost Tribes: A World History*. Oxford. 2009.

4. Raisanen, Heikki. *The Rise of Christian Beliefs: The Thought World of Early Christinas*. Fortress. 2010. p. 20.

5. *BAR*. March/April, 2013. p. 20.

Chapter 11. The Exilic Chapter, the Apocalyptic Verse

1. Psychological studies show that "cognitive dissonance", a situation when a person is faced with two mutually incompatible ideas at the same time (think of the fervent end-of-the-world devotees when their predictions fail) often makes people firmer in their convictions. Psychologists figure that the cognitive dissonance is so painful that some, to avoid the pain, believe more strongly and bond even more tightly together to support their belief. See Seife, Charles. *Virtual Unreality*. Viking. 2014. chapter 4.

    Germaine to this is a review of Alex Beam's book, *American Crucifixion: the Murder of Joseph Smith and the Fate of the Mormon Church* by Benjamin Moser who notes the Mormon teaching that Earth was created near some planet called Kolab and that the Garden of Eden was near Kansas City. As for Smith himself, prosecuted and murdered, he cites Smith's delusions of being "president pro tem of the world" and his pronouncements of himself as "King, Priest and Ruler over Israel on the Earth". Not to mention that Smith added 14 chapters to the Book of Genesis and had dozens of wives. Then Moser skeptically goes on:

    "After all, it may be easy to make fun of Mormon theology, but it is surely no more absurd to believe that the resurrected Christ visited America in A.D. 34 [a Mormon belief] than it is to believe that Moses parted the Red Sea, or that Mohammad ascended to heaven on a winged horse, or that Jesus was born of a virgin. To see Mormonism in this broader context is to be constantly confronted with questions of belief, of how much nonsense humans will suffer for the sake of making sense of their lives." *New York Times Book Review*. Sunday, July 6, 2014. p. 17.

Speaking of the Mormons, their leaders, after more than a century of suppressing the facts about their founders, have bravely decided to post a series of blogs telling all. They have acknowledged for the first time that their founder, Joseph Smith had more than 40 wives including one 14 years old and several who were already married to other men. He was polygamous as was Brigham Young. His first wife, Emma, was, understandably, unhappy about this. The blogs so far have admitted their ban on blacks in the priesthood (lifted in 1978) which is still closed to women. See these books:

Krakauer, Jon. *Under the Banner of Heaven*. Anchor Books. 2003. Abanes, Richard. *One Nation Under Gods: a History of the Mormon Church*. Four Walls Eight Windows. New York.

2. Kugler and Hartin. *op. cit.* p. 270.

3. MacCulloch, David. *Christianity: the First Three Thousand Years*. Viking. 2009. p. 7. The apocalyptic impulse is found in all three Abrahamic religions. It tends to surface in times of social and political crises. In our time the rise of the viciously radical Islamic State (or ISIS or ISIL) in 2014 in the Middle East political cauldron in the Syrian area has been fueled by apocalyptic fervor. The militants capture of Dabiq in northern Syria, for example, was deliberate, prompted by texts in the Qur'an and the Hadith (a collection of sayings attributed to Mohammed) that prophesized that there the end of the world drama will be played out. Dabiq is the Arab equivalent of Israel's Agamemnon and, significantly, is the name of the Islamic State's official magazine. Religious prophecy and millennial ideas fuel their aggression and lure recruits.

Chapter 12. The Late Writings

1. Kugel, James L. *How to Read the Bible*. Free Press. p. 469.

Chapter 13. The Messiah Narratives

1. Lohfink, Gerhard. *Jesus of Nazareth*. The Liturgical Press. 2012. p. 3.

2. *Church History*. Paulist Press. 1985. pp. 5-8. Italics his. Noted scholar John Meier says the same thing: "Like the variant forms of the Lord's Prayer, and the Beatitudes, the variant forms of the eucharistic words remind us that the early Church was interested in preserving the substance, the essence, the core message of what Jesus said, not the exact

wording. In that, the evangelists operated like many an historian in the ancient world: nobody told the evangelists that they had to operate like 20th-century historians instead."

3. *Kosher Jesus*. Gefen Books. 2012.

4. See Amy Jill-Levine's excellent essay on how the New Testament writers misrepresented Judaism: "Bearing False Witness." *The Jewish Annotated New Testament*. Oxford University Press. 2011.

5. Karban, Roger Vermalen. "Receive what you are." *National Catholic Reporter*. April 11 – 12, 2014.

6. *Church*. Winter, 2002. p. 64. italics mine except for the word "survival."

7. A fragment of a papyrus known as the "Gospel of Jesus' Wife" caused an uproar on 2012 when professor Karen King of Harvard made it a media event. After the brouhaha the papyrus' authenticity has been challenged as a crude forgery with Harvard protesting that it took no stand on the matter.

8. Vanauken, Shekdon. *A Severe Mercy*. HarperOne. 1977. p. 109.

9. Harrington, Daniel J. "What is Fact? What is Fiction?" *Encountering Jesus in the Scriptures*. edited by Daniel J. Harrington, S.J. and Christopher R. Matthews. Paulist Press. p. 11.

Chapter 14. Sir, We Wish to See Jesus

1. *The Hungering Dark*. Seabury Press. New York. 1969. p. 51ff.

2. *Jesus of Nazareth: the Infancy Narratives*. Image Books. 2012.

3. Bowden, J. (trans.). *Between Jesus and Paul: Studies in the Earliest History of Christianity*. London. 1983. p. 3.

4. Fitzmyer, S.J., Joseph. *op. cit.*

5. Broshi, Magen. "What Jesus Learned from the Essenes." *BAR*. January/February, 2004. p. 32ff.

6. Harrington, S.J., Daniel J. *Jesus*. St. Anthony Press. 2007. pp. 103 ff.

7. Albert J. Edmunds' 1902 book, *Buddhist and Christian Gospels* is still a standard text here.

8. *America*. October, 2002. Italics mine. (A must read book is *Partings: How Judaism and Christianity Became Two.* edited by Hershel Shanks, *BAR*. See also Levine, Amu-Jay. *Short Stories by Jesus*. HarperOne. 2014.)

9. "The Canon of the Bible" in *The Bible Today*.

10. Witherup, Robert D. *The Bible Companion*. Crossroad. 1998. p. 11. Italics mine.

11. Young, Brad. *Jesus an His Jewish Parables*. Paulist Press. 1989.

Chapter 15. Kingdom and Divinity

1. See: Wright, N.T. *How God Became King: The Forgotten Story of the Gospels* (and Marcus Borg's *Speaking Christian*.)

2. *My God and I: A Spiritual Memoir*. Eerdmans. 2003. p. 175.

3. Harrington, Wilfrid. *ibid*. 24.

4. Hoppe, Leslie. *op. cit*. p. 109-110.

5. Kinn, James W. "Jesus, the Image of God." *The Bible Today*. May/June 2011. p. 175, 176.

6. Martin, S.J., James. *Jesus; a Pilgrimage*. HarperOne. 2014. p. 8.

7. Carroll, James. "Jesus and the Modern Man." *New York Times*. November 7, 2014.

8. Martin, S.J., James. *ibid*. p. 94

Chapter 16. Last Days

1. "The Catholic Priesthood: A New Testament Reflection." *New Theology Review*. August, 2004. pp. 6ff.
A Catholic priest, Tony Flannery, has been censured by Rome for writing, "Whatever Jesus intended, I don't think anyone can credibly claim that he intended the type of system we now have in the Church...I no longer believe that the priesthood, as we currently have it in the

Church, originated with Jesus." Irish theologian, Father Gabriel Daly, defends Flannery citing his qualifying words, "as we currently have it in the Church". Daly notes the vast difference between the gathering of disciples around a first century Jesus and today's Catholic Church. See his book, *The Church: Always in need of Reform*.

2. *Mere Christianity*

3. *America*. September 22, 2008.

4. *National Catholic Reporter*. October 12 – 15, 2012. p. 35.
The disputes over the atonement goes on, most recently over the dropping of the beloved hymn, "In Christ Alone" in the Presbyterian hymnal, a hymn that seemingly turns God into an angry deity demanding to be appeased by Jesus' blood.

5. Raisanen, Heikki. *op. cit.* p. 191.

6. Wright, N.T. *Surprised by Scripture*. HarperOne. 2014. pp 52 – 53.

7. *The Human Being Jesus and the Enigma of the Son of Man*. Fortress. 2002. p. 152.

8. Raisanen, Heikki. *op. cit.* p. 204.

9. Ferder, Fran. *Enter the Story*. Orbis. 2010. p. 147. italics hers.

10. *Sacra Pagina: The Gospel of Luke*. p. 389.

11. Pecklers, Keith F. *The Genius of the Roman Rite*. Pueblo. 2009. pp. 2-5.

12. Two recent representative books (as of this writing) are *Partings – How Judaism and Christianity Became Two*, edited by Hershel Shanks. *BAR*. 2013; and *"Is This Not the Carpenter?" The Question of the Historicity of Jesus*, edited by Thomas L. Thompson and Thomas S. Verenna. Durham. 2013.

13. Spufford, Francis. *Unapologetic: Why Despite Everything, Christianity Can Still Make Surprising Emotional Sense*. HarperOne. 2012. p. 149.

Chapter 17: Sir, We Wish to See Mary

1. Pilch, John J. *Cultural Tools for Interpreting the Good News*. Liturgical Press. 2002. p. 9.

2. *Catholic Encyclopedia*. Volume 14. p. 693. italics mine.

3. *Signs of Life*. Doubleday. 2009. p. 115. His italics.

4. *When Jesus Became God*. Hardcourt. 1999. p. 20.

Chapter 18. Interpretation Tensions

1. Joachim Kahl, a former Lutheran pastor, quoted in Bullivant, Stephen. *Faith and Unbelief*. Paulist Press. 2013. p. 58.

2. *How to Read the Bible*. Free Press. 2007. pp. 15, 16.

3. *ibid*. pp. xix, xv. italics his.

4. Tov, Emanuel. "Searching for the 'Original' Bible." *BAR*. July/August, 2014. pp. 48ff.

5. *The Bible As It Was*. Belknap Press. Cambridge. 1997. p. 5.

6. Eerdmans. 2009. pp. 181-182. (See also David Darnell's masterful, *The Bible in English: Its history and influence*. Yale University Press. 2003.)

7. "The Bible Jesus Knew." *Priests & People*. August – September, 2002.

8. See "The Next Age of Discovery." *The Wall Street Journal*. May 8, 2009.

9. MacGregor, Neil. *A History of the World in 100 Objects*. Penguin Books. 2010. p. 503.

10. Levy, Sandra M. *Imagination and the Journey of Faith*. Eerdmans. 2008. pp. 96, 97. Yes, "as they saw it."

Chapter 19. Theory in Tensions

1. Circumcision is very much in contemporary news as some would make it illegal as it violates a children's "fundamental right to

bodily integrity." For a defense of it see Galston, William A. "Mark of Belonging." *Commonweal.* May 16, 2014. pp. 15ff.

2. Wenig, Lauren. *op. cit.* p. 32.

3. *Liguorian Magazine.* September, 2003. p. 28.

4. Revised Edition. Paulist Press. 2003.

5. Sanchez, Patricia. "Preaching Resources." *Lumen Gentium #16 and Gaudium et Spes, #22.* September 27, 2009.

6. *A Generous Orthodoxy.* Zondervan. 2004. pp. 186, 188.

7. *Evolution of the Word.* HarperOne. 2012. p. 6.

8. Witherup, S.S., Ronald. "Scripture from Scratch." *St. Anthony Messenger.* August, 1999.

9. Schultz, Karl A. and Duquin, Lorene Hanley. *Our Sunday Visitor.* December 1, 2008. p. 10.

Chapter 20. Three Modern Tensions

1. In England, for example, a newspaper uncovered instances of women getting abortions solely because they did not want female babies. This is strictly against the Abortion Act but the government choses to ignore it. Radical feminists, so vocal about abortion "rights" are silent about the abortions of females. See Gearty, Conor. "Victims on Inaction." *The Tablet.* 21 September, 2013. p. 12. (See also, "'It's a girl!' Joyful, Dangerous Words." *America.* September 30, 2013.)

2. "Letters to the Editor." *Commonweal.* April 25, 2008. p. 35.

3. Dulles. *America.* October 21, 2002.

4. *America.* October 21, 2002.

5. Nolan. *Good News.* February, 2003. p. 37.

6. Wright, N.T. *Scripture and the Authority of God.* HarperCollins. 2013. p. 103.

Chapter 21. The Tensions Continue

1. *Commonweal.* June 15, 2007. pp. 14ff. Italics mine.

2. *The Last Word.* HarperOne. 2006.

3. *An Acceptable Sacrifice? Homosexuality and the Church.* SPCK.

4. December 12, 2003. p. 2.

5. All this, by the way, is politically moot for gay marriage is pretty much a done deal as European countries, our Federal government and more and more States, churches and synagogues legalize it. On June 26, 2013 the Supreme Court made the historical ruling by striking down the 1966 Defense of Marriage Act and ruled that same sex couples must receive the same benefits as heterosexual couples. It is fairly certain that the courts will eventually nationalize gay marriage. Note also the rapid progress from the pleading for equality of the 2008 *Newsweek* article to the theme of *superiority* of gay marriages in the 2013 *The Atlantic* article, "What Straights Can Learn from Same-Sex Couples: Why Gay Marriages Tend to be Happier and More Intimate." Roman Catholicism, the most public foe of legalizing gay marriage, has suffered a severe set back by the reversals of some prominent Republican Senators and the former Secretary of State Colin Powell who have come out in favor of gay marriage. Now some very prominent conservative Catholics such as Joseph Bottum, former editor of the conservative magazine *First Things*, has moved from opposition to support. See *Commonweal* online, "The Things We Share: a Catholic's case for Same-Sex Marriage." August 23, 2013.

Chapter 22. The Tension Breaker

1. Paulist Press. 2003. p. ix. (See also Lacey, Michael J. & Oakley, Francis. *The Crisis of Authority in Catholic Modernity.* Oxford University Press. 2011.)

2. p. 287.

3. April 17, 2006.

4. pp. 288-289.

5. *op. cit.* p. 24

6. Kelly, Joseph F. *History and Heresy.* The Liturgical Press. 2012.

7. Reviewing Noonan's book, *A Church That Can and Cannot Change. The New York Times Book Review*, May 22, 05. Italics mine. See (Trevett, Christine. *Montanism: Gender, Authority, and the New Prophecy.* Cambridge University Press. 1996.)

8. See the article: Clifford, Nichols. "Historical Amnesia." *Commonweal.* September 27, 2013. pp. 8,9.

9. O'Malley, John. *What Happened at Vatican I.* Belkamp Press. Harvard. 2010.

10. *By What Authority?* Liturgical Press. 2002. pp. 49-50. His italics.

Chapter 23. The Tensions of Pluralism

1. August 9, 2003.

2. Q&A in the *New York Times.*

3. *National Catholic Reporter.* September 19, 2003. p. 4.

4. HarperOne. 2008. p. 79.

5. HarperOne. (See also Berger, Peter. *The Many Altars of Modernity.* DeGruywe. 2014.)

6. *A People's History of Christianity.* HarperOne. 2009. p. 241.

7. *A New Religious America: How a "Christian Country" Has Become the World's Most Religiously Diverse Nation.* HarperSanFrancisco. pp.21-23.

8. *op. cit.* p. 293. It would go beyond the topic of this book but it should be noted that in the aftermath of the depressing European religious warfare, Inquisitions and killings of the opposition, across the oceans tolerance was the norm. Three examples:

   In the 17th century one would find a great Christian cathedral built for the Armenian Christians right in the capital city of Muslim Iran. It was built by Shah Abbas I (a contemporary of England's Elizabeth I), its Muslim ruler and member of the Safavid dynasty. Iran decided early on after the Protestant Reformation that it could hold more than one monolithic faith even though the tolerance was sometimes fragile. Unlike the bloody intolerance of Christian Europe Muslims, Christians and Jews, each with their own places of worship, lived peacefully. Iran, for all of our contemporary impression of an implacable foe bent on acquiring atomic war capacity, is still a multi-faith society.

Similarly in early seventeenth over in India under the Islamic Mughals the Hindus, a non-people "of the book", found inclusion and its Islamic rulers worked with many faiths. Hindus mingled easily and even, unusual for Muslims, intermarried. The kings, reverential towards holy men of every stripe, were not only tolerant but also decidedly friendly. (See MacGregor, p. 533ff). Religious tolerance among Muslims, Christians and Jews was the norm in India.

Finally, today, while some Muslim countries shamelessly war on Christians, in Sierra Leone religious tolerance is a given. Sierra Leone is a Muslim country that has quite cordial relations with Christianity. In fact, it is not unusual to be both Christian and Muslim, known as "ChrisMus." Christians and Muslims interact every day and often pray side by side. Its president Ernest Bai Koroma, is Christian. His vice president is Muslim. Marriage across sectarian lines is common (*The Economist*, May 31, 2014, p. 43). The prophet Elijah would be out of work in these countries.

We should take careful note that the tolerance listed in these examples, unlike today in the United States, is not a mere disdainful constitutional acceptance while actively sidelining and excluding religion from the public square with an aggressive secularism that seeks an ideal world without God, but a respectful, genuine, positive openness. (see this insightful book: Smith, James K.A. *How (Not) To Be Secular: Reading Charles Taylor*. Eerdmans. 2014.)

9. Lane, Dermont, ed. "Biblical Scholarship: Past, Present and Future." *Catholic Theology Facing the Future* Paulist Press. 2003. p. 36.

10. Paulist Press. 2000.

Chapter 24. Nostalgic Searching

1. Zannoni, Arthur E. *op.cit.* pp. 22, 35. italics mine.

2. *op. cit.* pp. 106, 107.

3. *ibid.* p. 322.

4. *ibid.* pp. 201-202.

5. December, 2001.

6. Gomes, Peter. *The Good Book.*

7. *The Critical Meaning of the Bible.* p. 3.

8. Kugler, Joachim. *Theological Digest.* Summer, 2010. p. 137.

9. Dworkin, Ronald. *Religion Without God.* Harvard University Press. 2013.

Chapter 25. Searching Through the Lens of Reason and Myth

1. *The Wall Street Journal.* September 12-13, 2009. p. W1.

2. *How to Read Literature.* Yale University Press. 2013. p. 3. He also goes
   on to say, "The narrator of Genesis uses the phrase 'In the beginning'
   because, like 'once upon a time' it is a time-honoured way of starting a
   story." (p. 18)

3. *The New York Review.* December 3, 2009. p. 24.

4. *Enter the Story.* Orbis. 2010. p. 1.

5. *The Heart Is a Little To The Left.*

6. Vintage Books. 2008. p. 469. Science and religion remain pitted against
   each other with one side arguing that all belief systems are factually
   mistaken and the other arguing that scientists deny the differences
   between realms of human experience and existence and simplify reality.
   Read the lively debate between Steven Pinker and Leon Wieseltier in
   The New Republic (Pinker's article, "Science is Not the Enemy" is in
   the August 6, 2103 issue; and Wieseltier's rebuttal, "Crimes Against
   Humanities" is in the September 3, 2013 issue.)

   Of note are the words of Michael Ruse evolutionary biologist: "In my
   view, none of our knowledge, including science, just 'tells it like it is.'

Knowledge, even the best scientific knowledge, interprets experience through human cultural understanding and experience, and above all (just as it is for poets and preachers) metaphor is the key to the whole enterprise. As I developed my own career path, as a historian and philosopher of evolutionary biology, this insight grew and grew. Everything was metaphorical – struggle for existence, natural selection, division of labor, genetic code, arms race and more." (*The New York Times*, "Does Evolution Explain Religious Beliefs?" an interview by Gary Gutting, July 8, 2014.)

7. *op. cit.* p. 121.

Chapter 26. A Searcher's Epilogue

1. *Pulpit Reflections.* August 7, 2011. p. 26.

2. *Making Loss Matter.* Riverhead Books. 1999. p. 10.

3. Beck, John A. *God as Storyteller: Seeking Meaning in Biblical Narrative.* Chalice Press. St. Louis, Missouri. 2008. p. 61. Italics mine.

4. April 17, 2013. p. 3.

5. Quoted in the *New York Times* Opinion Pages in the article, "Evolution and the American Myth of the Individual" by John Edward Terrell, November 20, 2014.

6. Phrase is from Mark Lilla. (See Brooks, David. "The Spiritual Recession." *New York Times.* June 26, 2014.) See also Schneck, Stephen. "Ridiculing Mercy, Love and Faith: An Ayn Rand Dystopia" *Catholics in Alliance for the Common Good.* June 25, 2014.

7. Douthat, Ross. "Of New Atheists and Noble Lies." *New York Times.* Op Ed. January 13, 2014.

8. One only has to read the constant editorial moral hectoring of the liberal *New York Times* to confirm this.

9. Higgins, Michael. "Infinite Horizon." *Commonweal.* September 12, 2014. p. 18.